The Second Formation of Islamic Law

The Second Formation of Islamic Law is the first book to deal with the rise of an official school of law in the post-Mongol period. Guy Burak explores how the Ottoman dynasty shaped the structure and doctrine of a particular branch within the Ḥanafī school of law. In addition, the book examines the opposition of various jurists, mostly from the empire's Arab provinces, to this development. By looking at the emergence of the concept of an official school of law, the book seeks to call into question the grand narratives of Islamic legal history that tend to see the nineteenth century as the major rupture. Instead, an argument is formed that some of the supposedly nineteenth-century developments, such as the codification of Islamic law, are rooted in much earlier centuries. In so doing, the book offers a new periodization of Islamic legal history in the eastern Islamic lands.

Guy Burak is the Middle Eastern and Islamic Studies Librarian at New York University's Bobst Library. Previously, Burak was a postdoctoral Fellow at the Max Planck Institute for the History of Science, Berlin, and in the Islamic Legal Studies Program at Harvard Law School. His articles have appeared in the *International Journal of Middle East Studies*, *Comparative Studies in Society and History*, the *Mediterranean Historical Review*, and the *Journal of Islamic Studies*.

Cambridge Studies in Islamic Civilization

Other titles in the series are listed at the back of the book.

The Second Formation of Islamic Law

The Ḥanafī School in the Early Modern Ottoman Empire

GUY BURAK
New York University

CAMBRIDGE
UNIVERSITY PRESS

CAMBRIDGE
UNIVERSITY PRESS

32 Avenue of the Americas, New York NY 10013-2473, USA

Cambridge University Press is part of the University of Cambridge.

It furthers the University's mission by disseminating knowledge in the pursuit of education, learning and research at the highest international levels of excellence.

www.cambridge.org
Information on this title: www.cambridge.org/9781107090279

First published 2015

A catalogue record for this publication is available from the British Library

Library of Congress Cataloguing in Publication data
Burak, Guy, author.
The second formation of Islamic law : the Ḥanafī school in the early modern Ottoman empire / Guy Burak.
pages cm. – (Cambridge studies in islamic civilization)
Includes bibliographical references and index.
ISBN 978-1-107-09027-9 (hardback)
1. Islamic law – Turkey – History. 2. Hanafites – History. 3. Turkey – History – Ottoman Empire, 1288–1918. I. Title.
KBP295.B87 2015
340.5'901811–dc23 2014043072

ISBN 978-1-107-09027-9 Hardback

Contents

Acknowledgments

This book started as a dissertation at NYU almost a decade ago. I would like to thank my dissertation committee. Tamer el-Leithy's creative and critical approach to historical sources and legal documents was illuminating. Zvi Ben-Dor Benite's ever-expanding intellectual horizons took this project into several unexpected places. The post-Mongol turn of this project is to a considerable extent a result of Zvi's insistence on a global approach to historical questions. Everett Rowson's erudition and generosity were indispensable: he was the best guide one could ask for through the intricacies of Islamic thought and legal discourses. I also thank him for his assistance when I was lost in translation. Baki Tezcan commented on several drafts of the dissertation. Baki also offered useful advice when the manuscript was in preparation. Finally, I am grateful to Leslie Peirce, my main adviser. It is thanks to Leslie that the book is imperial in scope. Leslie has been a careful reader and editor: her lucid style and elegant narratives are superb examples to follow. Moreover, Leslie's encouragement and confidence in me and in this book have been absolutely crucial.

The first draft of this book was written during two short postdoctoral fellowships at the Max Planck Institute for the History of Science in Berlin and the Islamic Legal Studies Program at Harvard Law School. In Berlin, Anthony Grafton, Glenn Most, and the research group on premodern textual practices commented generously on Chapter 4 of this book. At Harvard, Shahab Ahmed invited me to discuss my dissertation in his seminar at HLS. Shahab also invited me to submit this book to Cambridge University Press. Our long conversations shaped this book in numerous ways. Also at Harvard, I benefited immensely from conversations with Baber Johansen, Maaike Voorhoeve, Nir Shafir, Zeynep Oğuz,

Ünver Rüstem, Himmet Taşkömür, Avigail Noy, Andrew Halladay, and Noit Banai. They all made my stay in Boston/Cambridge enjoyable and stimulating.

Jonathan Brown had understood that the project was about the madhhab before I did. His invitation to write an entry on the madhhab for the *Oxford Encyclopedia of Islamic Law* and his editorial insights completely changed the framework of the book. Brinkley Messick's encouragement and inspiring comments improved this project substantially. I would also like to thank Selim Kuru, Wheeler Thackston, Ehud Toledano, Amy Singer, Michael Gilsenan, Robert McChesney, Jane Burbank, James Baldwin, Bruce Grant, Sibel Erol, and Mohammad Mehdi Khorrami.

Several institutions supported the research for this book. At NYU, the MacCracken Fellowship and the Dean's Dissertation Award enabled me to complete the dissertation. The Max Planck Institute and Harvard Law School supported me during my stay in Berlin and Cambridge, Massachusetts, respectively.

The research for this book was conducted in several libraries. I thank the staff of the Süleymaniye Library (Istanbul) for their welcoming hospitality and assistance. I also thank the staff at Beyazit Library, Milli Yazmalar Kütüphanesi, the Center for Islamic Studies (ISAM), the Staatsbibliothek zu Berlin, the Khalediyya Library in Jerusalem, the library at Haifa University, the rare books and manuscripts section at Firestone Library (Princeton), the New York Public Library, and Butler Library at Columbia. Special thanks go to Peter Magierski, formerly of the Middle Eastern and Islamic Studies department at Bobst Library at NYU and now my colleague.

The Conclusion of this book is based on an article I published in *Comparative Studies in Society and History*. I thank Andrew Shryock, David Akin, and the four anonymous reviewers for their comments and suggestions.

I thank William Hammell, Kate Gavino, Shari Chappell, the staff at Cambridge University Press, and the reviewers of the book manuscript for the useful comments and suggestions. I also thank my editor, Allison Brown, for her careful reading of the manuscript and for her invaluable suggestions.

Many friends heard more than they could care about this project. I am grateful for their friendship, patience, and long conversations. I thank Omar Cheta, Hasan Karataş, Tuna Artun, Nada Moumtaz, Rebecca Wiggins, Ayelet Zoran-Rosen, Dale Correa, Samy Ayoub, Ilan Diner, Shuki Ecker, Roni Weinstein, Nira Reiss, Ori Kleiner, Gerald Heverly,

Lyuba Grinberg, and Yassine Touati. I am especially grateful for Selma Zecevic's friendship and advice. I could not have written this book without her work and thoughts about the other end of the empire. Finally, Yigal Nizri, an amazing friend and intellectual companion, is present in every page of this book.

Last but not least, I thank my parents for their support of my academic pursuits. This book could not have been written without you. I dedicate this book, with great love, to my sister, Adi.

Note on Transliteration and Dates

As is well known, the Ottoman Empire was multilingual. This multilingualism is also reflected in the sources I have consulted. Most of the sources are in Arabic and Ottoman Turkish, but there are a few in Persian. The vocabularies of these languages often overlap, but their pronunciations differ. For extended citations, I use the *International Journal of Middle East Studies*'s transliteration system to Arabic and modern Turkish. For Ottoman Turkish, I use the ALA-LC (1997) transliteration system. For convenience's sake, several words I use frequently – such as *madrasa*, *fatwā*, *muftī*, (and not *medrese*, *fetvâ*, *müftî*) – follow the Arabic transliteration system. I use the English spellings whenever they are widely recognized (e.g., Cairo, Damascus). Some names appear throughout the book in their Turkish and Arabic forms (Muḥammad and Meḥmet, for instance). If the individual is from the Arab lands, I follow the Arabic transliteration system, but if she or he is from the Turkish-speaking parts of the empire, I use the Turkish transliteration. No one person will have his or her name spelled differently on different occasions.

Whenever I cite a Muslim *Hijri* date, it is followed by its Gregorian equivalent. For the most part, I cite the Gregorian date exclusively.

Introduction

> Fine distinctions among groups attain an importance that appears exaggerated to observers outside a particular time and place but reflects participants' certain knowledge that they are struggling not just over symbolic markets but over the very structure of rule.
>
> – Lauren Benton, *Law and Colonial Cultures*[1]

In 1535, soon after the Safavid army evacuated the city, Ottoman troops, led by Sultan Süleymân (r. 1520–66), marched into Baghdad. The Ottoman excitement about this military achievement is understandable: within a time period of twenty years, all the major cities and the most important learning centers of the eastern part of the Arabic-speaking world had come under Ottoman rule. Baghdad was a prestigious addition to the expanding Ottoman Empire for another reason – it was there that the eponymous founder of the Ḥanafī school, Abū Ḥanīfa (d. 767), was buried. Sixteenth- and seventeenth-century chroniclers did not fail to recognize the symbolic significance of the seizure of the tomb of the Greatest Imam (al-Imām al-Aʿẓam). Some describe in detail how the sultan himself visited the tomb upon its conquest and ordered its purification, for, in Sunnī Ottoman eyes, it was contaminated by the heretical Safavids.[2]

[1] Lauren Benton, *Law and Colonial Cultures: Legal Regimes in World History 1400–1900* (Cambridge: Cambridge University Press, 2002), 2.

[2] Naṣūḥü's-Silāḥī (Maṭrāḳçī), *Beyān-ı Menāzil-i Sefer-i ʿİrāḳeyn-i Sulṭān Süleymān Ḫān* (Ankara: Türk Tarih Kurumu, 1976), 46b–61a; Celālzāde Muṣṭafā (Ḳoca Nişāncı), *Ṭabaḳāt ül-Memalīk ve Deracāt ül-Mesālik* (Wiesbaden: Franz Steiner Verlag GMBH, 1981), 258b–259a; Eyyûbî, *Menâḳib-i Sulṭan Süleyman (Risâle-i Pâdişâh-nâme)* (Ankara: Kültür Bakanlığı, 1991), 88; İbrâhîm Peçevî, *Târîḫ-i Peçevî* (Istanbul: Maṭbaʿa-i ʿÂmire, 1865–67), 1:184–85; (Aḥmad Çelebi b. Sinān) al-Qaramānī, *Ta'rīkh salāṭīn Āl ʿUthmān*

This symbolic reconstruction of the tomb of Abū Ḥanīfa was the third of its kind within less than a century. During the siege on Constantinople, Meḥmet the Conqueror is said to have discovered the grave of Abū Ayyūb al-Anṣārī, one of the companions of the Prophet Muḥammad who died when he tried to conquer Constantinople in the seventh century.[3] Later, in 1516, the Ottoman seizure of another tomb, that of the famous yet controversial Sufi master Muḥyī al-Dīn b. al-ʿArabī, in the Ṣāliḥiyya suburb of Damascus, was celebrated with great pomp, and Sultan Selîm I, the conqueror of Syria and Egypt, ordered the restoration of the tomb and the construction of the mausoleum complex.[4] These ceremonial reconstructions of important tombs, as real acts and narrative tropes, are intriguing not only because members of the Ottoman dynasty play an important role but also because each of the three figures whose tombs were discovered and reconstructed represent a pillar of what some modern scholars have called "Ottoman Islam."[5] Abū Ayyūb al-Anṣārī embodies the Ottoman dynasty's ideal of holy war against the infidels; Ibn al-ʿArabī was one of the most prominent figures in the Ottoman pantheon of Sufi masters; and Abū Ḥanīfa was the founder of the school of law (madhhab) that the Ottoman dynasty adopted as its official school. In other words, the discovery-reconstruction of their tombs was an act of appropriation. In this book, I am particularly interested in the third pillar – the Ottoman Ḥanafī school of law.

(Damascus: Dār al-Naṣā'ir, 1985), 45; Gülru Necipoğlu, *The Age of Sinan: Architectural Culture in the Ottoman Empire* (Princeton, NJ: Princeton University Press, 2005), 60–64; Zeynep Yürekli, *Architecture and Hagiography in the Ottoman Empire: The Politics of Bektashi Shrines in the Classical Age* (Farnham, Surrey, UK: Ashgate, 2012), 17–18.The seizure and reconstruction of the tomb is also mentioned in other genres and documents. See, for example, the preamble of the endowment deed of Süleymân's wife: *Waqfiyyat Khāṣakī Khūram (Ḫürem) Sulṭān ʿalā al-Ḥaramayn al-Sharīfayn Makka al-Mukarrama wa'l-Madīna al-Munawwara* (al-Karak: Mu'assasat Rām lil-Tiknūlūjiyā wa'l-Kumbiyūtar, 2007), 39. In addition to Abū Ḥanīfa's grave, the new Ottoman rulers became the custodians of numerous other tombs of great significance, both for Sunnīs and Shiʿīs.

3 Çiğdem Kafescioğlu, *Constatntinopolis/Istanbul: Cultural Encounter, Imperial Vision, and the Construction of the Ottoman Capital* (University Park: Pennsylvania State University Press, 2009), 45–51.

4 Çiğdem Kafescioğlu, "'In the Image of Rūm': Ottoman Architectural Patronage in Sixteenth-Century Aleppo and Damascus," *Muqarnas* 16 (1999): 70–96. Selîm I also commissioned a polemical treatise to defend Ibn al-ʿArabī's teachings, which stood at the center of a heated debate among jurists and scholars across the empire. Şeyh Mekkî Efendi and Ahmed Neylî Efendi, *Yavuz Sultan Selim'in Emriyle Hazırlanan İbn Arabi Müdafaası* (Istanbul: Gelenek, 2004).

5 See, for example, Tijana Krstić's recent study: Tijana Krstić, *Contested Conversions to Islam: Narratives of Religious Change in the Early Modern Ottoman Empire* (Stanford, CA: Stanford University Press, 2011).

Süleymân's seizure and reconstruction of Abū Ḥanīfa's grave captures broader developments that predate the conquest of Baghdad. Since the early fifteenth century (and possibly even earlier), the Ottoman dynasty had gradually developed a distinctive branch within the Sunnī Ḥanafī school of law, one of the four legal schools of Sunnī Islam. The development of a distinctive branch that was exclusively associated with the dynasty was coupled by another important development: the rise of an imperial learned hierarchy. Although the institutional aspects of the development of an imperial hierarchy have been studied in detail, the doctrinal dimensions of this development have received considerably less attention.[6] Furthermore, despite the fact that the Ottoman adoption of the Sunnī Ḥanafī school is almost a scholarly truism among students of Islamic societies, the implications of this adoption – a radical innovation in Islamic legal history – remain fairly understudied.

One of the few exceptions is Rudolph Peters's short yet thought-provoking article, in which he raises the question that guides my inquiry: "What does it mean to be an official madhhab?"[7] In this article, Peters points to the instrumental role the Ottoman state played in the emergence of the Ḥanafī school as the official and dominant school in the Ottoman domains and to its intervention in regulating, to some extent, the school's doctrines. Following some of Peters's insights concerning the pivotal role the Ottoman dynasty played in the emergence of the official madhhab, the present study pursues his investigation further by looking at multiple sites, discourses, and practices that formed the Ottoman Ḥanafī school over the course of the fifteenth through the eighteenth centuries.

The rise of an Ottoman official legal school may be also seen as a new chapter in the history of canonization of Islamic law. In recent years, several studies have looked at Islamic legal history, especially at its earlier

6 Richard C. Repp, *The Müfti of Istanbul: A Study in the Development of the Ottoman Learned Hierarchy* (London: Ithaca Press, 1986); Abdurrahman Atcil, "The Formation of the Ottoman Learned Class and Legal Scholarship (1300–1600)" (PhD diss., University of Chicago, 2010). As to the doctrinal aspects of this development, see Colin Imber, *Ebu's-Su'ud: The Islamic Legal Tradition* (Stanford, CA: Stanford University Press, 1997); Rudolph Peters, "What Does It Mean to Be an Official Madhhab? Hanafism and the Ottoman Empire," in *The Islamic School of Law: Evolution, Devolution, and Progress*, ed. Peri Baerman, Rudolph Peters, and Frank E. Vogel (Cambridge, MA: Islamic Legal Studies Program, Harvard Law School, distributed by Harvard University Press, 2005), 147–58; Snejana Buzov, "The Lawgiver and His Lawmakers: The Role of Legal Discourse in the Change of Ottoman Imperial Culture" (PhD diss., University of Chicago, 2005); Haim Gerber, *State, Society, and Law in Islam: Ottoman Law in Comparative Perspective* (Albany: State University of New York, 1994).

7 Peters, "What Does It Mean to Be an Official Madhhab?"

centuries, through this lens.[8] But while canonization is pivotal to the emergence of any tradition, legal or otherwise, it may assume different forms. *The Second Formation of Islamic Law* focuses on the particular features of the canonization practices that the Ottoman dynasty and its learned hierarchy employed to shape an Ottoman madhhab and compares them with other canonization mechanisms and perceptions of legal canons that prevailed in earlier centuries, as well as in various scholarly circles throughout the Ottoman Empire.

My investigation of the history of the Ottoman official madhhab oscillates between the provincial and the imperial levels. At the provincial level, this study examines the encounter between the followers of different branches and traditions within the Ḥanafī school of law in the Ottoman province of Damascus (Bilād al-Shām, or Greater Syria, roughly modern day's south and central Syria, Lebanon, Palestine/Israel, and parts of Jordan) in particular, although much of what will be said in the following chapters may be applied to other Arab provinces as well. At the imperial level, it seeks to draw attention to how the conquest and subsequent incorporation of the Arab lands into the empire produced a clearer articulation of the boundaries of the learned hierarchy and, more generally, of the branch within the Ḥanafī school that members of the dynasty were expected to follow.

I have chosen the Ottoman province of Damascus for three reasons. First, although the Arab provinces were conquered over the course of the sixteenth century, their incorporation assumed different forms.[9] Moreover, sixteenth- to eighteenth-century sources often differentiate between the various districts that constituted the "Arab lands" of the

[8] Brannon M. Wheeler, *Applying the Canon in Islam: The Institutionalization and Maintenance of Interpretive Reasoning in Ḥanafī Scholarship* (Albany: State University of New York Press, 1996); Ahmed El Shamsy, *The Canonization of Islamic Law: A Social and Intellectual History* (Cambridge: Cambridge University Press, 2013).

[9] Haghnar Zeitlian Watenpaugh, *The Image of an Ottoman City: Imperial Architecture and Urban Experience in the 16th and 17th Centuries* (Leiden: Brill, 2004); Doris Behrens-Abouseif, *Egypt's Adjustment to Ottoman Rule: Institutions, Waqf, and Architecture in Cairo, 16th and 17th Centuries* (Leiden: Brill, 1994). This was even the case in later centuries as various Arab provinces were integrated differently into the empire, some significant similarities notwithstanding. See, for example, Amy Singer, *Palestinian Peasants and Ottoman Officials: Rural Administration around Sixteenth-Century Jerusalem* (Cambridge: Cambridge University Press, 1994); Jane Hathaway, *The Politics of Household in Ottoman Egypt: The Rise of the Qazdağlıs* (Cambridge: Cambridge University Press, 1997); Dina Rizk Khoury, *State and Provincial Society in the Ottoman Empire: Mosul, 1540–1834* (Cambridge: Cambridge University Press, 1997); Charles L. Wilkins, *Forging Urban Solidarities: Ottoman Aleppo 1640–1700* (Leiden: Brill, 2010).

empire. Therefore, it is necessary to pay attention to the particularities of each province. Second, since a major concern of this study is the organization of the Ottoman legal administration, it is convenient to preserve the provincial setting. Third, as Kenneth Cuno has demonstrated, there were, at times, significant doctrinal differences between the Ḥanafī jurists of each province.[10]

That said, this study seeks to undermine the rigidity that the focus on the imperial administration implies. Accordingly, the term "the Ottoman province of Damascus" – and, more generally, the term "Arab lands" – is used to demarcate a territory in which the encounters and exchanges between people, ideas, and traditions occurred. To be sure, certain traditions and practices were rooted in these regions, as many sixteenth- to eighteenth-century jurists and chroniclers observed. Yet it is necessary to differentiate between the territory and certain cultural practices, albeit for analytical ends. This approach also enables us to account for the multiple contacts and ties between the disparate parts of the empire and between certain provinces and other parts of the Islamic world. For example, one has to account for the fact that some of the Greater Syrian jurisconsults received questions from neighboring provinces as well as from the central lands of the empire. Moreover, many jurists traveled to and from other learning centers across the Arab lands (namely, Cairo and the holy cities in the Hijaz) and the imperial capital. In addition, the circulation of texts and students tied Greater Syrian jurists to other provinces across the empire and beyond.

The book's chronological framework is from the second half of the fifteenth century though the late eighteenth century. The relatively long time frame enables us to trace the gradual incorporation of Greater Syria into the empire and to examine the impact of this incorporation on different perceptions of the legal school.[11] Furthermore, examining the history

[10] Kenneth M. Cuno, "Was the Land of Ottoman Syria Miri or Milk? An Examination of Juridical Differences within the Hanafi School," *Studia Islamica* 81 (1995): 121–52.

[11] Dror Ze'evi has suggested considering the seventeenth century as the "Ottoman century." In his words, "The second century of Ottoman rule, forming the time frame for this study, is perhaps the clearest manifestation in this region of the 'Ottoman way' – the distinct set of norms and methods that represents the empire's rule in all realms." Dror Ze'evi, *An Ottoman Century: The District of Jerusalem in the 1600s* (Albany: State University of New York Press, 1996), 4–5. For the purposes of this study, Ze'evi's periodization is somewhat rigid and essentialist. Instead, I seek to draw attention to the complex dynamics that characterized the incorporation of the Arab lands into the empire, processes that are, to some extent at least, open-ended, yet equally "Ottoman." Other studies of the incorporation into the empire of the Arab provinces in general and of Greater Syria in

of the official madhhab up to the late eighteenth century may provide a better understanding of the more widely studied developments of the nineteenth century.

The Madhhab

In order to appreciate the novelty of the rise of the official school of law, the main development this book aims to describe, it would be helpful to introduce – admittedly, in very broad strokes – the notion and features of the pre-Mongol Sunnī madhhab. As I have suggested above, this notion of the school did not disappear in the post-Mongol period, and jurists in certain circles adhered to this understanding of the school of law.

The pre-Mongol madhhab (plural *madhāhib*, *mezheb* in Turkish) was a fairly loose social organization whose main function was to regulate the legal interpretation of divine revelation and to determine the authority of a given interpreter to do so. The word "madhhab" is derived from the Arabic root *dh-h-b* (generally associated with walking or following a path) and means "a way, course, or manner, of acting or conduct." More generally, the term is used to denote a doctrine, tenet, or an opinion concerning a certain issue. In certain cases "madhhab" may refer to the opinion of a leading jurist on a specific issue, but it may also denote, as is more commonly the case, a general hermeneutic approach.[12]

particular have tended to focus on the sixteenth-century consolidation and organization of Ottoman rule in the newly conquered territories. Among these studies are Muhammad ʿAdnan Bakhit, *The Province of Damascus in the Sixteenth Century* (Beirut: Librarie du Liban, 1982); Leslie Peirce, *Morality Tales: Law and Gender in the Ottoman Court of Aintab* (Berkeley: University of California Press, 2003); Astrid Meier, "Perceptions of a New Era? Historical Writing in Early Ottoman Damascus," *Arabica* 51, no. 4 (2004): 419–34; Timothy J. Fitzgerald, "Ottoman Methods of Conquest: Legal Imperialism and the City of Aleppo, 1480–1570" (PhD diss., Harvard University, 2009). Nevertheless, as this study intends to show, an examination of the last decades of the sixteenth century and the seventeenth century highlights significant dimensions of the incorporation that are not easily discernable in the sixteenth century.

12 The literature on the formation of the schools of law is vast. Among the most important works on this issue are Christopher Melchert, *The Formation of the Sunni Schools of Law, 9th–10th Centuries CE* (Leiden: Brill, 1997); Jonathan E. Brockopp, *Early Maliki Law: Ibn ʿAbd al-Hakam and His Major Compendium of Jurisprudence* (Leiden: Brill, 2000); Wael B. Hallaq, *Authority, Continuity and Change in Islamic Law* (Cambridge: Cambridge University Press, 2001); Nimrod Hurvitz, *The Formation of Hanbalism: Piety into Power* (London: Routeledge Curzon, 2002); Nurit Tsafrir, *The History of an Islamic School of Law: The Early Spread of Hanafism* (Cambridge, MA: Islamic Legal Studies Program, Harvard Law School, distributed by Harvard University Press, 2004); El Shamsy, *The Canonization of Islamic Law*.

During the late ninth and tenth centuries, the madhhab emerged as a legal discourse, or canon, around which a community of jurists galvanized. Moreover, much greater efforts were invested in regulating the range of permissible opinions within each school, and, perhaps more importantly, in limiting the authority of later followers of the schools to employ independent discretion or reasoning (*ijtihād*) and new hermeneutic approaches to derive new rules. This does not mean that jurists of later centuries did not employ independent reasoning to solve new problems they encountered, but that, discursively, followers of the schools emphasized their commitment to the doctrines of their schools' respective founders and leading authorities. Later jurists affiliated with a school were expected to derive new rules on the basis of the rulings and doctrines of the school's founder, the hermeneutic principles he set, and those developed by his disciples and later authorities within the school. The commitment to these hermeneutic and doctrinal principles is what made a jurist a follower (or an imitator, *muqallid,* the performer of *taqlīd*) within a school.[13]

As part of the evolution of the madhhab as a communal legal discourse, since the late tenth and eleventh centuries, and even more so in the following centuries, all four Sunnī schools of law developed a hierarchy of authorities. This hierarchy of authorities was often reflected in a growing textual body of chronological typologies of the jurists who were affiliated with the different schools. Generally, in most typologies, jurists of later centuries were limited in their authority to exercise independent discretion, although many of them, in practice, did. By establishing a hierarchy of authorities, the schools emerged as a corpus of doctrines and arguments that their followers had to study and memorize. These typologies drew on, and were accompanied by, an extensive biographical literature (known as the *ṭabaqāt* literature) whose main purpose was to serve as reference works for the schools' followers by documenting the intellectual genealogies of the schools (most commonly starting with the eponym), mapping out the schools' leading authorities, and reconstructing the genealogies of authoritative opinions and doctrines within the schools.

The typologies, as we shall see in Chapters 2 and 3, vary in structure and scope. Some are quite comprehensive, while others only outline general principles. Moreover, some typologies begin with the highest

[13] Hallaq, *Authority*, chaps. 2 and 4; Mohammad Fadel, "The Social Logic of Taqlīd and the Rise of the Mukhtaṣar," *Islamic Law and Society* 3, no. 2 (1996): 193–233.

rank of *mujtahids*. The utmost *mujtahid* may derive new rules when he encounters new cases by resorting to the revealed texts. The eponymous founder of the school and often his immediate companions are included in this category. Other typologies start from the perspective of the follower least qualified to employ independent discretion, the utmost imitator, the *muqallid*. In any case, the typologies reflect a fairly wide and complex range of juristic activity in terms of the authority to employ independent reasoning, which is not limited to the dichotomy of independent reasoning versus imitation. Between the utmost *mujtahid* and the utmost *muqallid* are jurists who are allowed to use limited forms of *ijtihād* (known as *takhrīj*) as long as they conform to the hermeneutic principles set by their schools' eponym and his immediate followers. In most typologies, this form of judicial activity was performed by the jurists who studied with the founder and his immediate successors, but jurists of this category can be found, albeit to a lesser extent, in later centuries. Later jurists, who usually lived in the fourth and fifth Islamic centuries (tenth and eleventh centuries CE), were mostly concerned with weeding out weaker and less authoritative opinions and arguments while making other opinions preponderant (hence this activity is termed *tarjīḥ*, literally meaning to prefer). They did so on the basis of their understanding of their interpretation of the teaching of their predecessors. All the jurists who followed a school, except the founder of the school, performed *taqlīd* to varying degrees, as they followed hermeneutic and legal principles that already existed. Jurists of later centuries, for the most part, were considered utmost *muqallids*, although they, too, practiced at times different forms of *takhrīj* and *tarjīḥ*.[14]

Despite the consolidation of the legal schools around specific legal discourses and hermeneutic principles, at what Wael Hallaq calls the microlevel of the school, there were multiple opinions. Over the centuries, the Sunnī schools of law developed discursive conventions and other institutional practices to guide their followers through the different opinions of the schools and to point out what opinions and doctrines were considered more authoritative. These conventions were instrumental in articulating the schools' canons. While many of the less authoritative opinions, or the minority opinions, were preserved in the schools' texts and manuals, the authoritative opinions served as pedagogical tools that guided followers of the school to extrapolate and derive new rules on the

[14] Hallaq, *Authority*, chaps. 1 and 2.

basis of the hermeneutic principles that their more authoritative predecessors developed.[15]

For our purposes here, it is important to stress that, doctrinally, the evolution of the schools of law and the regulation of their jurisprudential content were not a state-sponsored enterprise. This is not to say that states and sovereigns did not contribute to the dissemination of the schools by extending support, employment, and patronage to specific jurists or did not in practice shape doctrine. As early as the seventh and the eighth centuries, the Umayyad (661–750) and the ʿAbbasid (750–1258) dynasties supported eminent jurists and appointed jurists to different positions in their realms.[16]

In other cases, while not intervening directly in the content of the law, rulers and sovereigns adopted a school (and sometimes several schools) to provide authoritative legal counsel. In the Ayyubid and the Mamluk sultanates, for example, it was fairly common that the sultan was a follower of the Shāfiʿī school of law, the most popular school in Egypt at the time.[17] In the Mamluk sultanate during the reign of Sultan al-Ẓāhir Baybars (d. 1277), the state constituted a legal system in which all four schools were represented and specific cases were directed to judges of different schools, according to the relative advantage of the most common

[15] On the preservation of minority opinions, see Hallaq, *Authority*, 121–65; Eyyup Said Kaya, "Continuity and Change in Islamic Law: The Concept of Madhhab and the Dimensions of Legal Disagreement in Hanafi Scholarship of the Tenth Century," in Baerman, Peters, and Vogel, *Islamic School of Law*, 26–40. On the pedagogical use of authoritative opinions, see Wheeler, *Applying the Canon in Islam*.

[16] For example, Steven C. Judd, "Al-Awzāʿī and Sufyān al-Thawrī: The Umayyad Madhhab?," in Baerman, Peters, and Vogel, *Islamic School of Law*, 10–25; Tsafrir, *History of an Islamic School of Law*. There were also a few instances in early Islamic history, it is worth mentioning, in which caliphs or members of the ruling elite sought to promulgate a standardized legal code. Ibn al-Muqaffaʿ (d. ca. 756), a courtier at the court of the eighth-century ʿAbbasid caliph al-Manṣūr, compiled a treatise in which he encouraged the caliph to promulgate a standardized legal code because legal diversity among the various jurists was too inconvenient, in the courtier's mind, for running the vast empire. In response to this treatise, the eminent jurist and the eponymous founder of the Mālikī school, Mālik b. Anas (d. ca. 795), allegedly wrote his own treatise in which he defied any attempt by a single person, even by a prominent jurist, to draw a binding legal code. Instead, he endorsed plurality and diversity in legal matters. As a result of the events of the following decades, and especially the ʿAbbasid inquisition (the miḥna) during the reign of Hārūn al-Rashīd's son, al-Maʾmūn (r. 813–833), jurists increasingly asserted their independence from the state in regulating the content of Islamic law. Muhammad Qasim Zaman, "The Caliphs, the ʿUlamāʾ and the Law: Defining the Role and Function of the Caliph in the Early ʿAbbasid Period," *Islamic Law and Society* 4, no. 1 (1997): 1–36.

[17] Sherman Jackson, *Islamic Law and the State: The Constitutional Jurisprudence of Shihāb al-Dīn al-Qarāfī* (Leiden: Brill, 1996), 53–56.

view of the school for the Mamluk ruling elite.[18] Although the Mamluk state regulated the adjudication procedures of cases dealing with specific issues, it did not intervene doctrinally in the regulation of the structure of the school, its authorities, and the content of the law, and it accepted the opinion of eminent jurists as to what the preponderant opinion of the school was. Furthermore, although the Mamluk (like many other contemporary and early Islamic dynasties) employed jurists, for the most part there was no institutionally identifiable group of jurists that were affiliated with the ruling dynasty.[19] In Sherman Jackson's words, "The idea, thus, of state sovereignty entailing the exclusive right to determine what is and what is not law, or even what is and what is not an acceptable legal interpretation, is at best, in the context of classical Islam, a very violent one."[20]

The Official Madhhab

How the Ottomans (and, it appears, other contemporary polities) understood the madhhab diverges markedly from the classical, pre-Mongol understanding, for the Ottoman sultan and ruling dynasty assumed the right to intervene doctrinally in regulating and structuring the school. One should allow some room for contingency in the development of the official school of law, but it is fairly clear that at least from the second half of the fifteenth century the Ottoman ruling and judicial elite sought to single out a particular branch within the school.

The present study follows four major, closely interlocking developments that contributed to the evolution of the state madhhab: (1) the rise of the imperial learned hierarchy, (2) the emergence of the practice

[18] Yossef Rapoport, "Legal Diversity in the Age of Taqlīd: The Four Chief Qāḍīs under the Mamluks," *Islamic Law and Society* 10, no. 2 (2003): 210–28.

[19] See, for example, Jonathan Porter Berkey, *The Transmission of Knowledge in Medieval Cairo: A Social History of Islamic Education* (Princeton, NJ: Princeton University Press, 1992); Michael Chamberlain, *Knowledge and Social Practice in Medieval Damascus, 1190–1350* (Cambridge: Cambridge University Press, 1994); Daphna Ephrat, *A Learned Society in a Period of Transition: The Sunni "Ulama" of Eleventh-Century Baghdad* (Albany: State University of New York Press, 2000); Yossef Rapoport, "Royal Justice and Religious Law: Siyāsah and Sharī'ah under the Mamluks," *Mamluk Studies Review* 16 (2012): 71–102; Amalia Levanoni, "A Supplementary Source for the Study of Mamluk Social History: The Taqārīz," *Arabica* 60, nos. 1–2 (2013): 146–77.

[20] Jackson, *Islamic Law*, xv. See also Baber Johansen, "Secular and Religious Elements in Hanafite Law. Function and Limits of the Absolute Character of Government Authority," in *Islam et politique au Maghreb*, ed. E. Gellner and J. C. Vatin (Paris: Editions du CNRS, 1981), 281–303.

of appointing muftīs by the dynasty, (3) the dynasty's/state's regulation of the structure and doctrine of the school, and (4) the rise of dynastic law in the post-Mongol eastern Islamic lands. These developments are so closely related that it is almost impossible to treat one without considering the other three. Nevertheless, I will argue, the first three depend upon the fourth.

Since the early fifteenth century, and particularly since the conquest of Istanbul in 1453, the Ottoman dynasty gradually developed an imperial learned hierarchy, with fairly standardized career and training tracks and a hierarchical network of teaching institutions whose graduates manned many of the senior judicial and bureaucratic positions throughout the empire. This hierarchy was structured and regulated by the Ottoman dynasty through a series of imperial edicts, regulations, and legal codes, perhaps the most famous of which is the legal code ascribed to Meḥmet II.[21] Furthermore, as we shall see in Chapter 4, in addition to regulating the structure of the hierarchy, certain legal codes regulated the curriculum taught in these institutions. By regulating the curriculum – and by specifying an imperial jurisprudential canon – the Ottoman dynasty also regulated the doctrine of its branch of the Ḥanafī school of law and limited the range of permissible hermeneutic principles that jurists who were affiliated with it could follow when deriving new rules.

An integral component in the evolution of the learned hierarchy was the emergence of the practice of the appointment of jurisconsults (muftīs) by the sultan and the rise of the chief imperial muftī (the *şeyḫülislâm*) to preside over the learned hierarchy as a whole.[22] Although many of the officially appointed muftīs were graduates of the imperial educational system, in the Arab provinces of the empire, the Ottoman dynasty and its learned hierarchy also gave appointments to muftīs educated elsewhere. In addition, many of these muftīs served as professors in the imperial madrasa system either before or during their tenure in the position of muftī. From the mid-sixteenth century, when the chief imperial muftī became the head of the imperial hierarchy as a whole, he became institutionally its chief judicial and scholarly authority. In that capacity, as I show in Chapter 4, he also regulated the imperial jurisprudential canon that members of the hierarchy were to apply. In so doing, the chief muftī regulated the doctrine of the branch within the Ḥanafī school of law that the learned hierarchy followed. Furthermore, he could enforce specific

21 Repp, *The Müfti of Istanbul*.
22 Ibid.; Imber, *Ebu's-Su'ud*; Buzov, "The Lawgiver and His Lawmakers," 135–89.

legal arguments and doctrines out of a wider range of opinions within the Ḥanafī school, and, in some cases, the *şeyḫülislâm* opted for a minority opinion within the school and asked the sultan to issue an imperial edict that would enforce it within the learned hierarchy.

As we shall see in Chapter 2, as part of the consolidation of the imperial learned hierarchy, its members sought to document the hierarchy's intellectual genealogy within the Ḥanafī school of law (and, to some extent, their personal genealogy as well). To this end, from the second half of the sixteenth century, high-ranking members of the hierarchy compiled intellectual genealogies (*ṭabaqāt*) of the school. The aim of these compilations was twofold: first, they were intended to reconstruct and record a continuous chain of transmission of knowledge and authority leading from the eponymous founder of the school, Abū Ḥanīfa, to members of the hierarchy; second, they sought to reconstruct the authoritative genealogies of certain legal arguments and jurisprudential texts within the Ḥanafī legal school that often constituted part of the imperial jurisprudential canon. Roughly around the same time as they were developing the genealogies, members of the learned hierarchy also started compiling biographical dictionaries that were dedicated to the upper echelon of the Ottoman learned hierarchy, the most famous of which is Aḥmad b. Muṣṭafā Taşköprüzâde's *al-Shaqā'iq al-nu'māniyya*. Through these biographical dictionaries, members of the hierarchy demarcated its institutional boundaries and cemented its career and training tracks.

Taken together, the institutional consolidation of the learned hierarchy and, as I argue in Chapter 1, the practice of appointing jurisconsults were instrumental in shaping the structure of the particular branch within the Ḥanafī school, or a specific Ottoman Ḥanafī canon, that members of the hierarchy followed. In earlier periods in Islamic history, the sovereign (the caliph, the sultan, or the state) appointed judges, but, as Norman Calder, following the fourteenth-century Shāfi'ī jurist Taqiyy al-Dīn al-Subkī (d. 1355) points out, "Though both [the teaching/writing jurist's and the muftī's] functions might be marked by the acquisition of posts (a teaching post in a madrasa, the mufti-ship of a particular community), they were essentially informal. They permitted, but did not require, institutional realisation."[23] This was clearly not the case in the Ottoman Empire.

The Ottoman dynasty, it is worth reiterating, contributed immensely to the emergence of an Ottoman Ḥanafī school through certain

[23] Norman Calder, *Islamic Jurisprudence in the Classical Era* (Cambridge: Cambridge University Press, 2010): 128–29.

administrative practices, edicts, and legal codes, which together constituted part of a legal corpus and discourse that I call throughout this book "dynastic law." Furthermore, this set of administrative practices and legal codes was associated with and, to a large extent, drew its legitimacy from the dynasty and its ancestors (hence its definition as dynastic law). As I suggest in the Conclusion, the rise of Ottoman dynastic law was part of a broader development across the eastern Islamic lands in the post-Mongol period that drew heavily on the shared real and imagined political-legal heritage of Chinggis Khān.

The Official School of Law and the Imperial Legal Order

The conquest of the Arab lands set in motion an intense encounter between different jurists who claimed affiliation to different branches within the Ḥanafī school and perceived their relationship with the Ottoman dynasty quite differently. The exchanges and debates between the different jurists were not only centered on legal controversies concerning specific issues. They were also – or, perhaps, mainly – about the role the sultan and the dynasty were to play in regulating and shaping the structure of the Ḥanafī school of law and its doctrine. While jurists who were affiliated with the Ottoman dynasty accepted, and at times actively promoted, the sultan's intervention in regulating the branch within the Ḥanafī school to which they claimed affiliation, other jurists, mostly from the empire's Arab provinces, argued for much greater autonomy for the jurists, as was the case, at least theoretically, in the pre-Ottoman (and, more generally, in the pre-Mongol) period. In other words, generally speaking, the position of a jurist in relation to the Ottoman dynasty/sultan corresponded to a large degree to his position within the Ḥanafī school of law.

Throughout this volume, I pay considerable attention to the critique raised by discontents and rivals who called into question the validity of the legal order the Ottoman dynasty sought to advance. Their critique, I would argue, helps illustrate how radically novel, within the context of Islamic legal history, the emergence of an official state school was. Furthermore, these dissenting voices qualify the connection between the Ottomans and the Ḥanafī school of law as a whole. Put differently, this book argues that the Ḥanafī school in the Ottoman period was not, and should not be treated as, a homogenous school either socially or intellectually.[24]

[24] Haim Gerber's work deserves special mention in this respect. In his study of the Ottoman legal system, and particularly in his comparison of the rulings of jurists from the core

In recent years several studies have emphasized the role law and legal regimes played in different imperial and colonial contexts. While some studies have looked comparatively at various legal administrations, others have focused on the interactions between different legal systems within a single empire (as well as on inter-imperial legal arrangements). Among the latter, Lauren Benton's studies of the organization and function of imperial legal regimes are particularly noteworthy. Benton's work offers an analytical framework that allows numerous legal actors as well as the imperial state to be woven into the narrative. In addition, Benton has defined two main types of imperial legal orders. The first is a multicentric legal order in which the imperial state is one among many legal authorities. The second, by contrast, is state-centered, with the state claiming dominance over other legal authorities.[25] More recently, Benton has elaborated her study of legal regimes and pointed to the importance of the geographical spread of "legal cultures," institutions, and "carriers" of certain legal concepts, such as imperial officials, merchants, soldiers, and even captives. "Empires," she has argued, "did not cover space evenly but composed a fabric that was full of holes, stitched together out of pieces, a tangle of strings. Even in the most paradigmatic cases, an empire's spaces were politically fragmented; legally differentiated; and encased in irregular, porous, and sometimes undefined borders."[26]

This study draws on Benton's insights concerning the administration of law in different empires and pays attention to the overlapping topographies of administrative practices and legal-scholarly traditions across the Ottoman Empire. More concretely, it examines how the Ottoman dynasty and its learned hierarchy functioned in – but also shaped – the empire's multicentric legal landscape. As I have mentioned, the new rulers did not ban the activity of some eminent jurisconsults who did not hold a state appointment, although they did ban the activity of nonappointed judges (*qāḍīs*). Yet, in order to cope with this plurality of Ḥanafī jurists and traditions, the Ottoman dynasty and its affiliated jurists emphasized

lands of the empire to those of the Palestinian jurist Khayr al-Dīn al-Ramlī, whom we shall meet in several instances throughout this book, Gerber points to the existence of multiple legal cultures within the scholarly judicial circles across the empire. Although my interpretations and conclusions are at times different from Gerber's, I fully agree with his suggestion to look at the empire's different scholarly circles comparatively. Gerber, *State, Society, and Law in Islam*; Haim Gerber, *Islamic Law and Culture* (Leiden: Brill, 1999).

25 Benton, *Law and Colonial Cultures*, 11.

26 Lauren Benton, *A Search for Sovereignty: Law and Geography in European Empire, 1400–1900* (Cambridge: Cambridge University Press, 2010), 2.

the importance of the official appointment and the importance of the affiliation with the imperial learned hierarchy, whose center was at the imperial capital.

The encounter between the different scholarly and legal traditions transformed all the parties involved, as jurists tried to adopt some of the discourses and practices of their rivals and opponents. Members of the Ottoman learned hierarchy, as we shall see in the following chapters, employed conventions and genres that prevailed in the preconquest period (and well into centuries of Ottoman rule) throughout what was following the conquest the Arab lands of the empire. On the other hand, as Chapter 1 examines, jurists who were not affiliated with the imperial hierarchy attempted in various ways to justify and retain their position within the imperial landscape on the basis of legal arguments that were accepted by members of the learned hierarchy as well. Moreover, the vast majority of the jurists that inhabit the chapters that follow were loyal Ottoman subjects, and some of the locally acclaimed jurists who were not members of the learned hierarchy authored treatises in which they praised the Ottoman dynasty.

This book also argues that the debates and exchanges between the jurists were not merely scholarly debates. Since these debates shaped to a considerable degree the legal landscape of the empire, they affected many individuals and groups who were not necessarily scholars or jurists. Furthermore, the multifaceted and diverse legal landscape meant that Ḥanafī jurists, regardless of their affiliation with the Ottoman dynasty, had to maintain ongoing dialogues with their colleagues, the Ottoman dynasty, and their own constituency (or constituencies) in order to preserve and negotiate their position within the imperial framework. Members of the Ottoman learned hierarchy were keenly aware that the ruling elite as well as many of their constituents across the central lands of the empire (the Balkans and central and western Anatolia) could address and consult Ḥanafīs from the Arab lands, for though the Ottoman ruling and judicial elites tried to prevent this constituency from turning to jurists who were followers of the other Sunnī schools (the Shāfiʿī, Ḥanbalī, and Mālikī schools), they did not prevent them from addressing Ḥanafī jurists who were not affiliated with the imperial learned hierarchy.[27] Similarly, Ḥanafīs from the Arab lands understood that their constituency, too, had new options to resolve their legal issues. Many Ḥanafīs from the Arab lands retained their teaching positions in madrasas across these

[27] Peters, "What Does It Mean to Be an Official Madhhab?," 154–57.

provinces and were appointed as deputies of the chief provincial judge,[28] but, within the imperial legal system, they did not enjoy the same level of support that members of the dynasty (and particularly graduates of the Ottoman madrasa system) did, as the former acutely perceived. The concerns of both members of the learned hierarchy and their colleagues who were not officially appointed were grounded in reality: as I show in Chapter 5, individuals and groups, not necessarily members of one of the empire's scholarly circles, made use of the multiple jurists who were at their disposal to promote their legal and other interests.

Paying attention to the complexity of the empire's legal landscape and to the exchanges between the different jurists also casts light on additional dimensions of the conquest and incorporation of the Arab lands that have not received much attention in modern historiography. This gap in modern historiography may be attributed, at least in part, to the subtle and indirect nature of these debates and exchanges. There were relatively few instances of major debates that attracted the attention of contemporary and modern historians. This historiographical silence may seem surprising given the doctrinal significance of the rise of an official school of law and the formation of a well-defined and structured learned hierarchy. On the other hand, the multicentric nature of the empire's legal landscape may account, to some extent at least, for this relative silence.

My analysis in the following pages, which concentrates on specific aspects of the relationship between the dynasty and the jurists, does not intend to question the sincerity of either the Ottoman dynasty or of the jurists who were affiliated with it (as some cynics may be tempted to do). In fact, my goal is to draw attention to both parties' sophisticated responses, solutions, and adjustments in the face of the serious challenge

[28] Some jurists from the Arab lands entered the Ottoman madrasa system, although never reached its upper echelon. Baki Tezcan, "Dispelling the Darkness: The Politics of 'Race' in the Early Seventeenth-Century Ottoman Empire in the Light of the Life and Work of Mullah Ali," in *Identity and Identity Formation in the Ottoman World: A Volume of Essays in Honor of Norman Itzkowitz*, ed. Baki Tezcan and Karl Barbir (Madison: University of Wisconsin Press, 2007), 75–76.

Despite clear administrative continuities in the years following the conquest, there are some indications that the Ottomans introduced certain changes that affected Greater Syrian jurists. For example, the sixteenth-century Damascene chronicler and jurist Shams al-Dīn Muḥammad b. ʿAlī b. Ṭūlūn complained that "the Rūmīs [the Ottomans] [did] not follow the stipulations of the endowers, unless it serve[d] their interests (*illa fīmā lahum fīhi maṣlaḥa*)." Shams al-Dīn Muḥammad b. ʿAlī b. Ṭūlūn, *Ḥawādith Dimashq al-yawmiyya ghadāt al-ghazw al-ʿUthmānī li'l-Shām, 926–951H: ṣafaḥāt mafqūda tunsharu li'l-marra al-ūlā min Kitāb Mufākahat al-khillān fī ḥawādith al-zamān li-Ibn Ṭūlūn al-Ṣāliḥī* (Damascus: Dār al-Awāʾil, 2002), 270.

posed by the encounter between the post-Mongol notion of dynastic law and the pre-Mongol notion of Islamic law. After all, the Ottoman dynasty invested considerable efforts and resources to develop a learned hierarchy in order to justify its claim to be an Islamic dynasty.

The Rise of an Ottoman Official Madhhab and the Grand Narratives of Islamic Legal History

Despite the particularities of the Ottoman Ḥanafī school, it appears that the emergence of the notion of an official state madhhab is not uniquely Ottoman. The rise of the official school of law and the dynasty's intervention in its regulation may have been broader phenomena that spanned most polities throughout the eastern Islamic lands, from the Indian subcontinent to the Balkans, in the post-Mongol period. Herein lies the justification for the title of this book: in one of his last public talks, the late art historian Oleg Grabar suggested a supplement to his classic study *The Formation of Islamic Art*, which focuses on monuments from Syria, North Africa, and Islamic Spain from the eighth century to the tenth century. The suggested supplement, which would be entitled *The Second Formation of Islamic Art*, would concentrate on the art produced in the eastern Islamic lands in the thirteenth and the fourteenth centuries, roughly the century and a half following the Mongol invasions of the thirteenth century.[29] Inspired by Grabar's suggestion, *The Second Formation of Islamic Law* seeks to offer an analytical framework that would account for the recurring discursive and administrative patterns across the eastern Islamic lands in that period, and particularly in the various Sunnī (and Ḥanafī) polities of the region. These patterns, I believe, may be attributed to the introduction of new notions of law and rulership in the wake of the Mongol invasions of the thirteenth century. Moreover, they enable us to speak of a new era in Islamic legal history – indeed, a second formation of Islamic law.

Of particular importance in this context is the rise of the post-Mongol notion that each ruling dynasty has a corpus of legal and administrative practices that is distinctively associated with it, what I call throughout this study "dynastic law." The terms that were used to refer to these dynastic laws varied over time and space: the *yasa* of Chinggis Khān, the Timurid *töre*, or the Ottoman *ḳânûn*. Moreover, throughout the eastern

[29] Cited in Persis Berlekamp, *Wonder, Image, and Cosmos in Medieval Islam* (New Haven, CT: Yale University Press, 2011), 1–2.

Islamic lands in the post-Mongol period, the different dynastic laws were often perceived (as they also are in modern historiography) as incompatible with Islamic law, at least in the manner it was understood in the pre-Mongol period. The main reason for this real or imagined tension is that each of these legal corpuses/discourses had different historical and discursive points of reference: while the Islamic legal discourse claimed to derive new rules and laws by interpreting the divine revelation, dynastic law often drew its legitimacy from the authority of the dynasty's ancestors and ruling members (and in some cases, from their heavenly mandate to rule). The tensions between dynastic and the pre-Mongol perceptions of Islamic law, I would suggest, shape the immediate background to the rise of the official state madhhab in two important ways: first, by developing an official school of law, the different dynasties and the jurists who were affiliated with them sought to reduce the tension between the legal bodies as they perceived it; second, as I hope to illustrate in the Ottoman context, it was on the basis of dynastic law that dynasties and sultans were able to regulate the structure of the school and its doctrines. Put differently, adherence to dynastic law as a legal ideal was both a challenge that many post-Mongol dynasties were facing and one of the most important tools they had at their disposal to respond to this challenge.

As I contend throughout this book, tracing the history of the official madhhab and its practice provides an opportunity to reconsider the issue of "reconciliation" or "harmonization" of dynastic and Islamic law. Most studies of the incompatibility and reconciliation of dynastic law and sharīʿa have tended to focus on specific legal arguments or rules: if the sultan permitted or ordered acts that contradicted certain Islamic legal principles as some scholars perceived them (such as, for example, the construction of new churches and synagogues), his edict may have been considered contradictory to the tenets of Islamic law by certain jurists and modern scholars; on the other hand, if certain jurists succeeded in establishing the permissibility of certain practices on the basis of arguments they could find in the Ḥanafī jurisprudential tradition, these practices may have been considered licit according to Islamic law. This approach, however, fails to account for other dimensions of the relationship between Islamic and dynastic law, and seems to assume a very specific form of reconciliation or harmonization of the two discourses. Looking at the relationship between dynastic and Islamic law from the perspective of the Islamic school of law, the madhhab, considerably complicates this understanding of reconciliation.

The history of the rise of the official madhhab should also be examined in the context of other developments in Ottoman political thought and that of other contemporary dynasties. In recent years, growing attention has been paid to the self-perception of Muslim sovereigns in the post-Mongol period.[30] In the Ottoman context, as Hüseyin Yılmaz has demonstrated, the sixteenth century witnessed a fairly massive production of compilations on political theory. Many of these works were particularly interested in promoting a more legalistic view of the sultanate and stressed the importance of the dynastic legal tradition (*ḳânûn*) as the definitive law of government, at the expense of the personality of the ruler.[31] This study intends to elucidate additional dimensions of this legalistic worldview by focusing on another textual corpus – the jurisprudential production of jurists who were affiliated with the Ottoman dynasty. In so doing, the following chapters examine further the nature of the relationship between dynastic law, the ruling dynasty, and the jurists affiliated with it.

Finally, this book intends to call into question some key elements in certain dominant grand narratives of Islamic legal history. According to these narratives, the main rupture point in Islamic legal history is the nineteenth century, with its state-initiated (and often Westernizing) legal reforms and the codification of Islamic law. These reforms, so the narrative goes, replaced a more fluid and diverse Islamic law that was by and large regulated autonomously by the jurists (hence Islamic law is at times described as "jurists' law").[32] This book shares these grand narratives' emphasis on the role states/rulers played in regulating Islamic law, but it differs in its periodization of this important change, as the

[30] Hüseyin Yılmaz, "The Sultan and the Sultanate: Envisioning Rulership in Age of Süleymân the Lawgiver (1520–1566)" (PhD diss., Harvard University, 2004); Muzaffar Alam, *The Language of Political Islam: India, 1200–1800* (Chicago: University of Chicago Press, 2004); Anne F. Broadbridge, *Kingship and Ideology in the Islamic and Mongol Worlds* (Cambridge: Cambridge University Press, 2008); A. Azfar Moin, *The Millennial Sovereign: Sacred Kingship and Sainthood in Islam* (New York: Columbia University Press, 2012).

[31] Yılmaz, "The Sultan and the Sultanate." See also Colin Imber's discussion of the caliphate and Ottoman notions of sovereignty during the reign of Sultan Süleymân: Imber, *Ebu's-Su'ud*, 66–111.

[32] See, for example, Muhammad Qasim Zaman, *The Ulama in Contemporary Islam: Custodian of Change* (Princeton, NJ: Princeton University Press, 2002), chap. 1; Wael B. Hallaq, *Sharī'ah: Theory, Practice, Transformations* (Cambridge: Cambridge University Press, 2009); Chibli Mallat, *Introduction to Middle Eastern Law* (Oxford: Oxford University Press, 2009).

growing intervention of post-Mongol dynasties is observable from the fifteenth century (and perhaps even earlier). In the Conclusion, this study attempts to offer a historiographical framework, albeit a provisional one, that accounts for the developments in Islamic legal history in the post-Mongol period.

A caveat is in order here concerning the terminology. I make use of the terms "pre-Mongol" and "post-Mongol" quite freely throughout this study. Unless stated otherwise, these terms should not be taken as chronological terms in the narrow sense of the word. Rather, they are used to denote different relations between the ruling dynasty (or Muslim sovereigns, more generally) and the jurists. This usage reflects the book's argument that some pre-Mongol notions and practices remained in circulation in the centuries following the Mongol invasions of the thirteenth century.

1

Muftīs

Late in his career, after he had already served as the officially appointed Ḥanafī muftī of Damascus, the eighteenth-century jurist and chronicler Muḥammad Khalīl b. ʿAlī al-Murādī (d. 1791 or 1792) sat down to write a biographical dictionary of the Ḥanafī muftīs of Damascus from the Ottoman conquest of the city up to his own time.[1] In the introduction to this dictionary, al-Murādī explains why he decided to focus on those who held the office of the muftī of Damascus. In addition, he elaborates on the reasons for the chronological scope of the dictionary – the years of the Ottoman rule in Damascus. It is worth citing this fascinating passage in full:

> I wanted to compile a book that would include all the biographies of those who were appointed as muftīs [*waliya al-fatwā*] in it [in Damascus] from the time of the great sultan, the famous *khaqān*, the protector of the land and the frontiers, the grace of the eras and the times, the merciful and helper, he who makes flow the fountains of benevolence in this world and [the fountains] of justice, the queller of the people of evil and corruption, the bearer of the standards of the sharīʿa and righteousness, the uprooter of oppressors, the defeater of tyrants, he who holds the throne, he who is auspiciously assisted by God, the Iskandar of the time and its Anushervān, the Mahdi of the time and its Sulaymān, the Ottoman Sultan Selîm Khān, let him be enrobed with [God's] merciful contentment. This [the book starts] when he entered Damascus, renewed its affairs, implemented his edicts in it, and

[1] Muḥammad Khalīl b. ʿAlī b. Muḥammad b. Muḥammad al-Murādī, *ʿArf al-bashām fī-man waliya fatwā Dimashq al-Shām* (Damascus: Dār Ibn Kathīr, 1988), 144–52. For more on al-Murādī, see also Karl K. Barbir, "All in the Family: The Muradis of Damascus," in *Proceedings of the IIIrd Congress on the Social and Economic History of Turkey*, ed. Heath W. Lowry and Ralph S. Hattox (Istanbul: ISIS Press, 1990), 327–53.

> organized it according to his exalted qānūn, which is in accordance with the honorable sharīʿa (*al-sharʿ al-sharīf*). [He also] arranged its [the city's] offices of knowledge and siyāsa[2] according to his ability and his noble opinion. This was in 922 [1516]. Among these [new regulations] was the assignment of the position of the muftī [*takhṣīṣ al-iftāʾ*] of each school to a single person, and so he did with the judgeship. The kings and sultans before him, while they appointed a single person to the judgeship, left the affairs of issuing *fatāwā* to the jurists [ʿulamāʾ]: the jurists of each school issued their opinion when they were asked [about a certain issue], they answered [lit., wrote] questions, and constant dispute and strife prevailed among them [the jurists]. This was the state of affairs in Damascus until Sultan Selîm Khān entered the city, conquered it, and arranged its affairs. [Then] he eradicated from the stubborn people their rebelliousness. He perfected the [city's] regulation, which he conducted according to the pure sharīʿa. His successors, the honorable Ottoman kings, employed this manner of assigning the muftīship of each school to a single person from the jurists of the school, and prevented all the other [jurists] from answering questions, and so was the case with the judges, up until our time in the rest of their lands.[3]

In this introductory paragraph, al-Murādī points to the existence, on the eve of the Ottoman conquest of the Arab lands, of two radically different perceptions of the relationship between the muftī and the ruler. The pre-Ottoman, "Mamluk" model, explains al-Murādī, advances the independence of the muftī from state authorities, since the muftīship is an internal concern of the community of jurists and religious scholars. In the Ottoman perception of the muftīship, by contrast, it is the sultan who appoints the jurisconsult. Although al-Murādī does not explicitly discuss the implications of the different models, he seems to imply that the change was deeper than the mere appointment procedure: at stake were the nature of the institution of the muftī, its role within the legal (and political) system, and – perhaps most importantly – the authority of the Ottoman sultan and dynasty to regulate the structure of the Ḥanafī school of law and its content.

[2] Siyāsa (or *siyâset* in Turkish) refers to the executive powers granted to state officials (*ehl-i ʿörf*), whose authority derived ultimately from the Ottoman sultan. See Leslie Peirce, *Morality Tales: Law and Gender in the Ottoman Court of Aintab* (Berkeley: University of California Press, 2003), 134–35. For siyāsa in the Mamluk period, see Kristen Stilt, *Islamic Law in Action: Authority, Discretion, and Everyday Experiences in Mamluk Egypt* (Oxford: Oxford University Press, 2012); Yossef Rapoport, "Royal Justice and Religious Law: Siyāsah and Shariʿah under the Mamluks," *Mamluk Studies Review* 16 (2012): 71–102.

[3] Al-Murādī, *ʿArf al-bashām*, 2–3.

In al-Murādī's eyes, the Ottoman conquest of the Arab lands led to an abrupt and intense encounter of these perceptions (or models). The aftermath of this encounter was decisive: the "Ottoman perception" of the muftīship prevailed. Fittingly, the office of the muftī in general and specifically that of the Ḥanafī muftī of Damascus, which up to 1516 had followed the pre-Ottoman model, underwent considerable change as it was modeled after the Ottoman perception of the office.

Although al-Murādī's description of the three centuries that had elapsed since the Ottoman conquest should not be taken at face value, his understanding of the transformation the office underwent merits attention for three major reasons. First, in this passage al-Murādī articulates his perception of the history of the office he himself held for several years. Second, and perhaps more importantly, this passage may be read as an attempt by al-Murādī, as a religious scholar and a chronicler, to reconcile the tension between his knowledge of what he considered the pre-Ottoman understanding of the institution of the muftī and the current Ottoman practice. Third, it is quite possible, as we shall see in the following discussion, that al-Murādī was defending this change in response to some of his colleagues' discontent with the transformation the office of the muftī had undergone in the past three centuries – discontent that stemmed precisely from the tension between the different views of the institution of the muftī and from some of his colleagues' disenfranchisement.

This chapter takes al-Murādī's account as its point of departure for a reconstruction of the transformation the institution of the muftī underwent in the Ottoman Empire from roughly the early fifteenth century, namely, the rise of the officially appointed muftīship, which I locate as part of the emergence of an imperial learned hierarchy. I also seek to situate this account within a debate that took place from the sixteenth century onward between the supporters of this relatively recent innovation of the officially appointed jurisconsult and those who favored the pre-Ottoman perception and practice of the muftīship. Furthermore, as I suggest in the fifth and concluding sections of this chapter, the rise of the officially appointed muftī (and of an imperial learned hierarchy as a whole) was instrumental in the emergence of the official madhhab. At the same time, I also look at some of the jurists who were less sympathetic to the Ottoman dynasty's intervention in regulating the structure of the legal school and its doctrine, and how they formulated their own understanding of the relationship between the sultan and school of law.

Muftī: A Very Brief Introduction

Before we turn to an examination of the perception and practice of the muftīship in the late Mamluk and the Ottoman contexts, a few introductory words about the institution of the muftī in classical Sunnī legal theory are in order. One of the fundamental institutions of Islamic legal systems, a muftī (often glossed as jurisconsult) is an authority who issues opinions (*fatwā* pl. *fatāwā* in Arabic, *fetvâ* pl. *fetâvâ* in Turkish) in response to questions posed to him (or, in some cases, to her) on questions regarding sharīʿa rulings. Theoretically, a muftī should be a pious Muslim, adult, sane, and trustworthy, and should possess the necessary legal training. Slaves, women, and people who are blind or mute (assuming that they can communicate their opinions) may serve as muftīs as well. The legal requirements for issuing legal rulings are thus somewhat different from the requirements for other legal capacities (such as bearing witness, for example).

In classical Sunnī jurisprudence, the formalized concept of the muftī is different from that of the judge (the *qāḍī*) in several significant respects, although many scholars considered muftīs also serve as judges. First, for the most part, the muftī is not appointed by the leader of the Muslim community (the *imām*), whereas judges are. Second, the ruling of the muftī (the *fatwā*), unlike the judge's resolution (*ḥukm*), is not legally binding and enforceable. Therefore, the solicitor of the muftī's opinion does not have to follow the muftī's *fatwā*. Third, while judges deal only with issues of conflict between individuals or between individuals and the state, muftīs can be asked about issues ranging from proper ablution practices to the fundamentals of faith to the interpretation of obscure passages in jurisprudential texts – issues that would never be adjudicated in a court. Finally, the ruling of the muftī is intended to articulate a general legal principle, "an element of doctrine," on the basis of a concrete case. By contrast, the judge in his ruling aims to resolve a concrete dispute between two parties or litigants. As Brinkley Messick aptly explains,

> Their [the *fatwā*'s and the judgment's] interpretive thrusts are diametrically opposed. What is "constructed" in a fatwā is an element of doctrine: a fatwā is concerned with and based upon doctrinal texts, although it requires the specifics of an actual case as its point of departure. What is "constructed" in a judgment is a segment of practice: a judgment is concerned with and based upon practical information, although it requires a framework of doctrine as its point of reference. Fatwās use uncontested concrete descriptions as given instances necessitating interpretation in doctrine; judgments address the contested facts of cases as

problematic instances that are themselves in need of interpretation. Fatwās and judgments are thus interpretive reciprocals: they come to rest at opposed points on the same hermeneutical circle.[4]

As articulators of general legal principles, muftīs play a significant role in expanding and elaborating the Islamic legal corpus, especially in cases that are not explicitly addressed in the existing legal (as well as theological and even mystical) literature. Moreover, in many instances, their rulings, especially those of eminent muftīs, have been integrated into the literature of substantive law (or the "branches of the law," *furūʿ*). On the other hand, muftīs have interpreted the literature and applied it to new cases that it did not explicitly address. In other words, as several modern scholars have observed, muftīs serve as mediators between the legal text and the world.

Islamic legal literature – and especially the genre of the *etiquette of the muftī* (*adab al-muftī*), whose focus is the institution of the jurisconsult – is concerned with regulating the muftī's activity within the school of law. Unlike the judge, who is generally charged with applying the existing rules and laws of his *maddhab* exclusively (and is often considered a follower, *muqallid*, of the school), the muftī in classical Sunnī theory is often perceived as the performer of independent legal discretion (*ijtihād*), since he may well be asked about an issue that has no existing ruling yet (or that is hotly debated). Moreover, the terms *muftī* and *mujtahid* are frequently used interchangeably. In the Ḥanafī school, however, as we shall see in the fifth section of this chapter, the notion of a *muqallid* muftī existed as well.[5]

4 Brinkley Messick, *The Calligraphic State: Textual Domination and History in a Muslim Society* (Berkeley: University of California Press, 1993), 146.

5 The literature on muftīs is vast. See, for example, A. Kevin Reinhart, "Transcendence and Social Practice: Muftis and Qadis as Religious Interpreters," *Annales Islamologiques* 27 (1993): 5–25; Wael B. Hallaq, "From Fatwas to Furuʿ: Growth and Change in Islamic Substantive Law," *Islamic Law and Society* 1, no. 1 (1994): 29–65; Norman Calder, "al-Nawawi's Typology of Muftis and Its Significance for a General Theory of Islamic Law," *Islamic Law and Society* 3, no. 2 (1996): 137–64; Muhammad Khalid Masud, Brinkley Messick, and David S. Powers, eds., *Islamic Legal Interpretation: Muftis and Their Fatwas* (Cambridge, MA: Harvard University Press, 1996); David S. Powers, *Law, Society, and Culture in the Maghrib, 1300–1500* (Cambridge: Cambridge University Press, 2002); Etty Terem, "The New Miʿyar of al-Mahdi al-Wazzani: Local Interpretation of Family Life in Late Nineteenth-Century Fez" (PhD diss., Harvard University, 2007); Camilo Gomez-Rivas, "The Fatwas of Ibn Rushd al-Jadd to the Far Maghrib: Urban Transformation and the Development of Islamic Legal Institutions under the Almoravids" (PhD diss., Yale University, 2009); Muhammad Khalid Masud, "The Significance of

The Institution of the Muftī in the Late Mamluk Sultanate

The kings and sultans before him, while they appointed a single person to the judgeship, left the affairs of issuing *fatāwā* to the jurists: the jurists of each school issued their opinion when they were asked [about a certain issue], they answered questions, and there was constant dispute and strife among them.

Like many other jurists and religious scholars in the late Mamluk sultanate, the Ḥanafī scholar Muḥammad b. Ibrāhīm b. Muḥammad al-Ghazzī (1421–91) left his hometown (Gaza) to travel to Cairo to study with the great scholars of the time. One of his teachers in Cairo, Saʿd al-Dīn al-Dayrī,[6] granted him a permit to teach law and issue legal opinions (*idhn fī al-tadrīs wa'l-iftā'*). After he had spent a while in Cairo, he traveled to Damascus, where he eventually settled down and issued legal opinions.[7] Al-Ghazzī was not a prominent jurist or a distinguished scholar. Nevertheless, his career is similar to many other contemporary and earlier ones. It was a common practice among jurists and scholars in the Mamluk sultanate to travel to learning centers both within and without the Mamluk sultanate in order to obtain religious and jurisprudential knowledge (their earlier and contemporary counterparts elsewhere similarly traveled within and outside their respective polities in pursuit of knowledge). Of particular relevance to our discussion of the nature of muftīship in the late Mamluk sultanate is the license al-Ghazzī was granted to teach law and issue legal opinions, since this license turned him into a muftī in the most literal sense of the word – someone who is allowed to issue jurisprudential rulings.

Since George Makdisi published his seminal *The Rise of Colleges*,[8] scholars have been debating the degree to which the transmission of religious and jurisprudential knowledge in Sunnī Islam in general and in the Mamluk sultanate in particular was institutionalized. The key issue in

Istifta' in the Fatwa Discourse," *Islamic Studies* 48, no. 3 (2009): 341–66. The literature on muftīs in the Mamluk and the Ottoman periods will be discussed in the following.

6 On Saʿd al-Dīn al-Dayrī, see ʿAbd al-Raḥmān b. Muḥammad al-ʿUlaymī, *al-Uns al-jalīl bi-tārīkh al-Quds wa'l-Khalīl* (Najaf: al-Maṭbaʿa al-Ḥaydariyya, 1968), 2:227–28; Muḥammad b. ʿAbd al-Raḥmān al-Sakhāwī, *al-Ḍaw' al-lāmiʿ li-ahl al-qarn al-tāsiʿ* (Beirut: Dār Maktabat al-Ḥayāt, 1966), 3:249–53; Boaz Shoshan, "Jerusalem Scholars (*ʿUlamā'*) and Their Activities in the Mamluk Empire" [in Hebrew], in *Palestine in the Mamluk Period*, ed. Joseph Drory (Jerusalem: Yad Izhak Ben-Zvi, 1992), 95–96.

7 Aḥmad b. Muḥammad b. al-Mullāal-Ḥaṣkafī, *Mutʿat al-adhhān min al-tamattuʿ bi'l-iqrān bayna tarājim al-shuyūkh wa'l-aqrān* (Beirut: Dār Ṣādir, 1999), 2:589–90.

8 George Makdisi, *The Rise of Colleges: Institutions of Learning in Islam and the West* (Edinburgh: Edinburgh University Press, 1981).

this "institutionalization debate" is the importance of two specific institutions – religious colleges (madrasas) and certificates (*ijāzas*), including the permit to teach and issue legal opinions – in the transmission of religious knowledge. In their studies of the transmission of religious knowledge in Mamluk Cairo and Damascus, Jonathan Berkey and Michael Chamberlain,[9] respectively, have stressed the importance assigned to the individual transmitter or professor, rather than to the institution (the madrasa) in which he taught. In addition, while both scholars have acknowledged the importance of the transmission from a teacher to his student, they have downplayed the importance of the certificate (as document), which permitted the student to teach and issue legal rulings, as a significant institution within the Mamluk educational system. Instead, they have both emphasized the personal, flexible, informal, and unsystematic nature of the transmission of religious and jurisprudential knowledge across the Mamluk sultanate.

Makdisi and more recently Devin Stewart, by contrast, have argued that both the madrasa and the certificates (*ijāzas*) played a pivotal role in the transmission of knowledge in Mamluk Egypt and Syria. Based on his reading of al-Qalqashandī's chancery manual and two biographical dictionaries from the fourteenth century and the first half of the fifteenth century, Stewart has shown that the permits (*ijāzas*) were divided into three types,[10] each of which followed specific literary patterns and scribal rules. Stewart has concluded that the license granted by the teachers to their students involved a document and that, furthermore, granting a permit to teach and issue legal opinions was highly institutionalized as part of the training of the student in the madrasa throughout the Mamluk period. From at least the fourteenth century, it was granted at a specific point in the student's training course, which most often took place in the

[9] Jonathan Berkey, *The Transmission of Knowledge in Medieval Cairo: A Social History of Islamic Education* (Princeton, NJ: Princeton University Press, 1992); Michael Chamberlain, *Knowledge and Social Practice in Medieval Damascus, 1190–1350* (Cambridge: Cambridge University Press, 1994).

[10] Al-Qalqashandī lists three types of ijāzas: a license to teach law and issue legal opinions (*ijāzat al-futyā wa'l-tadrīs*); a certificate granted after the student has memorized certain works and presented his knowledge before a number of scholars (hence, this certificate literally means "presentation," *'arḍ*); and a license of transmission (*ijāzat al-riwāya* or *ijāza bi'l-marwīyāt 'alā' al-istid'ā'āt*). For a translation of these certificates, see Devin Stewart, "The Doctorate of Islamic Law in Mamluk Egypt and Syria," in *Law and Education in Medieval Islam: Studies in Memory of Professor George Makdisi*, ed. Joseph E. Lowry, Devin J. Stewart, and Shawkat M. Toorawa (Cambridge: E. J. W. Gibb Memorial Trust, 2004), 66–78.

madrasa assigned to the teacher. Moreover, the *ijāza* (or at times *idhn*) to teach and issue *fatāwā* served as a credential necessary for employment as a judge, deputy judge, or professor of law (*mudarris*), as well as in several other offices.[11]

The institutionalization of the permit to teach law and issue *fatāwā* was bolstered by the recording of issued permits in the biographical dictionaries from the Mamluk (and later) periods.[12] As Chamberlain has noted, one of the functions of biographical dictionaries was to serve as communal archives of scholarly (and other) elites.[13] Through these "archives," as Stewart has contended, scholars and jurists sought "to establish [them]selves in authoritative chains of transmission, linking [their] own authority to that of the learned among earlier generations in the Muslim community,"[14] and perhaps to enhance their scholarly prestige among their peers.[15] To put it differently, the biographical dictionaries assisted in turning the permit into a "social fact" within the scholarly and learned circles.

It is difficult to assess the number of permits to teach law and issue *fatāwā*, but the data recorded in the biographical dictionaries suggest that they were granted regularly. Nevertheless, as Stewart has pointed out, the number of permits recorded in the dictionaries seems to represent a tiny fraction of those actually granted in the major learning center across the Mamluk sultanate. The key point for the purpose at hand is that all those who were granted this license could have issued legal opinions, even if they were not appointed to a teaching or judging position. Moreover, as al-Murādī correctly observes, granting a permit to teach and issue *fatāwā* was an exclusive prerogative of the jurists and the scholars.

Since the learned circles across the Mamluk sultanate independently produced a large number of graduates who could issue legal opinions, the relationship between the Mamluk ruling elites and these muftīs deserves a few words. Being a muftī was not an official religious position (*waẓīfa dīniyya*) in the Mamluk administration, a fact that is reflected in the absence of the muftī as an office from the administrative and chancery

[11] Ibid., 60–63.

[12] Ibid.

[13] Chamberlain, *Knowledge and Social Practice*, 18.

[14] Stewart, "The Doctorate of Islamic Law," 52.

[15] It should be noted that biographical dictionaries vary widely regarding the frequency with which they mention *ijāzat al-tadrīs wa'l-iftā'*. As Makdisi and Stewart have shown, fourteenth- and fifteenth-century biographical dictionaries, such as Ibn Ḥajar al-ʿAsqalānī's (d. 1449) and al-Sakhāwī's (d. 1497), mention the *ijāza* to teach and issue *fatāwā* quite frequently (ibid., 53).

manuals.[16] Moreover, although the biographical dictionary was a common genre throughout the Mamluk period, to the best of my knowledge, no biographical dictionary that was dedicated exclusively to muftīs, that is, to officially appointed muftīs, was ever compiled.[17] This is not to say that muftīs did not appear in Mamluk biographical dictionaries: as Stewart has pointed out, the division between muftīs and judges is not as strict as it might appear, as some of those who obtained a permit to issue legal opinions were appointed by the Mamluk state to judiciary positions (such as judges or deputy judges), and many judges also issued legal opinions.[18] Still, throughout the Mamluk period, muftīs were not considered holders of a religious position.

The only official muftīship was the muftīship of the Hall of Justice (*Dār al-ʿAdl*), the superior sultanic (*Maẓālim*) court presided over by either the Mamluk sultan (in Cairo) or his deputy (in Syria).[19] But the opinion of the

[16] Al-Qalqashandī, for instance, does not list muftīs as officeholders. Aḥmad b. ʿAlīal-Qalqashandī, *Ṣubḥ al-aʿshā fī ṣināʿat al-inshāʾ* (Cairo: al-Muʾassasa al-Misriyya al-ʿĀmma li'l-Taʾlīf wa'l-Tarjama wa'l-Ṭibāʿa wa'l-Nashr, 1964), 2:192–93. Chroniclers did not list muftīs who were not appointed to a specific position among the officeholders as well. For late Mamluk Damascus, see, for instance, ʿAlīb. Yūsuf al-Buṣrawī, *Tārīkh al-Buṣrawī: ṣafaḥāt majhūla min tārīkh Dimashq fī ʿaṣr al-mamālīk, min sanat 871 H li-ghāyat 904 H* (Damascus: Dār al-Maʾmūn li'l-Turāth, 1988), 189–90; Shihāb al-Dīn Aḥmad b. Muḥammad b. ʿUmar b. al-Ḥimṣī, *Ḥawādith al-zamān wa-wafāyāt al-shuyūkh wa'l-aqrān* (Beirut: al-Maktaba al-ʿAṣriyya, 1999), 2:191–92. Moreover, the Damascene chronicler and muftī Ibn Ṭūlūn adheres to this historiographical approach in his annals of the Ottoman conquest of Damascus. As in many other Mamluk chronicles, the account of the events that transpired in a certain year opened with the enumeration of all the officeholders (the sultan, the governors, the judges, and so on). Muftīs are absent from this list. See Shams al-Dīn Muḥammad b. Ṭūlūn, *Mufākahat al-khillān fī ḥawādith al-zamān: tārīkh Miṣr wa'l-Shām* (Cairo: al-Muʾassasa al-Miṣriyya al-ʿĀmma li'l-Taʾlīf wa'l-Tarjama wa'l-Ṭibāʿa wa'l-Nashr, 1962–64), vol. 2.

[17] In fact, al-Murādī seems to be the first chronicler from the Arab lands to compile such a work. In the core lands of the empire, Müstaḳîmzâde Süleymân Saʿdeddîn Efendi (d. 1787–88), roughly a contemporary of al-Murādī, wrote a biographical dictionary entitled *Devḥatü'l-Meşâyiḫ-i Kibâr* that is exclusively devoted to muftīs: Müstakîmzâde Süleymân Saʿdeddîn, *Devḥatü-l-Meşâyiḫ: Einleitung und Edition*, 2 vols. (Stuttgart: Steiner Verlag, 2005). See also Richard C. Repp, *The Müftī of Istanbul: A Study of the Development of the Ottoman Learned Hierarchy* (London: Ithaca Press, 1986), 11.

[18] Ibn al-Shiḥna comments on the permissibility of *qāḍī*s' issuing of *fatāwā*. He argues that a *qāḍī* should not issue *fatāwā* in court (*majlis al-qaḍāʾ*). There is a debate among the jurists, he continues, about whether a *qāḍī* should issue *fatāwā* when he is not serving as a judge. Some jurists suggested that he should issue *fatāwā* concerning rituals (*ʿibādāt*) but not concerning interpersonal issues (*muʿāmalāt*). Ibrāhīm b. Abī al-Yamn Muḥammad b. Abī al-Faḍl b. al-Shiḥna, *Lisān al-ḥukkām fī maʿrifat al-aḥkām* (Cairo: Muṣṭafā al-Bābī al-Ḥalabī, 1973), 219.

[19] On *Dār al-ʿAdl*, see Emile Tyan, *Histoire de l'organisation judiciaire en pays d'Islam* (Leiden: Brill, 1960), 433–525; Jon E. Mandaville, "The Muslim Judiciary of Damascus

muftī of the Hall of Justice, like any other muftī in the Mamluk sultanate, was not in and of itself officially enforceable. The appointment deed of the late fourteenth-century Abū Bakr al-Jaytī al-Ḥanafī (ca. 1358–1416) to the Ḥanafī muftīship of *Dār al-ʿAdl* in Cairo offers a glimpse into the manner in which this office was perceived.[20] As the Ḥanafī muftī of the Hall of Justice, al-Jaytī was to supervise the rulings (*al-aḥkām al-sharʿiyya*) of the hall. Moreover, the deed states that his legal opinions should be the "foundation of our illustrious rulings" and that he "should issue legal opinions for the people of the time courageously and knowledgably." It is important to note, however, that the appointment deed does not specify that the appointee's rulings are binding or that he has the right to abrogate the rulings of the judges.[21]

There was also a fairly large number of muftīs that did not hold a state appointment, as any scholar who held a permit to issue legal rulings was virtually a muftī. Some held a teaching position in madrasas and mosques across the sultanate; others might have earned their livings through issuing legal opinions. More troubling, in the eyes of some jurists, was the fact that every muftī could issue legal opinions freely, even when they lacked proper knowledge. The late fourteenth-century historian and Mālikī chief judge Ibn Khaldūn, for instance, commented that the Mālikī muftīs in Cairo, some of whom he considered "quacks or lacking in learning," served as legal advisers to anyone who asked for their opinions either before or after a case was adjudicated in court, and his account emphasized the burden these muftīs and their opinions posed on his court and presumably on the legal system at large.[22] Roughly around

in the Late Mamluk Period" (PhD diss., Princeton University, 1969), 5–11, 69–73; Jørgen S. Nielsen, *Secular Justice in an Islamic State: Maẓālim under the Baḥri Mamlūks 662/1264–789/1387* (Leiden: Nederlands Historisch-Archaeologisch Instituut te Istanbul, 1985), 49–173; Nasser O. Rabbat, "The Ideological Significance of the Dar al-ʿAdl in the Medieval Islamic Orient," *International Journal of Middle East Studies* 27, no. 1 (1995): 3–28; Rapoport, "Royal Justice and Religious Law." In the fourteenth century, there were official muftīs affiliated with the four legal schools present in every session of the hall in Cairo. In Damascus, on the other hand, in the late Mamluk period only the Ḥanafī and Shāfiʿī schools were represented. Jon Mandaville has suggested that in late fifteenth-century Damascus, only a Ḥanafī muftī attended the sessions of *Dār al-ʿAdl* in the city, although al-Ghazzī mentions a Shāfiʿī muftī as well. Najm al-Dīn Muḥammad b. Muḥammad al-Ghazzī, *al-Kawākib al-sāʾira bi-aʿyān al-miʾa al-ʿāshira* (Beirut: Jāmiʿat Bayrūt al-Amīrikiyya, 1945–58), 1:40–45.

20 Al-Sakhāwī, *al-Ḍawʾ al-Lāmiʿ*, 11:50.

21 Taqiyy al-Dīn Abī Bakr b. ʿAlī Ibn Ḥijja al-Ḥamawī al-Azrārī, *Kitāb qahwat al-inshāʾ* (Beirut: Klaus Schwarz Verlag, 2005), 112–13.

22 Morimoto Kosei, "What Ibn Khaldūn Saw: The Judiciary of Mamluk Egypt," *Mamluk Studies Review* 6 (2002): 109–31. Ibn Khaldūn's comment is an important indication

the same time, the Mamluk sultan al-Ẓahīr Barqūq issued a decree to curb the muftīs' activity. In his decree, Barqūq demanded that muftīs follow the accepted doctrine of their respective schools. In addition, each muftī was to obtain a permit from the chief *qāḍī* (*qāḍī al-quḍāt*) of his respective school to issue legal opinions (thus obtaining an approval of his competence). Subsequently, the chief Shāfiʿī *qāḍī* of Damascus nominated seven muftīs, while his Ḥanafī counterpart appointed only three.[23] Approximately three decades later, in 1424, the Ḥanafī chief *qāḍī* was asked by Sultan al-Ashraf Barsbay to oversee the competence of some Ḥanafī muftīs.[24] Although these incidences seem to be the exception, they tell us something about the problems the multiplicity of jurisconsults generated.

The sultan's demand to supervise the muftīs was an extreme measure. For the most part, muftīs were not institutionally restricted. It was left to jurists to cope with the multiplicity of muftīs, and, over the course of the fifteenth century, different jurists suggested various approaches. In his manual for judges, the early fifteenth-century jurist ʿAlī b. Khalīl al-Ṭarābulusī, for instance, explains how a judge should decide which muftī to follow. In addition, al-Ṭarābulusī offers several rules that the muftī should follow when issuing an opinion in cases where there are disagreements between the leading authorities of the Ḥanafī school. By doing so, al-Ṭarābulusī aimed at limiting the range of possible solutions to jurisprudential controversies within the school.[25] Several decades later, in another manual for judges, Ibrāhīm b. al-Shiḥna simply reiterates the

that obtaining a permit to issue legal opinions did not necessarily imply scholarly accomplishment.

23 Lutz Wiederhold, "Legal-Religious Elite, Temporal Authority, and the Caliphate in Mamluk Society: Conclusions Drawn from the Examination of a 'Zahiri Revolt' in Damascus in 1386," *International Journal of Middle East Studies* 31, no. 2 (1999):220.

24 Leonor Fernandes, "Between Qadis and Muftis: To Whom Does the Mamluk Sultan Listen?," *Mamluk Studies Review* 6 (2002): 101–2. There is one more interesting precedent to the practice of appointing muftīs: the Umayyad caliph ʿUmar b. ʿAbd al-ʿAzīz (d. 720) is said to have appointed three Egyptian jurists to issue *fatāwā*. Ahmad El Shamsy, *The Canonization of Islamic Law: A Social and Intellectual History* (Cambridge: Cambridge University Press, 2013), 101.

25 Al-Ṭarābulusī cites al-Ḥasan b. Ziyād's *Adab al-qāḍī*: If there is only a single jurist, the solicitor should follow his opinion. If there are two jurists and they disagree, he should follow the opinion of the jurist he deems sounder (*aṣwabihimā*). If there are three jurists, and two of them agree on a certain issue, he should follow their opinion, and not the third's. If the three disagree, however, the solicitor is to exercise *ijtihād* on the basis of the three opinions. Then he should follow the opinion he deems soundest. ʿAlāʾ al-Dīn Abī al-Ḥasan ʿAlī b. Khalīl al-Ṭarābulusī, *Muʿīn al-ḥukkām fīmā yataraddadu bayna al-khaṣmayn min al-aḥkām* (Cairo: Muṣṭafā al-Bābī al-Ḥalabī, 1973), 27–28.

distinction between the nonbinding (or, more accurately, nonenforceable) nature of the muftī's ruling and the binding ruling of the judge, thus placing the weight on the *qāḍī*'s resolution rather than on the muftī's opinion.[26] Nonetheless, he does not suggest that the muftīs should be institutionally supervised, as Ibn Khaldūn does in his *Muqaddima*.[27]

To be sure, the muftīs who operated throughout the Mamluk domains varied in their prominence and status, with some appearing as towering figures in the jurisprudential landscape of the Mamluk period. Contemporary biographical dictionaries and chronicles clearly allude to such an informal hierarchy of muftīs. The various epithets and designations attached to jurists and scholars served, in part, to create and advertise this hierarchy. His biographical dictionary, which draws heavily on the biographical works of the sixteenth-century jurist and chronicler Shams al-Dīn b. Ṭūlūn and the late fifteenth-century Ibn al-Mibrad, Aḥmad b. Muḥammad al-Ḥaṣkafī (d. 1595), at times attaches titles that point to the prominence of certain muftīs in specific towns during the late Mamluk period. Muḥammad b. Muḥammad b. Muḥammad b. al-Ḥamrāʾ al-Dimashqī (d. 1487), for example, was known as the "muftī of the Ḥanafīs" in Damascus,[28] and Ibn Ṭūlūn's uncle, Yūsuf b. Muḥammad

[26] Ibn al-Shiḥna, *Lisān al-ḥukkām*, 221.

[27] The fifteenth-century reality, however, was more complex than what both al-Ṭarābulusī and Ibn al-Shiḥna's manuals might lead one to believe. As Ibn Khaldūn's account of the state of affairs in late fourteenth-century Cairo suggests, using both muftīs and *qāḍī*s was a well-known practice. The Mamluk sultan and his ruling elite also manipulated both *qāḍī*s and muftīs in order to obtain legal approval of their deeds. When *qāḍī*s refused to approve of a decision made by a member of the Mamluk ruling elite, the latter often sought to obtain the opinion of some prominent muftī. As Leonor Fernandes has concluded, following some Mamluk chroniclers, this was especially true in the fifteenth century, when the status of the *qāḍī*s somewhat deteriorated, possibly because incompetent people were increasingly appointed to judiciary positions; see Fernandes, "Between Qadis and Muftis," 95–108.

According to the fifteenth-century chronicler and a Ḥanafī deputy *qāḍī* Ibn al-Ṣayrafī, for example, the Mamluk sultan Qāyitbāy respected the Ḥanafī muftī Amīn al-Aqṣarāʾī to the extent that in one of the sultanic processions al-Aqṣarāʾī is reported to have walked before the *qāḍī*s, and sometime earlier the sultan had asked al-Aqṣarāʾī to recommend jurists for judiciary positions. ʿAlīb. Dāwūd al-Jawharīal-Ṣayrafī, *Inbāʾ al-haṣr bi-abnāʾ al-ʿaṣr* (Cairo: Dār al-Fikr al-ʿArabī, 1970), 372, 251. This is not to say, however, that the judges in the late Mamluk sultanate lost their legal authority. As Fernandes has noticed, the muftīs' opinions had to be approved by a judge before being enacted by the sultan. Second, late Mamluk chronicles still portray the chief *qāḍī*s as fairly dominant figures in the late Mamluk "legal landscape" of both Egypt and in Syria, despite occasional controversies on the authority of a particular *qāḍī* (see, for example, Ibn al-Ṣayrafī, *Inbāʾ al-haṣr*, 375–77).

[28] Al-Ḥaṣkafī, *Mutʿat al-adhhān*, 2:748.

b. ʿAlī b. ʿAbd Allāh b. Ṭūlūn al-Ṣaliḥī al-Ḥanafī (d. 1530), served as the muftī of *Dār al-ʿAdl* and was known as the "shaykh of the Ḥanafīs in Damascus."[29]

It is appropriate to return at this point to al-Murādī's comment concerning the "constant dispute and strife" among the muftīs. It is true that the muftīs across the sultanate should not be perceived as a homogenous community that speaks in one voice. Jurisprudential disputes among adherents of the different jurisprudential schools as well as within a particular school were not unheard of. Consider, for instance, the following dispute that occurred in 1471 in Cairo between the descendants of the Mamluk Amir Īnāl and the officeholders in the madrasa endowed by Īnāl over the right of the former to benefit from the revenues of the endowment. Each of the parties involved solicited the opinion of the leading Ḥanafī muftīs in Cairo at the time – Amīn al-Dīn al-Aqṣarāʾī, al-Shaykh Muḥyī al-Dīn al-Kāfiyajī, and Qāsim b. Quṭlūbughā – and brought their opinions to the Mamluk sultan Qāyitbāy. The sultan decided to summon all the chief *qāḍī*s and the three muftīs to a session. Ibn al-Ṣayrafī records a heated debate in the session. While al-Kāfiyajī and al-Aqṣarāʾī approved the inclusion of Īnāl's descendants, Ibn Quṭlūbughā contended that only the position holders should enjoy the endowment's revenues. Al-Kāfiyajī, in response to Ibn Quṭlūbughā's opinion, approached the sultan, the chief Ḥanafī *qāḍī*, and the *dāwādār* and said: "This man – that is, Qāsim [b. Quṭlūbughā] the Ḥanafī – does not know syntax, grammar, the fundamentals [of law], and *fiqh*; but he knows the legal devices (*ḥiyal*), and he is not allowed to issue *fatāwā* (*maḥjūr ʿalayhi fī al-fatwā*), because he accepted a bribe."[30] These are serious accusations. Nevertheless, it should be stressed that most fourteenth- and fifteenth-century Mamluk chroniclers and jurists did not consider these disputes to be a major systemic problem that called for an institutional reform, as al-Murādī clearly did.

Finally, the chronological framework of the "Mamluk" model as presented by al-Murādī remains to be addressed. Al-Murādī marks the year 1516 as a turning point in the organization of the muftīship in Damascus and perhaps in the Arab lands in general. But Mamluk chroniclers who witnessed the Ottoman conquest of the Arab lands, such as the Damascene Ibn Ṭūlūn or the Egyptian Ibn Iyās, do not mention any reform in the muftīship, even though they provide elaborate accounts of administrative and legal reforms introduced by the new rulers. Furthermore, Ibn Ṭūlūn's

[29] Ibid., 2:843–44 and also 1:392–93.
[30] Al-Ṣayrafī, *Inbāʾ al-haṣr bi-abnāʾ al-ʿaṣr*, 352–54.

description suggests that the activity of Damascene nonappointed muftīs, such as Quṭb al-Dīn Muḥammad b. Muḥammad b. ʿUmar b. Sulṭān al-Dimashqī (d. 1543) and ʿAbd al-Ṣamad al-ʿAkkārī (d. 1558), continued unmolested in the first decades following the conquest.[31] As we shall see, sixteenth-century chronicles do mention the appointment of a Rūmī Ḥanafī muftī to be sent from Istanbul to Damascus, but they do not present the appointment as an abrupt and sweeping transformation of the office, as al-Murādī does. It is therefore necessary to pay attention to the continuity of "Mamluk" scholarly practices between the sixteenth and the eighteenth centuries.

Biographical dictionaries of the tenth, eleventh, and the twelfth Hijri centuries (roughly the sixteenth to the eighteenth centuries CE) may assist us in this task. A brief survey of the biographical literature reveals that permits to teach and issue legal rulings were still granted well after the Ottoman conquest. Consider, for instance, the following examples. At some point in the second half of the sixteenth century, the Gaza-based Ḥanafī jurisconsult Muḥammad al-Timurtāshī (d. 1595) left his hometown and traveled for Cairo to study with some of the most renowned authorities of his time. One of his teachers in Cairo, the muftī of Egypt, Amīn al-Dīn b. ʿAbd al-ʿĀl, granted him a permit to teach and issue *fatāwā*.[32] The Ḥanafī Muḥyī al-Dīn b. Khayr al-Dīn al-Ramlī (d. 1660) of the Palestinian town of Ramla was also granted such a permit. Like his father, Khayr al-Dīn al-Ramlī, one of most eminent Ḥanafī jurists in the Arab lands (and beyond) in the seventeenth century, Muḥyī al-Dīn was trained as a jurist. At some point, presumably in an advanced stage of his studies, Khayr al-Dīn wrote him a permit to teach and issue legal rulings.[33] Roughly around the same time, the Shāfiʿī Ibn al-Naqīb al-Bayrūtī (d. 1650) obtained from his teachers in Damascus a permit to teach and issue *fatāwā*.[34] In other words, as these examples suggest, the certificate to teach law and issue *fatāwā* did not die out in 1516.

Nevertheless, a significant change did occur over the course of the sixteenth and the seventeenth centuries. This change was both quantitative

[31] Ibn Ṭūlūn records a dispute between these muftīs in 1538. See Ibn Ṭūlūn, *Ḥawādith Dimashq*, 325. On these muftīs, see al-Murādī, *ʿArf al-bashām*, 29–32.

[32] Taqiyy al-Dīn b. ʿAbd al-Qādir al-Tamīmī, *al-Ṭabaqāt al-saniyya fī tarājim al-Ḥanafiyya*, Süleymaniye Library MS Aya Sofya 3295, 346r. See also in al-Timurtāshī's biography, Anonymous, *Tarjmat Muḥammad al-Timurtāshī*, Süleymaniye Library MS Esad Efendi 2212–1, 4v.

[33] Muḥammad Amīn b. Faḍl Allāh al-Muḥibbī, *Khulāṣat al-athar fī aʿyān al-qarn al-ḥādī ʿashar* (Beirut: Dār al-Kutub al-ʿIlmiyya, 2006), 4:324–25.

[34] Al-Muḥibbī, *Khulāṣat al-athar*, 4:301–2.

and qualitative. Quantitatively, there is a drastic decline in the number of times the practice of granting permits to teach and issue *fatāwā* is mentioned in biographical dictionaries from the seventeenth and the eighteenth centuries in comparison to earlier periods. In his biographical dictionary, which focuses on the second half of the fifteenth century and the early decades of the sixteenth century, Aḥmad b. Muḥammad al-Ḥaṣkafī mentions such a permit twenty-three times.[35] Similar figures emerge from Najm al-Dīn al-Ghazzī's centennial biographical dictionary of the tenth Hijri century (roughly the sixteenth century CE).[36] There the term *ijāza fī tadrīs wa-iftā'* appears thirty-two times, equally spread over the course of the century. In al-Ghazzī's biographical dictionary of the early decades of the seventeenth century, the term appears four times.[37] Al-Ghazzī is of particular importance for our purposes, since he documents both the sixteenth century and the early decades of the following century. The decline in the number of permits recorded is indicative of the change this scholarly practice underwent around the turn of the century – a decline that was to continue well into the eighteenth century. In his centennial biographical dictionary of the seventeenth century, Muḥammad al-Muḥibbī records only six instances in which an *ijāza fī tadrīs wa-iftā'* was granted,[38] and for the eighteenth century, al-Murādī mentions only four jurists who were granted such a permit.[39] To be sure, it is problematic to deduce exact statistical data from the information provided in the biographical dictionaries. It is possible that permits to teach and issue legal rulings were granted more frequently than what these sources suggest. Nevertheless, the tendency is clear and points to a steady decline in the popularity of this practice among scholars and jurists.

Although the decline in granting permits to teach and issue legal opinions was a phenomenon that cut across legal schools, there were clear differences in the frequency with which permits were granted among the

[35] Al-Ḥaṣkafī, *Mut'at al-adhhān.*

[36] Al-Ghazzī, *al-Kawākib al-sā'ira.*

[37] Najm al-Dīn Muḥammad b. Muḥammad al-Ghazzī, *Luṭf al-samar wa-qaṭf al-thamar: Min tarājim a'yān al-ṭabaqa al-ūlā min al-qarn al-ḥādī 'ashar*, 2 vols. (Damascus: Wizārat al-Thaqāfa wa'l-Irshād al-Qawmī, 1981–82). Similar figures emerge from the biographical dictionary of al-Ghazzī's counterpart and rival al-Būrīnī. Al-Ḥasan b. Muḥammad al-Būrīnī, *Tarājim al-a'yān min abnā' al-zamān* (Damascus: al-Majma' al-'Ilmī al-'Arabī bi-Dimashq, 1959–63); ibid., *Tarājim al-a'yān min abnā' al-zamān*, Staatsbibliothek zu Berlin MS Weetzstein II 29.

[38] Al-Muḥibbī, Khulāṣat al-athar.

[39] Muḥammad Khalīl b. 'Alī b. Muḥammad b. Muḥammad al-Murādī, *Kitāb silk al-durar fī a'yān al-qarn al-thānī 'ashar* (Beirut: Dār al-Bashā'ir al-Islāmiyya, 1988).

adherents of the different schools. Out of all the cases recorded, the vast majority of receivers (and respective granters) were followers of the Shāfiʿī school. Only five Ḥanafīs are reported to have been granted such a permit in the sixteenth- and the seventeenth-century biographical dictionaries. Two questions ought to be addressed: First, how are we to explain the decline in the frequency of the practice of granting permits? And second, why did certain jurists preserve this practice more than others? (Or, to be more precise, why did biographical dictionaries record these specific cases and not others?)

The first question will be answered more fully in the following. At this point, suffice it to say that the decline in the frequency with which permits to teach law and issue legal opinions were granted corresponds to the emergence of the official appointment of muftīs in the Ottoman province of Damascus. These two trends suggest that the appointment of the muftī by the state rendered the permit superfluous.[40]

The answer to the second question is related to the first, but it may also be related to the Ottoman dynasty's adoption of the Ḥanafī legal school (or, to be more precise, a specific branch within the school) as its official school: it is possible that followers of the Ḥanafī school from the Arab lands, especially those who sought an official appointment to a position, were more inclined than their non-Ḥanafī colleagues to give up on the permit to teach and issue legal rulings. Many non-Ḥanafīs, it appears, while not utterly renouncing the authority of the sultan or the chief muftī, still relied on their affiliation with certain authoritative genealogies more than their Ḥanafī counterparts did. This may also explain why in these particular circles the permit to teach and issue legal rulings preserved some of its preconquest prestige – a fact that is also reflected in the "communal archives" of the scholarly circles, the biographical dictionaries.

The same can be said about Ḥanafīs who did not hold any officially appointed position in the late sixteenth to eighteenth centuries. As the cases of al-Tīmūrtāshī and Khayr al-Dīn al-Ramlī's son indicate, these muftīs based their authority on their teachers and their affiliation to a specific scholarly tradition rather than on an official appointment by the state. This last point is exemplified in al-Muḥibbī's account of the Ḥanafī muftīship of the Palestinian town of Gaza. When the Ḥanafī muftī of

[40] In a mid-sixteenth-century legal code that was intended to regulate the function of the imperial learned hierarchy, *Ḳânûnnâme-i Ehl-ʿİlm*, the *ijāza* (*icâzet*) appears as an official certificate that can be validated in case of official inspection. Ahmed Akgündüz, ed., *Osmanlı Kanunnâmeleri ve Hukukî Tahlilleri* (Istanbul: Fey Vakfı, 1992), 4:663.

Gaza, ʿUmar b. ʿAlāʾ al-Dīn, died in 1648,[41] there was not any Ḥanafī jurist in Gaza who could man the vacant muftīship that had previously been held by Muḥammad al-Timurtāshī and his son, Ṣaliḥ. The governor of Gaza and the city's notables forced a Shāfiʿī jurist, ʿUmar b. al-Mashriqī, to switch to the Ḥanafī legal school. Subsequently, he was sent to study with Khayr al-Dīn al-Ramlī, who granted him a permit to teach and issue legal opinions. Since he apparently did not hold any appointment from Istanbul, the permit he obtained from the eminent muftī was crucial for his jurisprudential authority.[42]

But the change was not merely a quantitative decline in the frequency with which the permits to teach and issue *fatāwā* were granted. The change had a qualitative dimension as well. Sixteenth-century Greater Syria, for example, witnessed the weakening of the link between the permit and the training career in the madrasas, a link that, as Makdisi and Stewart have demonstrated, was fairly prominent in the Mamluk period and particularly in the fourteenth and the fifteenth centuries. In the late Mamluk period, as we have already seen, the permit to teach and issue *fatāwā* was granted to the student at a specific point in his training course in the madrasa. Moreover, if in the late Mamluk period the permit was a document that followed specific conventions, by the late sixteenth century this was not always the case. Although Khayr al-Dīn al-Ramlī wrote a license for his son, the following anecdote related by the Shāfiʿī chronicler and jurist al-Ghazzī about how he obtained the permit to issue *fatāwā* deserves attention, for it captures some of these qualitative transformations. ʿAbd al-Qādir b. Muḥammad al-Ṭarābulusī (d. 1592) was a Damascene Shāfiʿī jurist. One night al-Ṭarābulusī saw al-Ghazzī's deceased father, Badr al-Dīn, in a dream. Al-Ṭarābulusī wanted to ask the esteemed jurist a question, but the latter sent him to ask his son, Najm al-Dīn. The leading Shāfiʿī jurist and al-Ghazzī's teacher, Shihāb al-Dīn Aḥmad al-ʿAythāwī (d. 1616),[43] interpreted this dream as Badr al-Dīn's granting his son a license to teach and issue *fatāwā*. Here clearly the permit was not granted as an integral part of the training career of the jurist, nor was a document similar to those described by the Mamluk encyclopedist al-Qalqashandī involved. It is difficult to estimate how sweeping this change was, but the qualitative change this anecdote reflects is noteworthy.

[41] Al-Muḥibbī, *Khulāṣat al-athar*, 3:209.
[42] Ibid., 3:203–5.
[43] Al-Ghazzī, *Lutf al-samar*, 1:308–24.

To conclude, the decline in the popularity among jurists and scholars of the permit to teach law and issue legal rulings, together with the possible change the permit's institutional nature underwent and the jurisprudential affiliation of such a permit's recipients, might reflect a twofold change that occurred over the first three centuries of Ottoman rule in the Arab lands. First, it seems that the practices of transmitting jurisprudential knowledge, or at least some of them, changed. In the new reality, the certificate carried significantly less weight. This change dovetails with the transformation in the appointment patterns of muftīs, Ḥanafīs and non-Ḥanafīs alike. In this respect, al-Murādī's observation that jurisconsults were increasingly appointed by the Ottoman dynasty and its learned hierarchy seems quite accurate. But, as has already been argued, the process was not as sweeping and abrupt as al-Murādī envisioned it. The institution of the permit to teach and issue legal rulings (*ijāzat al-tadrīs wa'l-iftā'*), albeit perhaps in a modified form, and the "Mamluk" perception of the muftīship were preserved in certain circles throughout the Arab provinces of the Ottoman Empire (and perhaps in other provinces as well).

There is still an unresolved question: Why was al-Murādī so anxious about the constant dispute and strife among the jurists? To understand al-Murādī's anxiety, we have to look at a different set of concerns, one that echoes, I would argue, the perception held by members of the Ottoman religious-judicial and ruling elites with regard to the Mamluk institution of the muftī. For this purpose, one has to explain the Ottoman understanding of the muftīship.

The Ottoman Perception of the Institution of the Muftī

Cling to the opinion of Meḥmet [Efendi] and according to this [opinion, you] should rule. [*Amsikū qawl Meḥmet wa-ʿalayhi al-fatwā.*]

– Muṣṭafâ Naʿîmâ, *Târîḫ-i Naʿîmâ*[44]

When the early eighteenth-century Ottoman historian Naʿîmâ commemorated the date of Meḥmet Efendi's appointment (in the year 1024/1615) as the imperial chief muftī, a post that had previously been occupied by Ṣunʿullah Efendi, he decided to do so by composing the above chronogram. The chronogram, however, is not merely a rhetorical device or a decorative word game. It captures Naʿîmâ's understanding of the nature of the office of the chief imperial muftī (the *şeyḫülislâm*) and of the

[44] Mustafa Naʿîmâ, *Târih-i Naʿîmâ: Ravzatü'l-Hüseyin fî Hulâsati Ahbâri'l-Hâfikayn* (Ankara: Türk Tarih Kurumu, 2007), 2:424.

importance of his legal opinion. This section sets out to clarify Na'îmâ's chronogram and the assumptions on which it rests.

From around the mid-fifteenth century, roughly at the time of the conquest of the new imperial capital, the still-evolving Ottoman ruling and religious elites gradually developed a hierarchy of judiciary positions and madrasas. An integral dimension of this process was the emergence of the chief muftī, the *şeyḫülislâm*, "to become, by the mid-sixteenth [century], the supreme office in the Ottoman judicial hierarchy."[45] Although many jurists and chief muftīs took part in the articulation and the development of the office in this period, it is hard to overstate the importance of the eminent sixteenth-century chief imperial muftī Ebû's-Su'ûd Efendi in this process, a fact that did not escape contemporary observers as well as modern scholars. Toward the mid-sixteenth century the chief muftī became, as Colin Imber has put it, "the chief source of juristic authority in the empire."[46]

To understand the implications of the emergence of the chief muftī as the "chief source of juristic authority" it is necessary to examine the doctrinal definition of this office in tandem with its evolution. As will be suggested in the following, the establishment of a hierarchy was accompanied by a doctrinal reconfiguration of the institution of the chief muftī and of its role within the burgeoning learned hierarchy. This section looks at how the office was defined from the early sixteenth century onward by members of the Ottoman religious-judicial elite. Special attention will be paid to the relations between the chief imperial muftī (the *şeyḫülislâm*) and the provincial muftīs, his subordinates.

Understanding this Ottoman hierarchy of muftīs is crucial for understanding the nature of the institution of the muftī in general – not only the chief muftī – in the Ottoman domains. In his *Telḫîsü'l-Beyân fi Ḳevânîn-i Âl-i Osmân*, the seventeenth-century historian and encyclopedist Hezârfen Ḥüseyin Efendi dedicates a section to the taxonomy of muftīs in the Ottoman Empire: "A muftī might be the *şeyḫülislâm*, or he might not. Those who are not the *şeyḫülislâm* are the provincial muftīs (*kenâr müftileri*)."[47] Hezârfen does not specify who the *kenâr müftileri*

[45] Colin Imber, *Ebu's-Su'ud: The Islamic Legal Tradition* (Stanford, CA: Stanford University Press, 1997), 7. See also Repp, *The Müfti of Istanbul*; Murat Akgündüz, *XIX. Asır Başlarına Kadar Osmanlı Devleti'nde Şeyhülislamlık* (Istanbul: Beyan Yayınları, 2002); Abdurrahman Atcil, "The Formation of the Ottoman Learned Class and Legal Scholarship (1300–1600)" (PhD diss., University of Chicago, 2010).

[46] Imber, *Ebu's-Su'ud*, 7.

[47] Although writing in the second half of the seventeenth century (the work was completed in 1675–76), Hezârfen relied on older documents, such as "ḳânûnnâmes, histories, old

were, what their position in the learned hierarchy was, why they were appointed, or in what manner. He merely explains that their rank is lower than the chief muftī's. Their lower rank is reflected in the requirement that they mention the authoritative text (*nuḳûl*) they consulted for their ruling, whereas the chief muftī was not expected to do so (see Chapter 4).[48]

The anonymous author of *Ḥırzü'l-Müluk*, a treatise written several decades earlier and dedicated to the structure of the Ottoman state, provides additional details concerning the history of the office of the provincial muftī. According to this treatise, the main reason for the appointment of jurists as muftīs in specific localities was to increase the access of provincial subjects to a muftī who could provide them with authoritative rulings. Presumably, before the appointment of the provincial muftī, a province's subjects had to send their questions to Istanbul or to travel to the capital. Moreover, this comment may suggest that before this development took place there had been only a single official muftī, who had resided in the Ottoman capital. Later, in the author's time, the main purpose of the provincial muftī was to check on oppressive officials and ignorant judges (*ẓaleme-i vulât ve cehele-i ḳuḍât*), who did not follow the rules of *şerî'at*. In addition, the anonymous author explicitly states that those who were to serve as provincial muftīs (*eṭrâf ve cevânibde fetvâ ḫidmetine*) could have been chosen from among the professors (*müderrisinden*) or from among the pious (*du'âci*) who were capable of issuing legal opinions (*fetvâ virmeğe iktidâri olan*).[49]

The fact that the provincial muftī could have been chosen from among the madrasa teachers should be clarified. As Richard Repp has pointed out, although it does not seem that there was a formal career track for muftīs, as was the case for judges (*ṭarîḳ-i ḳaẓâ*) or teachers (*ṭarîḳ-i tedrîs*), it appears that from the reign of Bâyezîd II onward the teacher in the most important madrasa built by the sultan (but at times by other members of the royal household or the Ottoman ruling elite) in major cities across the empire served as the local muftī as well. The professors in prominent madrasas – such as the ones built by Bâyezîd

and new registers," as well as on other documents and registers from the court and the Imperial Divan. Hezârfen Hüseyin Efendi, *Telhîsü'l-Beyân fî Ḳavânîn-i Âl-i Osmân* (Ankara: Türk Tarih Kurumu Basımevi, 1998), 38, 197.

48 Ibid., 200. See also Uriel Heyd, "Some Aspects of the Ottoman Fetva," *Bulletin of the School of Oriental and African Studies* 32, no. 1 (1969): 45–46.

49 Anonymous, "*Ḥırzu'l-Mülûk*," *in* Yaşar Yücel, ed., *Osmanlı Devlet Teşkilâtına dair Kaynaklar* (Ankara: Türk Tarih Kurumu, 1988): 191–92.

II in Amasya, by Süleymân's mother in Manisa, by Süleymân himself in Rhodes and Damascus, by Selîm II in Cyprus, and by Ḫüsrev Bey in Sarajevo – all served as the officially appointed provincial muftīs in these localities.[50] Nevertheless, not all of these professors/muftīs were at the same rank in the madrasa hierarchy, a fact that was reflected in the difference in their salaries, ranging from thirty to eighty *akçes* a day.[51] An important qualification is in order here. The attachment of the office of the muftī to a prominent provincial madrasa characterizes mostly large urban centers. As we shall see, in lesser urban centers, such as the Palestinian town of Ramla, there were jurists who held a state appointment to serve as muftī but were not appointed to a teaching position in an imperial madrasa.

Much more is known about the office of the *şeyḫülislâm* than that of his provincial subordinates. As already mentioned, by the mid-sixteenth century the *şeyḫülislâm* had emerged as the head of the hierarchy. As such, he had the authority to appoint jurists to various positions within the evolving hierarchy (perhaps in consultation with the vezir and the sultan). In addition, serving as the head of the learned hierarchy allowed the chief muftī to resolve disputes among its members.[52] Another aspect of this position, as will be seen in Chapter 4, was the authority to canonize jurisprudential texts.

The legal opinions issued by the chief muftīs offer an important insight into the way in which the heads of the Ottoman learned hierarchy perceived their position in relation to its other members. In particular, these legal rulings reveal the doctrinal articulation of the office as the chief muftīs understood it. Even before the chief muftī assumed all the authorities he would possess the mid-sixteenth century, officially appointed muftīs, and particularly by the chief muftī, attempted to establish the

[50] The *şeyḫülislam* himself held (at least nominally) the teaching position at the *medrese* of Bâyezîd II in Istanbul. See İsma'il Hakki Uzunçarşılı, *Osmanlı Devletinin İlmiye Teşkilâti* (Ankara: Türk Tarih Yurumu Basimevi, 1965), 205. On al-Madrasa al-ʿUthmāniyya in Jerusalem, see Guy Burak, "Dynasty, Law and the Imperial Provincial Madrasa: The Case of al-Madrasa al-ʿUthmāniyya in Ottoman Jerusalem," *International Journal of Middle East Studies* 45, no. 1 (2013): 111–25.

[51] Repp, "The Müfti of Istanbul," 62–68. Repp argues that the range was between thirty and sixty *akçe*. But as we shall see in the following, the salary of at least one muftī in Damascus was eighty *akçe*.

[52] The anonymous author of *Ḥırzu'l-Mülûk*, for instance, explains that the chief muftī is to resolve all the jurisprudential disputes among the jurists (*her kelâmi beyne'l-ʿulemâ naṣṣ-i ḳaṭiʿ okup*) and that the muftī, in turn, should provide the soundest reply to those who address their question to him (192).

authority of their legal opinions.[53] As part of this attempt, as early as the first decades of the sixteenth century, Ottoman muftīs ruled that the scornful treatment of a legal ruling presumably issued by an officially appointed muftī was blasphemy. The quite famous sixteenth-century chief imperial muftī Kemâlpaşazâde, for instance, was asked about a person who disparaged a ruling by questioning its relevance to an unspecified case. The chief muftī replied that this person should renew his faith and be severely punished (*ta'zîr balîğ*).[54] Perceiving disobedience to a legal ruling as blasphemy, however, was not an Ottoman innovation. In one of the debates that took place in 1359, the Ḥanafī jurist Sirāj al-Dīn al-Hindī and others declared that the school of Abū Ḥanīfa held that whoever disdained *fatāwā* and muftīs was an apostate.[55] But it seems that in the Ottoman context, this argument was employed particularly in cases involving the rulings of the chief muftī and his officially appointed subordinates. As Ömer Lütfi Barkan pointed out, questioning the validity of the chief muftī's ruling was considered "a major transgression against the religious and social order."[56]

Moreover, in the years and decades to come, chief muftīs increasingly underscored the binding and enforceable nature of their legal opinions, insisting that all members of the Ottoman learned hierarchy, muftīs and judges alike, were to follow their rulings. Consider, for example, the following ruling by Şeyḫülislâm Ṣunʿullah Efendi (d. 1612). When asked about a judge who was not, in his rulings, "following the şerîʿat, the imperial edicts, and the şerʿî *fatwā*," Ṣunʿullah Efendi replied that this judge should be removed from office, punished, and denounced as a heretic (*kâfir olur*) for abasing the sacred law.[57] In this case, it is clearer that the ruling was issued by an official jurisconsult, perhaps even by the chief muftī himself. In the same vein, at some point in the first half of the seventeenth century, Şeyḫülislâm Yaḥyâ Efendi (d. 1643) was asked about a provincial muftī

[53] The term used is *fetvâ-ı şerîfe*. In sixteenth- and seventeenth-century Ottoman sources, the term usually denotes legal opinions issued by officially appointed muftīs, often by the *şeyḫülislâms* themselves.

[54] Kemâlpaşazâde, *Fetâvâ*, Süleymaniye Library MS Darulmesnevi 118, 19v. On the practice of renewal of faith, see Guy Burak, "Faith, Law and Empire in the Ottoman 'Age of Confessionalization' (15th–17th Centuries): The Case of 'Renewal of Faith,'" *Mediterranean Historical Review* 28, no. 1 (2013): 1–23.

[55] Fernandes, "Between Qadis and Muftis," 104.

[56] Ömer Lütfi Barkan, "Caractère religieux et caractère séculier des institutions ottomanes," in *Contributions à l'histoire économique et sociale de l'Empire ottoman*, ed. Jean-Louis Bacqué-Grammont and Paul Dumont (Leuven: Peeters, 1983), 36.

[57] Ṣunʿullah Efendi, *Fetâvâ*, Süleymaniye Library MS Reşid Efendi 269, 43r.

who permitted the remarriage of a couple after the wife had been triple-divorced but had not married another husband in between (*ḥilla*). This permission was against the ruling of the chief muftī.[58] Accordingly, the chief muftī ruled that the provincial muftī should be punished (*taʿzîr*) and banned from issuing legal opinions (*iftâʾdan menʿ lâzimdir*). The same chief muftī also ordered the removal from office of a judge who ruled against a chief muftī's *fatwā* – perhaps even his own.[59]

Recent studies of provincial courts across Anatolia suggest that legal opinions issued by an officially appointed muftī carried significant weight and were indeed respected as binding and enforceable, presumably as long as they corresponded to the case at hand.[60] In seventeenth-century Bursa, for example, every *fatwā* bearer won his case in court.[61] Such was also the case in seventeenth- and eighteenth-century Kastamonu and Çankırı. There, as Boğaç Ergene has shown, *fatāwā* were frequently brought to court by the litigant and "carried significant weight in the proceedings, winning legal cases for their bearers almost every time."[62] The identity of the muftī in these cases is not always clear. In some cases the rulings were issued by the *şeyḫülislâm*, while in others it was the provincial muftī's ruling that was brought to court. It is worth pointing out that the legal opinion of the officially appointed provincial muftī carried significant weight in the eyes of the local judge, for the provincial muftī was, at least theoretically, following the ruling of the chief muftī.

Compared with Anatolia, little is known about the manner in which litigants across the Arab lands of the empire made use of *fatāwā*. Judith Tucker has argued that the reality in seventeenth- and eighteenth-century Syria and Palestine was different from the one in Anatolia, as "there is little evidence to suggest that the muftī and qāḍī [in Greater Syria] worked glove-in-hands," because of what she has termed "pivotal differences in the background, training, and official standing of the muftīs."

[58] Yaḥyâ Efendi, *Fetâvâ*, Süleymaniye Library MS Aya Sofya 1569, 88v.

[59] Ibid., 85r. A similar ruling is recorded in ʿAbdurraḥim Efendi's *fatāwā* collection. See Haim Gerber, *State, Society, and Law in Islam: Ottoman Law in Comparative Perspective* (Albany: State University of New York Press, 1994), 81, 201n3.

[60] Gerber, *State, Society, and Law in Islam*, 82–83; R. C. Jennings's findings for Kayseri, however, qualify Gerber's conclusions: in Kaysari, *fatwā* bearers did not necessarily win the case. R. C. Jennings, "Kadi, Court, and Legal Procedure in 17th c. Ottoman Kayseri," *Studia Islamica* 48 (1978): 133–72.

[61] Gerber, *State, Society, and Law in Islam*, 81.

[62] Boğaç Ergene, *Local Court, Provincial Society, and Justice in the Ottoman Empire: Legal Practice and Dispute Resolution in Çankırı and Kastamonu (1652–1744)* (Leiden: Brill, 2003), 31.

Nevertheless, she has drawn attention to the congruence between the muftīs' rulings and the judges' resolutions.[63] On the other hand, cases from sixteenth- and seventeenth-century Jerusalem, for example, suggest that litigants sought to obtain a *fatwā* from the chief muftī or from the officially appointed provincial muftī. These cases also indicate that the officially appointed Jerusalemite muftī's opinion carried particular weight in court.

A *fatwā* issued by an officially appointed provincial muftī in Jerusalem toward the end of the seventeenth century casts light on how the chief muftī's rulings were perceived from a provincial perspective. The officially appointed muftī of Jerusalem, ʿAbd al-Raḥīm b. Abī Luṭf, was asked about two appointment deeds (*berât*) for the same position. The solicitor wanted to know which appointment deed should be put into effect. In his reply, the muftī from Jerusalem states that the "*shaykh al-Islām*, the current muftī of the Sublime Sultanate, Yaḥyâ [Efendi] ... has ruled" that the earlier appointment deed should be implemented.[64] In other words, the Jerusalemite jurisconsult implemented the chief muftī's ruling. Nevertheless, ʿAbd al-Raḥīm b. Abī Luṭf himself (and probably other provincial muftīs) at times diverged from the rulings of the chief muftī, or at least avoided following some of his rulings.[65]

The hierarchical picture that emerges from these legal rulings is also mirrored in contemporary chronicles. When the accomplished jurist Meḥmet b. Meḥmet, known as ʿArabzâde (d. 1561), refused to admit one of Ebû's-Suʿûd's students as his reciter (*muʿīd*), Ebû's-Suʿûd issued a *fatwā*, which was accompanied by a sultanic edict, stating that no one was to oppose the *şeyḫülislâm*. Subsequently, ʿArabzâde was removed from office and exiled to Bursa for several years.[66]

Now that we have examined the relations between the chief muftī and other members of the imperial learned hierarchy, it seems appropriate to dedicate a few words to his relations with members of the Ottoman

63 Judith E. Tucker, *In the House of the Law: Gender and Islamic Law in Ottoman Syria and Palestine* (Berkeley: University of California Press, 1998), 20–22.

64 Based on Ibn Abī Luṭf's comment, it is plausible that he learned about the chief muftī's ruling after he had seen this ruling in an edict (*bi-khaṭṭihi al-sharīf al-maʿhūd*), though it is not clear if it was an imperial/sultanic edict that included the chief muftī's ruling or simply a *fatwā* issued by the chief muftī. ʿAbd al-Raḥīm b. Abī Luṭf al-Maqdisī, *al-Fatāwā al-Raḥīmiyya fi waqiʿāt al-sadāh al-Ḥanafiyya*, Firestone Library (Princeton University) MS Mach Yehuda 4154, 74r.

65 Burak, "Faith, Law and Empire."

66 ʿAlī b. Bālī Manq, *al-ʿIqd al-manẓūm fī dhikr afāḍil al-Rūm* (Beirut: Dār al-Kitāb al-ʿArabī, 1975), 349–53.

ruling elite, including the sultan himself, who appointed him to his exalted office. The anonymous author of *Ḥırzü'l-Müluk* states that "a pious man, scholar, and jurist should be appointed and ordered to the position of the muftī (*mesned-i fetvâ bir ehl-i taḳvâ ʿâlim ve faḳîhe taʿyîn ve tevcîh buyurulmak vech-i vecîhdir*)."[67] The use of the verb *buyurulmak* indicates that he was appointed by a sultanic order. Contemporary chronicles also confirm that the *şeyḫülislâm* was appointed by an imperial edict.[68] Hezârfen does not specify how the chief muftī is appointed, but it is clear that he is subordinate to the sultan.[69] In the seventeenth century (and possibly earlier), the newly appointed chief muftī was summoned, upon his appointment, to the palace, where the sultan would bestow upon him the *şeyḫülislâm*'s white cloak.[70] Occasionally, however, this understanding of the power relations between the sultan and the muftī was contested. Sultan Meḥmet IV reportedly reminded his chief muftī, Kara Çelebizâde, that he had appointed him to the muftīship, implying that Kara Çelebizâde owned his position to the sultan. Kara Çelebizâde, by contrast, replied that it was God who appointed him and not the sultan.[71] This is an interesting anecdote, for it reveals that even within the scholarly and judicial circles in the core lands of the empire the practice of appointing jurisconsults was debated, and that jurists who were affiliated

[67] Anonymous, *Ḥırzu'l-Mülûk*, 192. The personality of a chief muftī was occasionally the reason for his removal. When, for example, the news of the appointment of Memekzâde to the *şeyḫülislâmlik* reached the army (*ʿasker*), the troops objected to the appointment, claiming that they "do not want a drunkard muftī." Three hours later, so ʿÎsâzâde relates, the newly appointed chief muftī was removed from office. ʿÎsâzâde, *ʿÎsâzâde Târîhi: Metin ve Tahlîl* (Istanbul: İstanbul Fetih Cemiyeti, 1996), 26.

[68] Silâḥdâr Fındıklılı Meḥmet Ağa, *Silâḥdâr Târîḫi* (Istanbul: Devlet Maṭbaʿası, 1928), 1:221.

[69] Hezârfen, however, holds the *şeyḫülislâm* responsible for the sultan's administrative deeds. In a passage entitled "advice" (*naṣîḥat*), he recommends that the sultans have a conversation (*müṣâḥebet*) from time to time with the *şeyḫülislâm*. Interestingly enough, Hezârfen includes in this passage hypothetical sentences from these recommended conversations, in which the sultan subtly reproaches his chief muftī for not drawing his attention to the oppression taking place in his domains. For instance, the sultan is to say to the *şeyḫülislâm*: "There is oppression and transgression in the provinces, why haven't you woken me up? ... You will be responsible [lit. on your neck] for the consequence of this evil action on the Day of Judgment" (*Taşrada ẓülm u teʿaddî olurmuş, niçün beni îkâẓ eylemezsin.... Rûz-ı cezâde vebâli senin boynuna*). Hezârfen Hüseyin Efendi, *Telhîsü'l-Beyân*, 201.

[70] Uzunçarşılı, *Osmanlı Devletinin İlmiye Teşkilâti*, 189–92. See also Defterdâr Sarı Mehmet Paşa, *Zübde-i Vekiʿât (1066–1116)* (Ankara: Türk Tarih Kurumu Basımevi, 1995), 219; ʿAbdülazîz Kara Çelebizâde, *Târîḫ-i Ravżatü'l-Ebrâr* (Cairo: Maṭbaʿat Bulāq, 1248 [1832]), 473.

[71] Naʿîmâ, *Târîh-i Naʿîmâ*, 3:1165.

with the imperial learned hierarchy, including the chief imperial muftī, were not oblivious to the problems that a sultanic appointment posed.

The sultanic appointment also implied that sultans could and did remove chief muftīs from office. In fact, by the early decades of the sixteenth century the office was not considered life tenure as it had been until then.[72] Moreover, as the anecdote about Kara Çelebizâde and al-Murādī's introduction suggest, the notion that the sultan is the source, or at least one of the main sources, of the chief muftī's authority to issue legal opinions was fairly common. Late sixteenth- and seventeenth-century Ottoman chronicles are replete with instances in which chief muftīs were removed (*'azl*),[73] exiled (*nefy*),[74] and, in some rare cases, executed (usually after their removal from office).[75] Ma'lûlzâde, for example, was removed from the muftīship for issuing the "wrong *fatāwā*."[76] In another instance, Boluvî Muṣṭafâ Efendi, who served as *şeyḫülislâm* from 1657 to 1659,[77] refused to issue a legal ruling permitting the execution of Gâzî Deli Ḥüseyin Paşa, the chief commander (serdar) of Crete. Consequently, he was exiled to Cairo, with the *qāḍī*-ship of Giza as his *arpalık*.[78] Interestingly enough, while in Egypt, he was appointed muftī of Egypt, although, as Evliyâ Çelebi notes, no one asked for his rulings there.[79]

[72] Madeline C. Zilfi, "The Ottoman Ulema," in *Cambridge History of Turkey III: The Later Ottoman Empire, 1603–1839*, ed. Suraiya N. Faroqhi (Cambridge: Cambridge University Press, 2006), 214.

[73] For example, Defterdar Sarı Meḥmed Paşa, *Zübde-i Veki'ât*, 256–58; Aḥmad b. Luṭf Allāh Munajjim Bāshī, *Kitāb Jāmi' al-duwal: Qism salāṭīn Āl 'Uthmān ilā sanat 1083 H.* (Mecca: s.n., 2009), 2:1193; Silâḥdâr Meḥmet Ağa, *Silâḥdâr Târîḫi*, 1:31, 363; 2:245. Some, such as Koçi Bey (d. 1650), lamented the removal of muftīs and other jurists from their office without reason. Koçi Bey also deplored, however, the quality of many of the jurists of his time. Koçi Bey, *Risale-i Koçi Bey* (Istanbul: Ahmet Vefik Paşa, 1863), 9–12.

[74] Munajjim Bāshī, *Kitāb Jāmi' al-duwal*, 2:1248; Silâḥdâr Meḥmet Ağa, *Silâḥdâr Târîḫi*, 1:11–12.

[75] Uzunçarşılı, *Osmanlı Devletinin İlmiye Teşkilâti*, 223–26.

[76] Aḥmet Hasan Beyzâde, *Hasan Beyzâde Târîhi* (Ankara: Türk Tarih Kurumu Basımevi, 2004), 1:408.

[77] On Boluvî Muṣṭafâ Efendi, see Defterdâr Sarı Meḥmed Paşa, *Zübde-i Veki'ât*, 257.

[78] *Arpalık* was a source of revenue, often a judgeship, which was assigned to a member of the Ottoman learned hierarchy between postings. Madeline C. Zilfi, "Elite Circulation in the Ottoman Empire: Great Mollas of the Eighteenth Century," *Journal of the Economic and Social History of the Orient* 26, no. 3 (1983): 353–54.

[79] *Hanefi şeyḫülislâmı idi. Amma fetvâsına kimse muḥtâc değil idi.* Evliya Çelebi, *Seyahatnâmesi: Topkapı Sarayı Bağdat 304 Yazmasının Transkripsiyonu, Dizini* (Istanbul: Yapı Kredi Yayınları, 1996–2007), 10:86. The reason for the lack of interest in Muṣṭafā Efendi's rulings, Evliya Çelebi explains, was the prominence of the jurists of al-Azhar: "He who is in need of [a ruling] heads to al-Azhar mosque, he pays two or three mankır,

Less careful, or at least less fortunate, chief muftīs lost not only their appointments but also their lives. Ahîzâde Ḥüseyin Efendi (d. 1633) was the first chief muftī in Ottoman history to be executed, for conspiring against Sultan Murâd IV. Twenty-two years later, Sultan Meḥmet IV executed another chief muftī, Ḫocazâde Mesʿûd Efendi (d. 1656), for what some in Meḥmet IV's court perceived as the chief muftī's propensity for intervening in political affairs.[80] Despite the rarity of these cases, these executions reveal that the chief muftīs were not immune from the severest punishment, their religious and juridical status notwithstanding.

This is not to suggest, however, that the chief muftī necessarily tailored his rulings to suit the sultan's need or will. Contemporary chronicles mention disagreements between chief muftīs and sultans. In some cases, the muftī's opinion prevailed. Esʿad Efendi, for instance, denied Sultan Osmân II's request to execute his younger brothers before leaving the imperial capital for an expedition against the Polish-Lithuanian commonwealth, a denial that contributed to the eventual abolition of the Ottoman practice of fratricide.[81] Moreover, the legitimacy of some sultanic rulings rested, to a large degree, on the approval of the chief muftī. The importance of obtaining the *şeyḫülislâm*'s support is reflected in occasional attempts made by members of the Ottoman ruling elite to obtain a ruling supporting their cause. In 1588, for instance, before meeting the grand vezir, several cavalrymen (*sipâhî*s) solicited the chief muftī's opinion in support of their claims.[82] Indeed, political factions in the capital would occasionally demand the appointment of a sympathetic chief muftī, suggesting that such an appointment could be an effective means to promote their interests. In 1648, for example, the sipâhîs wanted to appoint Ebû Saʿîd Efendi, who supported their cause, as chief muftī. Ebû Saʿîd, however, turned down the offer.[83]

The demand posed by different parties within the Ottoman ruling elite to remove certain chief muftīs from office shed light on the Ottoman

according to his will and intention, and he gets a noble fatwā." See also Akgündüz, *XIX. Asır Başlarına Kadar Osmanlı Devleti'nde Şeyhülislamlık*, 176–183.

[80] Uzunçarşılı, *Osmanlı Devletinin İlmiye Teşkilâti*, 223–26.

[81] See, for example, Baki Tezcan, "The Ottoman Mevali as 'Lords of the Law,'" *Journal of Islamic Studies* 20, no. 3 (2009): 404–6. See also Baki Tezcan, "Some Thoughts on the Politics of Early Modern Ottoman Science," in *Beyond Dominant Paradigms in Ottoman and Middle Eastern/North African Studies*, ed. Donald Quataert and Baki Tezcan (Istanbul: Center for Islamic Studies [İSAM], 2010), 135–56.

[82] Muṣṭafā Selaniki, *Târîh-i Selânikî* (Istanbul: İstanbul Üniversitesi Edebiyat Fakültesi, 1989), 1:210.

[83] Naʿîmâ, *Târîh-i Naʿîmâ*, 3:1188.

understanding of the nature of the muftīship. Some sources, both prescriptive and descriptive, describe the office as a service (*ḫidmet*), to which the eligible candidate is appointed.[84] In other cases, the muftī is said to have a permit to issue legal rulings (*iftâ'ya me'zûn olan*).[85] Nevertheless, the permit seems to refer to the sultanic appointment and not to the muftī's competence. The definition of the chief muftīship as "service" bears important implications for the jurisprudential authority of the muftī (both the chief muftī and his provincial counterpart) to issue legal opinions once he is removed from office. It is clear that according to the Ottoman understanding of this office, only the muftī who holds an appointment has the right to issue enforceable legal rulings within the imperial legal system. Furthermore, the authority of the Ottoman muftī to issue legal rulings, unlike that of his Mamluk counterparts, was revocable. In other words, if in the Mamluk sultanate the muftīship was first and foremost a status, the Ottomans perceived the muftīship as an office. Accordingly, those who were not appointed could not have issued enforceable legal opinions.[86]

[84] For example: İbrâhîm Peçevî, *Târîḫ-i Peçevî*, 1:49; Cengiz Orhonlu, *Osmanlı Tarihine Âid Belgeler* (Istanbul: Edebiyat Fakültesi Basımevi, 1970), 132. Other sources consider muftīship to be a rank (*rütbe* or *paye*) as well as a service. See Uzunçarşılı, *Osmanlı Devletinin İlmiye Teşkilâti*, 209–11; Mehmet Zeki Pakalın, *Osmanlı Tarih Deyimleri ve Terimleri Sözlüğü* (Istanbul: Milli Eğitim Basımevi, 1993), 2:764.

[85] It is worth paying attention to Repp's discussion concerning the term *ma'dhūn* in the context of Müstaḳîmzâde's (d. 1787) treatment of the muftīship of Molla ʿAbdülkerîm (who served as muftī during the reign of Bâyezîd II):

> So vague, indeed, is Müstakimzade that one is led to suspect that he doubts the validity of Abdülkerim's claim to the Müftilik.... Strengthening the impression of Müstakimzade's uncertainty is his use of the term ma'dhūn bi'l-iftā' (or the variant ma'dhūn bi'l-fatwā) in regard to Abdülkerim, he uses it on only three other occasions, at least in his articles concerned with the Müftis under consideration: first, in the general statement which forms the basis for his rejection of the Müftilik of Molla Yegan to the effect that all the ulema are empowered to give fetvas; second, in connection with Molla Yegan himself; and third, twice in regard to Molla Shaykh ʿAbd al-Karīm al-Ḳādīrī (Şeyḫ Abdülkerim), who seems to have held an ad hominem müftilik, not connected with Müftilik of Istanbul, in the time of Süleyman.

Repp's comment, following Müstakîmzâde, points to the vagueness of the term even among Ottoman scholars (Repp, *The Müfti of Istanbul*, 126).

[86] The seventeenth-century chronicler Muṣṭafā b. Fatḥ Allāh al-Ḥamawī uses the term the "sultanic muftīship" (*al-iftā' al-sulṭānī*) to refer to the officially appointed muftīship. Muṣṭafā b. Fatḥ Allāh al-Ḥamawī, *Fawā'id al-irtiḥāl wa-natā'ij al-safar fī akhbār al-qarn al-ḥādī ʿashar* (Beirut: Dār al-Nawādir, 2011), 5:128.

The Emergence of the Provincial Muftī and the Reorganization of the Muftīship in the Ottoman Province of Damascus

The honorable Ottoman kings employed this manner of assigning the muftīship of each school to a single person from the jurists of the school, and prevented all the other [jurists] from answering questions.[87]

When the Ottoman troops conquered the city of Damascus in 1516, the Ottoman religious-judicial hierarchy was still undergoing significant developments. Although at that time the chief muftī had not yet assumed the responsibilities he would in the decades to come, the practice of officially appointing muftīs and a discernible hierarchy presided over by a chief imperial muftī were already in place in the core lands of the empire. Over the course of the next two centuries, as the province of Damascus and the other Arab provinces were incorporated into the empire, the Ottoman practice of officially appointing muftīs became increasingly dominant. But despite the clear tendency, it was not a sweeping process. In what follows, I aim to explore how the Ottoman notion of the officially appointed muftī was implemented in the newly conquered province of Damascus and how local jurists adapted.

A survey of the biographies of those who served as the muftī of Damascus in the first two centuries following the Ottoman conquest of the city may assist us in reconstructing the appointment process. Al-Murādī's biographical dictionary of the Ḥanafī muftīs of the city of Damascus, which includes twenty-six biographies of jurists who served as muftīs in the city from the Ottoman conquest of the city to the early eighteenth century, is a useful source for this purpose. Perhaps its most striking feature is that it challenges al-Murādī's own description of the process, which has been discussed in the previous sections. The first muftī to be appointed by Istanbul was Ibrāhīm al-Rūmī (d. 1566). As the epithet "Rūmī," which is usually employed to refer to objects and people that hailed from the core lands of the empire, suggests, he was a graduate of the Ottoman madrasa system and a member of the imperial learned hierarchy. But along with Ibrāhīm al-Rūmī and his Rūmī successors, al-Murādī records the activity, well into the sixteenth century, of other Ḥanafī muftīs who were not appointed by the new rulers of the province. In other words, al-Murādī describes in his biographical dictionary a reality that is quite different from the one he outlines in the introduction: instead of a single officially appointed muftī, who was the sole Ḥanafī jurisprudential authority in

[87] Al-Murādī, *'Arf al-bashām*, 2–3.

the city, in the first decades following the conquest there were Damascene muftīs who did not hold an official appointment and yet operated in the city along with the officially appointed muftī.

His description of the seventeenth century, on the other hand, resembles more closely the description he offers in his introduction and is corroborated by other sources as well. For the seventeenth century, only officially appointed muftīs are mentioned in his dictionary. This change may suggest that toward the end of the sixteenth century, the Ottoman learned hierarchy insisted more adamantly that the officially appointed muftī serve as the city's sole Ḥanafī jurisconsult. Al-Muḥibbī's centennial biographical dictionary, which al-Murādī had possibly consulted,[88] corroborates this impression. It appears that by the second half of the seventeenth century, the appointment of a sole Ḥanafī muftī to Damascus had become the norm. Al-Muḥibbī even specifically mentions a sultanic edict that had been issued by that time ordering "that there should be only a single Ḥanafī muftī" in the city. The issuance of this edict also meant that at least occasionally the state authorities had to prevent other jurists from issuing their rulings. Al-Muḥibbī recounts that while ʿAlāʾ al-Dīn al-Ḥaṣkafī served as the officially appointed muftī of Damascus, the Damascene Ḥanafī muftī ʿAbd al-Ḥalīm b. al-Dīn b. Muḥammad al-Bahnasī (d. ca. 1679) issued his legal opinions in Damascus without obtaining an official appointment. As a result, the chief judge of the city intervened by implementing an imperial edict preventing al-Bahnasī from issuing his legal opinions.[89] The late seventeenth-century chronicler Ismāʿīl al-Maḥāshinī confirms this practice: muftīs who did not hold an official appointment appear in his chronicle as "the former (*sābiqan*) muftī."[90]

The picture that emerges from al-Muḥibbī's and al-Maḥāsinī's descriptions warrants attention, for it points to the existence of two seemingly contradictory trends. On the one hand, as al-Bahnasī's incident demonstrates, the Ottoman authorities did attempt to prevent nonappointed muftīs from issuing legal opinions. On the other hand, as we shall see in the following sections, the experience of several prominent nonappointed

[88] In his centennial biographical dictionary of the twelfth century AH, al-Murādī cites another biographical work by al-Muḥibbī, *Dhayl Nafḥat al-rayḥāna wa-rashḥat ṭilāʾ al-ḥāna*. Therefore, it is very likely that he was familiar with his Khulāṣat al-Athar as well. Muḥammad Amīn b. Faḍl Allāh b. Muḥibb al-Dīn al-Muḥibbī, *Dhayl Nafḥat al-rayḥāna wa-rashḥat ṭilāʾ al-ḥāna* (Cairo: ʿĪsā al-Bābī al-Ḥalabī, 1971).

[89] Al-Muḥibbī, *Khulāṣat al-athar*, 2:310.

[90] Ismāʿīl al-Maḥāsinī, edited under the title "Ṣafaḥāt fī tārīkh Dimashq fī al-qarn al-ḥādī ʿashar al-hijrī," *Revue de l'Institut des manuscits arabes* 6 (May–November 1960): 104.

muftīs, such as Khayr al-Dīn al-Ramlī and the late seventeenth-century 'Abd al-Ghanī al-Nābulusī (d. 1731), indicates that the activity of certain muftīs who did not hold a state appointment continued unmolested. It is possible that at certain times Ottoman state authorities were more insistent on the exclusivity of the appointed muftīs than at others. Alternatively, the eminence of these particular nonappointed muftīs could explain their undisturbed activity.

Not coincidently, the rise of the officially appointed muftī in the early decades of the seventeenth century corresponds to the decline in the importance of the permit to teach and issue *fatāwā*. Since the appointment of muftīs was not the exclusive prerogative of the jurists any longer, and as the Ottoman dynasty and sultans (and the learned hierarchy) became increasingly dominant in the appointment procedure, the license lost much of its significance. As has been suggested, in the eyes of many jurists, the imperial appointment deed rendered the permit to teach law and issue legal opinions superfluous.

The procedure of obtaining an imperial appointment is not always fully clear. The following letter from 1607 from the grand vezir Dervîş Paşa to Sultan Aḥmet I, in which the former reports the appointment decision, sheds some light on who was involved in the appointment of the muftī of Damascus:

> the office of the muftī of Damascus is now vacant. The muftīship of Damascus has been assigned to your servant the judge of Kütahya, because he is capable of serving as muftī. In his place, the office of the judge of Kütahya will be assigned to the professor of the *s̱emânî* [madrasas in Istanbul] Mevlânâ Emîr Hâibî.... My illustrious Sultan, these issues have been settled in consultation with your servant the Şeyḫülislâm. He has considered the chain [of appointments] appropriate and he has promulgated it. [The authority to issue] this *fermân* [belongs to] my illustrious Sultan.[91]

The appointment, it seems, never materialized, as the sources do not provide any information concerning a muftī in Damascus who previously served as the judge of Kütahya. But the letter reveals interesting aspects of the appointment procedure. It clearly points to the three most important actors in this procedure – the sultan, the vezir, and the chief muftī. as According to Dervîş Paşa, all three should agree on the candidate. This

[91] "Şâm-ı şerif fetvâsı hâlâ mahlûldür. Kütahya kadısı dâ'îleri fetvâ hıdmetine ḳâdir olmağın Şâm fetvâsı tevcîh buyurulup anun yerine s̱emânîye müderrislerinden Mevlânâ Emîr Hâibî dâ'ilerine.... Devletlü pâdişâhum be ḫuṣûṣlar Şeyḫülislâmeyḫülislâm du'âcıları ile müşâvere olunup vech-i meşrûḥ üzere silsile olmak münâṣib görüp i'lâm eylemüşlerdür. Fermân devletlü pâdişâhumundur" (Orhonlu, *Osmanlı Tarihine Âid Belgeler*, 132).

may not have always been the case, but gaining the support of at least one of the three could have considerably increased a candidate's chance of obtaining the appointment. Both al-Muḥibbī and al-Murādī confirm the need to gain the support of at least one of the three. From the biographies of the appointed muftīs it is clear that traveling to Istanbul increased a jurist's chance at appointment. There they could obtain a sultanic appointment deed (*amr sulṭānī*), either directly or through the intervention of a senior official. ʿAbd al-Wahhāb b. Aḥmad b. Muḥammad b. Farfūr (d. 1662), for example, was appointed as the muftī of Damascus when Meḥmet Köprülü, who previously served as the governor of Damascus, was promoted to the grand vezirate, presumably as a result of the latter's support of Ibn Farfūr's candidacy. Other jurists tried to procure the appointment to a muftīship from the chief muftī. When, for example, Khayr al-Dīn al-Ramlī's nephew Muḥammad b. Tāj al-Dīn b. al-Muḥammad al-Ramlī (d. 1685) returned from Egypt after he had studied there for a while, his uncle wrote to the chief muftī and asked for his nephew's appointment to the Ḥanafī muftīship of his hometown, Ramla.[92] Occasionally local officials, such as the governor or the chief judge, also appointed muftīs. Some of these appointments, however, led to internal disputes within the Ottoman administration. Shihāb al-Dīn b. ʿAbd al-Raḥmān b. Muḥammad b. Muḥammad al-ʿImādī (d. 1667), for instance, was appointed to the Ḥanafī muftīship of Damascus by the chief *qāḍī* of the city, while the sultan (*ṭaraf al-salṭana*) wanted to appoint Khalīl al-Saʿsaʿānī.[93]

Jurists, then, made use of the different channels at their disposal to promote either their own appointment to the coveted position or the appointment of a member of their close circles. At times, a competing faction asked that an appointed muftī be removed from office. ʿAbd al-Ghanī al-Nābulusī, for example, was removed by the chief muftī from the muftīship of Damascus after a rival Damascene faction apparently solicited his removal. In other cases, however, petitioners were less successful. When, following the death of ʿAbd al-Raḥmān al-ʿImādī, Muḥammad b. Qubād (known as al-Sukūtī al-Būdīnī) was appointed to the muftīship of Damascus, members of the al-ʿImadī family petitioned the chief muftī and asked for the muftīship, but al-Būdīnī remained in office.[94]

As we have seen, lesser urban centers also had an officially appointed muftī. Like their colleagues from the major urban centers, jurists from

[92] Al-Muḥibbī, *Khulāṣat al-athar*, 3:396–97.
[93] Ibid., 2:223–26.
[94] Ibid., 4:125.

these towns traveled to Istanbul or at least sent their requests to the imperial capital in order to obtain the appointment to the muftīship of their hometown. In late seventeenth-century Jerusalem, for instance, the muftī Muḥammad b. ʿAbd al-Raḥīm b. Abī Luṭf states in the introduction to his father's *fatāwā* collection that he was appointed by the chief muftī Feyżullah Efendi "to the service (*khidma*) of the muftīship."[95] Al-Muḥibbī provides information about the Ḥanafī muftīs of smaller towns, such as Tripoli, Safed, and Ramla.[96] It is not clear, however, how and by whom these muftīs were appointed. The aforementioned episode concerning Muḥammad b. Tāj al-Dīn b. al-Muḥammad al-Ramlī suggests that the chief imperial muftī was involved in the appointment of muftīs to smaller towns. In the case of Gaza, as we have seen, local governors appointed the muftī, but it is not clear whether this was the case in other towns as well. Whatever the case may have been, it is clear that toward the end of the sixteenth century, at least in the major cities of the empire, there were officially appointed Ḥanafī muftīs.

An official appointment, nonetheless, had its price. Since the practice of appointing muftīs followed the Ottoman understanding of the office, the officially appointed muftī could issue legal opinions only as long as he held the appointment. When another jurist was appointed to the muftīship, he was forced to leave the office. Moreover, falling from the chief muftī's grace may have led to removal from office. Consider, for instance, the career of ʿAbd al-Raḥīm b. Abī Luṭf. He was removed from the muftīship of Jerusalem by Şeyḫülislâm Esîrî Meḥmet Efendi (chief muftī from 1659 to 1662) in 1659, a year after he had been appointed. Eventually, the next chief muftī, Ṣunʿîzâde Seyit Meḥmet Emîn Efendi (chief muftī in 1662), reappointed him to the office.[97]

So far I have used the phrase "the officially appointed muftīship of Damascus," or of any other city for that matter, without elaborating on

[95] Ibn Abī Luṭf al-Maqdisī, *al-Fatāwā al-Raḥīmiyya*, 3v. On Ibn Abī Luṭf, see al-Murādī, *Kitāb Silk al-durar*, 4:59.

[96] For example, al-Muḥibbī, *Khulāṣat al-Athar*, 1:333–34; 2:230; 3:396–97; 4:192–93. As for Nablus, al-Murādī reports that Ḥāfiẓ al-Dīn al-Nābulusī, "the muftī of the Ḥanafīs in Nablus," was in contact with ʿAbd al-Raḥim b. Abī Luṭf al-Maqdisī, the appointed muftī of Jerusalem. See al-Murādī, *Kitāb Silk al-durar*, 2:10–11.

[97] The chief muftī also granted him a salary that was equivalent to the salary of a professor of a *dākhil* madrasa. Later he was granted a rank equivalent to the Süleymâniye madrasa, with the *qāḍī*-ship of Safed as *arpalık* (*ʿalā wujh al-maʿisha*). On the structure of the learned, see Repp, *The Müfti of Istanbul*; Atcil, "The Formation of the Ottoman Learned Class"; Madeline C. Zilfi, *Politics of Piety: The Ottoman ulamā in the Postclassical Age (1600–1800)* (Minneapolis: Bibliotheca Islamica, 1988).

the phrase's geographical dimension. It is worth, however, delving into the implications of the phrase. As we have already seen, al-Murādī dedicates most of his biographical dictionaries to the officially appointed muftīs of Damascus and not, for instance, to the muftīs who were considered influential in the city (although some of the muftīs he mentions probably were). As has been already suggested and will be further discussed in Chapter 5, there were muftīs who operated simultaneously throughout Greater Syria (and beyond), such as the seventeenth-century Palestinian al-Ramlī or al-Shurunbulālī of al-Azhar, and were highly influential in the city. But since al-Murādī's dictionary concentrates on officially appointed muftīs, he follows the logic of the Ottoman practice of appointing provincial muftīs to specific localities (such as Damascus, Jerusalem, Amasya, or any other city across the empire).[98] Moreover, the "locality" of the officially appointed muftī stemmed precisely from his being part of the imperial religious-judicial hierarchy (even if the muftī was not, as was the case in seventeenth-century Damascus, a graduate of the imperial madrasa system). In other words, he was one of the representatives of this hierarchy in a given place. Further emphasizing the connection between the appointed muftī and the Ottoman dynasty, even at the provincial level, was the attachment of a teaching position in prestigious learning institutions endowed by the Ottoman ruling elite to the muftīship of important urban centers.

The "locality" of the officially appointed muftīs throughout Greater Syria also meant that many of them were raised and trained in Damascus, Cairo, and other learning centers throughout the provinces. Moreover, many were members of notable families that produced many jurists and scholars. Oftentimes the office of the muftī was seized by individual families, such as the al-ʿImādīs (and later the al-Murādīs) in Damascus or the Banū Abī Luṭf family in Jerusalem.[99] In the case of Damascus, as Abdul Karim Rafeq has noted, around the turn of the seventeenth century most muftīs were no longer sent from Istanbul; increasingly, leading Damascene jurists were appointed instead of their Rūmī

[98] See, for example, the orders from the capital to the muftīs of Jerusalem and Damascus in Uriel Heyd, *Ottoman Documents on Palestine 1552–1615* (Oxford: Clarendon Press, 1960), 180, 177. On the journey of the Damascene muftī to Jerusalem, see al-Murādī, *ʿArf al-bashām*, 33–34; al-Ghazzī, *al-Kawākib al-sāʾira*, 3:117–18. It is interesting to note that the muftī emerges from these sources as an administrative official. It seems that this dimension of the muftīship in the province of Damascus became less significant over the seventeenth century.

[99] John Voll, "Old ʿUlama Families and Ottoman Influence in Eighteenth Century Damascus," *American Journal of Arabic Studies* 3 (1975): 48–59.

counterparts.[100] In other towns across Bilād al-Shām, such as Jerusalem, local jurists had occupied the position of the officially appointed muftī from the outset.

It is somewhat unclear what the exact reasons for this change in Damascus were. It is possible that the Ottoman learned hierarchy's intention was to gain the support of the relatively newly conquered subjects by appointing local jurists.[101] When one considers that the chief judges were sent from Istanbul throughout the period, the implication of the change in the "ethnic" origin of the muftīs is even more apparent. While the Ottoman learned hierarchy was not willing to compromise on the juridical cohesiveness of its courts system, it perhaps intended to increase its legitimacy through the local officially appointed muftīs.

For this reason, the "ethnic" distinction between the officially appointed muftīs in the province of Damascus and their colleagues who were sent from Istanbul during the sixteenth century should not be overstated. Clearly, the fact that local scholars were members of prominent

[100] Abdul Karim Rafeq, *The Province of Damascus, 1723–1783* (Beirut: Khayats, 1966), 49. There were exceptions. The Bosnian-born Faḍl Allāh b. ʿĪsā al-Būsnāwī (d. 1629), for example, served as the muftī of Damascus in the early decades of the seventeenth century. Although he studied in Bosnia, probably in one of the madrasas there, he settled in Damascus on his way back from the pilgrimage to the holy cities. He served in several teaching positions in Damascus before he was appointed as muftī. Several decades later, Muḥammad b. Qubād (also known as al-Sukūtī) (d. 1643), who entered the city with the chief *qāḍī* Meḥmet b. Yûsuf al-Nihâlî in 1605, served as muftī. He was originally from the town of Vidin, but resided in Damascus and was appointed to several positions in the city before his appointment to the muftīship. It seems that neither of these muftīs was a graduate of the imperial madrasa system, nor did they hold a position in the imperial learned hierarchy prior to their appointment to the muftīship. See al-Muḥibbī, *Khulāṣat al-athar*, 4:124–25; al-Murādī, *ʿArf al-bashām*, 65–66, 72–73.

[101] Sixteenth-century sources document some tensions between members of the Ottoman learned hierarchy and Damascene jurists. Ibn Ayyūb criticized some of the appointed Anatolian muftīs for their lack of knowledge of both jurisprudence and Arabic. Therefore, he argues, they had to rely on Damascene jurists when answering questions. This, however, might be somewhat overstated. See Muhammad Adnan Bakhit, *The Ottoman Province of Damascus in the Sixteenth Century* (Beirut: Librarie du Liban, 1982), 133. See also Abdul Karim Rafeq, "The Syrian ʿUlamāʾ, Ottoman Law, and Islamic Shariʿa," *Turcica* 26 (1994): 9–32; Abdul Karim Rafeq, "Relations between the Syrian "Ulamā" and the Ottoman State in the Eighteenth Century," *Oriente Moderno* 79, no. 1 (1999): 67–95. On the opposition of the Egyptian jurists, see Abdul Karim Rafeq, "The Opposition of the Azhar ʿUlamāʾ to Ottoman Laws and Its Significance in the History of Ottoman Egypt," in Brigitte Marino, ed., *Études sur les Villes du Proche-Orient XVIe–XIXe siècle: Homage à André Raymond* (Damascus: Institut français d'études arabes de Damas, 2001): 43–54; Reem Meshal, "Antagonistic Sharīʿas and the Construction of Orthodoxy in Sixteenth-Century Ottoman Cairo," *Journal of Islamic Studies* 21, no. 2 (2011): 183–212.

families and were well respected by the scholarly community in their hometowns played an important role in the state's decision to appoint them to the muftīship. But, as will be further explored in the following chapters, over the course of the sixteenth and the seventeenth centuries, Damascene and Greater Syrian muftīs gradually adopted and defended legal arguments promoted by the Ottoman learned hierarchy. Moreover, some of the Greater Syrian officially appointed muftīs were trained in the learning centers across the Arab lands, mostly in Egypt, as well as in Istanbul. The seventeenth-century officially appointed muftī of Damascus al-Saʿsaʿānī, for instance, was a graduate of the Ottoman madrasa system and served as the judge in Kayseri and Tripoli.[102] The Jerusalemite ʿAbd al-Raḥīm b. Abī Luṭf, too, traveled to Istanbul, and in 1648 entered the Ottoman madrasa system.[103] The madrasa training of some jurists or the visits to the imperial capital by others contributed to the adoption of legal concepts and jurisprudential texts that other jurists, mostly those who were not appointed to an official post, did not readily accept and at times even openly rejected.

The last issue to address is the rank of the Greater Syrian provincial muftī within the Ottoman learned hierarchy. The sixteenth-century biographer ʿÂşiḳ Çelebi mentions that the salary of Ibrāhīm al-Rūmī, who served as the appointed muftī of Damascus and the professor at the Sulīmāniyya madrasa in the city, was eighty *akçe*. In comparison to other positions in the imperial learned hierarchy in the sixteenth century, this was a fairly high rank.[104] Nevertheless, the appointed muftī's rank was somewhat lower than that of the chief judge of the province. Writing almost a century later, Evliyâ Çelebi claims in his description of Damascus that the Ḥanafī muftī in the city was a mola – that is, a full member of the Ottoman learned hierarchy – whose salary was five hundred *akçe*, as was the salary of the chief *qāḍī*.[105] When Evliyâ visited the city around 1670,[106] the Ḥanafī muftī was not as a rule a full member of the imperial hierarchy. This salary, however, seems to be correct, as in the late eighteenth century, al-Murādī reports that the rank (*rutba*) of the late

[102] Al-Murādī, *ʿArf al-bashām*, 80.
[103] ʿAbd al-Raḥīm b. Abī Luṭf studied in Egypt as well. Among his teachers in Egypt was the eminent Ḥanafī jurist Ḥasan al-Shurunbulālī. Al-Murādī, *Kitāb Silk al-durar*, 3:2–5.
[104] ʿÂşiḳ Çelebi, Muḥammad b. ʿAlī Zayn al-ʿĀbidīn b. Muḥammad b. Jalāl al-Dīn b. Ḥusayn b. Ḥasan b. ʿAlī b. Muḥammad al-Raḍawī, *Dhayl al-Shaqāʾiq al-nuʿmāniyya* (Cairo: Dār al-Hidāya, 2007), 87.
[105] Evliya Çelebi, *Seyahatnâmesi*, 9:267.
[106] Ibid., 9:286.

seventeenth-century muftī al-Saʿsaʿāni was the equivalent to the judgeship of Jerusalem,[107] whose salary at the time was five hundred *akçe*.[108] It is important to note, however, that al-Murādī's statement implies that the rank of the chief *qāḍī* of Damascus was higher. Moreover, the local muftīs of Damascus, and of any other town in Greater Syria for that matter, were not full members of the imperial learned hierarchy. The fact that they were not full members of the hierarchy accounts for the absence of these muftīs from the numerous biographical dictionaries dedicated to the jurists who were affiliated with it, such as those of Nevʿîzâde Atâî, Şeyh̠î Meḥmed Efendi, and Uşşakîzâde.[109]

The muftīs' position raises important questions about the dynamics between the judges and the appointed muftīs. Did the judge always respect the ruling of the Damascene muftī? If so, was it because the muftī followed the ruling of the *şeyh̠ülislâm*? Or was the appointed muftī a mediator of local, Damascene, or Greater Syrian legal practices for the Ottoman judiciary elite? Much more research into the court records remains to be done in order to answer these questions satisfactorily. While Judith Tucker's study suggests that the relationship between the muftī and the court in Ottoman Syria and Palestine was not as close as the one in Anatolia, there is evidence, as I have already argued, that the appointed muftī's opinion was respected in court and, if the *fatwā* corresponded to the case at hand, increased the solicitor's chances to win the case.[110]

To sum up, sixteenth- and seventeenth-century Greater Syria witnessed the encounter between two perceptions of the institution of the muftī. While the Ottoman dynasty and its learned hierarchy were fairly successful in disseminating the practice of officially appointing muftīs throughout the province, other jurists held to "pre-Ottoman" practices and to a different understanding of the muftīship. As will become clear

[107] Al-Murādī, *ʿArf al-bashām*, 80. Nevertheless, the rank was not always fixed. As the example of ʿAbd al-Raḥīm b. Abī Luṭf suggests, certain muftīs obtained higher ranks than others.

[108] See Evliya Çelebi, *Seyahatnâmesi*, 9:231.

[109] Nevʿîzâde Atâî, "Hadâiku'l-Hakâik fî Tekmileti'ş-Şakâik," in Abdülkadir Özcan, ed., *Şakaik-i Nuʿmaniye ve Zeyilleri* (Istanbul: Çağri Yayinlari, 1989); Şeyhî Meḥmed Efendi, "Vekâyiʿü'l-Fudalâ" in Abdülkadir Özcan, ed., Şakaik-i Nuʿmaniye ve zeyilleri (Istanbul: Çağri Yayinlari, 1989); in *Şakaik-i Nuʿmaniye ve Zeyilleri*; Uşşâkîzâde es-Seyyid İbrâhîm Hasîb Efendi,*Uşşâkîzâde Tarihi* (Istanbul: Çamlıca, 2005). On the other hand, graduates of the Ottoman madrasa system who served as muftīs in Damascus are mentioned. See ʿAlī b. Bālī Manq, *al-ʿIqd al-manẓūm*, 383.

[110] As we shall see in Chapter 3, the opinions of some eminent muftīs who did not hold an official appointment were adopted by members of the learned hierarchy. In this case, their appearance in court records may be interpreted as their adoption by the hierarchy.

in Chapter 5, it seems that over the course of the first two centuries following the Ottoman conquest, an equilibrium between these perceptions was achieved. This equilibrium, however, should not obscure the ongoing debate that took place among Greater Syrian jurists concerning the Ottoman practice of officially appointing muftīs. It is to this debate that we now turn.

Al-Nābulusī Responds to al-Ḥaṣkafī (and an Imaginary Dialogue with Al-Murādī)

Late in the seventeenth century or early in the next,[111] ʿAbd al-Ghanī al-Nābulusī penned an epistle in which he responded to a treatise composed by an al-Ḥaṣkafī, most likely the mid-seventeenth-century ʿAlāʾ al-Dīn al-Ḥaṣkafī. Although al-Ḥaṣkafī's treatise is not known to have survived, it is clear that the debate was centered on the nature of the muftīship from the sixteenth through the eighteenth centuries.[112] Like al-Murādī, al-Ḥaṣkafī was an officially appointed muftī in Damascus. Although al-Ḥaṣkafī's own voice in this debate is absent,[113] it seems that al-Murādī, in the introduction to his biographical dictionary, echoes some issues that al-Ḥaṣkafī presumably touched upon in his treatise. To be sure, none of the three participants in this debate was a contemporary of the others. Nevertheless, it appears fruitful to engage al-Nābulusī and al-Murādī in a conjectural dialogue with each other, for through such a dialogue it is possible to reconstruct more fully a range of opinions and arguments that circulated in Damascene scholarly circles.

The biography of ʿAbd al-Ghanī al-Nābulusī should not detain us here. Suffice it to say at this point that he held the muftīship of Damascus

[111] The epistle was copied by Muḥammad b. Muṣṭafā, most likely Muhammad al-Dakdakjī, a close disciple of al-Nābulusī and an acclaimed copyist. He is known to have written several works for al-Nābulusī. Al-Dakdakjī died in 1718, so the treatise must have been completed earlier. On al-Dakdakjī, see Barbara von Schlegell, "Sufism in the Ottoman Arab World: Shaykh ʿAbd al-Ghanī al-Nābulusī (d. 1143/1731)" (PhD diss., University of California at Berkeley, 1997), 55–60.

[112] Martha Mundy and Richard Saumarez-Smith have noticed this treatise; see Martha Mundy and Richard Saumarez-Smith, *Governing Property, Making the Modern State: Law, Administration, and Production in Ottoman Syria* (London: I. B. Tauris, 2007), 22.

[113] Al-Ḥaṣkafī discusses some of these issues in his commentary on *Multaqā al-abḥur*, entitled *al-Durr al-muntaqā fī sharḥ al-Multaqā*, but he does not address the sultanic appointment of muftīs. Muḥammad b. ʿAlī b. Muḥammad al-Ḥiṣnī al-Maʿrūf bi'l-ʿAlāʾ al-Ḥaṣkafī, *al-Durr al-muntaqā fī sharḥ al-Multaqā* (Beirut: Dār al-Kutub al-ʿIlmiyya, 1998), 3:214–16.

for a brief period of time, but for most of his career he did not hold any officially appointed office.[114] As such, he represents a group of non-appointed muftīs who were active across Bilād al-Shām. These muftīs, such as Muḥammad al-Tīmūrtāshī and Khayr al-Dīn al-Ramlī, were not officially appointed to serve as muftīs, yet they issued legal rulings. Moreover, some of these muftīs were among the most prominent jurisprudential authorities in Bilād al-Shām and, to a large degree, in the empire at large. It should be emphasized that despite their disapproval of certain legal practices endorsed by members of the Ottoman learned hierarchy, the nonappointed muftīs were by and large loyal subjects of the empire. As discussed earlier, these muftīs and their activity serve as a good reminder that the Ottomans did not always attempt to prevent non-appointed muftīs from issuing legal opinions. This stands in remarkable contrast to the Ottomans' adamant approach to nonofficial courts.[115] Instead of banning the activity of these muftīs, the Ottoman legal system provided an appointed muftī, whose opinion, at least theoretically, was to be followed in court.

Al-Nābulusī opens his treatise with a discussion concerning who should be considered a muftī. He explicitly states that "the muftīship is not like judgeship, which is assigned by the sultan to a single person exclusively, as [opposed to what] the people of this time do [i.e., the Ottoman practice of appointing muftīs]."[116] Al-Nābulusī bases this statement on his understanding of the state of the Ḥanafī school in his time. Following Ibn Nujaym's (d. 1563) *al-Baḥr al-rāʾiq*[117] and Ibn al-Humām's (d. 1459 or 1460) *Fatḥ al-qadīr*,[118] al-Nābulusī claims that a muftī should be a *mujtahid*,[119] a jurist who is allowed to exert his own juristic effort (*ijtihād*) to

[114] Von Schlegell, "Sufism in the Ottoman Arab World," 1–112.

[115] See, for instance, MD 7, 2040/15/RA/976. In this imperial edict, the judge of Bursa is asked to close the illicit court the former professor of the Dâvûd Paşa madrasa had opened in his home. In the second half of the seventeenth century, the Ḥanafī Yāsīn b. Muṣṭafā al-Biqāʿi (d. 1693) held an unofficial court in the al-Maḥalla al-Jadīda neighborhood in Damascus. The chief *qāḍī* of Damascus ordered this court closed down. Al-Muḥibbī, *Khulāṣat al-athar*, 4:480.

[116] ʿAbd al-Ghanī al-Nābulusī, *al-Radd al-wafī ʿalā jawāb al-Ḥaṣkafī ʿalā masʾalat al-khiff al-Ḥanafī*, Süleymaniye Library MS Esad Efendi 1762, 154r.

[117] Al-Nābulusī, *al-Radd*, 154r–154v. Al-Ḥaṣkafī, in his commentary on *Multaqā al-abḥur*, shares this observation. Al-Ḥaṣkafī, *al-Durr al-muntaqā*, 3:215. Zayn al-Dīn b. Ibrāhīm b. Muḥammad b. Nujaym, *al-Baḥr al-rāʾiq* (Beirut: Dār al-Kutub al-ʿIlmiyya, 1997), 6:446–49.

[118] Al-Nābulusī, *al-Radd*, 154v.

[119] Ibid.

reach a rule or an opinion.[120] But the problem, according to al-Nābulusī, is that at his time no jurist can be considered a *mujtahid*; instead, there are only jurists who preserve and transmit the opinions of Abū Ḥanīfa and other previous *mujtahids*. Thus the muftīs of his time, al-Nābulusī concludes, are not truly muftīs but the transmitters of the sayings of the real muftīs, such as Abū Ḥanīfa, to the solicitor. The opinion of a "real muftī" can be transmitted either through a reliable chain of transmission or through well-known, widely accepted, and reliable texts, such as al-Marghīnānī's (d. 1196 or 1197) *al-Hidāya* or al-Sarakhsī's (d. ca. 1096) *al-Mabsūṭ*. If there are multiple opinions, issued by different "real muftīs," the follower (*muqallid*) is free to choose any of these opinions.[121] In other words, al-Nābulusī argues that the community of Ḥanafī jurists should not rule out any opinion that was issued by a "real muftī" and was reliably transmitted.[122]

Returning to the sultan's appointment of muftīs, at the heart of the debate between al-Ḥaṣkafī and al-Nābulusī was their interpretation of the opinion of the Egyptian jurist Zayn al-Dīn b. Nujaym. Writing in Egypt in the first decades following the Ottoman conquest, Ibn Nujaym argued that the imām, in this case the sultan, should examine who is eligible to issue legal rulings from among the jurists and should prevent incompetent jurists from obtaining this position. In other words, Ibn Nujaym advocated an institutional solution to the plurality of muftīs that some in the late Mamluk sultanate found disturbing. Nevertheless, it should be emphasized that his solution is substantially different from the Ottoman understanding of the office. As in many other cases, his opinion is somewhere in between the Mamluk and the Ottoman approaches.

In his treatise, al-Nābulusī accepts Ibn Nujaym's statement that the imām, the leader of the Muslim community (most often understood as the sultan), should examine who is eligible to issue legal rulings from among the jurists and should prevent incompetent jurists from obtaining the

[120] On *mujtahid* and *ijtihād*, see Wael B. Hallaq, *The Origin and Evolution of Islamic Law* (Cambridge: Cambridge University Press, 2005), 128–32; Wael B. Hallaq, *Authority, Continuity, and Change in Islamic Law* (Cambridge: Cambridge University Press, 2004), 1–24.

[121] Al-Nābulusī, *al-Radd*, 154v.

[122] The concept of *al-muftī al-muqallid* appears in the writings of some members of the imperial learned hierarchy as well. In the introduction to his *ṭabaqāt* work, ʿAlî Çelebi Kınalızâde mentions that al-muftī al-muqallid should know the hierarchy of the authorities of the Ḥanafī school of law. ʿAlî Çelebi Kınalızâde, *Ṭabaqāt al-Ḥanafiyya* (Amman: Dār Ibn al-Jawzī, 2004–5), 93.

position of muftī.[123] But, as opposed to al-Ḥaṣkafī's alleged opinion that the sultan should appoint a sole jurisconsult in each locality, al-Nābulusī insists that Ibn Nujaym's statement should not be understood as a justification for appointing a sole muftī whenever there are several eligible jurists. Therefore, al-Nābulusī concludes, every person who fulfills the requirements in terms of knowledge and competence could issue legal rulings.[124]

It is worth paying attention to the manner in which al-Nābulusī employs the terminology of the madhhab, and particularly the concept of following/imitation (*taqlīd*), in his treatise. Specifically, the link he makes between the appointment procedure of the jurisconsults and the structure of the school of law is noteworthy. For al-Nābulusī, preserving a relative doctrinal plurality within the school of law was predicated on a multiplicity of muftīs. Concurrently, the notion of a wide range of opinions within the madhhab is employed to prevent, or at least to limit, the intervention of the state. In this sense, al-Nābulusī's argument is reminiscent of the argument made almost five centuries earlier by the Egyptian Mālikī jurist Shihāb al-Dīn al-Qarāfī (d. 1285), who argued, in the words of Sherman Jackson, that the madhhab is "a corporate constitutional unit" that is intended to protect its followers from the intervention of the state and followers of other, perhaps more dominant, schools of law.[125]

There were also, of course, other practical dimensions to al-Nābulusī's concerns. As far as al-Nābulusī and his nonappointed colleagues were concerned, the plurality of muftīs was crucial and not simply a theoretical discussion. Threatened by the Ottoman appointment policy, al-Nābulusī

123 In another treatise, *Iḍāḥ al-dalālāt fī samā' al-ālāt*, al-Nābulusī argues that incompetent muftīs should not be allowed to deliver their rulings. For a discussion of this treatise, see Andrew Lane, "'Abd al-Ghanī al-Nābulusī (1641–1731): Experience of a Sufi Shaykh on the Margins of Society," in *Marginal Voices in Literature and Society: Individual and Society in the Mediterranean Muslim World*, ed. Robin Ostle (Strasbourg: European Science Foundation in collaboration with Maison mediterraneenne des sciences de l'homme d'Aix-en-Provence, 2000), 89–116 and particularly 98–99. I thank Nir Shafir for bringing this article to my attention. By the eighteenth century, the removal of muftīs from office by the sultan was approved by non-Ḥanafī jurists as well. Ḥāmid b. 'Alī al-'Imādī (d. 1758), the officially appointed Ḥanafī muftī of Damascus, collected the opinions of several eminent Ḥanafī and non-Ḥanafī Damascene jurists who supported the Sultan's right to remove incompetent muftīs from office. See Ḥāmid b. 'Alī al-'Imādī, *Ṣalāḥ al-'ālam bi-iftā' al-'ālim* (Amman: Dār 'Ammār, 1988), 27–46.

124 Al-Nābulusī, *al-Radd*, 155r–155v. For Ibn Nujaym's opinion, see Ibn Nujaym, *al-Baḥr al-rā'iq*, 6:446–49.

125 Sherman A. Jackson, *Islamic Law and the State: The Constitutional Jurisprudence of Shihāb al-Dīn al-Qarāfī* (Leiden: Brill, 1996).

wrote a defense of a scholarly practice that permitted his (and others') activity as muftīs. More broadly, al-Nābulusī's treatise brings to the surface a different understanding of jurisprudential authority and its transmission. Furthermore, he poses a serious challenge to the officially appointed muftīs in particular, and to the soundness of the Ottoman appointment policy of muftīs in general.

Given al-Nābulusī's immense popularity, al-Murādī must have been familiar with at least some of the arguments raised in al-Nābulusī's treatise, and perhaps even with the treatise itself. Specifically, he must have been aware of the tension between the understanding and practice of the muftīship as it appears in pre-Ottoman, namely, Mamluk, jurisprudential texts, as well as in later compilations from the Arab lands, and the manner in which it was practiced within the Ottoman learned hierarchy. Aware of the novelty of the Ottoman's officially appointed muftīship, al-Murādī's introduction might be read as a justification of the Ottoman practice in response to the arguments advanced by his colleagues who did not hold a state appointment. It is perhaps for this reason that al-Murādī resorts to several arguments, such as the need to prevent disputes among the jurists, that are not the arguments made in Mamluk jurisprudential texts. Instead, al-Murādī is compelled to admit that the practice of appointing muftīs is rooted in the Ottoman *ḳânûn*, which in turn is "compatible with the sharīʿa."

The imaginary dialogue between al-Nābulusī and al-Murādī illuminates different aspects of the emergence of the state madhhab and the appointment of muftīs: on the one hand, al-Nābulusī's critique reveals how the Ottoman practice of appointing jurisconsults served to mark a specific range of legal opinions and doctrines within the Ḥanafī school; and, on the other, al-Murādī's account exposes that relationship between the Ottoman dynasty and its *ḳânûn* and this range of doctrines with the school.

Conclusion: The Ottoman Muftī, *Ḳânûn*, and the Ottoman Ḥanafī Legal School

> When he entered Damascus, he renewed its affairs, implemented his edicts in it, and organized it according to his exalted *qānūn*, which is in accordance to the honorable *sharīʿa*. [He also] arranged its [the city's] offices of knowledge and *siyāsa* according to his ability and his noble opinion.[126]

[126] Al-Murādī, *ʿArf al-bashām*, 2–3.

The definition of ḳânûn (*qānūn*) and *şerîʿat* (*sharīʿa*) in the Ottoman context, together with the relationship between these concepts, has drawn considerable scholarly attention over the past decades.[127] One of the approaches to these questions perceives ḳânûn and *şerîʿat* first and foremost as two supplementary, often "kneaded together" components of the Ottoman legal discourse. Other scholars, however, have approached this question somewhat differently. While not disregarding its discursive dimension, these scholars have pointed to the fact that ḳânûn also denotes various administrative and institutional practices prevalent across the empire. Although the institutional practices were not always codified and were constantly negotiated and reconfigured,[128] the ḳânûn as a legal discourse served to legitimize these practices. Whether codified or not, the task is to define what ḳânûn means in a specific historical context and to examine the bearings of this definition on the definition of *şerîʿat*, and specifically on the rise of an Ottoman Ḥanafī official school.

As Richard Repp has demonstrated, the consolidation of the Ottoman learned hierachy was a direct outcome of a series of imperial edicts and legal codes (*ḳânûnnâme*s).[129] The emergence of the officially appointed muftī was an integral part of the development of the hierarchy as a whole. To be sure, the fact that the hierarchy was established through these edicts does not necessarily preclude the participation of jurists in this process.

[127] Several studies have dealt with different aspects of these issues. Some notable examples include Halil Inalcik, "*Kanun*," *EI*[2]; *Uriel Heyd, Studies in Old Ottoman Criminal Law* (Oxford: Clarendon Press, 1973); Imber, *Ebu's-Suʿud*; F. Babinger, s.v. "Nishandji," *EI*[2]; Molly Greene, *A Shared World: Christians and Muslims in the Early Modern Mediterranean* (Princeton, NJ: Princeton University Press, 2000), 27–32; Snjezana Buzov, "The Lawgiver and His Lawmakers: The Role of Legal Discourse in the Change of Ottoman Imperial Culture" (PhD diss., University of Chicago, 2005); Yunus Koç, "Early Ottoman Customary Law: The Genesis and Development of Ottoman Codification," in Walter Dostal and Wolfgang Kraus, eds., *Shattering Tradition: Custom, Law and the Individual in the Muslim Mediterranean* (London: I.B. Tauris, 2005), 75–121; Dror Ze'evi, *Producing Desire: Changing Sexual Discourse in the Ottoman Middle East, 1500–1900* (Berkeley: University of California Press, 2006), 50; Timothy J. Fitzgerald, "Ottoman Methods of Conquest: Legal Imperialism and the City of Aleppo, 1480–1570" (PhD diss., Harvard University, 2009), 188–95; Sabrina Joseph, *Islamic Law on Peasant Usufruct in Ottoman Syria: 17th to Early 19th Century* (Leiden: Brill, 2012), chap. 4.

[128] Başak Tuğ, "Politics of Honor: The Institutional and Social Frontiers of 'Illicit' Sex in Mid-Eighteenth-Century Ottoman Anatolia" (PhD diss., New York University, 2009), 40–96; Cornell H. Fleischer, *Bureaucrat and Intellectual in the Ottoman Empire: The Historian Mustafa Âli (1541–1600)* (Princeton, NJ: Princeton University Press, 1986), 191–200.

[129] Repp, *The Müfti of Istanbul.*

Moreover, one should be careful not to assume that the jurists' involvement was instrumental. Instead, it is possible that the jurists in the core lands of the empire genuinely tried to articulate a religious-political vision that would be compatible with their understanding of Ḥanafī (and other Sunnī) legal traditions. Yet this does not alter the fact that, as al-Murādī observes in his introduction, it was the imperial edicts that legitimized these institutional and administrative developments – and specifically the emergence of the chief muftī as the chief jurisprudential authority within the Ottoman hierarchy.

By appointing jurisconsults, the Ottoman dynasty, either directly or, from the mid-sixteenth century, through the chief imperial muftī (and the learned hierarchy in general), sought to craft a particular version of the Ḥanafī school out of a wider range of possible opinions. From an institutional perspective, then, ḳânûn and *şerîʿat* were not exactly equal in the Ottoman context, for the content of the imperial madhhab was defined by officeholders, the chief muftī and his subordinates, whose authority to define which opinion within the Ḥanafī school should be followed rested on the ḳânûn. Put differently, the rise of an Ottoman official school of law was predicated on the emergence of an Ottoman dynastic legal corpus, a point to which we shall return in the following chapters.

An anecdote recorded in Maḥmud Kefevî's biography of Ebû's-Suʿûd Efendi illustrates these dynamics: "In certain cases he [Ebû's-Suʿûd] followed the path of [independent] judgment (*ra'y*). Then he took counsel with Sultan Süleymân … on whether he could give fatwas according to what he saw fit, and to whichever he preferred of the solutions which occurred to him. A decree was issued accordingly."[130] Put differently, the chief muftī needed the sultan's edict (and approval) to rule according to a minority opinion within the school, and by issuing this edict the Ottoman sultan (and dynasty) shaped the doctrine of the school. Nevertheless, as al-Murādī argues, many members of the Ottoman imperial learned hierarchy claimed, in what seems to be a cyclical argument, that this practice was compatible with *şerîʿat*, as if the two discourses were independent.

[130] Ibid., 279; see also Imber, *Ebu's-Suʿud*, 106–10.

2

Genealogies and Boundaries

Situating the Imperial Learned Hierarchy within the Ḥanafī Jurisprudential Tradition

In the entries dedicated to members of the Ottoman learned hierarchy in sixteenth- to eighteenth-century biographical dictionaries from the Arab provinces of the empire, the biographers often describe a certain biographee as "Rūmī" and "Ḥanafī."[1] At first glance, there is nothing remarkable in the juxtaposition of these epithets, as the Ottoman dynasty's adoption of the Sunnī Ḥanafī legal school as its state school is well known among students of Islamic societies. Accordingly, the combination "Rūmī Ḥanafī" may be read in a narrow geographical sense, denoting that the origin of a certain follower of the Ḥanafī school is from the core lands of the empire (central and western Anatolia and the Balkans). Nevertheless, as this chapter suggests, "Rūmī" is not merely a geographical epithet but one that has doctrinal implications as well.

[1] For example: Najm al-Dīn al-Ghazzī, *al-Kawākib al-sāʾira bi-aʿyān al-miʾa al-ʿāshira* (Beirut: Jāmiʿat Bayrūt al-Amīrikiyya, 1945–58), 1:20–23, 2:58; Muḥammad Amīn b. Faḍl Allāh al-Muḥibbī, *Khulāṣat al-athar fī aʿyān al-qarn al-ḥādī ʿashar* (Beirut: Dār al-Kutub al-ʿIlmiyya, 2006), 1:553, 3:386. Each of these terms has a long history with its meaning changing over the centuries. On the change the meaning of the term "Ḥanafī" underwent during the first century and a half of the school's existence, see Nurit Tsafrir, *The History of an Islamic School of Law* (Cambridge, MA: Harvard University Press, 2004). For the different meanings of the term "Rūmī," see C. E. Bosworth, "Rum," *EI*²; Halil Inaclik, "Rumi," *EI*²; Salih Özbaran, *Bir Osmanlı Kimliği: 14.–17. Yüzyıllarda Rûm/Rûmi Aidiyet ve Imgeleri* (Istanbul: Kitab, 2004); Benjamin Lellouch, *Les Ottomans en Égypte: Historiens et conquerants au XVIe siècle* (Paris: Louvain, 2006), 184–99; Cemal Kafadar, "A Rome of One's Own: Reflections on Cultural Geography and Identity in the Lands of Rum," *Muqarnas* 24 (2007): 7–25; Michael Winter, "Ottoman Qāḍīs in Damascus in 16th–18th Centuries," in *Law, Custom, and Statute in the Muslim World: Studies in Honor of Aharon Layish*, ed. Ron Shaham (Leiden: Brill, 2007), 87–109; Tijana Krstić, *Contested Conversion to Islam: Narratives of Religious Change in the Early Modern Ottoman Empire* (Stanford, CA: Stanford University Press, 2011), 1–7, 51–74.

In the previous chapter, I argued that the Ottoman dynasty attempted to regulate the structure and the doctrine of a specific branch within the Ḥanafī school of law by appointing muftīs and, more generally, developing an imperial learned hierarchy. This chapter looks at other aspects of this attempt and explores a hitherto understudied body of several intellectual genealogies of the Ḥanafī school. Known as *ṭabaqāt* (*tabaḳât* in Turkish), these genealogies, which were produced by jurists who were affiliated with the imperial learned hierarchy, offer a better understanding of the way in which these jurists, and most likely other members of the hierarchy, perceived their position, and the position of the hierarchy as a whole, within the Ḥanafī jurisprudential tradition.

The first original genealogy by a member of the imperial hierarchy was apparently compiled in the early decades of the sixteenth century. Subsequently, over the course of the sixteenth and seventeenth centuries, at least three members of the imperial learned hierarchy authored their own versions of the hierarchy's genealogy within the Ḥanafī school. The first genealogy, penned by the eminent chief imperial muftī Kemâlpaşazâde (d. 1534), was different from the later genealogies in terms of its chronological scope, structure, and goals. Its primary aim was to classify in declining order the leading figures of the school according to their authority to exert independent reasoning in relation to the eponymous founder of the school, Abū Ḥanīfa. Kemâlpaşazâde's treatise marks the first attempt by a senior member of the evolving imperial hierarchy to offer a systematic account of the history and the structure of the Ḥanafī school. The fact that all his successors who undertook similar projects included in their works a classification of the authorities of the school (some differences notwithstanding) and the large number of copies of the work found in various libraries throughout Istanbul and beyond point to its importance.

The authors of the other three genealogies from the second half of the sixteenth century onward, which constitute the focus of this chapter, had a somewhat different set of concerns. These concerns shaped to a considerable extent the structure and the content of their genealogies. Mostly preoccupied with establishing the position of the imperial learned hierarchy within the Ḥanafī tradition, all these *ṭabaqāt* works adhere by and large to a similar view of the Ḥanafī school. According to this view, from around the conquest of Istanbul in the mid-fifteenth century, the hierarchy became an independent branch with a particular genealogy within the Ḥanafī school. This branch, or sub-school, within the Ḥanafī school differed from other branches whose followers operated throughout the

Mamluk sultanate (and elsewhere). The authors of these *ṭabaqāt* works were interested in documenting the genealogy of, and cementing the authority of, specific legal arguments and texts within the Ḥanafī tradition that were endorsed by members of the imperial learned hierarchy.[2]

This is not to say that there were no significant differences in the way each of these authors perceived the history of the Ḥanafī school. Much attention will be paid in the following pages to these differences, which surely reflect the sensibilities of the different authors but also suggest that how members of the imperial learned hierarchy perceived the school and its history changed over time. Of particular importance is their selective incorporation of sixteenth-century Ḥanafī jurists from the Arab lands into these genealogies, while still preserving the aforementioned divergence of the mid-fifteenth century.

Although these genealogies were compiled in the sixteenth century (and later), that does not mean that they were invented in the sixteenth century. It is likely that at least some of the elements that the sixteenth-century authors utilized in their texts had already been circulating in the fourteenth and fifteenth centuries. But only in the sixteenth century did the need to compile systematic accounts of the genealogies of the imperial learned hierarchy within the Ḥanafī school emerge. Furthermore, the difference among the genealogies raises the possibility that several, at times contradicting, accounts of the history of the school coexisted, although they may also be the product of narrative layers that were added in later stages.

Finally, this chapter links the emergence of these intellectual and authoritative genealogies to the appearance of another important genre in the second half of the sixteenth century: the biographical dictionaries that were mostly devoted to senior members of the Ottoman learned

[2] Bibliographical works mention three additional *ṭabaqāt* works that were compiled in the Ottoman lands in that period. The first is a *ṭabaqāt* work by Ak Şems Çelebi that is very similar to Kınalızâde's work (see note 16). In the second half of the sixteenth century, the Meccan historian Qutb al-Dīn Muḥammad b. Aḥmad b. Muḥammad b. Qāḍīkhān al-Nahrawānī al-Makkī (d. 1583) wrote a *ṭabaqāt* work, now lost. In the seventeenth century, Khalīl al-Rūmī, known as Ṣolâkzâde (d. 1683), wrote another *ṭabaqāt* work, entitled *Tuḥfat al-tarājim*. Despite some slight variations, the work draws heavily on Ibn Quṭlūbughā's *Tāj al-tarājim* (even the title of the work makes clear reference to Ibn Quṭlūbughā's title). Ṣolâkzâde, *Tuḥfat al-tarājim*, Bayezit Library MS Velyüddin 1606. See also Kâtip Çelebi, *Kashf al-ẓunūn ʿan asāmī al-kutub waʾl-funūn* (Istanbul: Milli Eğitim Basımevi, 1972), 2:1097–99; Ismāʿīl Bāshāal-Bābānī, *Īḍāḥ al-maknūn fī al-dhayl ʿalā Kashf al-ẓunūn ʿan asāmī al-kutub waʾl-funūn* (Istanbul: Milli Eğitim Basımevi, 1945–47), 2:78.

hierarchy. There are some important similarities between the genres. First, both genres were intended to delineate the boundaries of the hierarchy against the background of an expanding empire where multiple Ḥanafī traditions coexisted. Second, as both genres are different manifestations of the Islamic (Arabic) biographical traditions, there is clear discursive continuity between the biographical dictionaries and the genealogies (at times they even draw on the same sources or cite each other). Nevertheless, I treat them separately because my intention is to draw attention to the fact that these two genres carry different semiotic baggage, follow somewhat different conventions, and aim to achieve, to some extent, different goals.[3]

Ṭabaqāt: A Very Short Introduction

While *ṭabaqāt* works produced before the sixteenth century have received a considerable deal of attention, scholars of Ottoman history have not by and large studied systematically the *ṭabaqāt* compiled throughout the empire over the course of the sixteenth and seventeenth centuries. This does not mean that Ottomanists have not consulted some of these works, especially for the information they preserve concerning the imperial learned hierarchy. But most studies have not examined the logic that lies at the basis of these works or read these texts in the context of the long historiographical-epistemological tradition of the *ṭabaqāt* genre. What follows, then, is a brief survey of some of the main features of the genre and its history up to the sixteenth century.

The word *ṭabaqa* (pl. *ṭabaqāt*) has several interrelated meanings. Most generally, the word denotes a group or a layer of things of the same sort. In the Islamic historiographical-bibliographical tradition, the word is often used to refer to a "rank, attributed to a group of characters that have played a role in history in one capacity or another, classed according to criteria determined by the religious, cultural, scientific, or artistic order." Moreover, the word often connotes a chronological dimension, and many of the works in this genre are organized chronologically according to "generations."[4]

[3] The close semiotic connection between the works in these genres is also evident from the ways in which they were preserved and copied. In several manuscripts (or, more precisely, *mecmûʿas*), biographical dictionaries or excerpts from biographical dictionaries were copied along with *ṭabaqāt* works. See, for example, Staatsbibliothek zu Berlin Mss. Or. Peterm II 688 and Houghton Library (Harvard University) MS Arab 411.

[4] Cl. Gilliot, "Ṭabaḳāt," *EI*².

By the early decades of the sixteenth century, when the first Ottoman *ṭabaqāt* works were produced, the genre already had a history of approximately eight centuries. Moreover, by that time, the genre had become fairly diverse in terms of structure, scope, and the groups of people classified. This diversity makes it difficult to offer a generalization that will do justice to all the works that were considered *ṭabaqāt* by their authors or their readers. Our focus, therefore, will be on a particular, and arguably the most dominant, group of works within the *ṭabaqāt* genre – the works dealing with the transmission of religious and jurisprudential knowledge and authority.

Over the course of the eight centuries up to the sixteenth century, the genre had become increasingly specialized according to the different disciplines of knowledge. Thus, for example, there are *ṭabaqāt* works dedicated to transmitters of prophetic traditions (*ḥadīth*), Sufis, theological schools, physicians, and lexicographers, as well as to the followers of the legal schools. Despite some differences between the specialized "subgenres," all these texts share the notion that religious scholars and jurists are metaphorically descendants of the Prophet Muḥammad, the source of knowledge.[5] The *ṭabaqāt* works' main purpose was to meticulously document these intellectual lineages through which the Prophet's knowledge was transmitted to different specialized groups, each of which inherited a particular type of knowledge. From the individual scholar's perspective, his (and in some cases her) authority rested precisely on his/her affiliation to a specific chain of transmission that linked him to the Prophet.

The genealogical/generational nature of the *ṭabaqāt* works implies, of course, a relationship between one generation and the other, but the relationship between the generations varies from one *ṭabaqāt* work to the other. Some works perceive the relation between the generations as one of decline in intellectual capacity, piety, or morals. Other works stress the transmission of knowledge and authority over time. The different

[5] Over the past decades, several studies have been dedicated to the *ṭabaqāt* genre. For example: Ibrahim Hafsi, "Recherches sur le genre ṭabaqāt dans la litterature arabe," pt. 1, 2, and 3, *Studia Arabica* 23 (1976): 227–65, 24; (February 1977): 1–41, 24; (June 1977): 150–86; Michael Cooperson, *Classical Arabic Biography: The Heirs of the Prophets in the Age of al-Ma'mun* (Cambridge: Cambridge University Press, 2000), 8–13; George Makdisi, "Ṭabaqāt-Biography: Law and Orthodoxy in Classical Islam," *Islamic Studies* 32, no. 4 (1993), 371–96; R. Kevin Jaques, *Authority, Conflict, and the Transmission of Diversity in Medieval Islamic Law* (Leiden: Brill, 2006); Felicitas Opwis, "The Role of the Biographer in Constructing Identity and School: al-ʿAbbādi and His Kitāb Ṭabaqāt al-Fuqahā' al-Shāfiʿīyya," *Journal of Arabic and Islamic Studies* 11, no. 1 (2011): 1–35.

perceptions, however, are not mutually exclusive, and, as we shall see in the following sections, a single work can accommodate both.

The *ṭabaqāt* works served other goals beyond documenting intellectual-spiritual genealogies. Over the centuries, *ṭabaqāt* works were used by different groups as a means to outline the "orthodoxy" or canonical views within their discipline. Moreover, as Kevin Jaques, following George Makdisi, has pointed out, since there is no "orthodoxy" without "heterodoxy," the *ṭabaqāt* works offer a glimpse into the internal debates within the community of scholars. In the context of the legal schools, the *ṭabaqāt* works demarcate the boundaries of permissible opinion and establish the authority of specific legal arguments within a particular school.[6] Furthermore, since different *ṭabaqāt* works record different chains of transmission, the variations between the different works point to concurrent, at times contradicting, visions of the history of specific disciplines or legal schools. For historians, the difference among the works permits the reconstruction, albeit a partial one, of the process through which "orthodoxy" was negotiated and determined.

A survey of the *ṭabaqāt* genre cannot be complete without addressing the relationship between this genre and the broader historiographical tradition of the Islamic biographical dictionary. Most notably, both the ṭabaqāt works and the biographical dictionaries utilize the same building block for constructing their narrative. As its name indicates, the biographical dictionary is a collection of independently standing biographies (*tarjama* pl. *tarājim*), comparable to modern "who's who" works. The individual biographies, however, form a mosaic from which a larger narrative emerges.[7] Furthermore, both genres are enmeshed in a shared discourse of authority. As far as the biographies of jurists and religious scholars are concerned, each biography preserves and reiterates the logic that lies at the basis of the *ṭabaqāt* works, that is, the idea that knowledge is transmitted through chains of transmission, and that the jurist's authority is constituted through his teachers. This logic underlies almost every biography, regardless of the organizing principle of the entire work.[8]

Further, much like the "who's who" works, the genealogies (but also, as we have seen in Chapter 1, the biographical dictionaries) served as

[6] Jaques, *Authority*, 17.

[7] Extensive work has been done on the biographical literature in Islamic historiography. For a comprehensive list, see Jaques, *Authority*, 11n56.

[8] For an analysis of the function of these discursive patterns in a fifteenth-century Shāfiʿī *ṭabaqāt* work, see Jaques, *Authority*. There might be, of course, some variations between the dictionaries and the *ṭabaqāt* works, though this issue requires further research.

reference works and pedagogical tools for jurists. As the introductions to some of the *ṭabaqāt* works discussed in this chapter explain, these works were intended to be consulted by jurists and muftīs. In addition, it appears that the works were also taught as part of a jurist's training. Moreover, it should be noted that "the *ṭabaqāt* project" was a living tradition, which was continuously updated and supplemented, as the comments on the margins of the extant copies of the genealogies attest. At least in some cases these marginal comments were consulted as well: Taqiyy al-Dīn al-Tamīmī, for instance, explicitly says that the Egyptian scholar Zayn al-Dīn b. Nujaym cited comments he read in the margins of several copies of al-Qurashī's fourteenth-century *ṭabaqāt*, *al-Jawāhir al-muḍiyya*.[9] Al-Tamīmī himself, in turn, points to pieces of information he could find only in the comments added to *al-Jawāhir*.[10] In other words, the genealogies as both texts and artifacts played a central role in maintaining the coherence of the legal school, or, at least, of its branches.

Early Stages: Kemâlpaşazâde's *Risāla fī Ṭabaqāt al-Mujtahidīn*

It is not fully clear when members of the Ottoman learned hierarchy got interested in the *ṭabaqāt* genre. It is very likely that in the fifteenth century many were familiar with important pre-Ottoman *ṭabaqāt* works, and particularly with ʿAbd al-Qādir al-Qurashī's (d. 1373) *al-Jawāhir al-muḍiyya*.[11] Moreover, the issue of authority and transmission of

[9] Taqiyy al-Dīn b. ʿAbd al-Qādir al-Tamīmī, *al-Ṭabaqāt al-saniyya fī tarājim al-Ḥanafiyya*, Süleymaniye Library MS Aya Sofya 3295, 473r–473v. Moreover, Ibn Nujaym mentions al-Qurashī's *ṭabaqāt* among the lists consulted while compiling his *al-Ashbāh wa'l-naẓā'ir*. Zayn al-Dīn b. Ibrāhīm b. Nujaym, *al-Ashbāh wa'l-naẓā'ir ʿalā madhhab Abī Ḥanīfa al-Nuʿman* (Cairo: Mu'assasat al-Ḥalabī, 1968), 18.

[10] Taqiyy al-Dīn b. ʿAbd al-Qādir al-Tamīmī, *al-Ṭabaqāt al-saniyya fī tarājim al-Ḥanafiyya* (Riyad: Dār al-Rifāʿī, 1983), 4:429–30; al-Tamīmī, *al-Ṭabaqāt*, Süleymaniye Library MS Aya Sofya 3295, 259r.

[11] According to his library's catalog (which was compiled around 1502–3), Sultan Bâyezîd II (d. 1512) held a copy of the *Jawāhir* in his palace library. He also kept a copy of another *ṭabaqāt* work, *Kitāb al-Darajāt al-ʿaliyya fī ṭabaqāt al-Ḥanafiyya*, which I have not been able to identify. Anonymous (possibly Khiḍr b. ʿUmar al-ʿAṭūfī), *Asmā' al-kutub al-khizāna al-ʿāmira*, Magyar Tudományos Akadémia, Könyvtár (Budapest), MS Török F 59, 97, 101. On this catalog, see Miklós Maróth, "The Library of Sultan Bayazit II," in *Irano-Turkic Cultural Contacts in the 11th–17th Centuries*, ed. Éva M. Jeremiás (Piliscsaba, Hungary: Avicenna Institute of Middle Eastern Studies, 2003 [2002]), 111–32; İsmail E. Erünsal, "909 (1503) Tarihli Defter-i Kütüb," in *The Archival Sources of Turkish Literary History*, ed. Cemal Kafadar and Gönül Alpay Tekin (Cambridge, MA: Department of Near Eastern Languages and Literatures, Harvard University, 2008),

knowledge must have concerned many Anatolian jurists during the fifteenth century, as they invested considerable efforts in obtaining permits (*ijāzas*) from leading jurists in prominent learning centers across central Asia and the Arab lands.[12] Nevertheless, it seems that fifteenth-century Anatolian Ḥanafī jurists were not particularly interested in committing their credentials and chains of transmission to paper. One may only speculate why these jurists did not record their intellectual genealogies systematically. It is possible, however, that only when the imperial learned hierarchy reached a certain degree of consolidation and assumed a distinct character did this concern became increasingly urgent. After all, during the second half of the fifteenth century, jurists from learning centers in the Mamluk sultanate and central Asia still entered the service of the Ottoman dynasty.

Things changed, however, during the early decades of the sixteenth century, and members of the imperial hierarchy became increasingly concerned with producing a systematic narrative of the history of the school and its authorities. Kemâlpaşazâde's *Risāla fī ṭabaqāt al-mujtahidīn* is one of the earliest treatises, perhaps the earliest one, on the history and structure of the Ḥanafī school compiled by a member, let alone a senior member, of the Ottoman learned hierarchy. Moreover, Kemâlpaşazâde's short treatise became an important reference for later jurists who

251–70. In the first half of the sixteenth century, the eminent jurist Ibrāhīm al-Ḥalabī (d. 1549) compiled an abbreviated version (*mukhtaṣar*) of ʿAbd al-Qādir b. Muḥammad al-Qurashī's *ṭabaqāt* of the Ḥanafī school, *al-Jawāhir al-muḍiyya fī ṭabaqāt al-Ḥanafiyya*. See Ibrāhīm b. Muḥammad b. Ibrāhīm al-Ḥalabī, *Mukhtaṣar al-jawāhir al-muḍiyya fī ṭabaqāt al-Ḥanafiyya*, Süleymaniye Library MS Esad Efendi 605–001. Kâtip Çelebi explains that al-Ḥalabī "selected [from the *Jawāhir* only those] that compiled a work or is mentioned in the books (*man lahu taʾlīf aw dhukira fī al-kutub*). Kâtip Çelebi, *Kashf al-ẓunūn ʿan asāmī al-kutub waʾl-funūn* (Istanbul: Maarif Matbaası, 1941), 1:616–17. The *Jawāhir* was copied several times over the course of the late fifteenth and sixteenth centuries. Out of the fourteen copies of the work located in different libraries in Istanbul, at least five were copied during the sixteenth century (Süleymaniye Library MS Yozgat 170, copied in 957/1550; Süleymaniye Library MS Murâd Buhari 252, copied in 947/1540; MS Esad Efendi 405, copied in 929/1522; Süleymaniye Library MS Süleymaniye 823, copied in 964/1556; Süleymaniye Library MS Fatih 4311, copied in 980/1572). In addition, another copy (Süleymaniye Library MS Damad Ibrahim Paşa 508) was copied late in the fifteenth century (890/1485).

[12] Taşköprüzâde mentions several jurists who traveled to the Arab lands to study with prominent authorities. Molla Khuḍur Shāh (d. 1449) left Anatolia for Cairo, where he spent fifteen years. Aḥmad b. Muṣṭafā Ṭaşköprüzâde, *al-Shaqāʾiq al-nuʿmāniyya fī ʿulamāʾ al-dawla al-ʿUthmāniyya* (Beirut: Dār al-Kitāb al-ʿArabī, 1975), 59–60. Another example is Ḥasan Çelebi b. Muḥammad Shāh al-Fenārī, who was granted permission by Meḥmet II to travel to Cairo to study with a well-known Maghribī scholar (ibid., 114–15; for additional examples, see ibid., 130, 288).

undertook similar projects.[13] The authors of the works discussed in the following three sections were clearly familiar with, and to a large extent followed, Kemâlpaşazâde's treatise. In this sense, Kemâlpaşazâde may be considered as the harbinger of the genre among members of the Ottoman learned hierarchy.[14]

In his treatise, Kemâlpaşazâde divides the jurists of the Ḥanafī school into seven ranks (*ṭabaqāt*). Each rank is unique as far as the jurisprudential authority of its jurists is concerned. More precisely, the jurists of each rank from the second rank onward are increasingly limited in their ability to employ independent reasoning. Kemâlpaşazâde's general narrative is thus one of decline in the authority of jurists to employ independent reasoning as their chronological distance from the eponymous founder of the school increases. The decline apparently reaches a steady level by the fourteenth century, as the latest jurist explicitly mentioned lived in that century. It is plausible that Kemâlpaşazâde considered himself and his peers to be members of the seventh rank, perhaps suggesting that they were the most limited in terms of the authority to employ independent reasoning, although Kemâlpaşazâde's narrative does not elaborate on the history of the school from the fourteenth century onward.

As we shall presently see, although the later authors referred to Kemâlpaşazâde's treatise (either explicitly or implicitly), and offered their own interpretations of the hierarchy of authorities of the school, they also sought to address other issues. In particular, they strove to establish the authority of the imperial hierarchy within the school and not only the relationship between the authorities up to the fourteenth century. Despite the interesting differences in the authors' understanding of the classification and the hierarchy of the authorities of the school, it is their view of the fifteenth and the sixteenth centuries, the period Kemâlpaşazâde's treatise does not cover, that will be the focus of the following sections.[15]

[13] The treatise exists in numerous copies. Ibn Kamāl Pāshā (Kemâlpaşazâde), *Risālat ṭabaqāt al-mujtahidīn*, New York Public Library MS M&A 51891A, 195v–196v. Modern scholars, such as Ibrahim Hafsi and Wael Hallaq, have thoroughly discussed this treatise. See Hafsi, "Recherches sur le genre *ṭabaqāt*," pt. 2, 14–15; Wael B. Hallaq, *Authority, Continuity, and Change in Islamic Law* (Cambridge: Cambridge University Press, 2004), 14–17.

[14] The treatise was so popular that the eighteenth-century dragoman of the Swedish embassy in Istanbul, Ignatius Mouradega d'Ohsson, translated it into French and included it in his *Tableau general de l'Empire othman*. Ignatius Mouradega d'Ohsson, *Tableau general de l'Empire othman* (Paris: L'imprimerie de monsieur, 1788), 1:10–21.

[15] For a more detailed discussion of the different articulations of the hierarchy see Appendix A.

Kınalızâde's *Ṭabaqāt al-Ḥanafiyya*

As argued above, the later three *ṭabaqāt* works compiled by members of the imperial learned hierarchy built on Kemâlpaşazâde's treatise but at the same time considerably diverged from it. The earliest of the three *ṭabaqāt* works was penned by Kınalızâde ʿAlî Çelebi (d. 1572).[16]

The grandson of the tutor of Meḥmet II and a relative of senior members of the Ottoman learned hierarchy, Kınalızâde held several teaching positions as well as senior judgeships throughout the empire. Prior to his appointment as the military justice of Anatolia, the most senior office he held, Kınalızâde was appointed to the judgeships of Damascus, Cairo, Aleppo, Bursa, Edirne, and Istanbul. He was also famous for several works he authored, perhaps the most important of which is the moralistic advice work *Aḫlâk-i ʿAlâʾî*.[17] According to the Ottoman historian Peçevî, Kınalızâde was so esteemed that it was only his death at the age of sixty-two that prevented him from becoming the imperial chief muftī.[18] For this reason, Kınalızâde's view of the school may be considered the view of a very senior member of the Ottoman hierarchy.

The work consists of 275 biographies organized in twenty-one generations/ranks (*ṭabaqāt*). Most biographies include information concerning the biographee's teachers, students, and texts he compiled, although in some biographies this information is missing. The number of biographies in each *ṭabaqa* varies greatly. While earlier ones include tens of biographies, each of the latest (*ṭabaqāt* 17 through 21) comprises fewer

[16] Kınalızâde ʿAlāʾ al-Dīn ʿAlī Çelebī Amr Allāh b. ʿAbd al-Qādir al-Ḥumaydī al-Rūmī al-Ḥanafī, *Ṭabaqāt al-Ḥanafiyya* (Amman: Dār Ibn al-Jawzī, 2003–4). The work has been wrongly attributed to Taşköprüzâde and has been published as such: Aḥmad b. Muṣṭafā Taşköprüzâde, *Ṭabaqāt al-fuqahāʾ*, 2nd ed. (Mosul: Maṭbaʿat al-Zahrāʾ al-Ḥadītha, 1961). It appears that Kınalızâde's work is the earliest to outline this particular narrative concerning the history of the school and the imperial learned hierarchy. Nevertheless, it is possible that some of these ideas were also articulated a decade or two earlier by Ak Şems Çelebi. For a more detailed discussion of the relationship between Kınalızâde's and Şems Çelebi's works, see Guy Burak, "The Abū Ḥanīfah of His Time: Islamic Law, Jurisprudential Authority and Empire in the Ottoman Domains (16th–17th Centuries)" (PhD diss., New York University, 2012), appendix 3.

[17] Hasan Aksoy, "Kınalızâde Ali Efendi," *Türkiye Diyanet Vakfı Islam Ansiklopedisi*. See also Şefaattın Severcan, "Kınalı-zade ʿAli Efendi," in *Kınalı-Zade Ali Efendi (1510–1572)*, ed. Ahmet Hulusi Koker (Kayseri: Erciyes Üniversitesi Matbaası, 1999), 1–11; Baki Tezcan, "The Definition of Sultanic Legitimacy in the Sixteenth Century Ottoman Empire: The Ahlak-ı Ala'i of Kınalızâde Ali Çelebi (1510–1572)" (MA thesis, Princeton University, 1996).

[18] Tezcan, "Definition of Sultanic Legitimacy," 20.

than ten entries. Interestingly enough, only a single biography, that of Kemâlpaşazâde, occupies the last *ṭabaqa*.

The decision to dedicate the last generation/rank to the eminent jurist bears important implications. But in order to gain a better understanding of these implications, one has to look at how Kınalızâde perceives the project as a whole. Kınalızâde describes his work as an abridged book (*mukhtaṣar*), thus implying that he had to choose between different accounts on the history of the school and multiple pieces of information. Therefore, it is worth paying attention to his explanation of how he decided which Ḥanafī jurists to include in his work:

> This is an abridged book in which the generations [*ṭabaqāt*] of the Ḥanafī school are mentioned. I have mentioned in it the [most] famous among the imāms, who transmitted the knowledge of the sharīʿa in every generation and spread it throughout the [Muslim] community [*umma*], with their chains of transmission [and recorded them] according to their generations ... so that the jurist's ignorance will not increase, [and when] he [is in] need, he will know whose opinion should be relied upon when there is a consensus [among the jurists in cases of agreement and consensus]; whose [opinion should be] considered when there is a controversy [in cases of] disagreement and controversy; and who[se opinion] is needed when [he has to determine which opinion] should be preferred and followed [*al-tarjīḥ wa'l-iʿmāl*] when opinions contradict [each other], [and he will be able to follow] the [opinion of] the most knowledgeable and most pious jurist of the time.[19]

Kınalızâde's work is organized along two axes, a diachronic and a synchronic one. Diachronically, the notion of dividing the jurists into generations indicates that he was interested in reconstructing a continuous chain of transmission. The phrase Kınalızâde employs to point to the transition of knowledge over the generations, "then the jurisprudential [knowledge] was transmitted to *ṭabaqa* [X]" (*thumma intaqala al-fiqh*),[20] suggests that Kınalızâde aims at producing a chain of transmission leading from Abū Ḥanīfa to Kemâlpaṣazâde.

On the other hand, Kınalızâde intends to point out the leading jurisprudential authorities in every generation. Fittingly, Kınalızâde urges the muftī to "know the positions [of the jurists] and [their] ranks, so he would be able to prefer one of them in cases of controversy and dispute [among the opinions of the school]." Although in most cases Kınalızâde does not explicitly state which opinion is preferable, this comment offers a glimpse into how Kınalızâde envisioned this compilation. The work,

19 Kınalızâde, *Ṭabaqāt al-Ḥanafiyya*, 91.
20 For example: ibid., 103, 190, 216, 252.

according to this vision, is not merely a history of the Ḥanafī school, but rather a tool for resolving jurisprudential disputes within the school. In other words, the work aims at determining the canonical doctrine, at least for the members of the Ottoman learned hierarchy. Kınalızâde, however, does not address in this work concrete debatable jurisprudential issues. Instead, he offers general guidelines for choosing between different contradicting opinions within the school, namely, in cases of disagreement between the eponym and his disciples.

Kınalızâde's attempt to define a canon is also reflected in the importance he places on jurisprudential texts. In Kınalızâde's view, the lore of the Ḥanafī school was transmitted from one leading jurist to the other until it was "preserved among the pages of the books." He explains, "These books widely circulate among the pious and they are consulted during adjudication (*qaḍāʾ*) and issuance of legal opinions (*fatwā*)."[21] This statement reflects a tendency discernable during the period under discussion here. As we shall see in Chapter 4, authoritative texts became increasingly important in the Ottoman understanding of the Ḥanafī school over the course of the sixteenth and the seventeenth centuries. The importance of the jurisprudential texts and manuals is evident in the sources Kınalızâde uses. When sources besides other ṭabaqāt works, such as the fourteenth-century comprehensive *ṭabaqāt* work *al-Jawāhir al-muḍiyya*,[22] are mentioned, they are often important jurisprudential texts, such as al-Marghīnānī's *al-Hidāya* or al-Sarakhsī's *al-Mabsūṭ*.[23] In other words, it seems that one of Kınalızâde's guiding principles was to document the genealogy of particular legal arguments.

An important goal Kınalızâde sets in his *Ṭabaqāt al-Ḥanafiyya* is to establish the authority of the Ottoman learned hierarchy within the Ḥanafī tradition.[24] The last seven *ṭabaqāt*, which cover the time period

[21] Ibid., 92–93.

[22] Kınalızâde also draws on Ibn Khallikān's and al-Khaṭīb al-Baghdādī's works. In addition, he cites Abū Isḥāq al-Shirāzī's *ṭabaqāt* and Muḥammad b. Iṣhāq's *Fihris al-ʿulamāʾ*.

[23] Here is, for example, the entry of Abū Jaʿfar al-Hindūwānī: "Abū Jaʿfar al-Hindūwānī, Muḥammad b. ʿAbd Allāh b. Muḥammad. Studied with al-Aʿmash. The author of *al-Hidāya* [al-Marghīnānī] mentioned him in the chapter on the description of prayer [*bāb ṣifat al-ṣalāt*]. [He was] a great imām from Balkh. Al-Samʿānī said: He was called the minor Abū Ḥanīfa due to his [knowledge] of jurisprudence. He studied *fiqh* [*tafaqqaha*] with his master Abū Bakr Muḥammad b. Abī Saʿīd, known as al-Aʿmash; al-Aʿmash was the student of Abū Bakr al-Iskāf; al-Iskāf was the student of Muḥammad b. Salama; [Muḥammad] was the student of Abū Sulimān al-Jūzjānī; al-Jūzjānī was the student of Muḥammad b. al-Ḥasan, the student of Abū Ḥanīfa" (Kınalızâde, *Ṭabaqāt al-Ḥanafiyya*, 180–81).

[24] Ibid., 321–22.

from the late fourteenth century to the early sixteenth century, that is, the period during which the Ottoman dynasty in general and its learned hierarchy in particular emerged, merit a closer examination. In the *ṭabaqāt* that cover the fourteenth century, jurists who operated in the Ottoman domains or were affiliated with the evolving Ottoman state are totally absent. Moreover, prominent religious and judicial figures that operated in the early days of the Ottoman polity, such as the famous Ede Bâlî, a leading religious-spiritual figure and the father-in-law of the first Ottoman sultan, are excluded from Kınalızâde's account. Most of the jurists in the *ṭabaqa* that covers the early decades of the fifteenth century (*ṭabaqa* 17) are Ḥanafīs who were not affiliated with the Ottoman dynasty. Nevertheless, the seventeenth *ṭabaqa* includes the biography of the renowned early fifteenth-century jurist Ibn al-Bazzāz (d. 1424), who entered the Ottoman domains and met Şemsuddîn Fenârî (or Shams al-Dīn al-Fanārī, d. 1430), who was the first jurist to serve as chief imperial muftī.[25]

The mid-fifteenth century evidently marks a turning point in Kınalızâde's account. The last *ṭabaqāt* (*ṭabaqāt* 18–21), which cover roughly the second half of the fifteenth century and the early decades of the sixteenth, include almost exclusively Ḥanafīs who were affiliated with the Ottoman learned hierarchy. The only important exception is the Cairene Ḥanafī Ibn al-Humām, who appears in the eighteenth *ṭabaqa*.[26] On the other hand, Kınalızâde does not mention any of Ibn al-Humām's students, either those who operated in the Mamluk sultanate or in the Ottoman domains. Moreover, Kınalızâde excludes luminary Ḥanafī jurists who operated in the Mamluk sultanate, such as Muḥyī al-Dīn al-Kāfiyajī, Qāsim b. Quṭlūbughā, and Amīn al-Dīn al-Aqsarā'ī,[27] of whom he must have heard.[28] In addition, Kınalızâde excludes many

[25] Ibid., 306–10.

[26] Ibid., 310–11.

[27] On al-Kāfiyajī, see the following. On Ibn Quṭlūbughā, see Ibrāhīm b. Ḥasan al-Biqā'ī, *'Inwān al-zamān bi-tarājim al-shuyūkh wa'l-aqrān* (Cairo: Maṭba'at Dār al-Kutub wa'l-Wathā'iq al-Qawmiyya, 2006), 4: 144–45; Ibrāhīm b. Ḥasan al-Biqā'ī, *'Unwān al-'unwān bi-tajrīd asmā' al-shuyūkh wa-ba'ḍ al-talāmidha wa'l-aqrān* (Beirut: Dār al-Kitāb al-'Arabī, 2002), 139–40; Shams al-Dīn Muḥammad b. 'Abd al-Raḥmān al-Sakhāwī, *al-Ḍaw' al-lāmi' li-ahl al-qarn al-tāsi'* (Cairo: Maktabat al-Qudsī, 1934), 6:184–90; Jalāl al-Dīn 'Abd al-Raḥmān b. Abī Bakr al-Suyūṭī, *al-Munjam fī al-mu'jam* (Beirut: Dār Ibn Ḥazm, 1995), 166–67; Shams al-Dīn Muḥammad b. Ṭūlūn, *al-Ghuraf al-'āliyya fī muta'akhkhirī al-Ḥanafiyya*, Süleymaniye Library MS Şehid Ali Paşa 1924, 188r–189r. On Amīn al-Dīn al-Aqsarā'ī, see al-Biqā'ī, *'Unwān al-'unwān*, 227; al-Sakhāwī, *al-Ḍaw' al-lāmi'*, 10:240–43; al-Suyūṭī, *al-Munjam*, 238–39; Ibn Ṭūlūn, *al-Ghuraf*, 330r–330v.

[28] In his supplement to Ṭaşköprüzâde's *al-Shaqā'iq al-nu'māniyya*, the sixteenth-century biographer 'Âşıḳ Çelebi, for example, records an *ijāza* he obtained from 'Abd al-Raḥman

other Ḥanafīs of lesser importance throughout Anatolia (and even the Ottoman domains), the Mamluk sultanate, and elsewhere. In short, the exclusion of Ḥanafīs from the other parts of the Islamic world and particularly from the Mamluk sultanate is intended to stress the rise of an independent authoritative genealogy in the Ottoman domains.

The problem, however, was that different jurists who joined the burgeoning Ottoman learned hierarchy in the fifteenth and sixteenth centuries were affiliated to various chains of transmission within the Ḥanafī school, as they came from different places in Anatolia, central Asia, and the Arab lands. Kınalızâde was most certainly aware of this fact, yet he often overlooks it in his text and does not always specify the different genealogies to which these jurists were affiliated. Furthermore, since he does not always mention the teachers of his biographees, it is somewhat difficult to reconstruct on the basis of Kınalızâde's *ṭabaqāt* a continuous chain of transmission. At the same time, it seems that Kınalızâde is interested in a meticulous recording of specific genealogies. For instance, out of the three members of the hierarchy mentioned in the eighteenth *ṭabaqa*[29] – the first *ṭabaqa* in which most of the jurists are affiliated with the Ottoman dynasty and its evolving learned hierarchy – Kınalızâde only mentions Sharaf b. Kamāl al-Qarīmī's teachers.[30]

In the concluding, twenty-first *ṭabaqa*, Kınalızâde closes his work with an entry on Kemâlpaşazâde, whom he dubs "the peerless of his time, and the unique of his era."[31] Kınalızâde's decision to situate Kemâlpaşazâde as the last link of the genealogy has important

al-ʿAbbāsī (d. 1555 or 1556), a scholar who entered the Ottoman lands for the first time as an envoy of the Mamluk sultan. After the conquest of Egypt, he migrated again to Istanbul, where he taught mostly *ḥadīth*. In the *ijāza*, al-ʿAbbāsī permits ʿÂşîḳ Çelebi to transmit what he learned from his teachers. The important point is that among the teachers of al-ʿAbbāsī that ʿÂşîḳ Çelebi lists are Muḥyī al-Dīn al-Kāfiyajī, Amīn al-Dīn al-Aqsarāʾī, and Muḥibb al-Dīn b. al-Shiḥna. ʿÂşîḳ Çelebi, Muḥammad b. ʿAlī Zayn al-ʿĀbidīn b. Muḥammad b. Jalāl al-Dīn b. Ḥusayn b. Ḥasan b. ʿAlīb. Muḥammad al-Raḍawī, *Dhayl al-Shaqāʾiq al-nuʿmāniyya* (Cairo: Dār al-Hidāya, 2007), 107–9. On al-ʿAbbāsī, see Ṭaşköprüzâde, *al-Shaqāʾiq*, 246–47; al-Ghazzī, *al-Kawakib al-sāʾira*, 2:161–65; Wolfhart P. Heinrichs, "ʿAbd al-Raḥman al-ʿAbbāsī (al-Sayyid ʿAbd al-Raḥīm) (12 June 1463–1555 or 1556)," in *Essays in Arabic Literary Biography 1350–1850*, ed. Joseph E. Lowry and Devin J. Stewart (Wiesbaden: Harrassowitz Verlag, 2009), 12–20. Interestingly enough, al-ʿAbbāsī is not mentioned in Ibn Ṭūlūn's *al-Ghuraf*. He is likewise absent from Kınâlızâde's and Kefevî's *ṭabaqāt*.

29 Kınalızâde, *Ṭabaqāt al-Ḥanafiyya*, 310–12.

30 Ibid., 311. Qarīmī's teacher was Ibn al-Bazzāz.

31 Ibid., 321.

implications, for Kemâlpaşazâde emerges as the sole channel of this branch of the Ḥanafī school and, according to Kınalızâde's explanation in his introduction, the sole authoritative figure to resolve disputes among Ḥanafīs. The role Kemâlpaşazâde plays in Kınalızâde's genealogy seems to reflect the latter's understanding of the role of the Ottoman chief muftī from the early decades of the sixteenth century. According to this view, the chief muftī (and the hierarchy he presided over) served as the channel of a particular genealogy within the Ḥanafī school. Moreover, the chief muftī appears as the ultimate authority when jurisprudential disputes emerge among Ḥanafī jurists affiliated with the imperial learned hierarchy.

It is worth dwelling on this view of the history of the school – and particularly the divergence of the Rūmī branch of the school around the mid-fifteenth century as well as the role Kınalızâde ascribes to the chief imperial muftī, a role that makes him guardian and arbiter of this branch. These features of Kınalızâde's narrative recurred in accounts by contemporary members of the imperial learned hierarchy and became, as we shall see in the next sections, tropes in histories of the school by members of the hierarchy in the centuries to come, some significant differences notwithstanding. A graduate of the Ottoman madrasa system and roughly a contemporary of Kınalızâde, the sixteenth-century chronicler Gelibolulu Muṣṭafâ ʿÂlî (d. 1600), for example, poignantly articulates this view in his writings. In his chronicle *Künhü'l-Aḫbâr*, ʿÂlî praises Sultan Meḥmet II for supporting the jurists who arrived in the Ottoman domains from the Arab and the Persian lands and for founding in the recently conquered imperial capital the famous eight madrasas (the *Ṣaḥn-ı Ṣemân* madrasas). Because of these projects, the central lands of the empire (Rûm) became a "fountain of wisdoms and sciences" (*menbaʿ-i ḥikem ve-ʿulûm*), and therefore Rūmī students were no longer required to travel to foreign lands.[32] Furthermore, Aḥmad b. Muṣṭafâ Taşköprüzâde (d. 1560), in his biographical dictionary dedicated to the members of the Ottoman learned hierarchy (and other religious scholars who operated in the Ottoman domains, such as Sufi shaykhs), also describes a rupture during the reign of Meḥmet II, as will be further discussed in the following. From Meḥmet II's reign onward, relates Taşköprüzâde, seekers of

[32] Muṣṭafâ b. Aḥmed ʿÂlî, *Künhü'l-Aḫbâr* (Istanbul: Darü't-Tibaʿâti'l-ʿÂmîre, 1860–61), 1:37. According to Muṣṭafâ ʿÂlî, this trend continued under Meḥmet II's successors, Bâyezîd II and Selîm I. The latter, following the conquest of Greater Syria and Egypt, brought to the capital scholars, poets, and jurists from these lands (ibid).

knowledge were drawn to Istanbul, instead of visiting Herat, Bukhara, and Samarqand, as their predecessors did.[33]

Maḥmûd b. Süleymân Kefevî's Katā'ib A'lām al-Akhyār min Fuqahā' Madhhab al-Nu'mān al-Mukhtār

The author of the second *ṭabaqāt* work that will concern us here, Maḥmûd b. Süleymân Kefevî (d. 1582), was born, as the epithet indicated, in Kefe in Crimea, where he began his studies. In 1542 Kefevî left his hometown for Istanbul, where he attended the classes of Ḳâdîzâde Aḥmad Şemseddîn Efendi and ʿAbdurraḥman Efendi. When the latter was appointed as the judge of Aleppo in 1546, Kefevî became the protégé (*mülâzim*) of Ma'lûlzâde Emîr Efendi. In 1554 Kefevî began his teaching career at the madrasa of Molla Gürânî in Istanbul. Later he was appointed as the judge of his hometown, Kefe. The next station in Kefevî's judgeship career was Gelibolu, where he served until 1579, when he was removed from office and returned to Istanbul. Three years later, in 1582, Kefevî died in the capital. Although Kefevî was not a senior member of the Ottoman learned hierarchy, his work gained popularity among members of the imperial hierarchy (and later, among modern scholars) and became known as one of the most comprehensive Ḥanafī *ṭabaqāt* works.[34]

Written slightly after Kınalızâde's *Ṭabaqāt*, Kefevî's *Katā'ib aʿlām al-akhyār min fuqahā' madhhab al-Nuʿmān al-mukhtār* shares some of the goals of the former work. Like his predecessor, Kefevî also wanted to compile a *ṭabaqāt* work that would comprise the biographies of

> our earlier and the later jurists [of the Ḥanafī school], those who are followers and those who are mujtahids [that is, those who have the right to employ

[33] Ali Anooshahr, "Writing, Speech, and History for an Ottoman Biographer," *Journal of Near Eastern History* 69, no. 1 (2010): 50.

[34] Ahmet Özel, "Kefevî, Mahmûd b. Süleyman," *TDVIA*. The work has also attracted the attention of several modern scholars as an important source for the history of the Ottoman learned hierarchy. See, for instance, Ekmeleddin İhsanoğlu, "The Initial Stage of the Historiography of Ottoman Medreses (1916–1965): The Era of Discovery and Construction," in *Science, Technology and Learning in the Ottoman Empire: Western Influence, Local Institutions, and the Transfer of Knowledge*, ed. Ekmeleddin İhsanoğlu (Burlington, VT: Ashgate/Variorum, 2004), 46–47; Ârif Bey, "Devlet-i Osmaniyye'nin Teessüs ve Takarrürü Devrinde İlim ve Ulema," *Darülfünün Edebiyat Fakültesi Mecmuası* 2 (May 1332/1916): 137–44; Imber, *Ebu's-Su'ud*, 22; Richard C. Repp, *The Müfti of Istanbul: A Study in the Development of the Ottoman Learned Hierarchy* (London: Ithaca Press, 1986), 139.

independently their jurisprudential skills to develop new rulings] from among the jurists of the times and the judges of the towns and the district, with their chains of transmissions [*asānīd wa-ʿanʿanātihim*], [and I have organized this work] according to their time and generations [*ṭabaqātihim*], including the rare issues [*al-masāʾil al-gharība*] transmitted from them in the famous collections of *fatāwā*. [I have also] appended the incredible stories which are heard about numerous scholars from the jurists of our time back to Abū Ḥanīfa, the imām of the imāms of our school, and through him to our Prophet, the lord of our sharīʿa.[35]

Kefevî explains that he decided to compile the work as a result of the absence of satisfactory compilations. The problem with the previous works, he continues, is that they "did not distinguish the student from the teacher, and they did not differentiate between the follower [*dhū al-taqlīd*] and [jurists] who are allowed to employ independently their jurisprudential skills to develop new rulings [*ahl al-ijtihād*]."[36] As we have already seen, by the time Kefevî wrote his *ṭabaqāt* there was at least one compilation, that of Kınalızâde, that was organized chronologically. Nevertheless, it is true that Kefevî's work is much more extensive. While Kınalızâde's *ṭabaqāt* includes 275 biographies of Ḥanafī jurists, the section in Kefevî's work that is devoted to the Ḥanafī school consists of 674 entries organized in twenty-two chronological clusters or groups, termed *katāʾib* (sing. *katība*), which function in a fashion similar to the *ṭabaqāt* in Kınalızâde's work.[37]

Kefevî's work, however, is not merely a history of the Ḥanafī school. Unlike his counterparts, he decided to frame his account of the history of the Ḥanafī school within the larger framework of the Islamic understanding of the history of the world. Therefore, Kefevî opens with the biography of Adam, the first Qurʾānic prophet. Only after listing the Qurʾānic prophets, the Prophet Muḥammad, his companions, and the eponymous founders of the Sunnī legal schools,[38] does he turn to the history of the Ḥanafī school and of the Ottoman learned hierarchy within it.

Following a discussion of the taxonomy of the Ḥanafī jurists, which refers indirectly to Kemâlpaşazâde's, Kefevî charts a fairly coherent narrative of the history of the school from the thirteenth century onward. Specifically, he seeks to describe what he considers a major development

35 Maḥmûd b. Süleymân Kefevî, *Katāʾib aʿlām al-akhyār min fuqahāʾ madhhab al-Nuʿmān al-mukhtār*, Süleymaniye Library MS Esad Efendi 548, 1r.

36 Ibid.

37 Kefevî's work is also more extensive than Ibn Quṭlūbughā's *Tāj al-tarājim*, on which he relies. On the other hand, the *Katāʾib* is more limited in scope than al-Qurashī's *al-Jawāhir al-muḍiyya*.

38 Ibid., 4v–21r.

in Ḥanafī history – the emergence of new Ḥanafī centers, and particularly the emergence of the Ottoman realms as a dominant Ḥanafī center in the centuries following the disastrous Mongol invasions. It is precisely at this point that Kefevî links his taxonomy of the Ḥanafī jurists (see Appendix A) to more general historical developments. Since the jurists of the last rank in his hierarchy of authorities were mostly active across central Asia and Iraq, the Mongol invasions were catastrophic for these jurists and, more broadly, for the Ḥanafī school. Following the destruction of these Ḥanafī scholarly centers, according to Kefevî, many of their jurists fled to the Mamluk sultanate, which emerged as a dominant Ḥanafī center. But the upheavals in the history of the school were not over yet: during the reign of the Circassian Mamluks, as the state of affairs in the Mamluk sultanate grew increasingly chaotic, "knowledge and competence traveled to Rūm," and a new Ḥanafī center emerged under the aegis of the Ottoman sultans. Kefevî concludes his survey of the history of the Ḥanafī school by praising the Ottoman sultan at the time, Murâd III. This is an important gesture, which serves to emphasize the pivotal role sovereigns in general and the Ottoman sultans in particular played in protecting and preserving the Ḥanafī tradition.[39]

Kefevî, nevertheless, is not only interested in compiling a general account on the emergence of the Ottoman domains as a major Ḥanafī center. He also aims at documenting particular chains of transmission that lead from Abū Ḥanīfa to jurists who were affiliated with the Ottoman learned hierarchy, and specifically, to Kefevî himself. In the brief introduction to the section of the *Katāʾib* that deals with the Ḥanafī jurists, Kefevî records three chains of transmission that lead from the eponym to him, all of which pass through important members of the Ottoman learned hierarchy, such as Kemâlpaşazâde, Molla Yegân, and Şemsuddîn Fenârî (see Appendix B). In addition to these chains, Kefevî claims to have several other chains of transmission within the Ḥanafī school.[40] This claim, it should be stressed, is not unique to Kefevî. As he explicitly explains in the introduction, many jurists are affiliated with multiple

[39] Ibid., 2v–3r. The practice of pledging allegiance to the sultan is evident in other genres as well. Tijana Krstić, in her study of sixteenth- and seventeenth-century self-narratives of conversion to Islam, has pointed out that the Ottoman sultanate plays a significant role in these narratives. In comparison to earlier Islamic conversion narratives, this "feature [of the Ottoman self-narratives of conversion] is entirely new and points to the politicization of religious discourse characteristic of the age of confessionalization" (Krstić, *Contested Conversion*, 103).

[40] Kefevî, *Katāʾib*, 2v–3r.

chains of transmission. At this point, however, Kefevî breaks from his predecessor's account. While Kınalızâde opted for a more institutional perspective, thus concluding his account with the chief imperial muftī, Kefevî also emphasized his own intellectual genealogies and his individual authority as a jurist, even if this authority was transmitted to him through members of the imperial learned hierarchy.

Let us now turn to the *katāʾib* themselves. My discussion will focus on the time period from the fourteenth century to the sixteenth century, the period during which, according to Kefevî's account, the Ottoman realms emerged as an important Ḥanafī center. This is also the period, as we have seen in the previous section, that Kınalızâde identified as the formative period of the imperial learned hierarchy. Despite clear similarities, there are also significant, as well as nuanced, differences between the accounts, which may be taken as illustrative of the manner in which different members of the imperial hierarchy narrated the history of the school. Admittedly, it is at times difficult to explain the difference between the works. Kefevî's work may reflect the change that the perception of the history of the school and the hierarchy underwent over time, although it is possible that some of Kefevî's ideas had already circulated in Kınalızâde's time (and perhaps even earlier).

Unlike the *ṭabaqāt* in Kınalızâde's work, which are more or less coherent clusters, Kefevî breaks most of the *katāʾib* into three subclusters. The first subcluster consists of Ḥanafī jurists who were affiliated with the main genealogy (or genealogies) within the Ḥanafī school that Kefevî was interested in documenting. The second subcluster, termed the "miscellanea part" (*mutafarriqāt*), includes prominent Ḥanafī jurists who were not part of the main intellectual genealogy documented in the general section. The third subcluster, which will not concern us here, is devoted to Sufi shaykhs and is labeled "the heart of the *katība*" (*qalb al-katība*). This internal division merits attention, for it fulfills an important function in Kefevî's grand narrative of the history of the Ḥanafī school in general and the history of the Ottoman hierarchy in particular.

Echoing his treatment of his own intellectual/authoritative genealogy, Kefevî's *Katāʾib* emphasizes the meticulous recording of the links of the chain of transmission leading to the biographees affiliated with the Ottoman learned hierarchy. Consider, for example, Kefevî's biography of Ede Bâlî, the father-in-law of the first Ottoman sultan, Sultan Osmân, and an important spiritual-juridical figure in the nascent Ottoman state, with which he begins his account of the history of the Ottoman hierarchy. Kefevî bases this entry on Taşköprüzâde's biographical dictionary of the Ottoman imperial learned hierarchy, *al-Shaqā'iq al-nu'māniyya*. Nevertheless, Kefevî modifies Taşköprüzâde's biography:

The shaykh, the imām, the pious Ede Bâlî. The pious jurist, [who served as] muftī in Rūm [*al-diyār al-Rūmiyya*] during the time of 'Uthmān the holy warrior, the ancestor of the Ottoman sultans.... He was a prominent shaykh. He met exalted [?] jurists in the lands of Qarāmān and in the Shām. He was born in the lands of Qarāmān, where he studied [*akhadha al-'ilm*] with the jurists of this land. He studied [*istaghala*] in the town of Larende in Qarāmān. He read [*qara'a*] *furū'* in Larende with the shaykh Najm al-Dīn al-Zāhidī, the author of Qunyat al-Fatāwā and of al-Ḥāwī. He studied [*akhadha*] [al-Zāhidī's teachings] with the author of *al-Baḥr al-muḥīṭ*, the pride of the community [of Islam] and the [Muslim] religion, Badī' al-Qarīnī,[41] and with Sirāj al-Dīn al-Qarīnī [d. 1258].[42] Then he traveled to the Shām and he studied [*akhadha al-'ilm*] with Ṣad[r] al-Dīn Sulīmān [b.] Abī al-'Izz, [who transmitted from] the imām [Jamāl al-Dīn Maḥmūd] al-Ḥaṣīrī, [who transmitted] from the *qāḍī*, the imām, Fakhr al-Dīn Qāḍīkhān. He collected various sciences, both in the fundamentals of law and in substantive law. He met many of the jurists of the Shām. He reached the level of excellence. He taught [law] and issued legal opinions.[43]

In this entry, Kefevî adds many details to the account that appears in Taṣköprüzâde's biographical dictionary, *al-Shaqā'iq al-nu'māniyya*. Although both accounts agree on the outline – the fact that Ede Bâlî was born in Qarāmān, where he also studied; that he traveled to Greater Syria and studied there; and that he eventually entered the service of the Ottoman sultan Osmân – Taṣköprüzâde does not mention any of Ede Bâlî's teachers. Kefevî, by contrast, is concerned with recording Ede Bâlî's authoritative lineage. Therefore he links the biographee to two important Ḥanafī authorities: al-Zāhidī and Sulaymān [b.] Abī al-'Izz (and through the latter, he links Ede Bâlî to the prominent Ḥanafī jurist Qāḍīkhān). In other words, Ede Bâlî emerges in Kefevî's *Katā'ib* as an integral part of the Ḥanafī tradition and the transmitter of the teachings of the authors of important jurisprudential texts.

As we have already seen in the previous section, many members of the Ottoman learned hierarchy shared a specific perception of the history

[41] Ibid., 148r–148v.

[42] Ibid., 163v–164r.

[43] Ibid., 184r–184v. Sulimān b. Wuhayb Abū al-Rabī' b. Abī al-'Izz (595–677/1197–1278) studied *fiqh* with al-Ḥaṣīrī. He served as judge in Egypt and Syria. On Ibn Abī al-'Izz, see 'Abd al-Qādir b. Muḥammad al-Qurashī, *al-Jawāhir al-muḍiyya fī ṭabaqāt al-Ḥanafiyya* (Cairo: Dār Iḥyā' al-Kutub al-'Arabiyya, 1978), 2:237 (and the references therein). Kınalızâde also mentions Ibn Abī al-'Izz in his *Ṭabaqāt* but does not mention Ede Bâlî among his students. Kınalızâde, *al-Ṭabaqāt*, 261. On Jamāl al-Dīn Maḥmūd al-Ḥaṣīrī, see al-Qurashī, *al-Jawāhir*, 431–33; Kınalızâde, *Ṭabaqāt al-Ḥanafiyya*, 252.

of the school from the mid-fifteenth century onward, a perception that excluded jurists who were not affiliated with the Ottoman enterprise. In his *Ṭabaqāt*, it should be recalled, Kınalızâde excludes leading late fifteenth-century jurists who were not affiliated with the evolving Ottoman learned hierarchy. Kefevî by and large follows this view. An examination of the *katāʾib* that cover the fourteenth and early fifteenth centuries reveals that a considerable number of entries are dedicated to jurists who were affiliated, or at least had some relations, with the emerging Ottoman learned hierarchy. In the *katāʾib* of the second half of the fifteenth century and the sixteenth century (*katāʾib* 18–22), Ḥanafīs who were not associated with the Ottoman learned hierarchy are virtually absent.

Kefevî's decision to include a biography of Muḥyī al-Dīn al-Kāfiyajī (d. 1474) may assist us in gaining a better understanding of his narrative strategies.[44] Al-Kāfiyajī was one of the most prominent Ḥanafī jurists who operated in the Mamluk sultanate during the fifteenth century. Although he was based in Cairo, previously he had studied with prominent Ḥanafīs who operated in the Ottoman lands, such as Şemsuddîn Fenârî, Ibn al-Bazzāz, and Burhān al-Dīn Ḥaydar al-ʿAjamī al-Harawī. It is on the basis of this relationship with these early fifteenth-century jurists in the Ottoman lands that Kefevî includes al-Kāfiyajī's biography (as did Taşköprüzâde in his *Shaqāʾiq*). At the same time, he excludes those of other senior Ḥanafīs from the Mamluk lands, is his relations with early fifteenth-century jurists who operated in the Ottoman realms. It is also noteworthy that al-Kāfiyajī's student Ibn al-Humām, an eminent jurist in his own right, has an entry in the *Katāʾib* as well.[45]

On the other hand, the prominent fifteenth-century jurist Qāsim b. Quṭlūbughā is absent from the *Katāʾib*. Supposedly, Kefevî could have included Ibn Quṭlūbughā, a student of Ibn al-Humām, who, in turn, was a student of al-Kāfiyajī.[46] Moreover, it is clear from the *Katāʾib* that Kefevî was familiar with Ibn Quṭlūbughā, since he draws on the latter's *ṭabaqāt* work, *Tāj al-tarājim*. The exclusion of Ibn Quṭlūbughā was intentional.

[44] Kefevî, *Katāʾib*, 230r–230v.

[45] It is worth mentioning that the contacts between al-Kāfiyajī and the Ottoman lands were not severed upon his migration to Cairo. An Ottoman soldier, who was captured by the Mamluks and spent several years in captivity, mentions in his report to the Ottoman sultan Bâyezîd II that he had studied with al-Kāfiyajī in Cairo several years before he was captured. The friends he made in al-Kāfiyajī's classes intervened on his behalf and helped to obtain his release. Emire Cihan Muslu discusses this episode at length; see Emire Cihan Muslu, "Ottoman-Mamluk Relations: Diplomacy and Perceptions" (PhD diss., Harvard University, 2007), 1–5. On Ibn al-Humām, see Kefevî, *al-Katāʾib*, 228r–228v.

[46] Kefevî, *al-Katāʾib*, 228r–228v.

Although it is difficult to assess the degree to which Kefevî was familiar with other late fifteenth-century Ḥanafīs who lived and worked in the Mamluk sultanate, it seems quite likely that he at least knew of some of them.

In his account of the sixteenth century (*katāʾib* 19–22), Kefevī slightly differs from Kınalızâde and expands the chronological scope into the second half of the sixteenth century. Kefevî's account, nonetheless, is consistent with Kınalızâde's view of the history of the Ḥanafī school in the sixteenth century and does not include Ḥanafī jurists who were not affiliated with the Ottoman learned hierarchy. Moreover, he ascribes a similar role to the imperial hierarchy in channeling the authority of the school.

To further clarify this point, it is necessary to turn to the miscellanea sections in Kefevī's *Katāʾib* and to dedicate a few words to their function in the work. Despite his interest in recording the chains of transmission that lead to the imperial hierarchy, Kefevî records in his work many jurists who were not affiliated with the main chains of transmission he sets out to reconstruct and document. Nevertheless, despite the fact that they are not affiliated with these particular chains, Kefevî considers these jurists important enough to mention. In some cases, such as that of the prominent early fifteenth-century Egyptian Ḥanafīs Badr al-Dīn al-ʿAynī (d. 1451) and Taqiyy al-Dīn al-Shummunī (d. 1468), Kefevî includes the biographies of these jurists because they were the authors of important jurisprudential works.[47] Other jurists whose biographies are recorded in the miscellanea section are fourteenth- and fifteenth-century members of the emerging Ottoman hierarchy who entered the Ottoman domains from different parts of the Islamic world (mostly central Asia) and were attached to other genealogies within the Ḥanafī school.[48] The miscellanea section, to put it differently, enabled Kefevî to incorporate these relatively prominent jurists in the broader narrative of the Ḥanafī school, while emphasizing the importance of a particular chain (or chains) of transmission within the school, which were recorded meticulously and continuously.

Not coincidentally, the miscellanea section is absent from the last two *katāʾib*, that is, the *katāʾib* that cover the second half of the sixteenth century.[49] The absence of this section reflects the consolidation of the

[47] Ibid., 232r–232v.

[48] See, for example, Aḥmad al-Kurānī's (Gürânî's) biography in the eighteenth *katība* (ibid., 232v–233v).

[49] Ibid., 264v–272r, 273v–284v.

Ottoman learned hierarchy and the growing reluctance to accept Ḥanafī jurists who were affiliated with other chains of transmission within the school. Like Kınalızâde, Kefevî perceives the Ottoman hierarchy as the only channel through which his contemporaries could attach themselves to this specific genealogy, or branch, within the Ḥanafī school.[50]

Finally, much like his predecessor, Kefevî intends to establish the authority of specific jurisprudential texts and document the genealogies of relevant jurisprudential arguments. Although he relies on other ṭabaqāt works – such as al-Qurashī's *al-Jawāhir al-muḍiyya*, Jalāl al-Dīn al-Suyūṭī's *al-Ṭabaqāt al-Ḥanafiyya al-Miṣriyya*,[51] Ibn Quṭlūbughā's *Tāj al-tarājim*, and Taşköprüzâde's *al-Shaqā'iq*[52] – the vast majority of the sources are Ḥanafī jurisprudential manuals and other works by prominent jurists. It is important to stress that almost all the jurisprudential texts Kefevî cites are texts that members of the Ottoman learned hierarchy, including the officially appointed muftīs, considered reliable and were expected to consult in their rulings (see Chapter 4).[53]

[50] It is interesting to compare the emergence of a clearly defined Ottoman genealogy in the last two *katības* to the developments in other cultural fields, such as the arts. For the consolidation of an Ottoman style in the arts, see Gülru Necipoğlu, "A Kânûn for the State, a Canon for the Arts: Conceptualizing the Classical Synthesis of Ottoman Art and Architecture," in *Soliman le Magnifique et son temps*, ed. Gilles Veinstein (Paris: La documentation français, 1992), 195–213.

[51] Kefevî, *Katā'ib*, 231v.

[52] Kefevî also consulted al-Subkī's *Ṭabaqāt al-Shāfi'iyya* (64r–64v, 74v–75r, 192v–193v, 197r–198r, 204v–206r).

[53] Among the jurisprudential texts Kefevî cites are Fakhr al-Dīn Ḥasan b. Manṣūr b. Maḥmūd al-Ūzcandī's *Fatāwā Qāḍīkhān* (46v); Ḥāfiẓ al-Dīn Muḥammad b. Muḥammad al-Kardarī b. al-Bazzāz's *al-Fatāwā al-Bazzāziyya* (47r, 47v–48r); an unspecified work by al-Taḥāwī (48v, 61r); Muḥammad b. Aḥmad b. 'Umar Ẓahīr al-Dīn al-Bukhārī's *al-Fatāwā al-Ẓahīriyya* (48r–48v); Ṭāhir b. Aḥmad b. 'Abd al-Rashīd al-Bukhārī's *Khulāṣat al-fatāwā* (51v–52r, 108v); Raḍī al-Dīn Muḥammad b. Muḥammad al-Ḥanafī al-Sarakhsī's *al-Muḥīṭ al-Raḍawī fī al-fiqh al-Ḥanafī* (52r–52v, 144v–145r); 'Alī b. Abī Bakr al-Marghīnānī's *al-Hidāya* (54v–56v); Maḥmūd b. Aḥmad b. 'Abd al-'Azīz b. 'Umar b. Māza al-Marghīnānī's *Dhakhīrat al-fatāwā* (*al-Dhakhīra al-Burhāniyya*) (54v–56v); an unspecified work by Kemâlpaşazâde (54v–56v); an unspecified work by Ebû's-Su'ûd Efendi (54v–56v); Mukhtār b. Maḥmūd b. Muḥammad Abū al-Rajā' Najm al-Dīn al-Zāhidī's *Qunyat al-munya* (56v); an unspecified work by Aḥmad b. Muḥammad b. 'Umar al-Ḥanafī al-Nāṭifī, most likely *Jumlat al-aḥkām* (56v–57r); 'Abd al-Barr b. Muḥammad b. Muḥammad al-Ḥalabī b. al-Shiḥna's *Sharḥ al-Manẓuma* (58v–59v, 115r); Ḥusām al-Dīn 'Umar b. 'Abd al-'Azīz al-Ṣadr al-Shahīd's *Kitāb al-wāqi'āt min al-fatāwā* (59r, 62r–63r); Akmal al-Dīn Muḥammad b. Maḥmūd al-Bābartī's *'Ināyat al-Hidāya* (61r); Ḥammād al-Dīn b. 'Imād al-Dīn al-Marghīnānī's *al-Fuṣūl al-'Imādiyya* (61v, 115r); 'Uthmān b. 'Alī al-Zayla'ī's *Sharḥ al-Kanz* (63v–64r); an unspecified work by 'Alī b. Muḥammad al-Pazdawī (66r–66v); *al-Tuḥfa*, possibly *Tuḥfat al-mulūk fī al-furū'* by Zayn al-Dīn Muaḥmmad b. Abū Bakr Ḥasan al-Ḥanafī al-Razī (66v–67r);

In addition, Kefevî appears to be interested in compiling a collective bibliography of works authored by jurists who were affiliated with a particular genealogy within the Ḥanafī school. By listing the works – not only jurisprudential works[54] – his biographees compiled, Kefevî offers his readers a reference work with which they can situate specific texts within the history of the school. Furthermore, the connection made in the *Katāʾib*, but definitely not only there, between the biographies, the chains of transmission of authority, and the bibliographies is fundamental in the emergence of the Ottoman branch of the Ḥanafī school as an authoritative textual corpus. As we shall see in the following sections, this aspect of the school will become even more central over the course of the seventeenth century.

To conclude, in his *Katāʾib*, Kefevî attempts to achieve several interrelated goals. First, he intends to situate himself as an accomplished jurist within the Ḥanafī tradition. Concurrently, he tries to define particular chains of transmission within the Ḥanafī school that eventually lead to the Ottoman learned hierarchy. By doing so, he excludes other chains of transmission and jurists who were not affiliated to the particular genealogy Kefevî is interested in recording, most notably jurists who operated in the Mamluk sultanate. Last, Kefevî reproduces Kınalızâde's view of the role of the imperial learned hierarchy and stresses its monopoly over a particular chain of transmission of knowledge and authority. Many of these aims still concerned other members of the Ottoman learned hierarchy in the decades and centuries to come, even when they organized their *ṭabaqāt* works in a radically different manner, as Edirneli Meḥmed Kâmî did.

ʿAlim b. ʿAlāʾ al-Ḥanafī's *al-Fatāwā al-Tatārkhāniyya* (89r); Aḥmad b. Muḥammad al-Qudūrī's *Sharḥ al-Qudūrī* (100v); Maḥmūd b. Muḥammad b. Dawūd al-Lūʾlūʾī al-Ifsinjī's *Haqāʾiq al-Manẓūma fī al-khilāfiyāt* (100v, 106r–106v, 144v–145r); Najm al-Dīn ʿUmar b. Muḥammad b. Aḥmad al-Ḥanafī al-Nasafī's *Fatāwā al-Nasafī* (101r); Rukn al-Dīn Muḥammad b. ʿAbd al-Rashīd al-Ḥanafī al-Kirmānī's *Jawāhir al-fatāwā* (104v–105r, 139v–140r); Qiwām al-Dīn Amīr Kātib b. Amīr ʿUmar al-Fārābī al-Itqānī's *Sharḥ al-Hidāya* (109v–110r); ʿAlī b. Abī Bakr al-Marghīnānī's *Mashyakha* (128v); Maḥmūd b. Ayyūb al-Ṣūfī's *al-Fatāwā al-Ṣūfiyya* (123r–123v, 141v–142v); Najm al-Dīn Mukhtār b. Maḥmūd al-Zāhidī's *al-Ḥawī* (132v); Muḥammad b. Maḥmūd b. al-Ḥusayn al-Ustrūshanī's *Fuṣūl al-Ustrūshanī* (134r–134v, 145v–146r); Badr al-Dīn Maḥmūd b. Aḥmad al-ʿAynī's *Sharḥ al-Kanz* (136v–137v); Ḥasan b. Ibrāhīm b. Ḥasan al-Zaylaʿī's *Tabyīn* (136v–137v); Kemâlpaşazâde's *al-Iṣlāḥ wa'l-īdāḥ* (136v–137v); Rashīd al-Dīn Muḥammad b. ʿUmar b. ʿAbd Allāh al-Sanjī al-Wattār's *Fatāwā Rashīd al-Dīn* (*al-Fatāwā al-Rashīdiyya*) (137v–138r).

[54] See, for example, 62r–63r, 66r, 112v–113v, 182r–182v, 207r, 225r.

Edirneli Meḥmed Kâmî's *Mahāmm al-Fuqahā'*

To the best of my knowledge, no *ṭabaqāt* works were produced during the seventeenth century. It is somewhat difficult to account for this fairly sudden silence, but it is possible that the consolidation of the hierarchy in the second half of the sixteenth century rendered the compilation of new *ṭabaqāt* works unnecessary. Nevertheless, the fact that new works were not compiled does not mean that the view promoted by Kınalızâde and Kefevî lost its value. And indeed, early in the eighteenth century, a third *ṭabaqāt* work was penned. Authored by Edirneli Meḥmed Kâmî (d. 1724), this *ṭabaqāt* work shows remarkable continuity with the works of his predecessors, and serves as an indicator that the latters' view of the history of the school retained its relevance, at least in certain circles within the imperial learned hierarchy.[55] At the same time, the work also introduces interesting and meaningful changes to the earlier accounts.

Kâmî was born in 1649 in Edirne, where he also started his training path. In 1674, at the age of twenty-five, Kâmî moved to the imperial capital to continue his studies and a year later became the protégé (*mülâzim*) of Ankaravî Meḥmed Emîn Efendi. Between the years 1690 and 1704, Kâmî taught in different madrasas. Then he was appointed as the judge of Baghdad and, two years later, as secretariat of the chief muftī. After serving three years as secretary, Kâmî was without an appointment for a while, until he was appointed as the judge of Galata for a year. During his subsequent unemployment period, Kâmî wrote two poems (*ḳasîde*) and a poem in rhyming couplets (*mesnevî*), which he submitted to the grand vezir Damâd ʿAlî Paşa, who in return appointed him as the inspector of the endowments in 1716. In 1718, Kâmî was sent to Cairo to serve as judge there, an office he held for a year. At the age of seventy-five, Kâmî was offered the judgeship of Mecca, but he turned this offer down because of his advanced age.[56]

As his career path shows, Kâmî was a fairly senior member of the Ottoman learned hierarchy at the time. He was also known as an accomplished poet and writer. His literary skills, as we have seen, enabled him

[55] The biographical dictionaries devoted to members of the imperial learned hierarchy also preserved, albeit implicitly, this view, some differences notwithstanding (see the following).

[56] Gülgün Yazıcı, "Kâmî," *TDVIA*. Menderes Gürkan mentions *Mahāmm al-fuqahā'* in his article "Müctehidlerin Tasnifinde Kemalpaşazade ile Kınalızade arasında bir Mukayese," in *Kınalı-zade Ali Efendi (1510–1572)*, ed. Ahmed Hulusi Köker (Kayseri: Erciyes Üniversitesi Matbbası, 1999), 87–88.

to gain the favor of the grand vezir and obtain an appointment to a fairly senior office. Therefore, although it is difficult to assess the popularity of his *ṭabaqāt* work, *Mahāmm al-fuqahā'*, it still reflects the view of a relatively senior and quite prolific late seventeenth-century early eighteenth-century member of the imperial hierarchy.

Over the course of his career, Kami witnessed some turbulent times for the empire in general and for the learned hierarchy in particular. The bloody events of the so-called "Edirne Event" (*Edirne Vak'ası*) of 1703, and especially the removal from office and execution of the eminent *şeyḫülislam* Feyżullah Efendi (d. 1703), must have left their mark on Kâmî and many of his colleagues who were affiliated with the hierarchy.[57] It is possible that he decided to compile *Mahāmm al-fuqahā'*, at least in part, in response to this crisis. If this interpretation of Kâmî's motives is correct, *Mahāmm al-fuqahā'* is an attempt to secure the position of the learned hierarchy and its authority in the decades following the Event.

Written during his stay in Cairo in 1718,[58] fifteen years after the "Edirne Event," Kâmî's *Mahāmm al-fuqahā'* is structured differently from the earlier two *ṭabaqāt* works we have examined so far. While Kınalızâde and Kefevî organize their works chronologically, Kâmî organizes his alphabetically. In addition, along with the biographical sections, Kâmî includes bibliographical ones in which he lists alphabetically Ḥanafī jurisprudential texts. Nevertheless, it seems that Kâmî shares Kınalızâde and Kefevî's narrative concerning the emergence in the mid-fifteenth century of the Ottoman domains as an important Ḥanafī center. Indeed, most of the jurists he mentions from the second half of the fifteenth century and onward are affiliated with the Ottoman learned hierarchy. This similarity might be attributed to the fact that, as Kâmî admits, he relies on Kefevî's *Katā'ib*.[59]

There are also noteworthy differences between Kâmî's work and those of his earlier counterparts. First, Kâmî does not include many jurists that appear in Kefevî's *Katā'ib* either as part of the continuous chains of transmission or in the miscellanea subcluster. Ede Bâlî, just to mention one

[57] The modern historiography on the "Edirne Event" and Feyżullah Efendi is quite vast. For a recent study of Feyżullah Efendi and his involvement in Ottoman politics, see Michael Nizri, *Ottoman High Politics and the Ulema Household* (New York: Palgrave Macmillan, 2014) (and the bibliography therein). On the "Edirne Event," see Rifa'at Ali Abou-El-Haj, *The 1703 Rebellion and the Structure of Ottoman Politics* (Leiden: Nederlands Historisch-Archaelogisch Instituut de Istanbul, 1984).

[58] Edirneli Meḥmet Kâmî, *Mahāmm al-fuqahā' fī ṭabaqāt al-Ḥanafiyya*, Süleymaniye Library MS Aşir Efendi 422, 41r.

[59] Ibid., 41r–41v.

example, does not appear in Kâmî's *Mahāmm al-fuqahā'*. Furthermore, fifteenth-century Ḥanafīs who operated in the Mamluk sultanate and were included in Kefevî's work, such as Badr al-Dīn al-'Aynī and Taqiyy al-Dīn al-Shummunī, are excluded as well. At the same time, an examination of the list of jurists Kâmî decided to include in his work – a list of approximately five hundred jurists – reveals that Kâmî includes jurists who do not appear in Kınalızâde's *Ṭabaqāt* or Kefevî's *Katā'ib*. As opposed to his predecessors, Kâmî does include in his work, for example, an entry on Qāsim b. Quṭlūbughā.

Kâmî's biography of Qāsim b. Quṭlūbughā merits attention, for it provides important clues regarding the guidelines that shaped the author's narrative choices.

> Qāsim b. Quṭlūbughā is the shaykh and the *imām*. [He is the author of] *Tāj al-Tarājim*, *Taṣḥīḥ al-Qudūrī*, and a gloss [*ḥāshiya*] on *Sharḥ al-Majma'* [*al-baḥrayn*] by ['Abd al-Laṭīf b. 'Abd al-'Azīz] b. Malak. He died in AH879 [1474] and was born in AH802 [1399]. His father was Quṭlūbughā, one of the manumitted slaves of the amir Sūdūn al-Shijwānī, the deputy. [He] studied *fiqh* [*tafaqqaha*] with Ibn al-Humām, studied ḥadīth with Ibn Ḥajar [al-'Asqalānī]. He also compiled several works.... [He] died in AH879 [1474].[60]

It is worth paying attention to the information Kâmî includes in this biography. He begins by mentioning two works by Ibn Quṭlūbughā. Although Ibn Quṭlūbughā produced a fairly large corpus of jurisprudential texts, the entry suggests that the reason for his inclusion was precisely the attention that these particular texts drew. By the late seventeenth century, members of the Ottoman learned hierarchy had started citing Ibn Quṭlūbughā's *Taṣḥīḥ al-Qudūrī*, after more than a century during which the work had been ignored.[61] By contrast, other prominent fifteenth-century Ḥanafīs from the Mamluk sultanate, such as Amīn al-Dīn al-Aqṣarā'ī, do not appear in the biographical sections because their works were not widely used by members of the learned hierarchy.[62]

[60] Ibid., 120v–121r.

[61] The *şeyḫülislam* Çatacalı 'Alî Efendi (served as *şeyḫülislam* from 1674 to 1682 and in 1692) and Meḥmet 'Ataullah Efendi (served as *şeyḫülislam* in 1713), for example, cite this work in some of their rulings. Çatalcalı 'Alî Efendi, *Fetâvâ-ı Çatalcalı*, Süleymaniye Library MS Aya Sofya 1572, 299v. Meḥmet 'Ataullah Efendi, *Fetâvâ-ı 'Atâiyye*, Süleymaniye Library MS H. Hüsnü Paşa 427, 323v.

[62] Muḥyī al-Dīn al-Kāfiyajī is included in Kâmî's work and in Kefevî's *Katā'ib*. Kâmî, *Mahāmm al-fuqahā' fī ṭabaqāt al-Ḥanafiyya*, Süleymaniye Library MS Aşir Efendi 422, 126r. Another interesting example is 'Abd al-Barr b. al-Shiḥna (d. 1515), who appears in the biographical section, probably because of the popularity of his commentary on Ibn Wahbān's *Manẓūma*. The entry, however, does not mention the commentary (ibid.,

This tendency to exclude Ḥanafīs from the Mamluk sultanate and the empire's Arab provinces is even clearer in the biography of Muḥammad al-Timurtāshī, a sixteenth-century scholar and muftī from the Palestinian city of Gaza who did not hold an official state appointment. Nevertheless, as we will see in Chapter 5, al-Timurtāshī was known and well respected for his scholarly excellence in Greater Syria and beyond. Two of the texts he compiled – *Tanwīr al-abṣār* and *Minaḥ al-ghaffār* (a commentary on the *Tanwīr*) – were adopted by the Ottoman learned hierarchy. His brief biography in one of the copies of Kâmî's *Mahāmm al-fuqahā'* reads: "Shams al-Dīn Muḥammad b. al-Timurtāshī, one of the Ḥanafī jurists. [He is the author of] Tanwīr al-abṣār and [of] its commentary, which he entitled Minaḥ al-ghaffār. The text [matn] and the commentary are both accepted among the jurists."[63] Except for the titles he authored, very little information is provided on al-Timurtāshī. Kâmî's emphasis on the popularity of al-Timurtāshī's works suggests that in this case, too, the texts paved the way for the inclusion of their author in the biographical sections. On the other hand, the fact that this entry appears in some manuscripts of the work while being absent from others suggests that there was uncertainty among the copyists of the work or, alternatively, that Kâmî himself produced two versions of his *Mahāmm al-fuqahā'*.[64] At any rate, it is clear that the inclusion of al-Timurtāshī was not trivial and required explanation. It is thus possible that Kâmî's concluding comment concerning the popularity of al-Timurtāshī's works among members of the hierarchy serves this purpose.

The emphasis on jurisprudential texts in Ibn Quṭlūbughā's and al-Timurtāshī's biographies is characteristic of Kâmî's *Mahāmm al-fuqahā'* in general. As I have already pointed out, in addition to the biographical sections dedicated to the jurists, Kâmî includes bibliographical sections dedicated to Ḥanafī jurisprudential texts. The bibliographical sections, like the biographical ones, are organized alphabetically, according to the titles of the works. Each entry consists of the title of the work and a list of commentaries on the work, not unlike the structure of the entries in Kâtip Çelebi's comprehensive bibliographical work, *Kashf al-ẓunūn*.

An examination of the lists of the texts in *Mahāmm al-fuqahā'* reveals some inconsistencies between the biographical sections and the

55r). On Ibn al-Shiḥna, see also al-Ghazzī, *al-Kawākib al-sā'ira*,1:219–21; Ibn Ṭūlūn, *al-Ghuraf*, 265r–266r.

[63] Kâmî, *Mahāmm al-fuqahā'*, Süleymaniye Library MS Aşir Efendi 422, 65r–66v.

[64] The entry appears in Süleymaniye Library MS Aşir Efendi 422; Süleymaniye Library MS Pertev Paşa 495, 21v–22r; Süleymaniye Library MS Carullah 896, 26v.

bibliographical ones. Following the logic presented in al-Timurtāshī's biography, Kâmî should have included in the biographical sections every jurist whose works were well received by members of the Ottoman learned hierarchy.[65] This, however, is not the case. Instead, Kâmî includes in the bibliographical sections many jurisprudential texts and commentaries by authors who do not appear in the biographical sections. Zayn al-Dīn b. Nujaym's (d. 1563) work *al-Ashbāh wa'l-naẓā'ir*, just to mention one salient example, appears in the bibliographical section,[66] but does not appear in the biographical sections. Moreover, Kâmî mentions several commentaries on this work, including one by the eminent sixteenth-century Egyptian Ḥanafī Ibn Ghānim al-Maqdisī (d. 1596), who is also not included in the biographical sections.

It is difficult to reconcile these discrepancies between the bibliographical and the biographical sections of Kâmî's work – although the absence of Ibn Nujaym from the biographical section is compatible with the version of the work that excludes al-Timurtāshī from the biographical section.[67] In that case, Kâmî does not include any sixteenth-century jurist who is not affiliated with the Ottoman learned hierarchy. Yet, as the difference between the manuscripts indicates, there were two contending approaches to the inclusion of sixteenth-century jurists. At any rate, it seems that Kâmî intended to compile a fairly comprehensive bibliography of Ḥanafī texts and commentaries on these texts, not only those consulted by members of the hierarchy. It is evident from the concluding comment of al-Timurtāshī's bibliography concerning the popularity of his work that Kâmî knew that not all the texts were equally accepted among the members of the imperial learned hierarchy. Moreover, both the biographical sections and Kâmî's comment at the end of al-Timurtāshī's biography demonstrate that texts were incorporated into the Ottoman jurisprudential canon (as we shall see in Chapter 4) and referred to by members of the Ottoman learned hierarchy regardless of the genealogy of their authors within the Ḥanafī school.

To sum up, despite noticeable differences, the three *ṭabaqāt* works – by Kınalızâde, Kefevî, and Kâmî – shed light on how members of the Ottoman learned hierarchy perceived the history of the Ḥanafī school in general and the position of the Ottoman learned hierarchy within the Ḥanafī

[65] Another example, as we have seen, is Ibn al-Shiḥna.

[66] Kâmî, *Mahāmm al-fuqahā'*, Süleymaniye Library MS Aşir Efendi 422, 57v.

[67] Edirneli Meḥmet Kâmî, *Mahāmm al-fuqahā' fī ṭabaqāt al-Ḥanafiyya*, Süleymaniye Library MS H. Hüsnü Paşa 844, 2r–71v.

tradition in particular. As we have seen, the differences notwithstanding, all three jurists share the view that in the mid-fifteenth century the Ottoman realms – and specifically the core lands of the empire – emerged as an important, perhaps even the most prominent, Ḥanafī center. Kâmî's work illustrates the longevity of the view of the hierarchy that appeared, or at least was documented, in the mid-sixteenth century. By the time Kâmî authored his *Mahāmm al-fuqahā'*, the imperial learned hierarchy was well established. Nevertheless, as the differences between the copies and the inconsistencies within the work suggest, the debates about the history of the Ḥanafī school and the boundaries of the branch endorsed by the imperial hierarchy were ongoing. While the *Mahāmm* reveals that specific jurists from the Arab lands and their works entered the hierarchy's view of the school, it also shows that members of the hierarchy still insisted on delineating the boundaries of their branch of the school and prevented, albeit selectively, a full assimilation of other followers of the school into the imperial learned hierarchy. Furthermore, the selective inclusion of jurists from the Arab lands illustrates the tensions within the *ṭabaqāt* genre in the Ottoman period: on the one hand, the authors of these works sought to record a chain of transmission of knowledge and authority, but, on the other, they were willing the incorporate jurists whose genealogies did not fit squarely into the learned hierarchy's main chain(s) of transmission.

Recontextualizing Taşköprüzâde's *al-Shaqā'iq al-Nu'māniyya*

In the second half of the sixteenth century a distinctively Ottoman genre appeared: the biographical dictionaries devoted to senior members of the imperial learned hierarchy. The founder of this genre was Aḥmad b. Muṣṭafâ Taşköprüzâde (d. 1560), whose acclaimed *al-Shaqā'iq al-nu'māniyya* became the model for authors of subsequent works.[68] Because both the aforementioned *ṭabaqāt* and the *Shaqā'iq* were compiled around the same time and focus on, or at least pay considerable

[68] Several studies have examined different aspects of this genre. Among these are Aslı Niyazioğlu, "Ottoman Sufi Sheikhs between This World and the Hereafter: A Study of Nev'īzāde 'Atā'ī's (1583–1635) Biographical Dictionary" (PhD diss., Harvard University, 2003); Abdurrahman Atcil, "The Formation of the Ottoman Learned Class and Legal Scholarship (1300–1600)" (PhD diss., University of Chicago, 2010); Ali Uğur, *The Ottoman 'Ulema in the Mid-17th Century: An Analysis of the Vaḳā'i 'ü'l-fużalā of Meḥmed Şeyhī Efendi* (Berlin: K. Schwarz, 1986).

attention to, the imperial learned hierarchy, it is worth considering the interconnections between the genres.

Taşköprüzâde's *Shaqā'iq* consists of biographies of leading jurists and Sufi masters who operated in the Ottoman domains and/or, for the most part, maintained connections with the Ottoman dynasty or the Ottoman lands (at least in the author's and probably his peers' perception of the scholarly history of the Ottoman enterprise). The biographies are organized in eleven *ṭabaqāt*. Nevertheless, his use of the concept is somewhat different from the meaning of the term in the genealogies of the Ḥanafī school. In the latter, as we have seen, the word denotes either "rank" or "generation." Taşköprüzâde, by contrast, devotes each *ṭabaqa* in the work to the reign of an Ottoman sultan, starting with the founder of the Ottoman dynasty, Osmân, up to Süleymân in chronological order. In so doing, Taşköprüzâde stresses the relationship between a particular group of jurists and the Ottoman dynasty.

An interesting introductory paragraph, in which Taşköprüzâde explains the reasons for the compilation of the *Shaqā'iq*, may assist us in gaining a better understanding of the way he envisioned his project:

> Since I [learned to] distinguish between right and left, between the straight [path] and trickery, I sought passionately the merits [*manāqib*] of the *'ulamā'* and their histories [*akhbār*], and I was obsessed with memorizing their important deeds and their works, until I would accumulate a large [body of knowledge] in my weak memory [so] it would fill the books and the notebooks. Historians have recorded the merits of the *'ulama'* and the notables according to what has been established through transmission or was confirmed by eyewitnesses, [but] no one has paid attention to the *'ulamā'* of these lands, and [consequently] their names and practices almost vanished from the tongues of every present [i.e., living person] and [their memory] perished. When the people of excellence and perfection noticed this situation, they asked me to gather all the merits of the *'ulamā'* of Rūm.[69]

The passage is perhaps somewhat exaggerated. Yet Taşköprüzâde claims that the main impetus for composing this work was a need to fill a historiographical lacuna. In other words, Taşköprüzâde situates this work in the Arabic historiographical tradition in general and within the genre of the biographical dictionaries dedicated to jurists and notables in particular.[70]

[69] Taşköprüzâde, *al-Shaqā'iq*, 5.

[70] Taşköprüzâde's encyclopedic work *Miftāḥ al-sa'āda wa-miṣbāḥ al-siyāda fī mawḍū'āt al-'ulūm* also points in this direction. In the section on historiography (*'ilm al-tawārīkh*), all the works listed were compiled in Arabic, mostly in the central Islamic lands. Although

It is noteworthy that Taşköprüzâde identifies the lacuna as a geographical-political one. He emphasizes therefore that the work is intended to introduce the jurists of Rūm. Rūm can be understood in the geographical sense of "these lands," that is, mostly central-western Anatolia and the Balkans. On the other hand, Rūm also has a political dimension – affiliation with the Ottoman dynasty. Following this meaning of the word, Taşköprüzâde decided to organize his work according to the reigns of the Ottoman sultans, for "this work was compiled under the shadow of their state (*dawla*)."[71]

More will be said about this issue in the next chapter. Here suffice it to say that the tension between the Arabic historiographical tradition and the Ottoman/Rūmī political context is also reflected in the author's and his successors' language choices. Taşköprüzâde decided to compile his work in Arabic. This choice deserves attention, for it may be attributed to Taşköprüzâde's attempt to take part in a historiographical project whose center in the fifteenth century and the early sixteenth century was in the Mamluk sultanate. It appears, therefore, that Taşköprüzâde, much like his counterparts who authored the genealogies of the Ḥanafī school, wanted his work to be read beyond the confines of the imperial learned hierarchy and particularly in the fairly recently conquered Arab provinces. Most of the authors of the supplements to the *Shaqā'iq*, however, opted for Ottoman Turkish, and even Taşköprüzâde's *Shaqā'iq* was translated a few decades after its completion.[72]

by Taşköprüzâde's time Arabic historiography had already had a long history, it is possible that Taşköprüzâde was particularly interested in (or those who asked him to compile this work were) the biographical dictionaries produced in the Mamluk lands, such as the biographical dictionaries by Ibn Khallikān and al-Suyūṭī. Moreover, in the introduction to his supplement to Taşköprüzâde's *Shaqā'iq*, 'Âşıḳ Çelebi makes a similar comment concerning the importance of focusing on the activity of Rūmī jurists and scholars. 'Âşıḳ Çelebi, *Dhayl al-Shaqā'iq*, 36–38. Aḥmad b. Muṣṭafā Taşköprüzâde, *Miftāḥ al-sa'āda wa-miṣbāḥ al-siyāda fī mawḍū'āt al-'ulūm* (Cairo: Dār al-Kutub al-Ḥadītha, 1968), 1:251–70. In this section Taşköprüzâde mentions the existence of historiographical works in Persian, but he says that he decided not to include them in this work (1:270). For an English translation of this section, see Franz Rosenthal, *A History of Muslim Historiography* (Leiden: Brill, 1968), 530–35.

71 Taşköprüzâde, *al-Shaqā'iq*, 3.

72 Anooshahr argues that Taşköprüzâde chose to write the work in classical Arabic, "the sacral language of Islam, a 'dead language' … that was no one's native speech by the sixteenth century." By doing so, Anooshahr contends, "Taşköprüzâde asserted his membership in what Benedict Anderson [in his *Imagined Communities*] calls a community of signs and sounds." My interpretation of Taşköprüzâde's intention is somewhat different, as Arabic was not, of course, a "dead language" for many of the work's intended Arab readers. Anooshahr, "Writing," 60. It is worth pointing out that two of the supplements

Another significant similarity between the *Shaqāʾiq* and the *ṭabaqāt* works by members of the hierarchy was the emphasis on the Ḥanafī framework. Unlike the authors of the genealogies, Taşköprüzâde does not make special efforts to situate the scholars within a particular genealogy (or genealogies) within the Ḥanafī school. Yet, as the title of the work – a play on the Arabic word for anemone (*al-shaqāʾiq al-nuʿmāniyya*) that also alludes to Abū Ḥanīfa's name (Nuʿmān b. Thābit) – suggests, he was interested in stressing the link, which overarches the entire compilation, between the Ḥanafī school and the Ottoman learned hierarchy. In this sense, Taşköprüzâde supports the claims of his colleagues who were affiliated with the imperial learned hierarchy in the intra-school competition between the various Ḥanafī jurists.

In a thought-provoking article, Ali Anooshahr has suggested that in the *Shaqāʾiq*, Taşköprüzâde is intent on responding to several accusations raised by members of the Ottoman elite against the jurists. Particularly, he argues, Taşköprüzâde attempts to respond to the charges of corruption and foreignness that were brought against jurists and scholars by late fifteenth-century chroniclers, who echoed the view of certain groups in the Ottoman elite ("the gazi/derviş milieu") and protested their marginalization within the Ottoman polity. Secondly, according to Anooshahr, Taşköprüzâde responds in his work to the challenge posed to the jurists by what Anooshahr considers "a dangerously intrusive imperial court that by the middle of the sixteenth century had perhaps reached the climax of absolutism." To this end, Taşköprüzâde attempts to define the proper relationship between the court and the jurists, and to defy the growing absolutism of the state, especially during the reigns of Meḥmet II and Süleymân. He does so, according to Anooshahr's interpretation, by adopting the genre of the dynastic history of the House of Osmân (*Tevârîh-i Âl-ı Osmân*) and the reigns of the sultans as its organizing principle. But instead of focusing on the dynasty and the deeds of the sultan, the focus is shifted to the affairs of jurists and scholars. At the same time, as Anooshahr points

to the *Shaqāʾiq* were also written in Arabic: ʿAlī b. Bālī Manq, *al-ʿIqd al-manẓūm fī dhikr afāḍil al-Rūm* (Beirut: Dār al-Kitāb al-ʿArabī, 1975); ʿÂşıḳ Çelebi, *Dhayl al-Shaqāʾiq*. As the compiler of a magisterial biographical dictionary dedicated to Ottoman poets in Ottoman Turkish, it is likely that ʿÂşıḳ Çelebi was fully aware of the implication of his language choice. Therefore, during the first decades after the completion of the *Shaqāʾiq*, it appears that works in this genre were supposed to be written in Arabic. For ʿÂşıḳ Çelebi's *tezkere* of poets, see ʿÂşıḳ Çelebi, *Meşâʿirü'ş-Şuʿarâ* (Istanbul: İstanbul Araştırmaları Enstitüsü, 2010).

out, Taşköprüzâde's work mirrors the increasing consolidation of the imperial learned hierarchy.[73]

Parts of Anooshahr's analysis are doubtlessly correct. The *Shaqā'iq* is clearly a rejoinder to many charges raised against certain scholarly circles and to the challenges they were facing. It also describes a process of growing institutionalization of the Ottoman hierarchy during the second half of the fifteenth and the first decades of the sixteenth century. Moreover, Taşköprüzâde promotes the notion of interdependence between the scholarly circles (jurists and Sufi shaykhs) and the imperial court as part of a broader process of change in the power relations between absolutists and their opponents.[74]

Nevertheless, Anooshahr's analysis fails to explain, in my view, why a work like the *Shaqā'iq* did not appear in earlier periods. Had the main concern been to respond to the accusations made by late fifteenth-century chroniclers and to the increasing involvement of the Ottoman dynasty in the affairs of the hierarchy, a member of the burgeoning learned hierarchy could have composed such a work several decades earlier. This is not to say that the *Shaqā'iq* does not echo this concern. But this does not seem to be the main reason for the compilation of the work.

Reading Taşköprüzâde's work in juxtaposition to the *ṭabaqāt* works by members of the hierarchy, however, raises the possibility that Taşköprüzâde was concerned with defining the relationship between the sultan and the emerging Ottoman learned hierarchy against the background of the growing incorporation of the Arab lands into the empire. In this new reality, members of the hierarchy, Taşköprüzâde and the authors of the genealogies included, felt the need to defend their positions within the expanding empire. Therefore, they wanted to remind members of the Ottoman ruling elite, and mostly the sultan, of the long relationship between a specific group of jurists (what would become the imperial learned hierarchy) and the Ottoman dynastic project. Moreover, they wanted to stress their unique position and genealogy within the Ḥanafī school and within the empire. This was to secure their position in their competition with followers of other branches within the Ḥanafī school of law that operated throughout the empire and were not affiliated with the imperial learned hierarchy.

[73] Anooshahr, "Writing," 43–62. See also Niyazioğlu, *Ottoman Sufi Sheikhs*, 1–145.

[74] See also Baki Tezcan, *The Second Ottoman Empire: Political and Social Transformation in the Early Modern World* (Cambridge: Cambridge University Press, 2010), chap. 2.

Concluding Remarks

Taşköprüzâde's compilation and the *ṭabaqāt* works document, and in turn contribute to, the Ottoman learned hierarchy's evolution over the course of the second half of the fifteenth and the sixteenth centuries. In particular, they contributed to the rise of what Cornell Fleischer termed "bureaucratic consciousness" among members of the hierarchy.[75] The textual corpuses examined in this chapter reveal that the emergence of the imperial learned hierarchy had important doctrinal dimensions. In fact, the institutional and the doctrinal developments go hand in hand: the hierarchy, with its standardized career and training paths, monopolized access to the particular branch within the Ḥanafī school of law associated with the Ottoman dynasty and secured the privileged position of the branch's followers within the Ottoman imperial framework. It is noteworthy that these developments did not escape seventeenth-century observers from the Arab provinces of the empire, who often mention the "Rūmī way" in their writings, referring to the Ottoman training and career track.[76]

Here, once again, we return to the issue of the dynasty's intervention in regulating the structure of the Ottoman branch within the legal school and canonizing its doctrine. The "Rūmī way" was a product of a series of imperial edicts and legal codes. Therefore, the picture that emerges is more complex than a story of jurists opposing intrusion on behalf of the state. From the vantage point of members of the learned hierarchy, their position was relatively secure, as members of the Ottoman ruling elite respected the hierarchy's exclusive position within the imperial framework. This respect may account for the fact that the idea of replacing the members of the hierarchy with other jurists who were not members of the learned hierarchy was never broached.[77] On the other hand, from the dynasty's perspective, the learned hierarchy was quite dependent on the Ottoman dynastic/sultanic edicts and regulations for securing its

[75] Cornell H. Fleischer, *Bureaucrat and Intellectual in the Ottoman Empire: The Historian Mustafa Âli (1541–1600)* (Princeton, NJ: Princeton University Press, 1986), 214–31.

[76] For example: Najm al-Dīn Muḥammad b. Muḥammad al-Ghazzī, *Luṭf al-samar wa-qaṭf al-thamar* (Damascus: Wizārat al-Thaqāfa wa'l-Irshād al-Qawmī, 1982), 2:511–13; al-Muḥibbī, *Khulāṣat al-athar*, 1:186–87, 1:241–49, 1:523, 2:130–31.

[77] In the early seventeenth century, when the court wanted to curb the power of the learned hierarchy it turned to charismatic mosque preachers. They did not, however, seek to replace the imperial learned hierarchy by "importing" Ḥanafī jurists from the Arab lands. By contrast, Osmân II considered recruiting a new army in the Arab lands. On these episodes see Tezcan, *Second Ottoman Empire*, chaps. 3 and 4.

exclusive status within the imperial setting. The hierarchy's dependence on its connection with the dynasty was also, at times, translated into specific solutions that members of the dynasty offered to legal problems and challenges that troubled the Ottoman dynasty and its ruling elite.[78] But more generally, the connection between the dynasty and this specific group of jurists enabled the dynasty to present itself as committed to Islamic tenets and as defender of Islamic Sunnī, and particularly Ḥanafī learning and law.

[78] For example: Imber, *Ebu's-Su'ud*; Johansen, *Islamic Law on Land Tax and Rent*; Jon E. Mandaville, "Usurious Piety: The Cash Waqf Controversy in the Ottoman Empire," *International Journal of Middle East Studies* 10, no. 3 (1979): 289–308; Reem Meshal, "Antagonistic Sharīʿas and the Construction of Orthodoxy in Sixteenth-Century Ottoman Cairo," *Journal of Islamic Studies* 21, no. 2 (2010): 183–212; Guy Burak, "Faith, Law and Empire in the Ottoman "Age of Confessionalization" (15th–17th Centuries): The Case of "Renewal of Faith," *Mediterranean Historical Review* (forthcoming).

3

Genealogies and Boundaries II

Two Responses from the Arab Provinces of the Empire

Members of the Ottoman imperial learned hierarchy were not the only ones to compile intellectual genealogies of the Ḥanafī school of law. In the sixteenth century, at least two jurists from the Arab provinces of the empire, one from Damascus and the other from Egypt, penned their own *ṭabaqāt* works.[1] Although their views of the school were substantially different from those of the members of the imperial hierarchy, the two works clearly point to the importance their authors attributed to documenting their position and genealogy within the Ḥanafī school of law. Furthermore, the compilation of these genealogies may also be interpreted as an attempt to preserve the authority of certain legal arguments and jurisprudential texts within the expanding imperial framework. But perhaps most importantly, these *ṭabaqāt* works reveal how different jurists from the Arab provinces of the empire perceived the notion of an official madhhab and the relationship between the sultan and the Ḥanafī school of law. The authors' views on the rise of an official school of law, much like the critique of their later counterpart ʿAbd al-Ghanī al-Nābulusī (discussed in Chapter 1), may shed light on the nature and implications of this development.

In addition, the genealogies from the Arab lands of the empire reveal the different strategies the region's jurists employed to cope with the challenges that their encounter with the Ottoman notion of a learned

[1] In addition, in the late sixteenth century, apparently in Mecca, the famous Ḥanafī jurist and scholar ʿAlī b. Sulṭān al-Qārī al-Harawī (d. 1605 or 1606) wrote an abridged version of al-Qurashī's *al-Jawāhir al-muḍiyya*. ʿAlī b. Sulṭān al-Qārī al-Harawī, *al-Athmār al-janniyya fī asmāʾ al-Ḥanafiyya*, 2 vols. (Baghdad: Jumhūrīyat al-ʿIrāq, Diwān al-Waqf al-Sunnī, Markaz al-Buḥūth waʾl-Dirāsāt al-Islāmiyya, 2009).

hierarchy and official school of law entailed. While some, like the author of the Damascene genealogy, emphasized the independence of the jurists from the sultan in regulating the structure of the school and its doctrine, others, like our Egyptian author, sought to carve out space for themselves within the imperial setting by endorsing, albeit partially, the imperial learned hierarchy's perception of the Ḥanafī school and the role of the sultan. What is more, the different approaches also mirror the manner in which the two jurists envisioned themselves in relation to the affiliates of the imperial hierarchy and to earlier generations of Ḥanafī scholars: the Damascene jurist wrote an exclusive work in which he strove to distinguish himself and many of his counterparts from the Arab lands of the empire from the members of the hierarchy, whereas the Egyptian scholar produced a more inclusive vision of the Ḥanafī school of law and its history.

More broadly, an examination of these two *ṭabaqāt* works helps illustrate how the Ottoman conquest of the Arab lands contributed to a clearer articulation of the different visions of the school of law. To be sure, with all likelihood, certain elements of these views of the Ḥanafī school of law circulated before the Ottoman conquest in the early sixteenth century. But the conquest, I submit, was the main impetus for the rise of this genre in the second half of the sixteenth century both in the core lands of the empire and its Arab provinces, as different Ḥanafī jurists throughout the empire felt the need to articulate their relation to the Ottoman dynasty on the one hand, and to their peers and fellow jurists on the other. Therefore, the concluding section of this chapter seeks to weave the genealogies discussed in Chapter 2 and in this chapter into a single narrative of imperial integration and the dialogues it produced.

Ibn Ṭūlūn's *al-Ghuraf al-ʿĀliyya fī Tarājim Mutaʾakhkhirī al-Ḥanafiyya*

Shams al-Dīn Muḥammad b. ʿAlī b. Aḥmad b. Ṭūlūn al-Ṣāliḥī al-Dimashqī al-Ḥanafī (d. 1546) was a prolific Damascene traditionist, historian, and jurist. Beyond his eminence during his lifetime, Ibn Ṭūlūn was an important link in the intellectual genealogy of many Damascene Ḥanafī jurists, such as the seventeenth-century officially appointed muftī ʿAlāʾ al-Dīn al-Ḥaṣkafī[2] and the nonappointed muftī ʿAbd al-Ghanī

[2] In the introduction to his commentary on *Multaqā al-abḥur*, al-Ḥaṣkafī records one of the chains of transmissions that stretch back to Abū Ḥanīfa through Ibrāhīm al-Ḥalabī, the

al-Nābulusī.[3] The importance attributed to Ibn Ṭūlūn in these genealogies renders Ibn Ṭūlūn's own account of the structure and history of the Ḥanafī school and of his position within this tradition into an important text for understanding the self-perception of many other Damascene Ḥanafīs (as well as of other followers of the school from the Arab lands of the empire).

Ibn Ṭūlūn was born in 1485 in the Damascene suburb of al-Ṣāliḥiyya. His father's family was well connected to scholarly circles in Damascus and beyond. For example, his paternal uncle Jamāl al-Dīn Yūsuf b. Ṭūlūn (d. 1530 or 1531), who played a major role in his upbringing after his mother's death, was the muftī and judge of the Hall of Justice (*Dār al-ʿAdl*) during the last decades of Mamluk rule in Damascus. Another family member who had great influence on the young Ibn Ṭūlūn was Burhān al-Dīn b. Qindīl, the half brother of Ibn Ṭūlūn's paternal grandfather, who was known in Damascus for a large endowment he had founded there before leaving for Mecca (where he died in 1482 or 1483).

Ibn Ṭūlūn started his studies at a very young age in an elementary school (*maktab*) and other educational institutions in Damascus. In the following years he attended the classes of several prominent Damascene jurists, such as Nāṣir al-Dīn b. Zurayq (d. 1486), Sirāj al-Dīn al-Ṣayrafī (d. 1511 or 1512), and Abū al-Fatḥ al-Mizzī (d. 1500 or 1501). Another important teacher was the eminent scholar and traditionist Jalāl al-Dīn al-Suyūṭī (d. 1505), who granted Ibn Ṭūlūn a permit to transmit his teachings (*ijāza*). After the completion of his studies, Ibn Ṭūlūn held several teaching and administrative positions in Damascus. He also served as imām in various institutions and, following the Ottoman conquest of the city, was appointed imām and reciter of the Qurʾān in the mosque the Ottoman sultan Selîm I built in the al-Ṣāliḥiyya suburb in the vicinity of Ibn al-ʿArabī's mausoleum. In addition to this office, Ibn Ṭūlūn served in other teaching and administrative positions.

author of *Multaqā al-abḥur*. Ibn Ṭūlūn and his paternal uncle Jamāl al-Dīn appear in this chain as direct transmitters from Ibrāhīm al-Ḥalabī. Muḥammad b. ʿAlī b. Muḥammad al-Hiṣnī, also known as ʿAlāʾal-Dīn al-Haṣkafī, *al-Durr al-muntaqā fī sharḥ al-Multaqā* (Beirut: Dār al-Kutub al-ʿIlmiyya, 1998), 1:9–13.

[3] ʿAbd al-Ghanī al-Nābulusī, *Sharḥ al-Ashbāh waʾl-naẓāʾir*, Süleymaniye Library MS Hamidiye 502, 3v. Moreover, as late as the early nineteenth century, jurists, such as the famous Muḥammad Amīn b. ʿUmar b. al-ʿĀbidīn (d. 1836), mentioned Ibn Ṭūlūn as an important link in their genealogy within the school. See Muḥammad Amīn b. ʿUmar b. al-ʿĀbidīn, *Thabat Ibn al-ʿĀbidīn al-musammā ʿUqūd al-lālī fī asānīd al-ʿawālī (Takhrīj li-Asānīd Shaykhihi Muḥammad Shākir al-ʿAqqād* (Beirut: Dār al-Bashāʾir al-Islāmiyya, 2010), 442–46.

The multiple positions he held did not prevent Ibn Ṭūlūn from compiling an enormous number of works in various disciplines. In his autobiography he mentions 750 works, out of which approximately 100 have survived. The surviving works reflect their author's wide range of interests, spanning jurisprudence, Sufism, and history.[4] Moreover, Ibn Ṭūlūn was an avid collector of prophetic traditions. For this purpose he even sought and obtained a meeting with the caliph, who entered Damascus as part of the Mamluk sultan's retinue during his campaign against the Ottomans.[5]

Let us turn to Ibn Ṭūlūn's *al-Ghuraf al-ʿāliyya*. As Ibn Ṭūlūn explains in the introduction and as the title suggests, the work is dedicated to the late Ḥanafīs (*muta'akhkhirī al-Ḥanafiyya*). The term *muta'akhkhirūn*, however, is a fairly loose chronological definition. Kemâlpaşazâde, for example, identifies the "late scholars" as scholars from the thirteenth and fourteenth centuries. Ibn Ṭūlūn seems to agree with Kemâlpaşazâde's definition, although he does not explicitly specify the exact time period. On the other hand, he does explain that this work is a supplement (*dhayl*) to ʿAbd al-Qādir al-Qurashī's fourteenth-century *al-Jawāhir al-muḍiyya*, which includes Ḥanafīs from the early days of the school up to the mid-fourteenth century.[6]

In the introduction, Ibn Ṭūlūn contextualizes this work within the genre of the *ṭabaqāt* by listing several *ṭabaqāt* works as his model. Among those mentioned are Ḥanafī *ṭabaqāt* works such as al-Qurashī's *al-Jawāhir* and five-volume work by Muḥibb al-Dīn Abū al-Faḍl Muḥammad b. Abī al-Walīd Muḥammad, known as Ibn al-Shiḥna (d. 1485).[7] In addition, he mentions several *ṭabaqāt* works that focus on a specific discipline, such as the *ṭabaqāt* dedicated to reciters of the Qur'ān or to transmitters of prophetic traditions.[8]

It is worth drawing attention to another possible context of the work. In Ibn Ṭūlūn's relatively close circle, two *ṭabaqāt* works devoted to the later (*muta'akhkhirūn*) Ḥanbalī and Shāfiʿī jurists were compiled. The

[4] Stephan Conermann, "Ibn Ṭūlūn (d. 955/1548): Life and Works," *Mamluk Studies Review* 8, no. 1 (2004): 115–21.

[5] Shams al-Dīn Muḥammad b. Ṭūlūn, *al-Ghuraf al-ʿāliyya fī muta'akhkhirī al-Ḥanafiyya*, Süleymaniye Library MS Şehid Ali Paşa 1924, 8v–9v.

[6] Ibid., 2r.

[7] Ibid., 8v. On this *ṭabaqat* work, see Kâtip Çelebi, *Kashf al-ẓunun 'an asamı al-kutub wa'l-funun* (Istanbul: Milli Eğitim Basımevi, 1972), 2:1098–99; Ismāʿīl Bāshā al-Bābānī, *Īḍāḥ al-maknūn fī al-dhayl ʿalā Kashf al-ẓunūn ʿan asāmī al-kutub wa'l-funūn* (Istanbul: Milli Eğitim Basımevi, 1945–47), 2:78.

[8] Ibn Ṭūlūn, *al-Ghuraf*, 8v–9v.

first work, entitled *al-Jawhar al-munaḍḍad fī ṭabaqāt muta'akhkhirī aṣḥāb Aḥmad* [b. Ḥanbal], was penned by the Ḥanbalī jurist and chronicler Yūsuf b. 'Abd al-Hādī (d. 1501), also known as Ibn al-Mibrad.[9] Ibn al-Mibrad had a noticeable impact on the young Ibn Ṭūlūn. The second work, entitled *Kitāb Bahjat al-nāẓirīn ilā tarājim al-muta'akhkhirīn min al-Shāfi'iyya al-bāri'īn*, was authored by Raḍī al-Dīn Abū al-Barakāt Muḥammad b. Aḥmad b. 'Abd Allāh al-Ghazzī (d. 1459 or 60).[10] Although Raḍī al-Dīn al-Ghazzī was not Ibn Ṭūlūn's contemporary, he was a central figure in Damascene intellectual life during the first half of the fifteenth century and was the ancestor of the al-Ghazzī family, many of whose members were dominant Shāfi'ī jurists in Damascus in the fifteenth and sixteenth centuries. It is therefore possible that Ibn Ṭūlūn knew about al-Ghazzī's work. Whatever the case may be, it is clear that Ibn Ṭūlūn's *al-Ghuraf* is part of a larger historiographical trend that started in the fifteenth century. But since Ibn Ṭūlūn concluded this work toward the end of his life, that is, almost three decades after the Ottoman conquest of the city, he was addressing other issues as well.

In his introduction, Ibn Ṭūlūn elaborates on the reasons that led him to compile *al-Ghuraf*:

> The subject matter [of this book] is the history of the jurists and the lineages, the length of their lives, the time of their death, the mention of who studied [*akhadhū al-'ilm*] with a [certain jurist] and who studied with [other jurists], so that the jurist will not be ignorant [concerning the issues he is] required to know as to whose opinion should be relied upon according to the consensus [*ijmā'*] and who should be consulted in [cases of] dispute.[11]

In other words, *al-Ghuraf* is meant to establish the school's consensus, so that jurists can use it to resolve disputes and controversies. Moreover, the work's main objective is to recover a continuous and reliable chain or chains of transmission through which jurisprudential knowledge and authority were transmitted from Abū Ḥanīfa to a specific jurist. Hence, Ibn Ṭūlūn stresses the importance of the dates of the jurists' deaths, their ages, and the identity of their teachers and their students.

[9] Yūsuf b. Ḥasan b. al-Mibrad, *al-Jawhar al-munaḍḍad fī ṭabaqāt muta'akhkhirī aṣḥāb Aḥmad* (Cairo: Maktabat al-Kanjī, 1987). Ibn Ṭūlūn mentions this work in his autobiography as well. See Shams al-Dīn Muḥammad b. 'Alī b. Ṭūlūn al-Ṣāliḥī, *al-Fulk al-mashḥūn fī aḥwāl Muḥammad b. Ṭūlūn* (Beirut: Dār Ibn Ḥazm, 1996), 24.

[10] Raḍī al-Dīn Muḥammad b. Aḥmad al-Ghazzī, *Kitāb Bahjat al-nāẓirīn ilā tarājim al-muta'akhkhirīn min al-Shāfi'iyya al-bāri'īn* (Beirut: Dār Ibn Ḥazm, 2000).

[11] Ibn Ṭūlūn, *al-Ghuraf*, 2r.

Ibn Ṭūlūn's focus on reconstructing continuous chains of transmission and his insistence on these biographical details may account for his choice in sources. Unlike Kınalızâde and Kefevî, for instance, who draw heavily on jurisprudential manuals and texts, Ibn Ṭūlūn uses sources that are mostly biographical dictionaries written during the Mamluk period, such as Ibn al-Mibrad's now lost *al-Riyāḍ al-yāniʿa*, al-Sakhāwī's *al-Ḍawʾ al-lāmiʿ*, and Ibn Taghrībirdī's *al-Manhal*. The only jurisprudential text he mentions is Ibn al-Shiḥna's commentary on al-Marghīnānī's *al-Hidāya* (entitled *Nihāyat al-nihāya*).

This frequent use of fifteenth-century Mamluk biographical dictionaries is reflected in the chronological and geographical scope of Ibn Ṭūlūn's work. It appears that Ibn Ṭūlūn sought to demarcate a specific community within the Ḥanafī school, with its own authoritative genealogies and, in some cases, particular jurisprudential arguments. To further illuminate this point, it is necessary to examine the approximately nine hundred Ḥanafīs that Ibn Ṭūlūn chose to include in *al-Ghuraf*. As a supplement to *al-Jawāhir al-muḍiyya*, the chronological focus of *al-Ghuraf* is from the fourteenth to the first half of the sixteenth century – a time period, as we have seen in the previous chapter, during which the Ottoman domains gradually emerged as a significant Ḥanafī center and a distinctively Ottoman branch within the school was evolving. Ibn Ṭūlūn ignores this momentous development. Accordingly, jurists who were affiliated with the Ottoman dynasty and with its evolving learned hierarchy are by and large excluded from *al-Ghuraf*.

Let us examine Ibn Ṭūlūn's treatment of Ibn al-Bazzāz, whom we have already met in the previous chapter, in order to demonstrate his general historiographical approach. Ḥāfiẓ al-Dīn b. Muḥammad b. Muḥammad al-Kardarī (d. 1423), known as Ibn al-Bazzāz, was a prominent Ḥanafī jurist who traveled quite extensively. After residing in Damascus for a while, he traveled to the Ottoman realms and eventually settled in Bursa. Ibn al-Bazzāz's residence in Anatolia, however, is totally absent from the entry dedicated to him in *al-Ghuraf*.[12] It is possible that Ibn Ṭūlūn's knowledge about the jurists of early fifteenth-century Anatolia was limited. His claim that he could not find any biographical data on Ibn al-Bazzāz in earlier *ṭabaqāt* works or in chronicles may support that assumption.

[12] Ibid., 280r–280v. It is noteworthy that al-Sakhāwī, in *al-Ḍawʾ al-lāmiʿ*, likewise does not provide any information on Ibn al-Bazzāz's career in the Ottoman realms. See Shams al-Dīn Muḥammad b. ʿAbd al-Raḥman al-Sakhāwī, *al-Ḍawʾ al-lāmiʿ li-ahl al-qarn al-tāsiʿ* (Cairo: Maktabat al-Qudsī, 1934), 10:37.

On the other hand, this omission raises some doubts. Given the popularity of Ibn al-Bazzāz's *al-Fatāwā al-Bazzāziyya*, including in Ibn Ṭūlūn's immediate circles,[13] it seems somewhat unlikely that such an important piece of information concerning this author's life could have escaped Ibn Ṭūlūn. The fact that so many other jurists who were affiliated with, or at least somehow related to, the Ottoman imperial learned hierarchy – including jurists whose works were consulted by Ḥanafī jurists in the Mamluk sultanate – are excluded from *al-Ghuraf* suggests that the omission was intentional. For instance, Mollâ Ḫüsrev (d. 1480), the author of the famous *Durar al-ḥukkām fī sharḥ al-aḥkām* and of the equally famous commentary on this work, does not have an entry in *al-Ghuraf*.

There are, however, some important exceptions to the general tendency to exclude affiliates with the Ottoman learned hierarchy. For instance, Ibn Ṭūlūn dedicates entries to Ibn ʿArabshāh,[14] Muḥyī al-Dīn al-Kāfiyajī,[15] Aḥmad b. ʿAbd Allāh al-Kurānī (Gürânî),[16] and Şemsuddîn Fenârî. In all these entries, he provides the reader with some information regarding the biographees' training and career in Anatolia. Şemsuddîn Fenârî's biography is an interesting example. In this entry, which draws on the entry in Ibn Ḥajar al-ʿAsqalānī's (d. 1442) *Inbāʾ al-ghumr fī anbāʾ al-ʿumr* and on Ibn Taghrībirdī's (d. 1470) *al-Manhal al-ṣāfī waʾl-mustawfā baʿda al-wāfī*,[17] Ibn Ṭūlūn lists al- Şemsuddîn Fenârî's teachers both in Anatolia and in Cairo. Moreover, the entry relates the years following Fenârî's return to Anatolia.[18] Nevertheless, it is evident that the main reason for the inclusion of the above-mentioned jurists in *al-Ghuraf* is the time they spent in the Mamluk lands. By emphasizing this aspect of their biographies, Ibn Ṭūlūn creates a hierarchy according to which the Mamluk

[13] Ibn Ṭūlūn says that his paternal uncle Jamāl al-Dīn, who was a dominant figure in Ibn Ṭūlūn's life, studied *al-Fatāwā al-Bazzāziyya*. Ibn Ṭūlūn, *al-Ghuraf*, 344v–345v.

[14] Ibid., 64r–67r. On Ibn ʿArabshāh, see R. D. McChesney, "A Note on the Life and Works of Ibn ʿArabshāh," in *History and Historiography of Post-Mongol Central Asia and the Middle East: Studies in Honor of John E. Woods*, ed. Judith Pfeiffer and Sholeh A. Quinn (Wiesbaden: Harrassowitz Verlag, 2006), 205–49.

[15] Ibn Ṭūlūn, *al-Ghuraf*, 217v–218r. The entry is very similar to al-Kāfiyajī's biography in Ibn Taghrībirdī's *al-Manhal* and al-Sakhāwī's *al-Ḍawʾ al-lāmiʿ*.

[16] Ibid., 48r–49r. On al-Kurānī's (or Gürânî's) career under the Ottomans, see Taşköprüzâde, *al-Shaqāʾiq*, 51–55.

[17] Aḥmad b. ʿAlīb. Ḥajar al-ʿAsqalānī, *Inbāʾ al-ghumr fī anbāʾ al-ʿumr* (Cairo: al-Majlis al-Aʿlā li'l-Shuʾūn al-Islāmiyya, 1972), 3:464–65; Abūal-Maḥāsin Yūsuf b. Taghrībirdī, *al-Manhal al-ṣāfī waʾl-mustawfā baʿda al-wāfī* (Cairo: Maṭbaʿat Dār al-Kutub al-Miṣriyya, 1956), 10:40–41.

[18] Ibn Ṭūlūn, *al-Ghuraf*, 212r–212v. Ibn Ṭūlūn also devotes an entry to Şemsuddîn Fenârî's son, who visited Cairo as well (ibid., 219v–220r).

lands were superior to other parts of the Islamic, and particularly the Ḥanafī, world in terms of scholarly activity.[19]

Almost all the jurists who are included in *al-Ghuraf* and had some connections with the emerging Ottoman learned hierarchy lived in the first half of the fifteenth century. From the mid-fifteenth century onward, the focus of the work is on jurists who operated in the Mamluk sultanate, and even more so in Damascus, Ibn Ṭūlūn's hometown. Moreover, almost all the biographies of jurists who died during the three decades following the Ottoman conquest were either Damascene or jurists from other parts of the Muslim world (but not from the core lands of the empire) who had passed through Damascus. Among the latter are several Ḥanafīs from central Asia who passed through Damascus on their way to the Hijaz and studied with Ibn Ṭūlūn during their stay in the city.[20]

It is therefore fairly evident that one of Ibn Ṭūlūn's main purposes in writing *al-Ghuraf* was to establish his own authority and that of other Ḥanafīs in Greater Syria (as well as in other Arab provinces of the empire). As we have already seen in our discussion of other *ṭabaqāt* works, the *ṭabaqāt* often serve as a means of establishing the authority of the author and his peers, or at least of the generation of his teachers. Fittingly, Ibn Ṭūlūn plays a central role in his own *ṭabaqāt* work, as many of his Ḥanafī teachers and students (in various disciplines, not only jurisprudence) are included therein.[21] Consolidating and cementing his scholarly and jurisprudential authority was a major concern of Ibn Ṭūlūn in other works as well. In his autobiography, for instance, Ibn Ṭūlūn says that one of the reasons for his composition of such a text is the loss of all his scholarly certificates during the rebellion of Jānbirdī al-Ghazzālī against the Ottomans.[22] Ibn Ṭūlūn's insistence on the preservation (and when needed

[19] In this sense, Ibn Ṭūlūn follows the conventions set by earlier Damascene biographer-chroniclers. Burhān al-Dīn Ibrāhīm b. ʿUmar b. Ḥasan al-Biqāʿī (d. 1480), in his biographical dictionary dedicated to his teachers, students, and peers – which Ibn Ṭūlūn consults extensively – does not include members of the nascent Ottoman learned hierarchy. He does, however, mention Aḥmad al-Kurānī, who entered the service of Meḥmet II, and Ibn ʿArabshāh, who spent several years in the Ottoman domains before his arrival in Cairo. See Ibrāhīm b. Ḥasan al-Biqāʿī, *ʿUnwān al-ʿunwān bi-tajrīd asmāʾ al-shuyūkh wa-baʿḍ al-talāmidha waʾl-aqrān* (Beirut: Dār al-Kitāb al-ʿArabī, 2002), 13–14, 33–34.

[20] Among these are Ḥusayn b. Muḥammad b. al-Khāwājāh Ḥusayn al-Saranī al-Ḥanafī (Ibn Ṭūlūn, *al-Ghuraf*, 105v); Muḥammad b. Ghiyāth b. Khāwājākī al-Samarqandī (ibid., 242r–242v); and Muḥammad b. Mīr b. Muḥammad b. Muḥammad b. Ṭāhir al-Bukhārī (ibid., 285r–286v).

[21] For example, Ibn Ṭūlūn, *al-Ghuraf*, 215v–216r, 290r–290v.

[22] Ibn Ṭūlūn, *al-Fulk*, 53. Ibn Ṭūlūn says that he recorded many of the permits he received in a notebook. In addition, he relates that he wrote the *ijāza* to teach the content of a specific book in the book itself.

restoration) of his scholarly credentials is an interesting indication of the social value of these documents for establishing the authority of a jurist. *Al-Ghuraf*, it seems, serves the same purpose, since the work, as the introduction states, was meant to reach a wide readership.

Ibn Ṭūlūn's attempt to establish his own position within the school seems to be one of the main reasons for *al-Ghuraf*'s exclusion of Ḥanafī jurists affiliated with the Ottoman learned hierarchy. The omission is particularly striking given the numerous encounters Ibn Ṭūlūn had with such jurists. For example, soon after the conquest, Ibn Ṭūlūn went to the Ottoman encampment to search for thirty-six madrasa professors who were sojourning in Damascus with the sultan and his troops.[23] In the following weeks, he had the opportunity to meet and talk with members of the imperial learned hierarchy: several days after his visit to the encampment, for instance, he met Mollâ Idrîs, possibly the renowned chronicler Idrîs-i Bidlîsî, who was spending some time in Damascus.[24] Furthermore, in his chronicles, Ibn Ṭūlūn provides information about chief imperial muftīs, such as Kemâlpaşazâde and Saʿdî Çelebi, and other jurists affiliated with the Ottoman learned hierarchy, such as the chief judges of Damascus.[25]

The exclusion of members of the Ottoman learned hierarchy in his *ṭabaqāt* thus may be read as Ibn Ṭūlūn's robust critique of the notion of the learned hierarchy and an official madhhab. The *ṭabaqāt* works by members of the Ottoman learned hierarchy, as we have observed in the previous chapter, made a clear connection between the Ottoman dynasty (through its learned hierarchy) and the Ḥanafī school of law (or, more accurately, a particular branch within the school). Ibn Ṭūlūn radically differs in this respect from these authors: *al-Ghuraf* does not make any connection between the dynasty (or a learned hierarchy, for that matter) and the school. The main reason for this separation is that during most of the Mamluk period the state did not adopt a single school.[26] On the other

[23] Shams al-Dīn Muḥammad b. Ṭūlūn, *Mufākahat al-khillān ḥawādith al-zamān: tārīkh Miṣr wa'l-Shām* (Cairo: al-Mu'assasa al-Miṣriyya al-ʿĀmma li'l-Ta'līf wa'l-Tarjama wa'l-Ṭibāʿa wa'l-Nashr, 1962–64), 2:31.

[24] Ibid., 2:59. Ibn Ṭūlūn mentions that Idrîs compiled a work entitled *Fatḥ al-mamālik al-Islāmiyya* (The conquest of the Islamic lands). On Idrîs-i Bidlîsî, see Abdülkadir Özcan, "Idrîs-i Bitlisî," *TDVİA*.

[25] For example, Shams al-Dīn Muḥammad b. ʿAlī b. Ṭūlūn, *Ḥawādith Dimashq al-yawmiyya ghadāt al-ghazw al-ʿUthmānī li'l-Shām, 926–951H: ṣafaḥāt mafqūda tunsharu li'l-marra al-ūlā min Kitāb Mufākahat al-khillān fī ḥawādith al-zamān li-Ibn Ṭūlūn al-Ṣāliḥī* (Damascus: Dār al-Awā'il, 2002), 187, 192, 283, 313, 324–25.

[26] Yossef Rapoport, "Legal Diversity in the Age of Taqlīd: The Four Chief Qadis under the Mamluks," *Islamic Law and Society* 10, no. 2 (2003): 210–28.

hand, since Ibn Ṭūlūn finished this work slightly after 1546, he must have been aware of the fact that he was promoting an alternate vision of the relationship between the school (or, more accurately, specific traditions within the schools) and the dynasty. This was clearly a very different vision from the one that his counterparts in the core lands of the empire sought to advance in the decades and centuries to come.

Moreover, Ibn Ṭūlūn's attempt to delineate a distinctive Ḥanafī (Mamluk) tradition with particular authorities and specific legal arguments – a tradition that was independent from the intervention of the Ottoman sultan and dynasty (or any other sultan for that matter) – may be read along the lines of the critique ʿAbd al-Ghanī al-Nābulusī later made, in the late seventeenth/early eighteenth century, of the Ottoman dynasty's practice of appointing muftīs and attempting to regulate the structure and doctrine of the school of law (discussed in detail in Chapter 1). In short, Ibn Ṭūlūn sought to establish the legitimacy of opinions within the school that were not endorsed by the Ottoman dynasty and its learned hierarchy.

This is not the say that *al-Ghuraf* excludes all mention of rulers who were followers of the Ḥanafī school of law. Among the rulers listed are the Timurids Shāhrukh (d. 1447) and Ulugh Beg (d. 1449)[27] and several sultans from the Indian subcontinent, such the sultan of Bengal Ghiyāth al-Dīn Aʿẓam (d. 1410) and the fourteenth-century sultan of Delhi Muḥammad b. Tughluk (or Tughluq) Shāh (d. 1388).[28] Ibn Ṭūlūn also includes the biographies of three Ottoman sultans – Bâyezîd I, Meḥmet Çelebi, and Murâd II[29] – and he mentions Selîm I in two entries.[30] The focus on these particular sultans is interesting and not fully clear, but in one of his chronicles of the Ottoman conquest of Damascus, Ibn Ṭūlūn criticizes Selîm I for not meeting the Damascene scholars and jurists during his stay in the city, explicitly contrasting Selîm I's comportment to that of his forefather Bâyezîd I.[31] In a similar vein, in his biographies of Bâyezîd I and of Murâd II in *al-Ghuraf*, Ibn Ṭūlūn emphasizes the piety of these sultans, their campaigns against Christian polities, and their support of religious scholars and jurists. The picture that emerges from these entries is, again, very different from that which the members of the

[27] Ibn Ṭūlūn, *al-Ghuraf*, 121r–121v, 90v–92r.
[28] Ibid., 88v–89r, 220v–221r.
[29] Ibid., 357r–358v, 318r–319r.
[30] Ibid., 162v–163r, 307v–308r.
[31] Shams al-Dīn Muḥammad b. ʿAlīb. Ṭūlūn, *al-Qalāʾid al-jawhariyya fī tārīkh al-Ṣāliḥiyya* (Damascus: Majmaʿ al-Lugha al-ʿArabiyya, 1949–56), 1:118–20.

learned hierarchy were promoting at the time: these rulers were indeed Ḥanafīs, but they do not seem to play an important role in Ibn Ṭūlūn's understanding of the function and nature of the school of law.

In his study of Ibn Ṭūlūn's biography, Stephan Conermann argues on the basis of his examination of Ibn Ṭūlūn's chronicles that "the occupation of his hometown by the Ottoman Sultan Selîm (r. 918–926/1512–1520) in 922/1516 does not seem to have represented a break for our author. In his writings he only mentioned this event in passing and did not attach much importance to it."[32] *Al-Ghuraf*, on the other hand, offers a glimpse into some of the author's, and probably many other jurists', anxieties and concerns in the wake of the Ottoman conquest of Damascus. These concerns, admittedly, are not addressed directly in *al-Ghuraf*. Still, the work, as I have suggested, challenges the view that Ibn Ṭūlūn did not attach much importance to the Ottoman conquest and subsequent incorporation of Bilād al-Shām into the Ottoman imperial framework. *Al-Ghuraf*, I propose, embodies some of the discursive strategies employed by Ibn Ṭūlūn and other jurists who shared his view of the madhhab and of the relationship between the sultan, the jurists, and school of law in order to cope with the new reality. Other Ḥanafī jurists from the Arab lands, meanwhile, opted for a different strategy and developed a different perception of the history and structure of the Ḥanafī school, as al-Tamīmī's *ṭabaqāt* will demonstrate.

Taqiyy al-Dīn al-Tamīmī's *al-Ṭabaqāt al-Saniyya fī Tarājim al-Ḥanafiyya*

Writing in Egypt a few decades after Ibn Ṭūlūn, Taqiyy al-Dīn b. ʿAbd al-Qādir al-Tamīmī al-Ghazzī produced his own *ṭabaqāt* work of the Ḥanafī school, *al-Ṭabaqāt al-saniyya fī tarājim al-Ḥanafiyya*. The compilation includes more than twenty-seven hundred entries, and it is thus one of the most extensive Ḥanafī *ṭabaqāt* works, and possibly the most extensive, to have survived. Al-Tamīmī's contemporaries clearly appreciated the achievement. In his supplement to *al-Shaqāʾiq al-nuʿmāniyya*, the chronicler Nevʿîzâde, for instance, claims that he examined the work and that it does not fall short of any of the *ṭabaqāt* works of the ancients (*salaf*).[33] Presumably it is because of this work that Nevʿîzâde

[32] Conermann, "Ibn Ṭūlūn," 119.
[33] Nevʿîzâde Atâyî, *Hadâʾiku'l-Hakâʾik fî Tekmîleti'ş-Şakâik* (Istanbul: Çağrı Yayınları, 1985), 408.

even included al-Tamīmī's biography in his supplement to *al-Shaqā'iq al-nu'māniyya* – quite a rare honor, as he usually did not include jurists who were not graduates of the imperial learned hierarchy's educational system. Moreover, it appears that several high-ranking members of the imperial learned hierarchy issued their endorsements (*taqrīẓ*) of al-Tamīmī's *Ṭabaqāt*. As we shall see in the next chapter, within the hierarchy, these endorsements played an important role in the incorporation of a text into the imperial jurisprudential canon.[34]

Another feature of al-Tamīmī's work that drew his contemporaries' attention is the number of entries he dedicated to members of the Ottoman learned hierarchy. The seventeenth/early eighteenth-century chronicler al-Muḥibbī says, in his centennial biographical dictionary's entry on al-Tamīmī, that he saw parts of al-Tamīmī's *Ṭabaqāt*, and he explicitly states that al-Tamīmī gathered in his work biographies of many Rūmī jurists and notables (that is, members of the imperial learned hierarchy).[35] It seems, however, that this characteristic of the work attracted the attention of its readers mostly because of al-Tamīmī's Arab origin. After all, al-Muḥibbī does not find it remarkable that Nev'îzâde, for instance, focuses in his biographical dictionary on members of the Ottoman learned hierarchy.

Al-Tamīmī's inclusion of members of the hierarchy has also drawn the attention of modern scholars.[36] In fact, most studies that make use of al-Tamīmī's work concentrate on the information he provides on jurists who were affiliated with the Ottoman learned hierarchy. The focus on this aspect of the work, nonetheless, overlooks its complexity. It is this complexity that I am interested in exploring in this section.

Al-Tamīmī, as the epithet "al-Ghazzī" suggests, was born in the Palestinian city of Gaza around 1543.[37] Originally Shāfi'ī, al-Tamīmī

[34] Kâtip Çelebi, in *Kashf al-ẓunūn*, mentions that four members of the hierarchy wrote approbations of the work (*qarraẓa lahu*) (2:1098).

[35] Muḥammad Amīn b. Faḍl Allāh al-Muḥibbī, *Khulāṣat al-athar fi a'yān al-qarn al-ḥādī 'ashar* (Beirut: Dār al-Kutub al-'Ilmiyya, 2006), 1:527.

[36] See, for instance, Ekmeleddin İhsanoğlu, "The Initial Stage of the Historiography of Ottoman Medreses (1916–1965): The Era of Discovery and Construction," in *Science, Thechnology and Learning in the Ottoman Empire: Western Influence, Local Institutions, and the Transfer of Knowledge*, ed. Ekmeleddin İhsanoğlu (Burlington, VT: Ashgate/Variorum, 2004), 46–47; Ârif Bey, "Devlet-i Osmaniyye'nin Teessüs ve Takarrürü Devrinde İlim ve Ulema," *Darülfünün Edebiyat Fakültesi Mecmuası* 2 (1916): 137–44.

[37] Al-Ṭalūwī attaches the epithet "al-Maqdisī" to al-Tamīmī, indicating that the family originated from Jerusalem or its environs. See Darwīsh Muḥammad b. Aḥmad al-Ṭalūwī, *Sāniḥāt dumā al-qaṣr fī muṭāraḥāt banī al-'aṣr* (Beirut: 'Ālam al-Kutub, 1983), 1:136–39.

switched at some point to the Ḥanafī school. At a young age he moved to Cairo, where he studied with some of the city's most prominent Ḥanafīs, such as Zayn al-Dīn b. Nujaym and Ibn Ghānim al-Maqdisī. After he completed his studies, he was appointed to several teaching positions in the city, including to the prestigious professorship at the Shaykhūniyya madrasa. Apparently at some point prior to his departure to Istanbul for the first time, al-Tamīmī traveled to Bilād al-Shām.[38] During his visit to his native town of Gaza, he met the famous jurist Muḥammad al-Timurtāshī. In Damascus he befriended other scholars, such as Darwīsh Muḥammad b. Aḥmad al-Ṭalūwī (d. 1606), who would later be appointed the official muftī of the city, and the city's chief judge, Nâẓirzâde Ramażân Efendi (d. 1574 or 1575), whom he later met again in Cairo.[39] In 1574, soon after the ascension to the throne of Murâd III (r. 1574–95), al-Tamīmī traveled for the first time to the imperial capital, where he met the famous teacher of the sultan, Saʿd al-Dīn, whose scholarly merits and excellence al-Tamīmī praises at length. During their meeting, al-Tamīmī introduced some of his works to Saʿd al-Dīn.[40]

Following his return to Egypt, al-Tamīmī was appointed to the judgeship of several Egyptian towns, with a salary of 150 *akçe*, apparently as a reward for his scholarly excellence. In 1588, he was removed from office and was demoted to the judgeship of the Egyptian town of Ibrīm because of an obscure conflict with some high-ranking authorities in Egypt. Al-Tamīmī then decided to travel again to Istanbul with the hope of improving his lot by gaining the support of some senior officials in the imperial capital. Eventually he was appointed in 1596 as a judge in a small town in Lower Egypt.[41] During his stay there, he compiled his *ṭabaqāt* work, a project that he may have been planning for several years, at least since his first visit to Istanbul.[42]

During his visits to the core lands of the empire, he was apparently granted permission to consult some of the capital's libraries and, in addition to his encounter with Saʿd al-Dīn, had the opportunity to meet other senior members of the Ottoman learned hierarchy. In Rhodes, he met

38 Nevʿîzâde, *Hadâ'ik*, 408.

39 Taqiyy al-Dīn b. ʿAbd al-Qādir al-Tamīmī, *Al-Ṭabaqāt al-saniyya fī tarājim al-Ḥanafiyya*, Süleymaniye Library MS Aya Sofya 3295, 3:250; on Nâẓirzâde Ramazân Efendi, see Nevʿîzâde, *Hadâ'ik*, 240–41.

40 Nevʿîzâde, *Hadâ'ik*, 408. See also al-Tamīmī's account in al-Tamīmī, *al-Ṭabaqāt*, Süleymaniye Library MS Aya Sofya 3295, 330r.

41 Nevʿîzâde, *Hadâ'ik*, 408.

42 Al-Tamīmī, *al-Ṭabaqāt*, Süleymaniye Library MS Aya Sofya 3295, 330r.

Bahâeddînzâde Efendi, a high-ranking member of the Ottoman hierarchy who eventually was appointed as the justice of Anatolia and Rumeli.[43] There, he also met the jurist Çivizâde ʿAlî Efendi, the paternal cousin of the chief imperial muftī Çivizâde Meḥmed Efendi, while the former was the island's muftī and the professor of the Süleymânîye madrasa there. Eventually, Çivizâde ʿAlî Efendi was appointed to several prestigious positions, including to the judgeship of Istanbul.[44]

It is important to pay attention to the differences between al-Tamīmī's biography and Ibn Ṭūlūn's. While the latter remained in Damascus until his death, the former was interested in gaining the support of leading jurists in Istanbul in order to obtain a position. Al-Tamīmī's case is not unique, however. Toward the end of the sixteenth century, with the growing integration of the Arab lands into the empire and the emergence of the imperial capital as an important political and scholarly focal point in the eyes of many Arab subjects of the empire in general and religious scholars in particular, more and more jurists from the Arab lands traveled to Istanbul and contacted members, at times high-ranking ones, of the Ottoman imperial learned hierarchy.[45] Al-Tamīmī's Ṭabaqāt mirrors this social and political shift as well as the integration of some, definitely more than a few, Arab scholars and jurists into the Ottoman imperial framework. As we have seen in Chapter 1, for the purpose of this study, one may list the officially appointed muftīs from the Arab lands among these jurists. This integration, however, also implied a new understanding of the history and structure of the Ḥanafī school and of the relationship between the school and the Ottoman dynasty.

It seems appropriate to turn at this point to a closer reading of al-Tamīmī's *Ṭabaqāt*. As opposed to the other *ṭabaqāt* works examined so far, both in this chapter and in the previous one, al-Tamīmī's *Ṭabaqāt* is not meant to defend the authority of a single lineage within the Ḥanafī school. In the introduction, al-Tamīmī explains that his main intention is to record the history of the school, in light of the destruction

[43] Taqiyy al-Dīn b. ʿAbd al-Qādir al-Tamīmī, *al-Ṭabaqāt al-saniyya fī tarājim al-Ḥanafiyya* (Riyad: Dār al-Rifāʿī, 1983–89), 4:180–81. On Bahâeddîn Efendi, see also Nevʿîzâde, *Hadâʾik*, 305–6.

[44] Al-Tamīmī, *al-Ṭabaqāt*, Süleymaniye Library MS Aya Sofya 3295, 276r.

[45] In the seventeenth century, more and more jurists from the Arab lands entered the Ottoman madrasa system and subsequently entered the learned hierarchy's career tracks as judges and teachers. ʿAwḍ b. Yūsuf b. Muḥyī al-Dīn b. al-Ṭabbākh, for example, was born in Damascus but was also educated in the madrasas of Istanbul. Then he was appointed to several judgeships, including some fairly senior ones, such as the judgeship of Medina (Al-Muḥibbī, *Khulāṣat al-athar*, 3:224).

of numerous works from different parts of the Islamic world (mostly in Iraq and Transoxania) dealing with the Ḥanafī school. Al-Tamīmī makes an interesting connection between the destruction and loss of this knowledge and the spread of disputes and discords. Therefore, he continues, he decided to compile "a single comprehensive [*jāmiʿ*] volume that would comprise the biographies of the Ḥanafī masters and would include all the information [about them], their virtues, and merits."[46] In this respect, one may wonder whether al-Tamīmī's concern with the spread of discord does not reflect the sensibilities of members of the Ottoman imperial learned hierarchy and its appointees. As I have suggested in Chapter 1, jurists in the Mamluk period and many of their counterparts in the Arab provinces of the Ottoman Empire did not, for the most part, consider differences among competent jurists a major problem needing to be remedied. Officially appointed jurists, by contrast, found the multiplicity of the opinions and doctrines within the madhhab more disturbing.

Al-Tamīmī's sensitivity to the issue of discord among the jurists seems to go hand in hand with the role he ascribes to the Ottoman sultan and dynasty. Unlike Ibn Ṭūlūn, al-Tamīmī praises at length the Ottoman sultan at the time, Murâd III, and states that he compiled the work following the sultan's order (*ʿamiltu bi-rasmihi*). This order attracted the attention of later jurists and scholars. In one of the copies of Edirneli Kâmî's *Mahāmm al-fuqahāʾ* the copyist included a list of several important *ṭabaqāt* works. Next to the entry of al-Tamīmī's *Ṭabaqāt*, the author added that the work was compiled upon a request of Sultan Murâd III.[47] It seems that much like the attention his inclusion of members of the learned hierarchy in his *ṭabaqāt* received, the emphasis that both al-Tamīmī and later jurists placed on the role of the sultan in the production of this work reflects precisely how atypical it was in the circles from which he hailed. Indeed, as we have seen, other Ḥanafī jurists from the Arab lands did not stress the role of the sultan and the dynasty in their *ṭabaqāt* works and did not compile them for the suzerain. In other words, by mentioning the sultanic order and his obedience, al-Tamīmī declares his loyalty to the Ottoman dynasty and, even more so, his endorsement of the logic the lies behind the Ottoman development of an imperial learned hierarchy and a state madhhab. Furthermore, al-Tamīmī's appreciation, or at least acceptance, of the notion of a learned hierarchy appears in other parts of his work as

[46] Al-Tamīmī, *al-Ṭabaqāt*, 1:4–5.
[47] Edirneli Meḥmet Kâmî, *Mahāmm al-fuqahāʾ fī ṭabaqāt al-Ḥanafiyya*, Süleymaniye Library MS Pertev Paşa 495, 83v.

well. In his biography of Ḳara Çelebizâde Ḥüsâm Efendi, who served as the military justice (*ḳâḍîasker*) of Anatolia and Rumeli, al-Tamīmī criticizes him for attempting (albeit unsuccessfully) to renew an obsolete practice, "an Ottoman ḳânûn." According to this practice, the appointment of jurists who were not members of the learned hierarchy was permissible. This is an intriguing comment, for al-Tamīmī seems like an obvious beneficiary of Ḳara Çelebizâde's proposed reform. But al-Tamīmī, perhaps echoing the opinions of jurists he met on his journey to Istanbul, defends the boundaries of the Ottoman imperial learned hierarchy.[48]

His stated attempt to compile a comprehensive *ṭabaqāt* work of the Ḥanafī legal school and his seeming acceptance of the notion of an imperial learned hierarchy calls for scrutiny of the manner in which al-Tamīmī engages with other *ṭabaqāt* and biographical works. More specifically, how does al-Tamīmī understand the relationship between the different jurisprudential traditions within the school in the context of the Ottoman imperial framework at the time? This question seems central, for its unlikely that al-Tamīmī was unaware of the fact that one of the main objectives of the *ṭabaqāt* genre is to document the genealogy of certain legal arguments. Further, he must have known that the multiple views of the madhhab that coexisted throughout the empire and were reflected in some of the *ṭabaqāt* works were radically different from one another. Although al-Tamīmī did not consult either Kınalızâde's or Kefevî's (at the time recently completed) *ṭabaqāt* work, he was familiar with and used Taşköprüzâde's *Shaqā'iq*, a work that excludes Ḥanafī jurists who were not affiliated with the Ottoman learned hierarchy.[49] On the other hand, he does draw on Ibn Ṭūlūn's *al-Ghuraf*, which excludes the members of the imperial hierarchy. For this reason, his decision to compile "a comprehensive study of all the Ḥanafī masters" was novel and challenged the approach of members of the learned hierarchy, on the one hand, as well as that of Ibn Ṭūlūn, on the other.

Nevertheless, despite his claim to inclusivity, al-Tamīmī is highly selective in his treatment of sixteenth-century jurists. He does not include all

[48] Al-Tamīmī, *al-Ṭabaqāt*, 3:158–59. The second half of the sixteenth century witnessed several attempts to reform the career tracks of the Ottoman learned hierarchy. See Yasemin Beyazit, "Efforts to Reform Entry into the Ottoman *İlmiye* Career towards the End of the 16th Century: The 1598 Ottoman *İlmiye Kanunnamesi*," *Turcica* 44 (2012–13): 201–18.

[49] It is possible that al-Tamīmī did not know about Kınalızâde's *ṭabaqāt*, as he does not mention the work in his biography of Kınalızâde. Al-Tamīmī, *al-Ṭabaqāt*, Süleymaniye Library MS Aya Sofya 3295, 258r–261v.

the Ḥanafīs whose work he is familiar with. Although al-Tamīmī cites Ibn Ṭūlūn's *al-Ghuraf* quite frequently, Ibn Ṭūlūn does not have his own entry. Moreover, almost all the sixteenth-century scholars who appear in the work were affiliated with the Ottoman imperial learned hierarchy. In addition, most of the Ḥanafīs from the Arab lands that appear in the centennial biographical dictionaries of the sixteenth century are excluded. The few sixteenth-century Ḥanafīs from the Arab lands are, not coincidentally, Ibn Nujaym and Ibn Ghānim al-Maqdisī, al-Tamīmī's most prominent teachers.[50] Another important Arab Ḥanafī is Muḥammad al-Timurtāshī, a student of Ibn Nujaym and an eminent jurist in his own right.[51] It is noteworthy that both Ibn Nujaym and al-Timurtāshī were acknowledged as eminent scholars by members of the Ottoman imperial learned hierarchy and that some of their works entered the Ottoman imperial canon, as we shall see in the next chapter.[52]

Al-Tamīmī's treatment of the second half of the fifteenth century, however, differs from accounts that focus on members of the imperial hierarchy. Whereas, for example, Kınalızâde and Kefevî exclude late fifteenth-century scholars from the Mamluk lands, al-Tamīmī does include a biography of such leading Ḥanafīs, namely, Qāsim b. Quṭlūbughā and Amīn al-Dīn al-Aqsarā'ī. The inclusion of these scholars has important implications, for it reintroduces many Ḥanafīs from across the Arab provinces who studied with these jurists (or whose authority relied on these jurists) into the "Ḥanafī ecumene."

Al-Tamīmī's attempt to include the late fifteenth-century jurists reflects the tension that jurists from the Arab lands who wanted to integrate into the Ottoman imperial framework experienced. Entering the Ottoman learned hierarchy and its educational system meant that they were required to practically denounce jurists whose authority they respected. In his *Ṭabaqāt*, al-Tamīmī intended to ease this tension and to offer a more comprehensive view of the school, one that would bridge the gaps between the hierarchy-affiliated jurists' vision of their position within the Ḥanafī school and that of many of their counterparts from the Arab provinces. This attempt, however, confirms the existence of different views within the school.

Al-Tamīmī's project had limited success. As we shall see in the following chapters, Ḥanafī jurists from the Arab lands who obtained a state

[50] Nev'îzâde, *Hadâ'ik*, 408.

[51] Al-Tamīmī, *al-Ṭabaqāt*, Süleymaniye Library MS Aya Sofya 3295, 349r. al-Timurtāshī's other teacher, 'Abd al-'Āl, on the other hand, does not have an entry.

[52] In addition, Nev'îzâde includes in his *Hadâ'ik* Ibn Nujaym's biography (34–35).

appointment tended to follow al-Tamīmī's vision (or some variation of it). The imperial learned hierarchy, in turn, permitted its appointees throughout the Arab provinces to follow al-Tamīmī's vision. Kâmî's *Mahāmm al-fuqahā'*, by contrast, suggests that although members of the imperial learned hierarchy did consult sixteenth- and seventeenth-century texts and authorities from the Arab lands of the empire, they by and large rejected al-Tamīmī's perception of the school and preserved a fairly clear distinction between the branches within the school well into the eighteenth century.

Concluding Remarks

Juxtaposing the ṭabaqāt works compiled during the sixteenth and the seventeenth centuries, both in the core lands of the empire and in its Arab provinces, reveals important dynamics that accompanied the Ottoman conquest of the Arab lands and their subsequent incorporation. Interestingly enough, contemporary chronicles, whether from Damascus or the core lands of the empire, provide very little information about these dynamics. The *ṭabaqāt* corpus we have examined in this and the previous chapter illustrates how the conquest and integration of the Arab lands into the Ottoman imperial framework contributed to a clearer written articulation of different perceptions of the school of law and of the relationship between the Ottoman dynasty and the madhhab. Furthermore, even though it is likely that many of the ideas and materials that shaped the different works had been circulating in earlier decades and centuries, this corpus demonstrates that the articulations of the various branches within the school of law were an outcome of an ongoing dialogue between their respective proponents.

The conquest of the Arab lands and the need that each of the authors we have met felt, in its wake, to establish his authority within the school and to propagate his view of the school may explain the surge in the production of *ṭabaqāt* works in the second half of the sixteenth century (as well as the rise of the biographical dictionaries devoted to members of the imperial learned hierarchy). In his groundbreaking study of an early fifteenth-century Shāfiʿī *ṭabaqāt* work, Kevin Jaques has observed the relatively massive production of *ṭabaqāt* works in the fourteenth and fifteenth centuries. The sudden rise in the production of *ṭabaqāt* works, Jaques has convincingly argued, should be attributed to a sense of a crisis of authority shared by many jurists in the centuries following the catastrophic events of the thirteenth and fourteenth centuries – namely, the

Mongol invasions and the outbreak of the Black Death. These developments wreaked havoc across the eastern Islamic lands, costing the lives of many, including many jurists. For the community of jurists, the destruction inflicted by these events had an important ramification: with the death of the jurists, many chains of transmissions were potentially cut off. Therefore, there was a need to reconstruct these chains in order to consolidate the authority of late fourteenth-century and fifteenth-century jurists. That severe sense of crisis accompanied jurists well into the fifteenth century, leading many to record their jurisprudential and scholarly genealogies in *ṭabaqāt* works, which later circulated among their followers and peers.[53]

The connection between a crisis of authority and the production of *ṭabaqāt* works may account for the Ottoman rediscovery of the *ṭabaqāt* genre as well. To be sure, the late fifteenth century and the early sixteenth century or the early eighteenth century were not fraught with disasters and events of apocalyptic scale.[54] Although from time to time there were outbreaks of plagues and epidemics, they did not match the Black Death of the fourteenth century. In other words, in terms of the physical well-being and safety of the jurists, the reality of the late fifteenth century and the early sixteenth century was worlds apart from that of the late fourteenth century and the early fifteenth century. Still, the *ṭabaqāt* works seem to reflect a sense of challenged authority, similar to the one experienced by fourteenth- and fifteenth-century jurists. On the one hand, as we have seen in Chapter 2, the *ṭabaqāt* corpus reflects the attempt made by some jurists, mostly members of the imperial learned hierarchy, to express and consolidate the connection between the Ottoman dynasty, members of the imperial hierarchy, and a particular branch within the madhhab. On the other, it reveals the attempt of jurists who were not affiliated with the hierarchy to establish their autonomy in regulating the structure and the doctrine of the branch within the school to which they claimed affiliation (as in Ibn Ṭūlūn's case).

53 R. Kevin Jaques, *Authority, Conflict, and the Transmission of Diversity in Medieval Islamic Law* (Leiden: Brill, 2006), 17–23, 255–79.

54 There were, of course, plagues and other natural disasters throughout the sixteenth and seventeenth centuries, but none of them reached the scale of the Black Death of the fourteenth century. On the plague in the Ottoman Empire, see Nükhet Varlık, "Disease and Empire: A History of Plague Epidemics in the Early Modern Ottoman Empire (1453–1600)" (PhD diss., University of Chicago, 2008). For a list of natural disasters in seventeenth- and eighteenth-century Syria, see Yaron Ayalon, "Plagues, Famines, Earthquakes: The Jews of Ottoman Syria and Natural Disasters" (PhD diss., Princeton University, 2009), 240–45.

But the *ṭabaqāt* literature does not solely tell a story of challenge and competition. The *ṭabaqāt* works of both al-Tamīmī in the sixteenth century and Kâmî in the early eighteenth century point to a gradual and selective co-optation and integration. Al-Tamīmī's work mirrors the attempts made by some Ḥanafī jurists from the Arab lands to combine the Ottoman genealogy of the Ḥanafī school with the one that prevailed in the former Mamluk territories. It is important to stress, however, that not all the jurists from the Arab lands followed this path, and some were reluctant to integrate the Ottoman vision of the Ḥanafī school into their own. It is worth pointing out that Kâmî's incorporation of eminent jurists and important jurisprudential texts from the Arab lands of the empire into his composition indicates that a similar process took place among members of the Ottoman learned hierarchy. At the same time, despite Kâmî's inclusion of jurists from the Arab lands, he was still reluctant to abandon the particular genealogy of the learned hierarchy within the Ḥanafī school that his predecessors advanced. But perhaps more telling here is the fact that he refused to abandon the connection with the Ottoman dynasty. In any case, as we have seen in the previous chapter, the adaptations the respective views of the schools underwent over the decades suggest that both synchronic and diachronic factors shaped the different branches within the school of law: on the one hand, the chain(s) of transmission that situated the branch within the history of the Ḥanafī school were crucial, but, on the other hand, jurists were willing to incorporate selectively authorities (and texts) from other branches without establishing their intellectual genealogy within the school.

Returning to the dialogic nature of the encounter between the different perceptions of the school of law, it is noteworthy that the dialogue was reflected in the decision of all the parties involved to follow the conventions of the same genre (despite certain modifications) and to compile their work in Arabic. There seems to be two main explanations for this decision. First, it appears that followers of each of the traditions within the school wanted the adherents of the others to read their works. Second, the members of the imperial learned hierarchy who authored the *ṭabaqāt* works, along with Taşköprüzâde and the authors of the supplements to his *Shaqāʾiq*, clearly strove to link their literary-jurisprudential production to medieval Islamic (Arabic) jurisprudential-historiographical traditions, with the intention of establishing and propagating their authority. It is precisely in this adoption and adaptation of medieval Arabic genres, however, that the tensions between the worldview of the medieval authors and that of their counterparts who were affiliated with the Ottoman enterprise become most evident. While accepting some of the fundamental notions underlying the genres, the works authored by members of the imperial learned hierarchy diverge from some of the genre conventions in significant ways. Most notably, as opposed to the medieval works, in both the *ṭabaqāt* works compiled by members of the Ottoman imperial learned hierarchy and the *Shaqā'iq*, the Ottoman dynasty and its hierarchy serve as the main narrative axis.

The rise in the production of the *ṭabaqāt* works and the appearance of the *Shaqā'iq* and its numerous supplements in the second half of the sixteenth century may serve as yet another indicator of the consolidation of the Ottoman Empire in that period. The second half of the sixteenth century witnessed the integration and unification of several monetary zones, the first wave of plague (1570–1600) to simultaneously hit the core lands of the empire and the provinces, and the rise of a distinctive Ottoman artistic language.[55] It is quite likely that the integration of the Arab provinces into the empire and the increasing interactions between the different scholarly circles and traditions throughout the Ottoman domains spurred different jurists to document their intellectual genealogies in general, and contributed to a clearer formulation of an Ottoman Ḥanafī school in particular.

As we have seen throughout this and the previous chapters, the *ṭabaqāt* works were instrumental in defining a repertory of legal arguments and texts that jurists were expected to consult in their rulings and writing. For this reason, the genealogies recorded in these *ṭabaqāt* works form the basis of – and in turn document – the emergence of jurisprudential "textual communities" within the Ḥanafī school and across the empire. It is to these communities that we now turn.

[55] Baki Tezcan, "The Ottoman Monetary Crisis of 1585 Revisited," *Journal of the Economic and Social History of the Orient* 52 (2009): 460–504; Varlık, *Disease and Empire*; Gülru Necipoğlu, "A Kânûn for the State, a Canon for the Arts: Conceptualizing the Classical Synthesis of Ottoman Art and Architecture," in *Soliman le Magnifique et son temps*, ed. Gilles Veinstein (Paris: La documentation français, 1992), 195–213.

4

Books of High Repute

On Saturday, the thirteenth of Dhū al-Ḥijja 995 (November 14, 1587), more than seven decades after the Ottoman conquest of the Arab lands, at the al-Kilāsa madrasa in Damascus, the sixteenth-century Damascene jurist Nūr al-Dīn Maḥmūd b. Barakāt al-Bāqānī (d. 1594) completed his commentary,[1] which he had started earlier that year, on one of the most important and popular jurisprudential manuals in the Ottoman domains: Ibrāhīm al-Ḥalabī's (d. 1549 or 1550) sixteenth-century *Multaqā al-abḥur*.[2] In his introduction, al-Bāqānī claims that he decided to compile the commentary upon the request of his Damascene peers, since he was the only one to have read parts of the *Multaqā* with Muḥammad al-Bahnasī (d. 1578 or 1579), an eminent Ḥanafī jurist and muftī (though not officially appointed) in Damascus.[3]

[1] Although he was not one of the most prominent jurists of Damascus, al-Bāqānī was significant enough to have his biography included in four of the most important centennial biographical dictionaries of the seventeenth century. The late seventeenth-century biographer Muḥammad Amīn b. Faḍl Allāh al-Muḥibbī states that al-Bāqānī taught in several madrasas in Damascus and in a teaching niche at the Umayyad Mosque, where he also served as a preacher. Despite numerous positions, it seems that al-Bāqānī gained most of his considerable wealth from selling books. Muḥammad Amīn b. Faḍl Allāh al-Muḥibbī, *Khulāṣat al-athar fī a'yān al-qarn al-ḥādī 'ashar* (Beirut: Dār al-Kutub al-'Ilmiyya, 2006), 4:312. See also Najm al-Dīn Muḥammad b. Muḥammad al-Ghazzī, *Luṭf al-samar wa-qaṭf al-thamar* (Damascus: Wizārat al-Thaqāfa wa'l-Irshād al-Qawmī, 1982), 2:638–39; al-Ḥasan b. Muḥammad al-Būrīnī, *Tarājim al-a'yān min abnā' al-zamān*, Staatsbibliothek zu Berlin MS Weetzstein II 29, 179r–179v; Muṣṭafā b. Fatḥ Allāh al-Ḥamawī, *Fawā'id al-irtiḥāl wa-natā'ij al-safar fī akhbār al-qarn al-ḥādī 'ashar* (Beirut: Dār al-Nawādir, 2011), 6:118–19.

[2] Maḥmūd b. Barakāt al-Bāqānī, *Majrā al-anhur 'alā Multaqā al-abḥur*, Süleymaniye Library MS Pertev Paşa 196, 2v.

[3] Al-Bāqānī was a prolific writer: in addition to his commentary on the *Multaqā*, he compiled a commentary on *al-Nuqāya* by 'Ubayd Allāh b. Mas'ūd al-Maḥbūbī, a supplement

Al-Bāqānī's commentary, entitled *Majrā al-anhur ʿalā Multaqā al-abḥur*, was one of approximately seventy commentaries on the *Multaqā* compiled in the core lands of the empire and its Arab provinces over the course of the sixteenth through the eighteenth centuries.[4] Of particular interest for our purpose is the reception of al-Bāqānī's commentary. At first, the scholars of Damascus looked at this commentary disparagingly, perhaps because of what the seventeenth-century Damascene historian Najm al-Dīn al-Ghazzī chronicler considered the author's infamous frivolity. Nevertheless, the work's fate changed dramatically after, in the words of the Damascene chronicler, "some of the most eminent jurists in Rūm [*akābir al-mawālī bi'l-Rūm*] asked for a copy [of the work]."[5] In the following decades, al-Bāqānī's commentary was apparently quite well received in scholarly circles both in his native town of Damascus and in the imperial capital, as later commentaries on the *Multaqā* that cite al-Bāqānī's attest.[6] In Damascus, for example, ʿAlā' al-Dīn al-Ḥaṣkafī, whom we have already met in Chapter 1, relied on al-Bāqānī's commentary in his commentary on the *Multaqā*, and in the central lands, slightly earlier, the mid-seventeenth-century eminent member of the imperial learned hierarchy ʿAbdurraḥmân b. Muḥammad Şeyḫîzâde (d. 1667 or 1668) also cited al-Bāqānī's commentary in his acclaimed commentary on al-Ḥalabī's work.[7]

(*takmila*) on Ibrāhīm b. Muḥammad b. al-Shiḥna's *Lisān al-ḥukkām fī maʿrifat al-aḥkām*, and another supplement on Zayn al-Dīn b. Nujaym's *al-Baḥr al-rā'iq*, as well as an abridged version of the *Baḥr* in one volume. Al-Muḥibbī, *Khulāṣat al-athar*, 4:311–12. Al-Bāqānī's teacher, al-Bahnasī, also had started his own commentary on the *Multaqā al-abḥur*, which he never completed because of his death eight or nine years before al-Bāqānī sat down to write his own commentary. Najm al-Dīn Muḥammad b. Muḥammad al-Bahnasī, *Sharḥ Multaqā al-abḥur*, New York Public Library MS M&A 51893A. The commentary is incomplete and ends with *Bāb Khiyār al-shurūṭ*. On al-Bahnasī, see Najm al-Dīn Muḥammad b. Muḥammad al-Ghazzī, *al-Kawākib al-sā'ira fī aʿyān al-qarn al-ʿāshira* (Beirut: Jāmiʿat Bayrut al-Amrikiyya, 1945–58), 3:13–15; Aḥmad b. Muḥammad b. al-Mullā al-Ḥaṣkafī, *Mutʿat al-adhhān min tamattuʿ bi'l-iqrān bayna tarājim al-shuyūkh wa'l-aqrān* (Beirut: Dār al-Ṣādir, 1999), 2:876–878.

4 For a comprehensive list of the extant commentaries on *Multaqā al-abḥur*, see Şükrü Selim Has, "A Study of Ibrahim al-Halebi with Special Reference to the Multaqa" (PhD diss., University of Edinburgh, 1981), 216–64. For the significance of the *Multaqā*, see Şükrü Selim Has, "The Use of Multaqa'l-Abḥur in the Ottoman Madrasas and in Legal Scholarship," *Osmanlı Araştırmaları* 7/8 (1988): 393–418.

5 Al-Ghazzī, *Luṭf al-samar*, 2:638–39.

6 The work exists in thirteen copies in libraries across Istanbul alone. Kefevî's *Katā'ib*, just for comparison's sake, exists in eleven copies in libraries throughout the city. Ebû's-Suʿûd Efendi's *fatāwā* collection, a widely cited work, exists in approximately fifty copies in libraries across Istanbul.

7 Muḥammad b. ʿAlī b. Muḥammad al-Ḥaṣanī al-ʿAlā' al-Ḥaṣkafī, *al-Durr al-muntaqā fī sharḥ al-Multaqā* (Beirut: Dār al-Kutub al-ʿIlmiyya, 1998), 1:146, 184, 194, 322; 2:42,

The history of al-Bāqānī's work, as this chapter hopes to demonstrate, is not unique. Over the course of the sixteenth and the seventeenth centuries (and possibly later), other jurisprudential texts underwent a similar review procedure. More broadly, its history reflects a concerted effort on behalf of the Ottoman dynasty, and particularly on behalf of the imperial learned hierarchy, to define a corpus of jurisprudential texts – what I call throughout this chapter the imperial jurisprudential canon – that members of the imperial learned hierarchy were to consult in their teachings and rulings.

It is not fully clear when the demarcation of an imperial jurisprudential canon assumed the institutional features that the aforementioned episode reveals. Jurists who were affiliated with the Ottoman enterprise in the fourteenth and the fifteenth centuries most probably consulted texts they considered authoritative and canonical. The jurisprudential texts, however, were not canonized in an official procedure. Canonization through an official procedure apparently reached maturity around the mid-sixteenth century, as indicated by an edict issued in 1556 by the Ottoman sultan Süleymân Ḳânûnî in which he lists the texts students of the imperial madrasa system were to study. In the following decades and centuries, the authority to canonize jurisprudential texts was conferred on the leading jurists of the imperial learned hierarchy, and particularly on the chief imperial muftī.

The emergence of the chief imperial jurisconsult as the gatekeeper of the imperial canon during the second half of the sixteenth century is significant, for it links the emergence of the imperial canon to the consolidation of the learned hierarchy and to the rise of the *şeyḫulislâm* as the

170, 260, 265, 330, 337, 365, 397, 429, 436; 3:154, 162, 417, 423; 4:56, 96, 112, 157, 297, 406, 459, 470, 481. ʿAbd al-Raḥmān b. Muḥammad b. Sulimān Shaykhīzāde (Şeyḫîzâde), *Majmaʿ al-anhur fī sharḥ Multaqā al-abḥur* (Beirut: Dār al-Kutub al-ʿIlmiyya, 1998), 1:316, 336, 553; 2:188, 345. It should be noted that in some cases Şeyḫîzâde has some reservations concerning al-Bāqānī's opinions and that al-Ḥaṣkafī cites al-Bāqānī's commentary much more frequently than his colleague Şeyḫîzâde does. Şeyḫîzâde's commentary, however, was fairly well known. He presented this commentary to the sultan in August 21, 1666, and the sultan, as a token of his appreciation, ordered the appointment of Şeyḫîzâde, until then the chief justice of Anatolia, to the chief judgeship of Rumeli. See Abdurrahman Abdi Paşa, *Abdurrahman Abdi Paşa Vekâyiʾ-Nâmesi* (Istanbul: Çamlıca, 2008), 246. On Şeyḫîzâde's appointment to *ḳâḍîaskerlik* of Rumeli, see Defterdar Sarı Mehmet Paşa, *Zübde-i Vekayiât* (Ankara: Türk Tarih Kurumu Basımevi, 1995), 261. The seventeenth-century chronicler and bibliographer Kâtip Çelebi also mentions al-Bāqānī's commentary and even records his introduction in his *Kashf al-Ẓunūn*. Kâtip Çelebi, *Kashf al-ẓunūn fī asāmī al-kutub wa'l-funūn* (Istanbul: Milli Eğitim Basımevi, 1971), 2:1814–15.

head of the learned hierarchy. Moreover, as we have observed in Chapter 2, the consolidation of the learned hierarchy over the course of the sixteenth century was paralleled by the articulation of the hierarchy's intellectual genealogies within the Ḥanafī tradition. One of the goals of the *ṭabaqāt* was to canonize specific legal arguments and texts by documenting their genealogy and establishing their authority. Moreover, the quite successful attempt to define an imperial jurisprudential canon was inextricably linked to the growing interest of the imperial learned hierarchy (and, more generally, of the Ottoman dynasty) in regulating the structure of its branch of the Ḥanafī school of law, including the doctrines its members were to apply.

The rise of the imperial jurisprudential canon took place against the background of the conquest of the Arab lands and their gradual incorporation into the empire. In fact, as was the case with the *ṭabaqāt* compilations, it was precisely the incorporation of the Arab lands that spurred members of the imperial learned hierarchy to specify what books were to be consulted as part of the imperial canon. From their vantage point, the incorporation of the Arab lands also meant that other Ḥanafī scholars, scholarly traditions, and jurisprudential texts became part of the imperial scholarly and jurisprudential landscape. In this new reality, jurists affiliated with the imperial learned hierarchy felt the need to defend their position and the authority of certain jurisprudential arguments and texts within the expanding imperial framework. The emergence of an imperial jurisprudential canon supplemented other textual and institutional practices and contributed to the emergence of an "establishment consciousness" among members of the learned hierarchy.

Situating the rise of an imperial jurisprudential canon against the backdrop of the incorporation of the Arab lands into the empire requires clarifying the relation between the canon endorsed by members of the imperial learned hierarchy and the canons of other scholarly, and particularly Ḥanafī, circles throughout the empire. Moreover, it calls for a comparison of an entire set of textual practices that accompanied and shaped the canonization practices of the different textual communities across the Ottoman realms.[8] As we will see in the following discussion,

[8] The phrase "textual communities" was coined by Brian Stock. Although the communities discussed here are somewhat different from those studied by Stock, in some important respects the concept is applicable here as well. In particular, texts played a pivotal role, similar to the one Stock describes, in organizing scholarly circles across the Ottaman Empire, and in defining the internal and external relationships of their members. Brian Stock, *The Implications of Literacy: Written Language and Models of Interpretation in the Eleventh and Twelfth Centuries* (Princeton, NJ: Princeton University Press, 1987), 90–91.

the organization of the scholarly community and its modes of transmission of knowledge (and texts) are closely related to its canonization procedures. The hierarchical and fairly centralized nature of the imperial hierarchy, and particularly of its educational system, enabled the chief imperial jurisconsult to instruct his subordinates which texts (or, more precisely, which parts of the texts) to consult. Other scholarly circles throughout the Arab lands, which were considerably less hierarchical, developed their canons on the basis of a consensus among their prominent members.

The relations and "dialogues" between the canons cast light on understudied dynamics that accompanied the incorporation of the Arab lands into the empire. Particularly, these relations uncover interesting aspects of the dynamics between different scholarly traditions within the Ḥanafī school and between various learning centers throughout the empire, such as Istanbul, Cairo, and Damascus. Moreover, the change in the composition of the different Ḥanafī jurisprudential canons enables us to explore the exchange, circulation, and co-optation of texts, arguments, and authorities across the Ottoman domains: while members of the imperial hierarchy consulted, albeit selectively, works authored by jurists from the Arab lands of the empire, some of their colleagues from the Arab lands, especially those who held a state appointment, began, over the course of the late sixteenth century and the seventeenth century, to consult jurisprudential texts compiled by their hierarchy-affiliated counterparts. In short, from the perspective of the madhhab and its structure, these "dialogues" and exchanges reveal the relative flexibility of some of the branches within the Ḥanafī madhhab to incorporate new texts and arguments from other branches.

This chapter is a preliminary foray into the history of the imperial jurisprudential canon. It is hoped that some of the points raised in the following pages will be further explored in future studies. Most notably, the composition of the canons and the change they underwent over time still await systematic study. Furthermore, much more work remains to be done on the ways in which the different canons were used, read, and applied. Here my goal is much more modest, and I am mostly interested in illustrating the importance of these questions for understanding the experience of jurists and religious scholars, and for understanding the different perceptions within the Ḥanafī school of law that coexisted throughout the empire.

A Methodological Note on Textual Canons and Their Formation

Drawing mainly on the insights and findings of students of literary and biblical canons, the scholarship on canon formation and canonization in the Islamic tradition has been growing steadily in the last decades.[9] My intention in this section is not to survey the historiography of canon formation in various Islamic contexts. Instead, I am interested in discussing some of the main issues and approaches that have shaped the study of canonization of texts in different Islamic societies and are relevant to our larger discussion. Since there are different sorts of canons (such as scriptural, literary, artistic, and legal), I will focus here mostly on legal/jurisprudential canons.

Two concepts are central in the historiography on textual canons, legal or otherwise, and their formation: canonical texts and the community of "users" (readers, scholars, and interpreters). In his seminal study of canonization in the Jewish tradition, Moshe Halbertal offers an incisive definition of "canonical texts." Halbertal's observations with regard to the Jewish jurisprudential tradition are pertinent to a large extent to the Islamic jurisprudential tradition as well, as both consider themselves text centered. The phrase "canonical text," Halbertal asserts, denotes the special status of a specific text. "Canonical texts," however, may function in different ways. For our purpose, I am specifically interested in what Halbertal calls normative texts. Texts that form a normative canon, such as scriptures and legal codes, are obeyed and interpreted, and they often constitute part of a curriculum. These texts establish what Halbertal terms a "formative canon," and, he explains, "they provide a society or a profession with a shared vocabulary." By adhering to this normative canon, a society or profession defines itself as text-centered. In other words, membership in this community is predicated on familiarity with these normative texts. It is important to stress the complex relations among various canonical texts of a certain tradition. While all the texts that constitute a canon are considered canonical, not all of them enjoy equal status; a text may be obeyed and followed, for instance, but not necessarily taught as part of a curriculum.[10]

[9] For a comprehensive survey on the different currents in canon studies in general and in the Islamic tradition in particular, see Jonathan Brown, *The Canonization of al-Bukhārī and Muslim* (Leiden: Brill, 2007), chap. 2.

[10] Moshe Halbertal, *People of the Book: Canon, Meaning, and Authority* (Cambridge, MA: Harvard University Press, 1997), 3–4. Canonical texts may also serve as "paradigmatic

In short, canons fulfill a dual function in the formation of a community. First, they demarcate the community's boundaries. Those who reject a particular canon (or follow another one) may be excluded from the community galvanized around it. At the same time, the canon offers the community a shared set of texts, which are referred to by community members to regulate and justify their actions, even when their interpretations of these texts may follow different hermeneutic principles and produce conflicting views. In this sense, canons contribute to the cohesiveness of the text-centered community.

This is not to say, however, that every member of a text-centered community enjoys equal status. As with the canonical texts, not every interpretation is equally accepted by the members of the community. Therefore, text-centered communities have to develop mechanisms to determine who has the authority to define the boundaries of the canon and to interpret canonical texts. It is for this reason that canonization is often accompanied by strong acts of censorship of different sorts that are meant to determine and regulate the range of legitimate interpretation.[11]

Turning to the particularities of canonization in the Sunnī tradition, two important studies, those of Brannon Wheeler and Jonathan Brown, inspired my inquiry in this chapter. Because of their importance to the discussion in the following sections, it is worth devoting a few words to how these studies approach the issue of canon and canonization.

Brannon Wheeler's study perceives the canon first and foremost as an interpretive standard. According to Wheeler, in the Ḥanafī context, the canon functions as a "device to promote the pedagogic agenda of those who use certain texts to represent the authority of the past."[12] Moreover, the canon is a set of hermeneutic principles or precedents for interpreting the revelation (i.e., the Qur'ān).[13] Wheeler's description of how the canon was employed in the postclassical period is particularly relevant. In this period, that is, from the fifth/eleventh century on, Ḥanafī jurists were particularly concerned with reconstructing the "hermeneutical moves" of their predecessors. Their main goal was to

examples of aesthetic value and achievement." These texts are not necessarily the best works of a specific genre but manifest its most typical conventions. Despite this distinction, a text may be both normative and exemplary (the Qur'ān, for instance, is both).

11 Halbertal, *People of the Book*, 6–10.

12 Brannon M. Wheeler, *Applying the Canon in Islam: The Authorization and Maintenance of Interpretive Reasoning in Ḥanafī Scholarship* (Albany: State University of New York Press, 1996), 2.

13 Ibid., 9–10.

comment on the work of previous jurists to illustrate how interpretive reasoning was epitomized in their opinions, so it could be learned and reproduced.[14] Wheeler, however, seems to disregard the possibility that jurists of the school's postclassical age actively shaped the boundaries of the canon they were consulting, and, by doing so, defined the tradition with which they claimed affiliation. This, I think, may be attributed to Wheeler's focus on canon as a criterion of interpretation, while, in Jonathan Brown's words, "downplaying the importance of the canon as a set of representative texts."[15]

Brown's fascinating study of the canonization of the *ḥadīth* collections of al-Bukhārī and Muslim traces the gradual process through which these collections became recognized as authoritative throughout the Sunnī world. Since Brown begins his account before the compilation of al-Bukhārī's and Muslim's collections, his study pays close attention to the reasons for the canonization of these particular texts. Unlike Wheeler, who accepts the canonical status of the texts as his departure point, Brown succeeds in demonstrating several important aspects of the canonization process that are by and large absent from the former's account. First, by focusing on the "canonical culture" that surrounded these texts, he shows how these specific collections gained their prominent status among medieval Muslims, with the "canonical culture" training the readers/listeners to "interpret a canonical text in a reverential manner and with suitable awe." This historiographical approach is especially fruitful, for it emphasizes the factors that shape the canonization of a particular text in a concrete historical setting. To put it differently, Brown's analysis stresses the existence of vying alternative traditions and the role the community of "users" played in shaping tradition.[16]

Both studies, despite their different methodological approaches, consider the canon and the canonization procedures internal concerns of the community of jurists and scholars. Members of the ruling elite, the ruling dynasty, or the "state" are absent from these accounts. This absence reflects a reality very different from the Ottoman context in which, as this chapter sets out to demonstrate, the dynasty and the sultan were much more prominent in the formation of the canon.

[14] Ibid., 169.
[15] Brown, *Canonization*, 33.
[16] Ibid., 42–46.

"The Reliable Books": The Imperial Hierarchy and Its Canon Consciousness

In his account of the removal of the chief imperial muftī Bostânzâde Meḥmed Efendi from office in 1592, the seventeenth-century Ottoman historian Ḥasan Beyzâde (d. 1636 or 1637) argues that one of the accusations raised against Bostânzâde was that his rulings contradicted the texts (*mütûn*) of the Ḥanafī school. Ḥasan Beyzâde did not specify what these texts were, which suggests that he assumed his readers, many of whom were probably members of scholarly and judicial circles in the central lands of the empire (and possibly beyond), knew which texts constituted the "texts" of the school. Moreover, the assumption underlying Ḥasan Beyzâde's account is that the authoritative texts reflect the sound opinions of the Ḥanafī school at the time.[17] The concept of "[authoritative] texts," then, suggests the existence of a specific text-centered epistemology or "canon consciousness" among members of the imperial learned hierarchy.

The notion that texts preserve the lore of the Ḥanafī school of law can be found in many pre-Ottoman legal manuals and works. In fact, as several modern scholars have pointed out, the formation of the Islamic schools of law from their early stages was inextricably linked to the emergence of respective textual corpuses that recorded the opinions of leading authorities of the evolving schools and served as repositories of guiding hermeneutic principles for interpreting the revelation.[18] In the post-formative period (from the tenth and eleventh centuries onward), as Wheeler has elegantly shown, jurisprudential texts became even more central as didactic tools to "teach students the epistemological foundations of the school by delineating the interpretive link between Ḥanafī scholarship and the revelation."[19] For example, the early fifteenth-century Ḥanafī jurist ʿAlī b. Khalīl al-Ṭarābulusī, in his *Muʿīn al-ḥukkām*, dedicates a

17 Ḥasan Beyzâde Aḥmed Paşa, *Ḥasan Beyzâde Târîḫi* (Ankara: Türk Tarih Kurumu Basımevi, 2004), 2:371. The seventeenth-century historian and bibliographer Kâtip Çelebi draws on Beyzâde's account. See Kâtip Çelebi, *Fezleke-i Tarîḫ* (Istanbul: Cerîde-i Ḥavâdis Maṭbaʿası, 1870–71), 1:3.

18 Norman Calder, *Studies in Early Muslim Jurisprudence* (Oxford: Clarendon Press, 1993); Wheeler, *Applying the Canon*; Jonathan E. Brockopp, *Early Maliki Law: Ibn ʿAbd al-Hakam and His Major Compendium of Jurisprudence* (Leiden: Brill, 2000); Devin Stewart, "The Structure of the *Fihrist*: Ibn al-Nadim as Historian of Islamic Legal and Theological Schools," *International Journal of Middle East Studies* 39 (2007): 369–87; Ahmed El Shamsy, *The Canonization of Islamic Law*.

19 Wheeler, *Applying the Canon*, 168.

few passages to the notion of the "books of the school" (*kutub al-madhhab*). Moreover, he even explicitly states that "at this time" a jurist is allowed to cite these books even if their content was not transmitted to him through a documented chain of transmission.[20]

This understanding of the function of the jurisprudential texts in the context of the emergence and function of the madhhab also appears in Kemâlpaşazâde's treatise on the structure the Ḥanafī school (discussed in Chapter 2). According to this treatise, many of the jurists included in the sixth rank (out of seven) in his classification of the authorities of the Ḥanafī school, most of whom lived in the thirteenth and fourteenth centuries, compiled authoritative legal works (*al-mutūn al-muʿtabara min al-mutaʾakhkhirīn*). Likewise, Kınâlızâde, in his introduction to his *ṭabaqāt* work, remarks that teachings of the Ḥanafī school were transmitted until they "ended up preserved in the pages of the books ... [and] these books circulate widely and are accepted among the pious, and are consulted by judge[s] and muftī[s] [*yustaʿān bi-ha*]." Furthermore, he recommends that the followers of the school (*muqallidūn*), "by a way of precaution at a time like this, should not act according to every book and chain of transmission [*isnād*], but [only] according to the books of high repute [*al-kutub al-muʿtabara*] [which were authored] by the best imāms."[21]

There is a clear continuity, then, in the manner in which jurists who were affiliated with the Ottoman imperial learned hierarchy, such as Kemâlpaşazâde and Kınâlızâde, and their earlier counterparts, such as al-Ṭarābulusī, perceived the role jurisprudential texts played in articulating the hermeneutic principles that organized the legal school. Nevertheless, there are two differences between the practice of earlier centuries (and in later centuries, too, in some of the scholarly circles across the empire, mostly in its Arab provinces) and that of the sixteenth-century Ottoman imperial learned hierarchy: in earlier centuries, states and sovereigns did not play a significant doctrinal role in determining which texts should be considered a hermeneutic standard to follow, nor was the idea of an official, clearly defined list of "texts/books of high repute" in circulation.

[20] ʿAlāʾ al-Dīn Abī al-Ḥasan ʿAlī b. Khalīl al-Ṭarābulusī, *Muʿīn al-ḥukkām fī mā yataraddadu bayna al-khaṣmayn min al-aḥkām* (Cairo: Muṣṭafā al-Bābī al-Ḥalabī, 1973), 28. This view appeared as early as the eleventh century: Baber Johansen, "Formes de langage et fonctions publiques: stéréopypes, témoins et offices dans la preuve par l'écrit en droit musulman," *Arabica* 44, no. 3 (1997): 341.

[21] Kınalızâde ʿAlāʾ al-Dīn ʿAlī Çelebī Amr Allāh b. ʿAbd al-Qādir al-Ḥumaydī al-Rūmī al-Ḥanafī, *Ṭabaqāt al-Ḥanafiyya* (Amman: Dār Ibn al-Jawzī, 2003–4), 92–93, 97.

According to Konrad Hirschler, who studied reading practices in the Ayyubid and Mamluk periods, the concept of "books of high repute" was rarely and very loosely used.[22]

It is difficult to pinpoint the exact date for the introduction of an official list of "texts" that supposedly epitomize the madhhab in the Ottoman realms, but the concept of "texts of high repute" was clearly in circulation as early as the first decades of the sixteenth century (and perhaps even earlier).[23] In any case, from the sixteenth century, references to the "authoritative texts" or "books of high repute" (*al-kutub al-muʿtabara/al-kutub al-muʿtamada*) became quite frequent in jurisprudential works compiled by members of the imperial learned hierarchy, in collections of legal opinions issued by the officially appointed muftī, and in imperial edicts.[24] The seventeenth-century chronicler, scholar, and bibliographer Kâtip Çelebi (d. 1657), for example, refers in his bibliographical compilation *Kashf al-ẓunūn* to canonical jurisprudential texts and specifies which texts should be consulted. In the entry dedicated to a fifteenth-century work, for instance, he states that this work is "a famous book that circulates widely among the judges and muftīs [i.e., members of the imperial learned hierarchy]." On the other hand, he comments that the sixteenth-century jurist Birgivî Meḥmet Efendi (d. 1573) argued that a certain thirteenth-century text was not one of the books of high repute (*laysat min al-kutub al-muʿtabara*) because it did not conform to the accepted principles of jurisprudence (*fiqh*).[25]

22 Konrad Hirschler, *The Written Word in the Medieval Arabic Lands: A Social and Cultural History of Reading Practices* (Edinburgh: Edinburgh University Press, 2012). I thank Prof. Hirschler for confirming that the term was rarely and loosely used in the scholarly circles of Ayyubid and Mamluk Egypt and Palestine (personal correspondence with Konrad Hirschler).

23 In the catalog of Bâyezîd II's library, which was compiled around 1502–3, the concept appears once. Anonymous, *Asmāʾ al-kutub al-khizāna al-ʿāmira*, Magyar Tudományos Akadémia (Könyvtár, Hungary) MS Török F 59, 6.

24 Several phrases are used to refer to the books that constitute the imperial jurisprudential canon: "books/texts of high repute" (*al-kutub/al-mutūn al-muʿtabara*), the most commonly used phrase; "reliable books" (*al-kutub/al-mutūn al-muʿtamada*); and, more rarely, "the famous book" (*al-kutub al-mashhūra*).

25 Kâtip Çelebi, *Kashf al-ẓunūn*, 2:1225. Kâtip Çelebi is also careful to draw his reader's attention to disagreements among members of the imperial learned hierarchy concerning the authoritative status of certain canonical texts. For example, when discussing Najm al-Dīn Mukhtār b. Maḥmūd al-Ghazmīnī al-Zāhidī's (d. 1259) *Qunyat al-munya li-tatmīm al-Ghunya*, he warns his reader that Birgîvi Meḥmet Efendi (d. 1573) considered the text somewhat problematic because of al-Zāhidī's Muʿtazilī leanings, despite the fact that other jurists who were affiliated with the learned hierarchy considered the *Qunya* reliable (ibid., 2:1357). Kâtip Çelebi's comments should serve as a good reminder

Despite the frequency with which the term "texts of high repute" is employed, few sources provide a systematic and comprehensive list of the texts that fall under this title. One of the few exceptions is an imperial edict (*fermân*) issued in 1556 by Sultan Süleymân Ḳânûnî. In this edict, the sultan lists the texts in various religious and judicial disciplines that students in the Ottoman madrasa system were to study.[26]

It is worth dwelling on the role the sultan played in the Ottoman canonization procedures. The 1556 edict illustrates how the sultan regulated the imperial canon. In the ensuing decades, as we shall see, when the chief imperial jurisconsult was appointed by the sultan to preside over the imperial learned hierarchy, he became the main gatekeeper of the imperial canon. At the same time, he served as the extension of the sultan who appointed him to this office.

In addition to listing the texts members of the imperial learned hierarchy were to read, the sultan also regulated the order in which they were to be read. In a sixteenth-century imperial legal code, also issued during Süleymân's reign, the sultan instructs that the "books of high repute" were to be studied in a particular order, according to the rank of the professor (and, supposedly, according to the rank of the madrasa in which he taught). Moreover, the edict urges jurists not to teach a given book in the curriculum until their students mastered the previous book and also warns that the knowledge and competence of the students would be subjected to inspection.[27] In other words, these canonization and reading practices were predicated on the existence of a learned hierarchy.

This rise of an Ottoman canon was particularly significant since the imperial jurisprudential canon shared many texts with other Ḥanafī canons across the empire and beyond its boundaries, in south and central Asia. The distinctive position of the imperial jurisprudential canon is

that even the canon that members of the imperial learned hierarchy were expected to consult (i.e., the imperial jurisprudential canon) was not a monolithic corpus, and that it was a product of internal debates and deliberations.

26 Shahab Ahmed and Nenad Filipovic, "The Sultan's Syllabus: A Curriculum for the Ottoman Imperial Medreses Prescribed in a Fermān of Qānūnī Süleymān, Dated 973 (1565)," *Studia Islamica* 98/99 (2004): 183–218. Other sources, mostly from later centuries, list books that comprise the curriculum taught in the imperial madrasa system. My impression is that their lists are extensive but not comprehensive. See, for example: Cahid Baltacı, *XV–XVI. Yüzyıllarda Osmanlı Medreseleri* (Istanbul: Marmara Üniversitesi İlahiyat Fakültesi Vakfı, 2005), 1:87–93; Cevat İzgi, *Osmanlı Medreselerinde İlim* (Istanbul: İz Yayıncılık, 1997), 1:61–127; Ömer Özyılmaz, *Osmanlı Medreselerinin Eğitim Programları* (Ankara: Kültür Bakanlığı, 2002).

27 Ahmed Akgündüz, ed., *Osmanlı Kanunnâmeleri ve Hukukî Tahlilleri* (Istanbul: Fey Vakfı, 1992), 4:662–63.

reflected in the entry a seventeenth-century Damascene biographer and Ḥanafī jurist devotes to Pîr Muḥammed b. Ḥasan el-Üskübî (d. 1620), a member of the Ottoman imperial learned hierarchy: he states that el-Üskübî's collection of legal rulings was considered important among members of the Ottoman learned hierarchy (Rūmīs), thus implying that many jurists from the Arab lands did not consult this work.[28] The distinctive status of the imperial canon also emerges from Edirneli Meḥmed Kâmî's *Mahāmm al-fuqahā'*. As we have seen in Chapter 2, the work consists of biographical and bibliographical sections, both organized alphabetically. The biographical section includes jurists who constitute part of the genealogy of the imperial learned hierarchy within the Ḥanafī school and those who compiled texts considered authoritative by members of the imperial hierarchy, or, in Kâmî's words, texts that were "accepted among the jurists."[29] The bibliographical section, by contrast, lists many Ḥanafī works that were not part of the imperial canon. The relationship between the exclusive biographical and the more inclusive bibliographical sections of Kâmî's work reproduces the status of the imperial canon against the backdrop of the much larger body of Ḥanafī texts.

The emergence of a corpus of "books of high repute" or "reliable texts" was accompanied by surveillance mechanisms that were meant to ensure that members of the imperial learned hierarchy consulted only these texts in their rulings and writings. It is in this context that we might recall Hezârfen Ḥüseyin Efendi's comment, discussed briefly in Chapter 1, that one of the main differences between the chief muftī (the *şeyḫülislâm*) and the provincial muftīs (*kenâr müftîleri*) is that the latter are required to cite the texts they consulted for their ruling (*nüḳûl*). Another example is Murâd III's (r. 1574–95) 1594 imperial edict to the judge and the local appointed muftī of the Anatolian town of Balıkesir, perhaps in response to a petition submitted by the judge himself, demanding the proper citation of the jurisprudential works on which he relied (*naḳl yazmak*). According to the submitted complaint, the muftī of Balıkesir used to reply by merely stating "yes" or "no" without referring to any legal authority.[30] By explicitly mentioning the texts, the appointed muftīs demonstrated their adherence to the imperial jurisprudential canon of "texts of high repute." What is more, they enabled their superiors, and also those who solicited their

[28] Al-Muḥibbī, *Khulāṣat al-athar*, 1:503.

[29] Edirneli Meḥmet Kâmî, *Mahāmm al-fuqahā' fī ṭabaqāt al-Ḥanafiyya*, Süleymaniye Library MS Aşir Efendi 422, 65r–66v.

[30] Uriel Heyd, "Some Aspects of the Ottoman Fetvā," *Bulletin of the School of Oriental and African Studies* 32, no. 1 (1969): 45.

opinions, to inspect their use of the texts. As late as the eighteenth century, appointed provincial muftīs were reminded to cite their sources properly. In his appointment deed issued in 1783, the muftī of Sarajevo was urged, "When issuing fatāwá, you must take into consideration the most correct opinions of the Ḥanafī imams – may God have mercy. You must write the sources on which you base your expert-opinions, and must sign your fatāwá clearly indicating your name and your position as the Muftī of Sarajevo."[31]

Jurists also internalized the requirement to consult specific texts. An anonymous mid-seventeenth-century jurist, who probably hailed from the central lands of the empire, recorded in his notebook rulings issued by important jurisconsults and other pieces of information he deemed necessary for his daily work. After several pages in which he records legal rulings related to land tenure issues, he lists all the works that a muftī may consult to resolve these issues.[32] The fact that members of different ranks consulted the same books indicates that the emergence of a binding bibliography was a crucial means to instill and reinforce a sense of "establishment consciousness" among members of the imperial learned hierarchy. This is of particular importance given the Ottoman dynasty and its learned hierarchy did not ban the circulation of other jurisprudential texts that were not part of the imperial canon.

Now that we have explored some central aspects of the "canon consciousness" among members of the learned hierarchy, we may turn to examine the mechanism whereby texts entered the imperial jurisprudential canon.

A Case Study: The Integration of *al-Ashbāh wa'l-Naẓā'ir* into the Ottoman Imperial Canon

The Ottoman imperial jurisprudential canon was an open canon, which could expand to include new texts, such as al-Bāqānī's commentary. As we have seen, works went through an official review procedure. The seventeenth-century account of the canonization of al-Bāqānī's commentary, however, leaves us with a patchy description of this procedure. In order

[31] Cited in Selma Zecevic, "On the Margin of Text, On the Margin of Empire: Geography, Identity, and Fatwa-Text in Ottoman Bosnia" (PhD diss., Columbia University, 2007), 87.

[32] The notebook is cataloged according to its various components. It is cataloged under Süleymaniye Library MS Fazil Ahmed Paşa 1581–1. The bibliographical list appears on 105r.

to gain a fuller understanding of how a text formally entered the canon, what follows explores the history of another sixteenth-century work: *al-Ashbāh wa'l-naẓā'ir*, by the accomplished sixteenth-century Egyptian Ḥanafī jurist Ibn Nujaym (d. 1563).

Zayn al-Dīn b. Nujaym completed his *al-Ashbāh wa'l-naẓā'ir 'alā madhhab Abī Ḥanīfa al-Nu'mān* in 1561. By that time, he had already established himself as a prominent Ḥanafī jurist in Egypt and across the empire. It is significant to note that Ibn Nujaym, like al-Bāqānī, was not a graduate of the Ottoman imperial educational system or a member of the imperial learned hierarchy. Nevertheless, *al-Ashbāh wa'l-naẓā'ir*, among his other works, drew the attention of senior members of the Ottoman learned hierarchy and was eventually incorporated into the imperial jurisprudential canon. In his biography of Ibn Nujaym, the biographer and scholar Nev'îzâde Atâyî (d. 1635) relates that "the deceased *şeyḫülislâm* Ebû's-Su'ûd approved [this work] [lit. signed it, *imżâ' eyleyip*], and several members of the imperial learned hierarchy compiled commentaries [on it] [*ba'ż-i 'ulemâ'-i Rûm şarḥ eylemiştir*]."[33]

The role of the chief imperial jurisconsult Ebû's-Su'ûd (d. 1574) in Nev'îzâde Atayî's account merits our attention. As we have seen, it was the sultan who issued the 1556 edict. Here, it is the chief imperial jurisconsult who approves the circulation of the text. It appears therefore that at some point between 1556 and 1574 the chief imperial jurisconsult was given the authority to approve new canonical texts. The logic of the 1556 edict was preserved, however, since both the edict and the new procedure manifest the understanding that the "reliability" of the canonical texts rests on their status within the Ḥanafī jurisprudential tradition and, equally importantly, on the endorsement of the sultan or, in later decades and centuries, of the chief imperial jurisconsult.

But what exactly does it mean to "canonize" a text? It seems that several members of the Ottoman learned hierarchy remained perplexed as to the status of *al-Ashbāh wa'l-naẓā'ir* in the decades following its completion and its approbation by Ebû's-S'ûd. This explains the question posed to one of Ebû's-Su'ûd's successors, the late sixteenth/early seventeenth-century chief imperial jurisconsult Hâcî Muṣṭafâ Ṣun'ullah Efendi

[33] Nev'îzâde Atâyî, *Hadâiku'l-Hakâik fî Tekmileti'ş-Şakâik*, in *Şakaik-i Nu'maniye ve Zeyilleri* (Istanbul: Çağri Yayinlari, 1989), 34. It is worth pointing out that this biography is one of the very few entries Atâyî dedicates to jurists who were not members of the Ottoman learned hierarchy in his biographical dictionary, which was mainly devoted to quite senior members of the hierarchy.

(who served in this capacity four times: 1599–1601, 1603, 1604–6, and 1606–8):

Question: [Do] the issues [*mesâ'il*] [discussed] in the book [entitled] *al-Ashbāh wa'l-naẓā'ir* correspond [*müvâfik ve 'amal olunmağla*] to the issues [discussed] in the other jurisprudential texts?

Answer: Although [parts of the work] are accepted [as sound] [*maḳbûlu var*], there are also [parts] that are rejected [*merdûdu var*].[34]

This short ruling illustrates two key issues. First, the question further clarifies that the role of the chief imperial jurisconsult as a "canonizing authority" entailed providing instructions on how to apply and interpret certain passages and texts.[35] In other words, the canonization was not an event, but rather an ongoing process whereby the canonical status of the work was defended and rearticulated. Second, the ruling indicates that the jurisprudential works were not necessarily canonized in their entirety, since only parts of the work are "accepted." This comment poses a serious methodological problem for students of Islamic law in the Ottoman context, for it implies that there may have been some sort of a "division of labor" between the texts within the imperial jurisprudential canon, and that jurists could not have used canonical texts arbitrarily.

Finally, it is worth dwelling on the approval itself. As we have seen, Ebû's-Su'ûd Efendi is said to have approved Ibn Nujaym's work. Fairly little is known about the nature and form of this approval. At least in some cases, it appears, at the end of the review procedure, senior members of the imperial learned hierarchy, including the *şeyḫülislâm*, compiled and published short reviews. For instance, when the late sixteenth-century/early seventeenth-century Celeb Muṣliḥuddîn Muṣṭafâ b. Ḫayreddîn Efendi (d. 1623) completed his commentary on *al-Ashbāh wa'l-naẓā'ir*, high-ranking members of the hierarchy, such as the former military judges of Anatolia and Rumeli as well as the *şeyḫülislâm*, issued their approvals/endorsements.[36] More commonly known as *taqrīẓ* (pl. *taqārīẓ*, *takrîẓ* in

[34] Ṣun'ullah Efendi, *Fetâvâ*, Süleymaniye Library MS Reşid Efendi 269, 42v. For instance, one of the passages in the work that members of the imperial learned hierarchy may have found problematic is Ibn Nujaym's ruling against the Ottoman practice of appointing judges to the provinces. See Zayn al-Dīn b. Ibrāhīm b. Nujaym, *al-Ashbāh wa'l-naẓā'ir 'alā madhhab Abī Ḥanīfa al-Nu'mān* (Beirut: Dār al-Fikr al-Mu'āṣir; Damascus: Dār al-Fikr, 1999), 288.

[35] Ebû's-Su'ûd Efendi, *Fetâvâ*, Süleymaniye Library MS Ismihan Sultan 226, 29r; Ṣun'ullah Efendi, *Fetâvâ*, 53v.

[36] See my forthcoming "Reflections on Censorship, Canonization and the Ottoman Practices of *Takrîẓ* and *imżâ*" (in Turkish). On this commentary, see: Lu'ayyy ibn 'Abd al-Raūf

Turkish) and occasionally as *imżâ'*, these documents were at times collected and preserved for their literary value but perhaps also as a proof that a certain work was reliable, especially in cases when the reviewed text was somewhat controversial.[37]

It is difficult to assess how common the practices were of issuing, circulating, and archiving endorsements. Whatever the case may be, these endorsements may tell us something about the identity of the "eminent jurists of Rūm" who approved al-Bāqānī's commentary. They also indicate that a jurisprudential text entered circulation only after several senior members had examined it and issued their approbation. At the end of the procedure, it was apparently the chief imperial jurisconsult who approved a new work, as Nevʿîzâde Atayî claims.

This circulation of approbations among members of the imperial learned hierarchy invites us to consider the function of these documents in a specific historical setting. Endorsements were and still are employed to varying degrees in different textual traditions – both Islamic and non-Islamic – as a means to canonize texts. Furthermore, within the Islamic textual tradition(s), the discursive continuity between pre-Ottoman endorsements and Ottoman ones is often striking. Yet, as our case study suggests, endorsements fulfilled a different role in the context of a learned hierarchy. Here, it seems, endorsements reflected formal approval, perhaps even an official instruction from senior members of the hierarchy to their subordinates to consult a specific work.

In light of the history of *al-Ashbāh wa'l-naẓā'ir* and its commentaries, one can draw a couple of conclusions with regard to the development of the imperial jurisprudential canon. First, unlike the canonization of jurisprudential texts in the pre-Ottoman and the Arab lands, the canonization within the Ottoman learned hierarchy was more formal and followed strict procedures. Second, upon its approval, the text entered circulation,

al-Khalīlī al-Ḥanafī, *La'ālī' al-mahār fī takhrīj maṣādir Ibn ʿĀbidīn fī ḥāshīyatihi Radd al-muḥtār, dhikr li-mā fī al-Ḥāshīya min muṣannafāt wa-rasā'il makhṭūṭa aw maṭbūʿa maʿa al-taʿrīf bi-hā wa-bi-aṣḥābihā* (Amman: Dār al-Fatḥ lil-Dirāsāt wa'l-Nashr, 2010), 1:93–94.

[37] The practice of issuing endorsements has a long history in various Islamic literary traditions. On *taqrīẓ* in the Mamluk sultanate, see: Franz Rosenthal, "'Blurbs' (taqrīẓ) from Fourteenth-Century Egypt," *Oriens* 27/28 (1981): 177–96; Amalia Levanoni, "A Supplementary Source for the Study of Mamluk Social History: The Taqārīẓ," *Arabica* 60, nos. 1–2 (2013): 146–77. On Ottoman endorsements, see Christine Woodhead, "Puff and Patronage: Ottoman *Takriz*-writing and Literacy Recommendation in the 17th Century," in *The Balance of Truth: Essays in Honour of Professor Geoffrey Lewis*, ed. Çiğdem Baalim-Harding and Colin Imber (Istanbul: Isis Press, 2000), 395–406; and my "Reflections."

which means that it was taught within in the imperial madrasa system and jurists could make use of it, or – if certain restrictions and limitations were imposed – of parts of it. The limitations could vary. As Ṣunʿullah Efendi's ruling states, sometimes the approval was partial. In other cases, as the history of al-Bāqānī's commentary suggests, it was permissible to use the approved work only for specific purposes or in specific genres. Thus, al-Bāqānī's commentary was apparently consulted in other commentaries on the *Multaqā*, but as far as I know it was not cited in other genres, such as legal rulings (*fatāwā*).

The Transmission and Canonization of Texts Outside the Ottoman Learned Hierarchy

So far, we have examined the imperial learned hierarchy's perception of the canon and the canonization practices it employed. To gain a better appreciation of the unique features of these practices, it would be useful to compare them with those prevailing in certain scholarly circles throughout the Arab lands of the empire. As opposed to the Ottoman learned hierarchy with its standardized career tracks, the scholarly circles across the Arab lands were considerably looser in terms of their hierarchy and educational practices. Since canonization and transmission of knowledge (and, for our purposes, of texts) are closely interlocking phenomena, the loose social organization of these scholarly circles shaped and, in turn, was reflected in their canonization practices. It is worth emphasizing that these canonization practices assisted these jurists in defining the doctrine and structure of their branch of the Ḥanafī school independently from the Ottoman dynasty and its learned hierarchy.

Darwīsh Muḥammad b. Aḥmad al-Ṭālūwī's (d. 1605) comments on his reading practices may serve to illustrate some of the issues at stake. Al-Ṭālūwī was on his maternal side a descendent of the Mamluk amir ʿAlī b. Ṭālū, while his father was one of the Ottoman (Rūmī) troops who conquered Damascus. Despite the military background of both his father and his maternal grandfather, al-Ṭālūwī pursued a scholarly career and studied in Damascus and Cairo, and most likely in Istanbul as well. The late sixteenth-century/early seventeenth-century jurist and chronicler Ḥasan al-Būrīnī says that al-Ṭālūwī was the protégé (*mülâzim*) of Bostânzâde Meḥmet Efendi, the future military justice of Anatolia and chief muftī (served 1589–92 and 1593–98), according to the procedures of the imperial learned hierarchy or the "*qānūn* of the jurists of Rūm." Apparently as Bostânzâde's protégé, al-Ṭālūwī entered the Ottoman madrasa system and taught in several madrasas until he reached the level of a daily salary of 50 *akçe*. Throughout his career he maintained contacts, some close, with high-ranking members of the Ottoman learned hierarchy. Al-Ṭālūwī was eventually removed from his teaching position in the Ottoman madrasa system after he composed satirical poems (*hajw*) against senior members of the imperial learned hierarchy. He succeeded, however, in securing an appointment to the Ḥanafī muftīship of his hometown, Damascus.[38]

Al-Ṭālūwī left a collection of letters, poems, and documents he exchanged with leading jurisprudents, scholars, and literati. This collection offers an invaluable glimpse into the wide network of contacts al-Ṭālūwī maintained both in the imperial capital and across Greater Syria and Egypt. Al-Ṭālūwī also recorded in the collection some of the permits (*ijāza*) he obtained from his teachers to transmit their teachings. These *ijāza*s may assist us in understanding practices of the transmission of knowledge and texts in scholarly circles outside the Ottoman imperial learned hierarchy. Let us, then, examine three permits al-Ṭālūwī obtained during his long stay in Egypt late in the sixteenth century and on his way back to Damascus.

The first *ijāza* was granted by the eminent Egyptian Ḥanafī jurist and scholar Ibn Ghānim al-Maqdisī, who was also the teacher of Taqiyy al-Dīn al-Tamīmī, whom we met in Chapter 2. Ibn Ghānim's *ijāza* includes a long enumeration of texts he had studied with various teachers and in turn taught al-Ṭālūwī. The list includes *ḥadīth* compilations, such as al-Bukhārī's *Ṣaḥīḥ*, as well as Ḥanafī jurisprudential works, such as al-Marghīnānī's *al-Hidāya*, Ibn al-Humām's commentary on the *Hidāya*, and al-Nasafī's *Kanz al-daqā'iq*. Ibn Ghānim also specifies the intellectual genealogies that linked him to al-Nasafī, to al-Marghīnānī, and to Abū Ḥanīfa himself. He claims, in addition, to have studied the works of Kemâlpaşazâde with several members of the imperial learned hierarchy.[39] Al-Ṭālūwī also cites a permit he obtained from another eminent teacher of his, Shams al-Dīn Muḥammad al-Naḥrāwī of al-Azhar, with whom he studied several Ḥanafī jurisprudential works.[40] On his way back from

[38] Al-Ghazzī, *Luṭf al-samar*, 2:439–62; al-Būrīnī, *Tarājim*, 2:201–21; al-Murādī, *'Arf al-bashām fī man waliya fatwā Dimashq al-Shām* (Damascus: Majma' al-Lugha al-'Arabiyya, 1979), 46–57.

[39] Darwīsh Muḥammad b. Aḥmad al-Ṭālūwī, *Shāniḥāt dumā al-qaṣr fī muṭarāḥāt banī al-'aṣr* (Beirut: 'Ālam al-Kutub, 1983), 2:52–91.

[40] Ibid., 2:80–81. Among the texts he studied with al-Naḥrāwī and mentioned in the *ijāza* the latter granted him are *al-Hidāya*, Ibn al-Humām's *Fatḥ al-qadīr*, *Mukhtaṣar*

Egypt, al-Ṭālūwī sojourned in Gaza, where he studied with Muḥammad al-Timurtāshī. Al-Ṭālūwī says that al-Timurtāshī taught him the school's "books of high repute" as well as his own works, such as *Tanwīr al-abṣar*. He also claims that al-Timurtāshī granted him a permit to teach the *Tanwīr* in its entirety.[41]

The fact that al-Ṭālūwī included the permits in the collection points to the importance he attributed to these permits in his self-fashioning as an accomplished scholar. Moreover, the image that emerges from these three permits is corroborated by contemporary and later sources, such as biographical dictionaries and bibliographical autobiographies (known as *thabat* or *mashyakha*) compiled by both Ḥanafī and non-Ḥanafī jurists. These sources often list the texts the biographee read and mention teachers with whom he read them. In terms of continuity and change, scholarly circles across the Arab lands tended to preserve the practice of transmitting texts from an individual teacher to his student.[42]

This aspect of the biographies is of particular relevance if one compares them with the entries in the dictionaries devoted to members of the imperial learned hierarchy, such as the *Shaqā'iq* and its supplements. Although the entries often identify the biographee's patron during his *mülâzemet* period (the period between the biographee's graduation and his appointment to a position within the hierarchy), they do not mention who the teachers of a certain jurist were during his training path in the imperial madrasa system. Furthermore, while the entries list the texts the biographee compiled and commented on, they rarely mention what texts he studied during his training path.

The differences between the biographical literature from the Arab lands and that authored by members of the imperial learned hierarchy reflect two scholarly traditions and, I would like to suggest, two different perceptions of the relationship between the sultan (and the dynasty), the jurists, and the school of law. In the imperial learned hierarchy, with its structured curriculum, even when permits were granted they served a

al-Qudūrī, al-Nasafī's *Kanz al-Daqā'iq* and its commentaries, Ibn al-Sā'ātī's *Majma' al-baḥrayn* and its commentaries, and 'Abd al-Rashīd al-Bukhārī's *Khulāṣat al-fatāwā*.

41 Ibid., 118–19.

42 See Daphna Ephrat, *A Learned Society in a Period of Transition: The Sunni 'Ulama' in Eleventh-Century Baghdad* (Albany: State University of New York Press, 2000); Jonathan Berkey, *The Transmission of Knowledge in Medieval Cairo* (Princeton, NJ: Princeton University Press, 1992). For eighteenth-century Damascus, see Stephen E. Tamari, "Teaching and Learning in 18th-Century Damascus: Localism and Ottomanism in an Early Modern Arab Society" (PhD diss., Georgetown University, 1998).

somewhat different purpose: in the words of the above-mentioned legal code intended to regulate the training of jurists affiliated with the hierarchy, the permit (*icâzet*) should testify to the student's proficiency and competence and "should not contradict the real state of affairs [*hilâf-i vâki'*]," and it may be subject to inspection (*teftîş*). In the less centralized scholarly circles, the transmission of knowledge and texts required, at least theoretically, individual permits for each transmission, because of the multiple centers of scholarly and jurisprudential authority. This is not to say that scholars and jurists could not read a text without the proper credentials, but their reading and interpretation became more authoritative if they held a permit from an eminent authority. It is for this reason that the permits were intended to circulate and, as contemporary biographers indicate, to remain accessible to other members of the scholarly community. The biographical dictionaries, in turn, increased the access of scholars and jurists to information concerning the credentials of their colleagues, as well as to the books that they were known to have read. It is fairly clear, then, that there was a strong "canon consciousness" among members of these scholarly circles, although their jurisprudential canon was a product of what Jonathan Brown calls an informal "canonization network," through which consensus among leading authorities concerning the quality of a specific text was obtained.[43]

An interesting indication to this strong canon consciousness is the use made since the late sixteenth century by some jurists from the Arab lands, such as Muḥammad al-Timurtāshī and his student al-Ṭālūwī, of the term "books of high repute" in their writings.[44] These jurists' adoption of the imperial hierarchy's concept, which, as we have seen, was not very common in the pre-Ottoman period throughout the Arab lands, was apparently in response to the hierarchy's use of the term. It would seem that the rise of a standardized and clearly defined canon among members of the hierarchy led Arab Ḥanafīs to more clearly demarcate their own canon. Concluding the introduction to his *al-Ashbāh wa'l-naẓā'ir*, Ibn Nujaym states: "I hereby mention the texts I refer to in my jurisprudential compilations [*naqalat minha mu'allafātī al-fiqhiyya*] that I have collected [by] the end of 968 [1561]."[45] This statement is followed by a detailed bibliography. Several decades later, al-Bāqānī also includes a

[43] Brown, *Canonization*, chap. 4.

[44] Muḥammad b. ʿAbd Allāh Khaṭīb al-Timurtāshī, *Musʿifat al-ḥukkām ʿalā al-aḥkām* (Amman: Dār al-Fatḥ li'l-Dirāsāt wa'l-Nashr, 2007), 150, 156.

[45] Ibn Nujaym, *al-Ashbāh wa'l-naẓā'ir*, 12–13.

comprehensive bibliography of the works he consulted while authoring his commentary.[46] Such comprehensive bibliographical lists were quite rare in jurisprudential texts prior to the sixteenth century.[47] The chronological proximity of Ibn Nujaym's statement (1561) and the imperial edict issued by Süleymân (1565) raises the possibility that these events are related.

Despite these similarities, the discourse of some Arab Ḥanafī jurists surrounding the jurisprudential texts diverges from that of the imperial learned hierarchy in a significant way. Although members of the hierarchy compiled copious commentaries and glosses on various texts, for the most part, they referred to all the texts they were permitted to consult merely as *mütûn* (or *kütüb*). On the other hand, their counterparts – and more specifically their counterparts who did not hold a state appointment – advanced a hierarchical tripartite taxonomy of texts: the authoritative texts (*mutūn*), the commentaries on the authoritative texts (*shurūḥ*), and collections of legal opinions (*fatāwā*).[48] The hierarchical relation between these texts meant that a jurist was expected to consult the authoritative texts first, then the commentaries, and the legal opinions last.[49]

This difference reflects the different perceptions of the school of law. As Baber Johansen has argued in his discussion of general and local customs in Ḥanafī jurisprudence, the authoritative texts are used for teaching the "classical" doctrine of the school and preserving its general framework, whereas the commentaries and the *fatāwā* are intended to apply the general rules of the school to a concrete setting.[50] In other words, it seems that the Ottoman hierarchy's rejection of the tripartite classification

[46] Al-Bāqānī, *Majrā*, 2r.

[47] On the issue of bibliographical lists in medieval Islamic works, see Shahab Ahmed, "Mapping the World of a Scholar in Sixth/Twelfth Century Bukhāra: Regional Tradition in Medieval Islamic Scholarship as Reflected in a Bibliography," *Journal of the American Oriental Society* 120, no. 1 (2000): 24.

[48] For example: Ibrāhīm b. Muḥammad al-Dimashqī al-Ḥanafī (Ibn al-Ṭabbākh), *'Ayn al-muftī li-ghayn al-mustaftī*, Hüsrev Bey Library (Sarajevo) MS 3069, 4v; Khayr al-Dīn al-Ramlī, *al-Fatāwā al-Khayriyya li-naf' al-bariyya 'alā madhhab al-Imām al-A'ẓam Abī Ḥanīfa al-Nu'mān* (Cairo: al-Maṭba'a al-Kubrā al-Miṣriyya bi-Bulāq, 1882), 2:81. According to al-Ramlī, following al-Ṭarasūsī's *Anfa' al-wasā'il ilā taḥrīr al-masā'il*, the authoritative texts should be given preference over the commentaries and the *fatāwā*.

[49] One should note, however, that the terms should not be taken too literally, as certain *fatāwā* collections and commentaries were considered "authoritative texts." See Wael B. Hallaq, "From Fatwās to Furū': Growth and Change in Islamic Substantive Law," *Islamic Law and Society* 1, no. 1 (1994): 39–45.

[50] Baber Johansen, "Coutumes locales et coutumes universelles aux sources des règles juridiques en droit musulman hanéfite," *Annales islamologiques* 27 (1993): 31.

corresponds to its attempt to turn its particular branch of the school into a fairly standardized imperial legal corpus.[51]

The different canons and canonization practices that coexisted across the Ottoman Empire's Ḥanafī circles raise some important questions about the relationship between these canons. This is the focus of the following pages.

Comparing Jurisprudential Canons

A Note on Reconstructing and Comparing Canons

The emergence of a canon is a contingent process, and the canon is the outcome of selection, for "other texts knock on the doors of the canon."[52] A text's inclusion or exclusion may be determined by various factors, such as its compatibility with other canonical texts, the eminence of its author, or the importance attributed to it by members of other text-centered communities. The crucial point is that canons often – though not always – emerge through interplay between communities and groups that seek to mutually differentiate themselves. In short, canons as a phenomenon are often relational, and any study of canons must take into account their interdependence as an influential factor in their formation. For this reason, it would be fruitful to look at multiple contemporary canons comparatively.

But how are we to determine which texts are considered canonical? Only rarely is a canon articulated in a treatise or edict. Moreover, in many cases canonical texts coexist with many other texts that are not considered canonical. One thus has to identify the texts that enjoy special status in a specific community or in the view of a particular scholar. In recent years, several studies have attempted to reconstruct the bibliographical (and intellectual) worlds of Muslim jurists and scholars in different time periods and places.[53] What distinguishes these studies from other works that

[51] Related to this issue are the different interpretations of the notion of "custom" (*ʿurf*/*ʿörf*) that coexisted throughout the Ottoman domains: while the understanding of *ʿurf* as local custom endured, the Ottoman dynasty employed the term to denote dynastic/imperial customs.

[52] Halbertal, *People of the Book*, 20.

[53] Ahmed, "Mapping the World of a Scholar," 24–43; Etan Kohlberg, *A Medieval Muslim Scholar at Work: Ibn Ṭāwūs and His Library* (Leiden: Brill, 1992); Tamari, *Teaching and Learning in 18th-Century Damascus*, chap. 5. In addition to these studies are works that focus on curricula, mostly in early modern Islamic societies: Ahmed and Filipovic, "The Sultan's Syllabus"; Maria Eva Subtelny and Anas B. Khalidov, "The Curriculum of Islamic Higher Learning in Timurid Iran in the Light of the Sunni Revival under Shah-Rukh,"

focus on libraries and book collections is that they reconstruct a scholar's intellectual world on the basis of his or her textual production.[54] In other words, these studies privilege the texts scholars used over the works they happened to possess in their library. This is not to say, of course, that jurists and scholars did not read other texts. But it is clear that the texts they cite in their works carried, in their view, particular symbolic meaning for them and for the scholarly circle to which they belonged.

Shahab Ahmed's study of an annotated bibliography compiled by a medieval central Asian scholar merits special mention here, since it offers a promising methodological approach for reconstructing and analyzing bibliographies that jurists consulted. Ahmed pays special attention to the chronological and geographical dimensions of the bibliography. By doing so, he is able to demarcate a specific scholarly tradition that prevailed in twelfth-century central Asia. However, precisely because the study concentrates on a bibliography, all the texts included therein appear to have similar status.[55]

While drawing on Ahmed's approach, I am interested in introducing into my analysis the "relative weight" of different texts. There are several ways to deduce the "weight" or "importance" of a certain work. In this study, I have decided to concentrate on the frequency with which different jurisprudential works appear in a given compilation. My assumption is that the frequency with which a work is cited is a good indicator to its importance. "Importance," however, does not necessarily imply agreement with the legal argument advanced in the cited work. A text may be frequently cited in order to repeatedly debunk its author's argument. Nevertheless, the denunciation of an argument reflects the importance of this work, albeit in a somewhat negative way, in a certain scholarly or jurisprudential tradition.

In order to calculate the relative frequency with which a certain work is cited, it is necessary to determine the ratio between the number of times

Journal of the American Oriental Society 115, no. 2 (1995): 210–36; Francis Robinson, "Ottoman-Safawids-Mughals: Shared Knowledge and Connective Systems," *Journal of Islamic Studies* 8, no. 2 (1997): 151–84; Zecevic, *On the Margin of Text*, 246–57.

[54] On Medieval and Ottoman libraries, see Ulrich Haarman, "The Library of a Fourteenth-Century Jerusalem Scholar," *Der Islam: Zeitschrift für Geschichte und Kultur des islamischen Orients* 61 (1984): 327–33; Daniel Crecelius, "The Waqf of Muhammad Bey Abu al-Dhahab in Historical Perspective," *International Journal of Middle East Studies* 23, no. 1 (1991): 57–81; Orlin Sabev, "Private Book Collections in Ottoman Sofia, 1671–1833," *Etudes balkaniques* 1 (2003): 34–82.

[55] Ahmed, "Mapping the World of a Scholar."

a text is cited and the total number of citations in the entire compilation. Granted, there are variations in the frequency with which a work is cited in different chapters and in different contexts throughout a compilation. In addition, at least as far as the Ottoman chief muftīs are concerned, one must keep in mind the ruling by Ṣunʿullah Efendi we discussed earlier and should not assume that the texts were canonized in their entirety. Nevertheless, the large number of citations analyzed enables us to get a sense of what texts were considered more reliable and/or more significant. It certainly leaves room for further, more nuanced examination.

My reconstruction of Ḥanafī jurisprudential canons and the dynamics between them is centered on two mid-seventeenth-century *fatāwā* collections. It would therefore be useful to dwell on the methodological challenges that these collections pose and on the implications of focusing on *fatāwā* collections for reconstructing jurisprudential canons in the Ottoman context.

The first major challenge concerns generic conventions. As the case of al-Bāqānī's commentary suggests, canonical works are not necessarily cited in all genres. While al-Bāqānī's commentary is cited by other commentators on *Multaqā al-abḥur*, the work is not cited at all in *fatāwā* collections. To put it somewhat differently, the canon is wider than what a specific genre may suggest. But even in the realm of a specific genre – in this case, the collections of legal rulings – it is worth paying attention to differences between the collections of the imperial chief muftī (and other muftīs who were members of the imperial learned hierarchy) and muftīs who did not hold a state appointment, such as the collection of the Palestinian muftī Khayr al-Dīn al-Ramlī, which will be further examined in the following sections.

One of the main methodological problems when dealing with *fatāwā* collections, and especially with collections from the late sixteenth century onward, is that the *fatāwā* collections of officially appointed muftīs from the core lands of the empire, the chief jurisconsults included, and the collections of their counterparts who did not hold a state appointment follow different conventions of citing references. While the seventeenth-century officially appointed muftīs (or those who collected their rulings) often mention, at the end of their answers, the jurisprudential texts on which they relied in their rulings, muftīs from the Arab lands do not. Furthermore, while the members of the imperial learned hierarchy usually cite a given text in support of their rulings, their Arab counterparts may attach to their answers a detailed analysis of the different available opinions within the Ḥanafī school (and at times in other schools).

In my analysis of al-Ramlī's collection, I assume that regardless of the Palestinian muftī's approval or disapproval of the texts he cites, the fact that he decided to mention specific works renders them important in his view. That said, I try to nuance this statement and draw attention to al-Ramlī's dialogue with the texts he read by looking to several instances in which al-Ramlī cites the opinions of the famous sixteenth-century chief imperial muftī Ebû's-Su'ûd Efendi.

Beyond the differences between the collection of the chief muftīs and that of their counterparts from the Arab lands in terms of the conventions they follow, it is worth reiterating that each collection is essentially unique, as it includes specific questions posed to the muftī in a concrete setting.[56] Therefore, the muftīs do not necessarily address the same jurisprudential issues. Nevertheless, an examination of the entire collection is intended to diminish the importance of the individual question, and point to more general trends.

The issue of change over time is central to any study of canons and canonization. The focus on roughly contemporary collections, admittedly, does not elucidate this aspect of canon formation. By looking at sources (not exclusively *fatāwā* collections) from earlier and later periods, I aim to emphasize the fact that these collections and the jurisprudential canons they represent are rooted in a specific moment. Although the picture for earlier and later periods is quite patchy at this stage, it still provides interesting insights about the mid-seventeenth-century canons.

Comparing the Bibliographies of Minḳarîzâde Yaḥyâ Efendi and Khayr al-Dīn al-Ramlī

Two collections form the basis of this section: Minḳarîzâde Yaḥyâ Efendi's and Khayr al-Dīn al-Ramlī's.[57] Minḳarîzâde Yaḥyâ Efendi served as *seyḫülislâm* between 1662 and 1674, making him the longest holder of the office in the seventeenth century. (The second-longest was his pupil

[56] See Guy Burak, "The Abū Ḥanīfah of His Time: Islamic Law, Jurisprudential Authority and Empire in the Ottoman Domains (16th–17th Centuries)" (PhD diss., New York University, 2012), 438–43.

[57] The *fatāwā* collections of the imperial chief jurisconsults were not standardized in terms of their content prior to the late seventeenth century. Instead, various collections of the rulings of a given jurisconsults were compiled. For this comparison I relied on a late seventeenth-century collection of Minḳarîzâde's ruling (Süleymaniye Library MS Hekimoğlu 421). It was compiled by one *'Aṭā'* Allāh Muḥammad and copied in 1725. As to al-Ramlī, I used the nineteenth-century printed edition of his rulings. For a discussion of the special features of the Ottoman *fatāwá* collections, see: Guy Burak, "The Abū Ḥanīfah of His Time," appendix I.

Çatalcalı ʿAlî Efendi.) This was a remarkable achievement in a century during which most chief imperial muftīs were replaced after much shorter tenures. Minḳarîzâde reached the upper echelon of the imperial learned hierarchy from its lower ranks – a particularly significant fact given that these upper echelons were the stronghold of the Saʿdeddîn family and their clients during the first decades of the century. As Derin Terzioğlu and Baki Tezcan have suggested, Minḳarîzâde's rise and long tenure should be attributed to his close contacts with the court, and especially with Vânî, a charismatic preacher and close adviser to the sultan.[58]

Some aspects of al-Ramlī's biography have already been discussed in Chapter 1. Here it suffices to remind readers that the Palestinian muftī represents a group of prominent muftīs who issued their legal opinions without holding a state appointment and that al-Ramlī was educated and trained in his hometown of Ramla and in Cairo. This educational background helps explain some aspects of his bibliography, as we shall see.

Which canons do these two muftīs represent? In the case of the chief muftī's collection, answering the question is a somewhat easier task. As the head of the imperial learned hierarchy, he served as the "gatekeeper of the canon." As such, he set, at least theoretically, the standard for his subordinates. It is still unclear, however, whether the frequency with which a work is cited by the *şeyḫülislâm* matches the frequency in works by other members of the imperial learned hierarchy. Al-Ramlī's collection poses more problems: although the Palestinian muftī was clearly a prominent figure in the jurisprudential landscape of Greater Syria and even across the empire, it is more difficult to assess the number of jurists who followed exclusively al-Ramlī's choices. On the other hand, the emergence of a provincial, Greater Syrian "Ottomanized" canon, as will be discussed in the following sections, indicates that al-Ramlī and other eminent muftīs who did not hold a state appointment were quite influential.

The institutional differences between these muftīs as well as their affiliation with different branches within the Ḥanafī school of law situate al-Ramlī's collection and that of his contemporary Seyḫülislâm Minḳarîzâde Efendi at two ends of a "continuum" within the Ḥanafī school in the Ottoman domains. This "continuum" is helpful, for it allows us to relationally locate many jurists, such as the aforementioned

[58] Derin Terzioğlu, "Sufi and Dissident in the Ottoman Empire: Miyāzī-i Miṣrī" (PhD diss., Harvard University, 1999), 231; Baki Tezcan, *The Second Ottoman Empire: Political and Social Transformation in the Early Modern World* (Cambridge: Cambridge University Press, 2010), 216–17.

al-Ṭālūwī, who were trained in both traditions or at least were appointed to the muftīship and other religious and scholarly positions by the Ottoman dynasty. As we shall shortly see, their positions contributed to (or were perhaps the result of) the development of yet another canon.

The bibliographies of al-Ramlī and Minḳarîzâde Efendi include more than 100 items each and are included in Appendix C. Here, my intention is to offer a brief analysis and a comparison.

Even a quick glance at these bibliographies reveals that they share many texts. Both jurists extensively cite postclassical texts, most of which were compiled between the eleventh and fifteenth centuries, such as the early fifteenth-century Ibn al-Bazzāz's *al-Fatāwā al-Bazzāziyya*, ʿĀlim b. ʿAlāʾ al-Anṣārī al-Dihlawī's (d. 1351) *al-Fatāwā al-Tātārkhāniyya*, Shams al-Aʾimma b. Bakr Muḥammad b. Abī Sahl Aḥmad al-Sarakhsī's (d. 1056) *al-Mabsūṭ fī al-furūʿ*, Iftikhār Ṭāhir b. Aḥmad b. ʿAbd al-Rashīd Ṭāhir al-Bukhārī's (d. 1147) *Khulāṣat al-fatāwā*, Burhān al-Dīn Maḥmūd b. Aḥmad b. al-Ṣadr al-Shahīd's (d. 1174) *al-Dhakhīra al-Burhāniyya*, and al-Ḥasan b. Manṣūr al-Ūzjandī's (d. 1196) *Fatāwā Qāḍīkhān*.

Several texts by Ḥanafī jurists who lived and wrote in the Mamluk realms are represented in both bibliographies as well. Among these are Fakhr al-Dīn ʿUthmān b. ʿAlī al-Zaylaʿī's (d. 1342 or 1343) *Tabyīn al-ḥaqāʾiq fī sharḥ Kanz al-daqāʾiq* (a commentary on al-Nasafī's *Kanz al-daqāʾiq*); Najm al-Dīn Ibrāhīm b. ʿAlī b. Aḥmad al-Ḥanafī al-Ṭarsūsī's (d. 1357) *Anfaʿ al-waṣāʾil ilā taḥrīr al-masāʾil*; Akmal al-Dīn Muḥammad b. Maḥmūd al-Bābartī's (d. 1384) *al-ʿInāya fī sharḥ al-Hidāya* (a commentary on al-Marghīnānī's *Hidāya*); and Muḥammad b. ʿAbd al-Wāḥid b. al-Humām's (d. 1459 or 1460) *Fatḥ al-qadīr* (his famous commentary on *al-Hidāya*).

In addition to these texts, both muftīs cite sixteenth-century texts that were penned in the Arab provinces of the empire, such as Ibn Nujaym's *al-Baḥr al-rāʾiq* (another commentary on al-Nasafī's *Kanz al-daqāʾiq*) and his *al-Ashbāh waʾl-naẓāʾir*, and Muḥammad al-Timurtāshī's (d. 1595) *Tanwīr al-abṣār* and *Minaḥ al-ghaffār* (a commentary on the *Tanwīr*). Moreover, both muftīs cite ʿAlī al-Maqdisī (d. 1574), possibly his commentary on al-Nasafī's *Kanz al-daqāʾiq*.

Furthermore, there are several works that were authored by jurists from the core lands of the empire and feature in both bibliographies. Molla Ḫüsrev's (d. 1480) *Durar al-ḥukkām fī sharḥ Ghurar al-aḥkām* is one example. Another is *al-Īḍāḥ fī sharḥ al-Iṣlāḥ fī al-fiqh al-Ḥanafī*, a jurisprudential manual by the famous chief muftī Kemâlpaşazâde (d. 1534), although neither Minḳarîzâde nor al-Ramlī cite this work frequently.[59] Both muftīs also cite the famous *şeyḫülislâm* Ebû's-Su'ûd Efendî, most likely his legal rulings. Nevertheless, it is important to stress that al-Ramlī does not always cite Ebû's-Su'ûd Efendî approvingly, but rather mentions the latter's opinion as one of the possible opinions within the school.[60]

Surprisingly, several texts that are known to be part of the imperial canon in the mid-seventeenth century are absent from Minḳarîzâde's bibliography. Perhaps the most striking example in this respect is Ibrāhīm al-Ḥalabī's *Multaqā al-abḥur* (the work does appear in al-Ramlī's bibliography). Other examples are 'Alī b. Khalīl al-Ṭarābulusī's (d. 1440 or 1441) *Mu'īn al-ḥukkām fī mā yataraddadu al-khiṣmayn min al-aḥkām*; 'Abdurrahman b. 'Alî Müeyyedzâde's (d. 1516) *Majmū'at al-masā'il*; Ya'ḳûb Paşa's (d. 1486) *Ḥashiyat sharḥ al-Wiqāya* (these works are cited by al-Ramlī); and Aḫî Çelebi's (d. 1499) gloss on *Sharḥ al-Wiqāya*.[61]

At the same time, the bibliographies differ in two substantial ways. First, there is a difference, at times great, in the frequency with which Minḳarîzâde and al-Ramlī consult works that appear in both bibliographies (see Figure 4.1). Minḳârîzâde cites *Fatāwā Qāḍīkhān*, just to mention one example, almost twice as frequently as al-Ramlī does. On the other hand, al-Ramlī consults much more frequently the works by sixteenth-century jurists from the Arab lands, such as Ibn Nujaym and al-Timurtāshī.

The second significant difference, as Figure 4.1 shows, concerns the composition of the bibliographies, that is, the jurisprudential texts that each muftī consults in addition to the shared texts. This difference reflects the diverse textual, interpretative, and jurisprudential traditions within the Ḥanafī school. A good example to illustrate this difference is the works of the fifteenth-century jurist Qāsim b. Quṭlūbughā. As we have already seen in Chapter 2, the *ṭabaqāt* works compiled by members of the Ottoman learned hierarchy throughout the sixteenth century excluded Ibn Quṭlūbughā from the intellectual genealogy of the imperial hierarchy. Although by the mid-seventeenth century, members of the

59 Another example is the collection of legal issues (*masā'il*) authored by Müeyyedzâde of Amasya (d. 1516). Müeyyedzâde 'Abd al-Raḥman al-Amâsî, *Majmū'at al-masā'il*, Süleymaniye Library MS Nafiz Paşa 16. It is noteworthy that both *Al-Durar* and *al-Īḍāḥ* appear in Ibn Nujaym's bibliography. Ibn Nujaym, *al-Ashbāh*, 13.

60 Al-Ramlī, *al-Fatāwā al-Khayriyya*, 1:48. For other cases in which al-Ramlī endorses the famous grand muftī's opinion, see ibid., 1:19, 20; 2:24, 95–96. See also Haim Gerber, *Islamic Law and Culture 1600–1840* (Leiden: Brill, 1999), 60–64.

61 The last two works appear in the notebook of the jurist from the early to mid-seventeenth century discussed above.

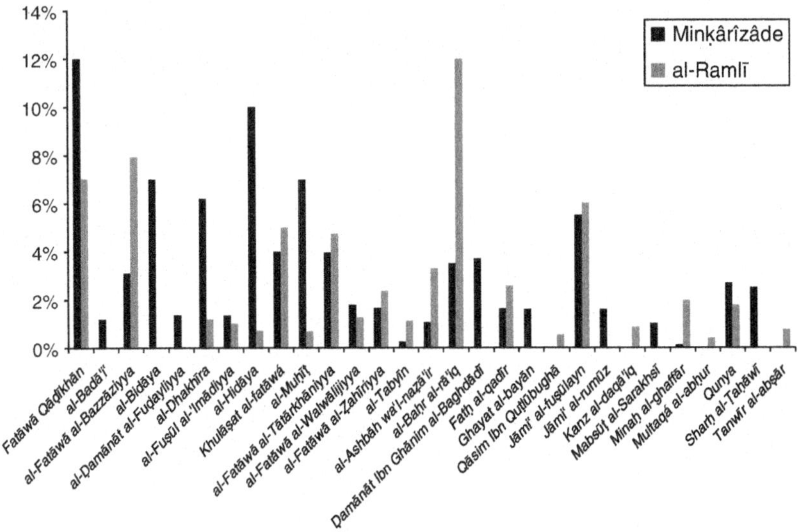

FIGURE 4.1. The frequency with which different jurisprudential texts are cited in Minkârîzâde's and al-Ramlī's *fatāwā* collections.

imperial hierarchy began consulting some of his works (such as *Taṣḥīḥ al-Qudūrī*), other works were not included in the imperial jurisprudential canon. Minkarîzâde, for instance, cites the *Taṣḥīḥ* only once, while al-Ramlī refers more frequently to the work, to Ibn Quṭlūbughā's *fatāwā* collection, and to his gloss on Muẓaffar al-Dīn Aḥmad b. ʿAlī al-Baghdādī b. al-Sāʿātī's (d. 1293) *Majmaʿ al-baḥrayn*.[62] Al-Ramlī's much more frequent consultation of Ibn Quṭlūbughā's works points to the prominence of the fifteenth-century jurist in Ḥanafī scholarly circles across the Arab lands well into the seventeenth century. The works of Saʿd al-Dīn al-Dayrī (d. 1462), an acclaimed Ḥanafī jurist in fifteenth-century Cairo, are a similar example of scholarship that was well known in Arab lands but apparently did not enter the Ottoman imperial canon.[63]

Al-Ramlī's bibliography mirrors his connections with other sixteenth- and seventeenth-century Ḥanafī jurists who operated throughout the Arab provinces of the empire, and particularly in Cairo, such as Muḥammad b. ʿUmar Shams al-Dīn b. Sirāj al-Dīn al-Ḥānūtī (d. 1601). Al-Ḥānūtī was an eminent jurist in Cairo and was described by the seventeenth-century historian and biographer al-Muḥibbī as the "head of the [Ḥanafī] school in

[62] Ibn Nujaym also owned a copy of Ibn Quṭlūbughā's *fatāwā* collection.
[63] On Saʿd al-Dīn al-Dayrī, see note 37.

Cairo after the death of the shaykh ʿAlī b. Ghānim al-Maqdisī." Moreover, al-Ḥānūtī was famous for his legal rulings, which were collected and consulted by "jurists in our time [i.e., the seventeenth century]."[64] Other *fatāwā* collections consulted by al-Ramlī but not by Minḳarîzâde are those of Muḥammad al-Timurtāshī and Muḥammad Amīn al-Dīn ʿAbd al-ʿĀl. The latter was an influential jurist in the sixteenth century and al-Timurtāshī's teacher; it is worth mentioning, too, that ʿAbd al-ʿĀl's son Aḥmad was al-Ramlī's teacher.[65] Another eminent jurist that al-Ramlī cites is his contemporary Ḥasan b. ʿAmmār al-Shurunbulālī (d. 1659).[66] Al-Shurunbulālī was one of the most distinguished Ḥanafī scholars (if not the most distinguished) in al-Azhar in the seventeenth century, the teacher of many Ḥanafī jurists from across Egypt and Greater Syria, and the author of several influential works and commentaries.[67]

While these three jurists loomed large in the intellectual and jurisprudential landscape of the Arab lands in the seventeenth century, they do not appear in Minḳarîzâde's bibliography. Al-Ramlī, on the other hand, sought to establish the authority of some of his rulings by referring to works and rulings of eminent Arab Ḥanafīs, whose authority in turn rested on their scholarly credentials and on their affiliation with a specific chain of transmission within the Ḥanafī school. Al-Ramlī, it should be stressed, was not the only one to refer to his own teachers in his jurisprudential writings. The late seventeenth-century/early eighteenth-century ʿAbd al-Ghanī al-Nābulusī, for example, cites his father, Ismāʿīl al-Nābulusī, a renowned jurist in his own right, in one of his treatises.[68] In other words, it seems that many Ḥanafīs from the Arab lands sought to establish their authority on the basis of their studies with well-known Ḥanafīs from across the Arab lands.

Conversely, many items that Minḳarîzâde tends to cite quite frequently are absent from al-Ramli's bibliography. Among these works one can mention *Ghāyat al-bayān wa nādirat al-aqrān* by Qiwām al-Dīn Amīr Kātib b. Amīr ʿUmar al-Itqānī (d. 1356);[69] *Jāmiʿ al-rumūz*, a popular

[64] Al-Muḥibbī, *Khulāṣat al-athar*, 4:76–77.
[65] Al-Ramlī, *al-Fatāwā al-Khayriyya*, 1:3.
[66] Ibid., 1:126, 183.
[67] On al-Shurunbulālī, see Nicola Melis, "A Seventeenth-Century Ḥanafī Treatise on Rebellion and Jihād in the Ottoman Age," *Eurasian Studies* 11, no. 2 (2003): 217–18.
[68] Barbara Rosenow von Schlegell, "Sufism in the Ottoman Arab World: Shaykh ʿAbd al-Ghanī al-Nābulusī (d. 1143/1731)" (PhD diss., UC Berkeley, 1997), 42.
[69] This work also appears in the *fermân* issued by Süleymân. Ahmed and Filipovic, "The Sultan's Syllabus," 203.

commentary on *al-Nuqāya* by Shams al-Dīn Muḥammad b. Ḥusām al-Dīn al-Quhistānī (d. 1554);[70] and *al-Ḍamānāt al-Fużayliyya* by Fużeyl Çelebi b. ʿAlî b. Aḥmad al-Jamâlî Zenbillizâde (d. 1583). Minḳarîzâde also consulted the works and rulings of other members of the imperial learned hierarchy, such as the rulings of Çivizâde Efendi (d. 1549), who served as chief muftī; an unspecified work by Ankaralı Zekeriyâ Efendi (d. 1592); and *Lawāzim al-quḍāt wa'l-ḥukkām fī iṣlāḥ umūr al-anām* by his contemporary Muṣṭafā b. Muḥammad b. Yardim b. Saruhān al-Sirūzī al-Dīkhī (d. 1679).

Minḳarîzâde also cites the works of Ghiyāth al-Dīn Abū Muḥammad Ghānim b. Muḥammad al-Baghdādī (d. 1620), who deserves particular attention in this context. Ibn Ghānim was not a graduate of the Ottoman madrasa system, but he was known for his scholarly excellence.[71] Moreover, he compiled several works that entered the imperial jurisprudential canon, the most important of which were his *Ḍamānāt* (known as *Ḍamānāt Ghānim al-Baghdādī*) and his *Tarjīḥ al-bayānāt*. It should be noted that despite the fact that Ibn Ghānim compiled his works in one of the Arab provinces, al-Ramlī does not cite his colleague's work. This fact indicates that al-Ramlī should not be taken as a representative of the textual traditions of the Arab lands in general. Instead, he seems to be a representative of a particular, local tradition, one of several that coexisted throughout the empire's Arab provinces.

Juxtaposing Minḳarîzâde's and al-Ramlī's collections and their respective bibliographies also sheds light on the relationship between the two muftīs. Minḳarîzâde cites al-Ramlī's opinion in several instances. Although it is difficult to date when Minḳarîzâde asked al-Ramlī for his opinion, or at least heard of it, the fact that the latter is called "Khayr al-Dīn al-Ghazzī" may suggest that al-Ramlī resided in the Palestinian city of Gaza at the time, that is, before settling down in his hometown of Ramla. The contacts between al-Ramlī and Minḳarîzâde are corroborated by other sources as well.[72] On the other hand, al-Ramlī does not cite the

[70] Al-Quhistānī's is one of the few texts compiled in the sixteenth century in central Asia (in Bukhara) that entered the Ottoman jurisprudential canon. On al-Quhistānī, see Muḥammad b. ʿAbd al-Raḥmān al-Ghazzī, *Dīwān al-Islām* (Beirut: Dār al-Kutub al-ʿIlmiyya, 1990), 4:35–36; ʿAbd al-Ḥayy b. Aḥmad b. al-ʿImād, *Shadharāt al-dhahab fī akhbār man dhahab* (Beirut: Dār al-Kutub al-ʿIlmiyya, 1980), 8:300.

[71] Kâtip Çelebi, *Fezleke-i Tarîh*, 2:4–5.

[72] Two questions from Minḳarîzâde to al-Ramlī are preserved in the collection of al-Ramlī's treatises and correspondences, which was compiled by his son. Khayr al-Dīn al-Ramlī (collected by Najm al-Dīn al-Ramlī), *Kitāb al-Lā'lī al-duriyya fī al-fawā'id al-Khayriyya ʿalā Jāmiʿ al-fuṣūlayn ta'līf Mawlānā Shaykh al-Islām al-wālid Khayr al-Dīn*, Khalediyya

chief muftī's rulings. The fact that the chief muftī based certain rulings he made on those of his Palestinian counterpart is significant for appreciating the latter's position within the imperial framework. Furthermore, Minḳarîzâde's reliance on al-Ramlī raises the question of the dichotomy between officially appointed muftīs and their colleagues who did not hold a state appointment. At any rate, in the following decades, some of al-Ramlī's rulings entered the imperial jurisprudential canon, as the collections of later chief muftīs indicate.[73]

Finally, a major difference between the two bibliographies is al-Ramlī's familiarity with and reference to the arguments and opinions of prominent Shāfiʿī jurists and muftīs. In his rulings, al-Ramlī occasionally cites or responds to the rulings of such prominent Shāfiʿī jurists and muftīs as Muḥyī al-Dīn Yaḥyā b. Sharf al-Nawawī (d. 1277), Taqiyy al-Dīn ʿAlī al-Subkī (d. 1355), Zakarīyā al-Anṣārī (d. 1520), and Aḥmad b. Aḥmad al-Ramlī (d. 1563). The reference to Shāfiʿī jurists may be attributed to the dominance of that school in the Arab lands, as opposed to its limited presence in the central lands of the empire. Moreover, as Kenneth Cuno and others have pointed out, al-Ramlī himself was of Shāfiʿī background, a fact that may account for his close familiarity with the arguments of specific jurists.[74]

Library (Jerusalem) MS 523/fiqh/450, 146r–156v. See also al-Muḥibbī, *Khāāṣat al-Athar*, 2:131–32.

[73] See, for example, Feyżullah Efendi, *Fetâvâ-i Feyżiyye maʿan-Nuḳûl* (Istanbul: Dar üt-Tıbaat ül-Amire, 1266 [1850]), 11, 17, 199, 203–4. The dichotomy between officially appointed muftīs and their colleagues who did not hold a state appointment emerges, for instance, from the biographical dictionaries dedicated to members of the imperial learned hierarchy. As Baki Tezcan notes, "Although al-Muḥibbī included a large number of Ottoman scholars, judges, and administrators in his biographical dictionary, al-Muḥibbī himself is not recorded in the biographical dictionary of seventeenth-century Ottoman scholars." The dictionaries also contribute to a somewhat misleading image of the relations between the jurists. Thus, Tezcan concludes that while "scholars in the periphery looked up to the center, those in the imperial capital seem to have ignored the intellectual production in the provinces." Although it is true that jurists from the Arab lands did not reach the higher echelon of the imperial learned hierarchy and in many ways, from the capital's vantage point, were marginalized, the analysis of the bibliographies indicates that members of the hierarchy did not ignore the production of their provincial colleagues. See Baki Tezcan, "Dispelling the Darkness: The Politics of 'Race' in the Early Seventeenth-Century Ottoman Empire in the Light of the Life and Work of Mullah Ali," in *Identity and Identity Formation in the Ottoman World: A Volume of Essays in Honor of Norman Itzkowitz*, ed. Baki Tezcan and Karl Barbir (Madison: University of Wisconsin Press, 2007), 76.

[74] Kenneth Cuno, "Was the Land of Ottoman Syria Miri or Milk? An Examination of Juridical Differences within the Ḥanafī School," *Studia Islamica* 81 (1995): 134–37. See also Chapter 5 of this volume.

The Emergence of the Greater Syrian "Ottomanized" Canon

So far, we have looked at the ends of the "continuum." Where on the continuum did the officially appointed provincial muftīs fall? As discussed in Chapter 1, across Greater Syria at least from the late sixteenth century (and in some cases possibly earlier), muftīs were appointed from among the notable Greater Syrian jurists. What follows is an attempt to outline in very broad strokes the seventeenth-century jurisprudential canon of an emininet Damascene officially appointed provincial muftī. This is, to be sure, a preliminary attempt, but even this sketch, based on the commentary on *Multaqā al-abḥur* compiled by the Damascene officially appointed muftī ʿAlāʾ al-Dīn al-Ḥaṣkafī (d. 1671), reveals interesting dynamics. It seems that the jurisprudential bibliography varies from genre to genre, as the example of al-Bāqānī's commentary, which is not mentioned in the *fatāwā* collections, illustrates. Nevertheless, the patterns that emerge from an analysis of the works al-Ḥaṣkafī mentions in the commentary convey a sense of his intellectual world and his position in the jurisprudential Ḥanafī landscape of the Ottoman realms.

Al-Ḥaṣkafī was an eminent and prolific jurist, and his works were well received, as their inclusion in the imperial canon in the last decades of the seventeenth century suggests.[75] For the purpose at hand, it is worth noting that al-Ḥaṣkafī studied with several jurists throughout Greater Syria and the Hijaz, including with Khayr al-Dīn al-Ramlī. Moreover, al-Ḥaṣkafī maintained good contacts with senior officials both in the imperial capital and in Damascus. Apparently through these contacts he was eventually appointed to serve as the muftī of Damascus.[76]

Al-Ḥaṣkafī's biography and career are crucial for understanding his bibliography. Officially appointed provincial muftīs across Greater Syria tended to be more attentive than muftīs without an official appointment to the arguments advanced by their colleagues who were affiliated with the imperial learned hierarchy.[77] This is also to a large degree the case as far as al-Ḥaṣkafī's bibliography is concerned. For instance, he cites quite frequently Shams al-Dīn Muḥammad b. Ḥusām al-Dīn

[75] For example: Feyżullah Efendi, *Fetâvâ-i Feyżiyye*, 5, 107, 447.

[76] Al-Muḥibbī, *Khulāṣat al-Athar*, 4:63–65.

[77] Martha Mundy and Richard Saumarez-Smith, *Governing Property, Making the Modern State: Law, Administration and Production in Ottoman Syria* (London: I. B. Tauris, 2007), chaps. 2–3; Burak, "The Abū Ḥanīfah of His Time," 355–96.

al-Quhistānī's *Jāmi' al-rumūz*,[78] as well as other works by members of the imperial learned hierarchy, such as Ya'ḳûb Paşa's *Ḥāshiyat sharḥ al-Wiqāya*,[79] Pîr Muḥammed b. Ḥasan al-Üskübî's *Mu'īn al-muftī fī al-jawāb 'alā al-mustaftī*,[80] Ebû's-Su'ûd Efendi's *Me'rûżât* and legal rulings,[81] Aḫî Çelebi's gloss on *Sharḥ al-Wiqāya*,[82] rulings by Çivizâde Meḥmed Efendi,[83] and rulings issued by seventeenth-century *şeyḫülislâm* Yaḥyâ Efendi.[84] Furthermore, al-Ḥaṣkafī also cites the commentary on the *Multaqā* completed a few years earlier, in 1666, by his contemporary Dâmâd Efendi.[85]

On the other hand, al-Ḥaṣkafī was not oblivious to the jurisprudential activity that was taking place across the Arab lands, namely, in Egypt and Greater Syria. Accordingly, he cites fairly frequently leading authorities from the Arab lands, such as the aforementioned Ḥasan al-Shurunbulālī,[86] Khayr al-Dīn al-Ramlī,[87] the fifteenth-century jurist Qāsim b. Quṭlūbughā,[88] and Muḥammad al-Timurtāshī.[89] In addition, like his teacher al-Ramlī, al-Ḥaṣkafī mentions specific influential non-Ḥanafī jurists and scholars, such as Aḥmad al-Ramlī;[90] Badr al-Dīn al-Ghazzī,[91] the father of the famous Damascene historian and an eminent jurist in his own right; and the Ḥanbalī traditionist 'Abd al-Bāqī al-Ḥanbalī.[92] Moreover, al-Ḥaṣkafī cites two other commentaries on the *Multaqā* by two Damascene scholars, al-Bahnasī and al-Bāqānī.

A juxtaposition of al-Ḥaṣkafī's bibliography with that of an eighteenth-century provincial muftī from the town of Mostar (in modern-day Bosnia) elucidates the difference between the provincial muftīs

[78] See, for example, al-Ḥaṣkafī, *al-Durr al-muntaqā*, 1:31, 62, 305, 326, 327, 331, 362, 363, 378, 389, 413, 433, 449, 501, 502, 532; 2:6, 12, 19, 28, 37, 40, 51, 65; 3:6, 19, 212; 4:198.
[79] Ibid., 2:365, 3:271.
[80] Ibid., 2:478.
[81] Ibid., 2:349, 536; 3:79, 212.
[82] Ibid., 2:579, 4:32.
[83] Ibid., 2:348–49.
[84] Ibid., 4:32.
[85] Ibid., 2:339.
[86] Ibid., 1:148, 164, 351, 361, 436, 445, 447, 512; 2:156, 186, 187, 195, 237, 302, 347, 363, 461; 3:83, 86, 155, 162, 194; 4:198, 210, 213.
[87] Ibid., 2:483–84.
[88] Ibid., 1:47; 2:175, 572.
[89] Ibid., 1:502, 532; 2:12; 3:4, 78, 234.
[90] Ibid., 2:71.
[91] Ibid., 2:350.
[92] Ibid., 2:411.

of the core lands of the empire and those of Greater Syria. As Selma Zecevic, who has studied the muftīship of Mostar in the eighteenth century, has pointed out, the provincial muftīs there were graduates of the Ottoman madrasa system. Although Zecevic has surveyed the library of an eighteenth-century muftī, which includes some works by late seventeenth- and eighteenth-century jurists that are naturally absent from bibliographies of earlier jurists, it is still possible to deduce from her reconstruction some pertinent conclusions. The Bosnian muftī, unlike his Greater Syrian colleague, did not consult works by sixteenth- and seventeenth-century Ḥanafī (let alone non-Ḥanafī) jurists from the Arab lands, with the exception of the works that entered the imperial canon, such as some of al-Timurtāshī's works.[93] In short, the examination of the different bibliographies and Zecevic's findings clearly indicate that the Ottoman learned hierarchy succeeded in achieving a remarkable coherence across great distance.

A Damascene Critique of the Imperial Jurisprudential Canon

The opposition of many jurists from the Arab lands to the Ottoman imperial canon was based, to a considerable extent, on their critique of the arguments and opinions that certain works that were part of the imperial canon advanced. In a treatise in which he presents his view of the structure of the Ḥanafī school of law and its authorities, the late eighteenth-century/early nineteenth-century Damascene jurist Muḥammad Amīn b. ʿUmar Ibn ʿĀbidīn (d. 1836) records an interesting critique of the Ottoman canon.[94] He cites his Damascene colleague Muḥammad Hibat Allāh b. Muḥammad al-Tājī al-Baʿalī (d. 1809),[95] who warns his readers that most of the "people of the time" (*ahl zamāninā*) tend to rule according to the unreliable opinions they find in the more recent books (*al-kutub al-mutaʾakhkhira*), such as al-Quhistānī's *Jāmiʿ al-rumūz*, al-Ḥaṣkafī's

[93] The bibliography of the eighteenth-century muftī of Mostar also illustrates this point. See Zecevic, *On the Margin of Text*, 246–57.

[94] On Muḥammad Amīn b. ʿUmar Ibn ʿĀbidīn, see Haim Gerber, *Islamic Law and Culture 1600–1840* (Leiden: Brill, 1999); Norman Calder, "The ʿUqūd rasm al-muftī' of Ibn ʿĀbidīn," *Bulletin of the School of Oriental and African Studies, University of London* 63 (2000): 215–28; Wael B. Hallaq, "A Prelude to Ottoman Reform: Ibn ʿĀbidīn on Custom and Legal Change," in *Histories of the Modern Middle East: New Directions*, ed. Israel Gershoni, Hakan Erdem, and Usrula Woköck (Boulder, CO: Lynne Rienner Pub, 2002), 37–61.

[95] On al-Baʿalī, see al-Ḥanafī, *Laʾāliʾ al-mahār fī takhrīj maṣādir Ibn ʿĀbidīn fī ḥāshīyatihi Radd al-muḥtār*, 1:91–93.

al-Durr al-mukhtār, and Ibn Nujaym's *al-Ashbāh wa'l-naẓā'ir*. Because of the brevity of the discussion in those books, al-Ba'alī complains, they tend to be obscure and often include opinions that are not reliable. Moreover, he further explains, the authors of those books prefer (*tarjīḥ*) the view that contradicts the preferable opinion within the Ḥanafī school (*rājiḥ*), and in some cases promote an opinion that is not ascribed to any authority within the madhhab. To support this view, al-Ba'alī alludes to the view of the eminent eighteenth-century Damascene jurist Ṣāliḥ al-Jīnīnī (d. 1757): "It is illicit to consult these books for issuing fatwas, unless [the muftī] knows the [authoritative] source on which [the authors] rely and looked at the books' [authoritative] sources (*lā yajūzu al-iftā' min hadhihi al-kutub illā idhā 'alima al-manqūl 'anhu, wa-l-iṭlā' 'alā maākhidihā*)."[96] Ibn 'Ābidīn himself further elaborates and points out that it is generally agreed that approximately twenty books by later authorities of the school may be consulted freely, but he still cautions his reader that mistakes tend to perpetuate themselves.[97]

The works on which al-Ba'alī chose to focus his attention, all of which were part of the Ottoman imperial canon of the eighteenth century, strongly suggest that by "people of the time" he refers to members of the Ottoman learned hierarchy and their provincial appointees. In other words, al-Ba'alī and the other Damascene jurists argued, some more explicitly than others, that the familiarity of jurists who were affiliated with the hierarchy with the Ḥanafī tradition was at best superficial. To remedy this state of affairs, they encouraged their readers to examine independently the references of the texts they read.

To sum up, Ibn 'Ābidīn and the jurists he cited challenged the Ottoman jurisprudential canon by advocating a different method of reading the Ḥanafī textual corpus than the one practiced by members of the learned hierarchy. Furthermore, and perhaps more importantly, they called into question the validity of certain legal arguments that the Ottoman learned hierarchy endorsed.[98] Furthermore, the Damascene critique of

[96] Ṣāliḥ al-Jīnīnī was one of the leading jurists in eighteenth-century Damascus. His was famous for his breadth of knowledge of the major texts of the Ḥanafī tradition. For his biography, see Muḥammad Khalīl b. 'Alī b. Muḥammad b. Muḥammad al-Murādī, *Kitāb silk al-durar fī a'yān al-qarn al-thānī 'ashar* (Beirut: Dār al-Bashā'ir al-Islāmiyya, 1988), 2:208–9. For al-Jīnīnī's scholarly credentials, see also his *thabat*: *Thabat Ṣāliḥ al-Jīnīnī*, Staatsbibliothek zu Berlin MS Wetzstein II 413, 77r–86r.

[97] Muḥammad Amīn b. 'Umar Ibn 'Ābidīn, *Majma' rasā'il al-imām Ibn 'Ābidīn al-Ḥanafī* (Cairo: al-Maktaba al-Azhariyya li-l-turāth, 2012), 1:41–46.

[98] In a recent study of the gloss (*ḥāshiya* pl. *ḥawāshī*) in the Shāfi'ī tradition, Ahmed El Shamsy pointed to a difference between Ibn 'Ābidīn's gloss on al-Ḥaṣkafī's *al-Durr*

the Ottoman canon and the forms of reading Ibn ʿĀbidīn proposes may be interpreted as an attempt to offer a different, perhaps more comprehensive view of the Ḥanafī school of law and its preponderant opinions from the one supported by the Ottoman learned hierarchy.

Concluding Remarks

The preliminary survey of different textual traditions and communities within the Ḥanafī school throughout the empire shows that the formation of different canons mirrors broader developments and processes, significant aspects of which we have examined in the previous chapters and will further investigate in the next ones. The analysis of the bibliographies sheds light on the dynamics that accompanied the incorporation of the Arab lands – and the scholarly and jurisprudential traditions prevalent in these lands – into the empire. As already said, over the course of the late sixteenth and seventeenth centuries, some Arab Ḥanafī jurists sought to integrate themselves in different ways into the imperial framework. As part of this attempt, these Ḥanafīs synthesized substantial elements of the "local" Ḥanafī tradition with that of the core lands of the empire. Following the concept offered by Ehud Toledano in his study of eighteenth- and nineteenth-century elites across the Arab provinces of the empire, one can interpret the synthesis promoted by al-Ḥaṣkafī and others as another aspect of the "dual process of localization and Ottomanization [that] produced ...

al-mukhtār and Shāfiʿī glosses: "Even though Ḥanafī scholars also composed *ḥawāshī* in abundance," El Shamsy observed, "they seem to have retained a greater interest in the earlier works of the school. This is indicated by the frequent direct quotations of early sources found in the most famous Ḥanafī *ḥāshiya* the *Radd al-mukhtār* [sic] of the Syrian jurist Ibn ʿĀbidīn, (d. 1252/1836)." El Shamsy speculated that the Ḥanafīs' engagement in the state of affairs of the Ottoman Empire "forced the Ḥanafīs to maintain as much doctrinal flexibility as possible and therefore to preserve as broad a textual corpus for the school as they could." In light of Ibn ʿĀbidīn and his colleagues' critique of the manner in which jurists who were affiliated with the learned hierarchy approached the Ḥanafī tradition, it appears, however, that Ibn ʿĀbidīn (and possibly other authors of *ḥawāshī*) were not particularly interested in assisting the Ottoman ruling elite by presenting a broad range of opinions within the school, but to demonstrate that the Ḥanafī madhhab's range of opinions is broader than the one members of the imperial learned hierarchy and its appointees followed. It is thus possible that at least some Ḥanafī *ḥawāshī* were another textual site where jurists who, like Ibn ʿĀbidīn, were not members of the imperial hierarchy could challenge the Ottomans' adoption of a particular branch within the Ḥanafī school and a specific and limited range of opinions. This point, however, remains to be further examined. Ahmed El Shamsy, "The Ḥāshiya in Islamic Law: A Sketch of the Shāfiʿī Literature," *Oriens* 41 (2013): 296.

Ottoman-local elites."[99] One may ask, however, if the "Ottomanized" canon is the outcome of this integration of Arab Ḥanafī jurists into the Ottoman judicial elite or an important development that facilitated their incorporation. At the same time, it is quite likely that through the growing integration of jurists from the Arab lands, texts authored and consulted in these provinces (such as Ibn Quṭlūbughā's works) entered, albeit selectively, the imperial canon.

Indeed, the fact that Minḳarîzâde cites his Palestinian contemporary indicates that members of the hierarchy were aware of towering jurisprudential figures who were active in the Arab provinces, consulted their opinions, and included their works in the imperial canon. It is not fully clear how members of the imperial hierarchy learned about the activity of these jurists, though there were several possible channels through which jurists in the core lands could have learned about the jurisprudential activity in the Arab provinces. After all, graduates of the Ottoman madrasa system traveled quite frequently across the Arab lands in various capacities (on their way to undertaking the pilgrimage, to serve as judges and bureaucrats, and such).[100] What is clear, however, is that senior members of the imperial learned hierarchy showed interest in the work of their counterparts in the Arab provinces. These dynamics, it should be noted, are obscured in other sources, namely, in the biographical dictionaries dedicated to members of the imperial learned hierarchy, which, as Baki Tezcan rightly notes, exclude the overwhelming majority of Ḥanafī jurists who operated in the Arab provinces. On the other hand, the case of al-Ramlī – and particularly the fact that his opinion was at times consulted by high-ranking members of the imperial hierarchy – attenuates the absoluteness of the dichotomy between jurists who were affiliated with the hierarchy and their counterparts who did not hold a state appointment.

[99] Ehud R. Toledano, "The Emergence of Ottoman-Local Elites (1700–1900): A Framework of Research," in *Middle Eastern Politics and Ideas: A History from Within*, ed. Ilan Pappé and Moshe Ma'oz (London: Tauris Academic Studies, 1997), 148–49.

[100] Ottoman officials were interested in the literary production of the Arab lands. Ibn Ṭūlūn, for instance, recounts that in 1530 the appointed judge of Damascus "took over" the libraries of Damascus and took the books he was interested in (while disregarding the stipulation of the endower). Then he banned access to these libraries, save for several Rūmīs and those they favored. Shams al-Dīn Muḥammad b. ʿAlīb. Ṭūlūn, *Ḥawādith Dimashq al-yawmiyya ghadāt al-ghazw al-ʿUthmānī li'l-Shām, 926–951H: ṣafaḥāt mafqūda tunsharu l'il-marra al-ūlā min Kitāb Mufākahat al-khillān fī ḥawādith al-zamān li-Ibn Ṭūlūn al-Ṣāliḥī* (Damascus: Dār al-Awā'il, 2002), 238–39.

The analysis of the bibliographies sheds light on the circulation of texts and, more broadly, on the relationships between the myriad intellectual centers across the empire. Specifically, the analysis clearly demonstrates the connections between the imperial center and the Arab provinces and between the different learning centers across the Arab lands. It should be stressed that the latter connections were not made by way of passing through the imperial capital. The connections traced here between the different textual traditions support the findings of recent studies of administrative practices as well as of cultural and intellectual activities throughout the empire that have pointed to the connections between the provinces, thus challenging the center-periphery dichotomy.[101]

Since the imperial learned hierarchy was intent on specifying the texts its members should consult and on regulating the readings of these texts, the study of the imperial canon, as well as those of other scholarly circles across the empire, emphasizes the importance of jurisprudential texts in defining the various jurisprudential traditions within the Ḥanafī school that coexisted in the Ottoman domains (and beyond).[102] Seen from this perspective, to paraphrase Brian Richardson, the circulation of texts and their canonization were not an issue at the margins of the study of legal content, but rather an integral part of law itself.[103] Moreover, the imperial canonization project indicates that the imperial learned hierarchy was interested in regulating a wide range of legal issues, including, for instance, rituals (*ʿibādāt*) and personal status, and did not limit itself to issues considered matters of "imperial interest," such as land tenure and charitable endowments.

Ultimately, the canonization mechanisms explored in this chapter also allow us to understand some of the practices employed by the imperial learned hierarchy to inculcate a sense of "establishment consciousness," and, equally important, to consolidate a distinctive branch within the

101 Khaled El-Rouayeb, "Opening the Gate of Verification: The Forgotten Arab-Islamic Florescence of the Seventeenth Century," *International Journal of Middle East Studies* 38, no. 2 (2006): 263–81; Alan Mikhail, "An Irrigated Empire: The View from Ottoman Fayyum," *International Journal of Middle Eastern Studies* 42, no. 4 (2010): 569–90.

102 Many of the jurisprudential texts that constitute the Ottoman imperial canon are absent from seventeenth- and eighteenth-century book endowments from the Bukharan Khanate. For a comprehensive study of these book endowments, see Stacy Liechti, "Books, Book Endowments, and Communities of Knowledge in the Bukharan Khanate" (PhD diss., New York University, 2008).

103 Brian Richardson, *Manuscript Culture in Renaissance Italy* (Cambridge: Cambridge University Press, 2009), ix.

Ḥanafī madhhab. Nevertheless, much like the story the *ṭabaqāt* corpus examined in the previous chapters tells, the study of the changes both the imperial canon and other Ḥanafī canons across the empire underwent over the centuries suggests that jurists at times were able to shape – at least to some extent – their own jurisprudential bibliography and consequently the jurisprudential tradition they adhered to.

5

Intra-Madhhab Plurality and the Empire's Legal Landscape

> [When] he entered the Aya Sofya mosque for prayer, as he entered the door [of the mosque] all the people, adults and children [*kibâr ü ṣiğâr*], stood up and opened the way to the *miḥrāb* for him. Mevlânâ [Mollâ Ḫüsrev] also greeted [the people] on both his sides as he was proceeding to the front row. Several times Sultan Meḥmet Khân watched this situation [occurring] from his upper prayer place and said to his vezirs: [in Arabic] "Behold, this is the Abū Ḥanīfa of his time!" [Returning to Ottoman Turkish] That is, he was proud [of Mollâ Ḫüsrev], saying, "This is the Grand Imam [i.e., Abū Ḥanīfa] of our era."

This is how the sixteenth-century historian Muṣṭafâ ʿÂlî, who apparently drew on Taşköprüzâde's *Shaqāʾiq*, describes the special relationship between the Ottoman sultan Meḥmet II and one of the most eminent jurists in the still-evolving learned hierarchy, Mollâ Ḫüsrev (d. 1480).[1] Note the sultan's exclamation was recorded in Arabic, a fact that suggests that the audience of this congratulatory statement, beyond the sultan's immediate circle, were other Arabic-speaking Ḥanafī jurists, mostly in what were at the time the Mamluk territories. By the late sixteenth century, when Muṣṭafâ ʿÂlî was writing this account, the audience of this statement may have been many Ḥanafī jurists and, equally important for our purposes here, their followers across Arab provinces of the empire. The possibility that the sultan (and those who cited him) had a broader audience in mind invites us to venture beyond the scholarly

[1] Gelibolulu Muṣṭafâ ʿÂlî, *Künhü'l-Aḫbâr, c. II: Fatih Sultan Mehmed Devri 1451–1481* (Ankara: Türk Tarih Kurumu, 2003), 187–88. For the passage in the entry in the *Shaqāʾiq*, see Aḥmad b. Muṣṭafâ Ṭaşköprüzâde, *al-Shaqāʾiq al-nuʿmāniyya fī ʿulamāʾ al-dawla al-ʿUthmāniyya* (Beirut: Dār al-Kitāb al-ʿArabī, 1975), 81.

circles and to weave into the narrative men (and possibly women) that hailed from different economic and social backgrounds, Muslims and non-Muslims, Sufis, and members of the imperial ruling elite who followed the different jurists and made use of their rulings and opinions for different ends.

By introducing the ways the different jurists tried to establish, preserve, and negotiate their authority within the diverse and complex Ḥanafī legal landscape of the Ottoman Empire, on the one hand, and by looking at the ways in which members of the ruling and scholarly circles as well as commoners made use of the different jurists at their disposal, on the other, I hope to cast light on the broader context of the scholarly debates discussed in the previous chapters. Moreover, I seek to show that non-jurists understood, at least to some extent, the tension and gaps between the different perceptions of the school of law and of the relationship between the jurists and the sultan. Finally, I aim to further demonstrate how the imperial learned hierarchy and its appointed muftīs promoted and secured their particular, state-affiliated branch of the Ḥanafī legal school within an imperial framework in which multiple traditions and legal venues coexisted.

Of particular interest are the questions the different jurists received and the opinions they dispensed in response (their *fatāwā*), for they reflect the dialogue between the muftīs and those who solicited their opinions. Moreover, as we shall see, *fatāwā* at times traveled long distances across the empire: the chief imperial muftī received questions from the most distant provinces, while some of the eminent jurists who did not hold a state appointment, such as Muḥammad al-Timurtāshī, Khayr al-Dīn al-Ramlī, or ʿAbd al-Ghanī al-Nābulusī, were asked to dispense their opinions on certain legal and theological issues by solicitors from places as distant from one another as Istanbul to the holy cities of the Hijaz, and Damascus to Cairo. The circulation throughout the empire of questions and subsequent responses points, to some degree at least, to the significance that the different questioners attributed to a specific jurist's ruling.

The following example captures much of what is at stake. Early in the eighteenth century, a question was sent to the chief imperial muftī, Şeyḫülislam Menteşîzâde Efendi (served 1715–16):

Question: What is the opinion of your Excellency *Shaykh al-Islām* ... concerning a river which reaches several villages, some of which are up [the stream and closer] to the spring, [while] others are down [the stream]. In some years in which the flow of the river declines, the inhabitants of the upper [villages] started damming the river [thus depriving] the inhabitant of the lower [villages of water]. Are they allowed to do so? Dispense your opinion to us, [may you] be rewarded.[2]

The question was written in Arabic, as was the *şeyhülislam*'s answer. Several decades earlier, the same question (with very slight variations) was submitted to the officially appointed muftī of Damascus, Ismāʿīl al-Ḥāʾik (d. 1701).[3] This question, in turn, resembles a question that was sent from Damascus to the Palestinian muftī, Khayr al-Dīn al-Ramlī (d. 1660), whom we have already met in the previous chapters. The question posed to al-Ramlī reveals more details about the setting than the other two do. First, the question explicitly discloses the whereabouts of the questioner, and the river is a concrete river, the Bardī River. Here the questioner mentions several endowments of the treasury (*awqāf bayt al-māl*) that are entitled to enjoy this water. The questioner also provides detailed information about the damming technique that caused the water shortage in the villages down the stream.[4] The three muftīs' answers are not equally detailed, but all three ruled that the inhabitants of the lower villages are entitled to use the water as well.

The fact that two of the questions were either sent from Damascus or addressed to the officially appointed muftī of the city, together with the similarities between the three questions, may support the assumption that the one sent to the eighteenth-century chief muftī also originated from this region. If this is indeed the case, we have a debate that took place in Damascus (or its environs) and spanned at least half a century. Since very little is known about the solicitors, much room is left for speculations concerning their decision to address a certain muftī. Given the similarity in the way the questions were articulated, it appears that the questioners, or those who articulated the question on their behalf, knew to employ specific phrases and perhaps were even aware of the previous rulings. In any case, the main point is that, for whatever reason, different solicitors made use of different jurisconsults to promote their interests. In some cases, clear doctrinal differences between the jurists may account for the decisions of the different solicitors – to the extent that they were indeed aware of these differences – to address specific jurists. In this case,

[2] Menteşîzâde ʿAbdurraḥim Efendi, *Fetâvâ*, Süleymaniye Library MS Haci Selim Ağa 440, 83v.

[3] Ismāʿīl b. ʿAlī b. Rajab b. Ibrāhīm al-Ḥāʾik, *al-Shifāʾ al-ʿalīl bi-fatāwā al-marḥūm al-Shaykh Ismāʿīl*, Dār Isʿāf al-Nashashibī MS 9mim-53dal, 175v.

[4] Khayr al-Dīn al-Ramlī, *al-Fatāwā al-Khayriyya li-nafʿ al-bariyya ʿalā madhhab al-Imām al-Aʿẓam Abī Ḥanīfa al-Nuʿmān* (Cairo: al-Maṭbaʿa al-Kubrā al-Miṣriyya bi-Bulāq, 1882), 2:187–88.

however, the fact that all the jurists ruled in the same manner clarifies that beyond the legal content of a specific ruling, there were other concerns that drove the Damascene solicitors to address particular muftīs.

Taking this example as my point of departure, in the following pages I intend to situate some of its key elements in the broader context of the empire's jurisprudential landscape.

Using the Officially Appointed Muftīs' Rulings

By the time the Damascene solicitor addressed Şeyḫülislam Menteşîzâde in the early eighteenth century, questioners from the Arab lands in general, and from Greater Syria in particular, had been sending their queries to Istanbul and to the officially appointed provincial muftīs for almost two centuries: The quite famous sixteenth-century chief imperial muftī, Kemâlpaşazâde (d. 1534), received questions from the Arab provinces within less than two decades following their conquest.[5] Still, the decision to address officially appointed jurisconsults is not self-evident, given the activity of competing authoritative jurists across the empire.

Since the identity of the solicitor (or solicitors) or the context in which the question was initiated is rarely disclosed either in the questions they sent or in the muftīs' answers, the attempt to explain their decision to solicit these particular muftīs' opinion poses two main interlocking challenges. The first is the reconstruction of the historical and legal context of the *fatāwā*. While in some cases this is practically impossible, in others the picture that emerges is patchy and leaves much room for speculation. Second, it is difficult to determine the intentionality of the inquirer, or, to be more precise, to determine the extent to which a solicitor was aware of – and skillfully used – the different opinions and authorities. Furthermore, it is difficult to account for the commitment of a certain solicitor to a specific muftī.

Nevertheless, since most of the *fatāwā* I am interested in were compiled in Arabic and issued by an identifiable muftī, it is possible to situate the solicitor in the Arab lands in a concrete time period (the duration of the muftī's tenure in office). Moreover, in some cases, by reading the *fatāwā* with and against other sources, one may situate them in the context of a specific jurisprudential debate or in a concrete historical setting.

[5] The earliest ruling by Kemâlpaşazâde that I have been able to find is discussed in the following.

In addition, certain patterns in the use of the chief muftīs and their provincial subordinates are discernible. These patterns raise important questions – but may also provide answers – with regard to the reasons that led the solicitors to consult officially appointed muftīs. What is more, these patterns point to a considerable degree of familiarity with the different authorities and the advantages of each, depending on the case at hand. This analytic approach is not exclusive to our discussion of the *fatāwā* issued by the chief muftī and the officially appointed provincial muftīs, but, as we shall see in the following discussion, may be applied to *fatāwā* dispensed by muftīs who did not hold a state appointment.

To convey a better sense of the instances and venues in which imperial subjects across the Arab lands utilized the institution of the chief muftī or officially appointed provincial muftīs, it would be helpful to submit several representative case studies to closer scrutiny. One of the most common reasons for obtaining a ruling from an officially appointed muftī or the *şeyḫülislâm* was to support the solicitor's claims in court. Court records from Jerusalem, which have been published by Amnon Cohen and others, provide rich information concerning the ways imperial subjects utilized rulings issued by the local officially appointed muftīs and the *şeyḫülislâm*. These records corroborate and supplement the findings of other studies based on court records from across the Arab lands and Anatolia. At this point, however, it is difficult to assess how frequently the officially appointed muftīs were approached. This will require more research into the court records. It is clear, on the other hand, that *fatāwā*, the majority of which were issued by officially appointed muftīs, were brought to court and recorded.

Many of the cases gleaned and translated by Cohen dealt with Jewish subjects, which should not be a problem for our purposes. Although there may be differences in the ways Muslims and non-Muslims made use of the different authorities, the fact that non-Muslims (Jews, in this case) did not have particular interests in preserving the authority of a specific tradition within the Ḥanafī school renders their use of the different muftīs illuminating. In other words, non-Muslims solicited the opinion of the muftī they thought would promote their legal interests most efficiently.[6]

[6] On non-Muslims' use of the various channels of the Ottoman legal system, see Richard Wittmann, "Before Qadi and Grand Vizier: Intra-Communal Dispute Resolution and Legal Transactions among Christians and Jews in the Plural Society of Seventeenth Century Istanbul" (PhD diss., Harvard University, 2008).

Consider, for example, the following case, which is preserved in the court records of Jerusalem. In 1597, several Jerusalemite Jews who failed to pay their debts and were consequently imprisoned in the local prison appeared before the Ḥanafī judge of Jerusalem. In prison, they complained, they had to share their cells with Muslim prisoners, and therefore could not pray and observe the Sabbath day. They proposed to be transferred to an adjacent cell, known as the Room of the Well, located near the prison. The judge summoned the Muslim lenders, who rejected the proposed arrangement. The Jews, or, more likely, someone on their behalf, approached Jār Allāh b. Abī Luṭf, the Ḥanafī muftī of Jerusalem at the time, and asked for his opinion:

[Question:] What is the opinion of our lord the *Shaykh al-Islām* concerning a case in which next to the prison of the judge there is a room suitable to serve as prison, [and given that] the Jewish community has a debt [which they have not paid], and they [the Jewish prisoners] asked to be imprisoned in the aforementioned room so the imprisoned Muslims would not suffer any harm inflicted by the Jews? Moreover, the Muslims will also harm the Jews, if they are to be imprisoned in a single place, for they [the Jews] are prevented from praying and [observing] the Sabbath among the Muslims, while they are not to be prevented according to the sharīʿa. If the judge deems it right to imprison them in the aforementioned room in a manner that guarantees that they will not flee and that they [the Jews will] perform all that is required from prisoners according to the law, is he [the judge] allowed to do so [i.e., to transfer the Jews to that room]? Dispense to us your opinion.

[Answer:] Praise be to God, may He guide me in the straight path. Yes, the judge is allowed to imprison them [the Jews] wherever he wishes, so they will not lose any of their rights. God knows best. Jār Allāh b. Abī al-Luṭf wrote this [answer].[7]

After examining the legal rulings, the judge ordered the warden to transfer the Jews to the Room of the Well. All this information, including the legal ruling issued by the Jerusalemite muftī, was recorded in the court record.

This case raises several issues that are relevant to our discussion: the Jews' decision to solicit the ruling of this particular muftī, the manner in which the question was articulated, and the circulation of the muftī's legal ruling in the context of the imperial legal system. Moreover, despite

[7] Amnon Cohen and Elisheva Ben Shimon-Pikali, *Jews in the Moslem Religious Court: Society, Economy and Communal Organization in the XVIth Century (Documents from Ottoman Jerusalem)* [in Hebrew] (Jerusalem: Yad Izhak Ben-Zvi, 1993), 1:29–30. At the end of Jār Allāh's answer, the Jews also grafted on the opinion of Isḥāq b. ʿUmar b. Abī al-Luṭf, the Shāfiʿī muftī of Jerusalem, who approved the opinion of his Ḥanafī colleague (and relative).

the case's local particularities, I would suggest examining it in the broader context of Greater Syria (and, to some extent, of other Arab provinces of the empire).

Let us start by dwelling on the identity of the Ḥanafī muftī the Jews approached. Jār Allāh b. Abī al-Luṭf was the officially appointed Ḥanafī muftī of Jerusalem and the professor of a madrasa known as al-Madrasa al-ʿUthmāniyya, a position that was stipulated to go to the Ḥanafī officially appointed muftīs of the city since the sixteenth century and was monopolized by the Banū Abī al-Luṭf in that period.[8] Although the Jews could have consulted a muftī who did not hold a state appointment, they decided to consult one who was officially appointed, assuming that his ruling would be the most effective.

In addition, this case shows how the muftī's ruling as a document functioned in the context of the legal procedure in the court. It is clear that the muftī had to be informed about the case and usually did not intervene in the procedure that took place at the court before the judge. Here, the muftī was informed by one of the parties involved, but it seems that in other cases the judge himself consulted the muftī. After the *fatwā* – the question and the muftī's answer – was brought to court, the judge examined the extent to which it matched the case under consideration. In some cases, as here, the muftī's ruling was recorded verbatim in the court record; in others, it was paraphrased.

This is not to say that the officially appointed muftī never intervened in the court procedure. According to Sharaf al-Dīn Mūsā b. Yūsuf al-Anṣārī (d. after 1592), who served as Shāfiʿī deputy judge in Damascus, in 1590 the secretary of the officially appointed provincial Ḥanafī muftī in the city, Muḥammad b. Hilāl al-Ḥanafī, sent him two rulings issued presumably by al-Ḥanafī. These *fatāwā*, which followed the rulings of Ebû's-Suʿûd Efendi, reiterated the regulation that cases that are older than fifteen years should

[8] See Najm al-Dīn Muḥammad b. Muḥammad al-Ghazzī, *Luṭf al-samar wa-qaṭf al-thamar: Min tarājim aʿyān al-ṭabaqa al-ūlā min al-qarn al-ḥādī ʿashar* (Damascus: Wizārat al-Thaqāfa wa'l-Irshād al-Qawmī, 1981–82), 2:584–85; al-Ḥasan b. Muḥammad al-Būrīnī, *Tarājim al-aʿyān min abnāʾ al-zamān* (Damascus: al-Majmaʿ al-ʿIlmī al-ʿArabī bi-Dimashq, 1959–63), 2:127–28; Muḥammad Amīn b. Faḍl Allāh al-Muḥibbī, *Khulāṣat al-athar fī aʿyān al-qarn al-ḥādī ʿashar* (Beirut: Dār al-Kutub al-ʿIlmiyya, 2006), 1:530. The use of the Shāfiʿī muftīs who held an official appointment deserves another study. Here suffice it to say that there are other instances of litigants bringing a *fatwā* from both the Ḥanafī and Shāfiʿī officially appointed muftīs. In some cases, litigants brought only the ruling of the officially appointed Shāfiʿī muftī (see, for instance, Cohen and Ben Shimon-Pikali, *Jews in the Moslem Religious Court*, 1:216).

not be adjudicated in court. Nevertheless, in most cases, it was one of the litigants who brought the jurisconsult's ruling to court.[9]

The practice of bringing a ruling of an officially appointed muftī to court in Jerusalem corresponds to similar practices elsewhere. Studies of other courts – such as Boğaç Ergene's study of the courts of seventeenth- and eighteenth-century Çankırı and Kastamonu, Haim Gerber's study of Bursa, and Hülya Canbakal's of the court of seventeenth-century Ayntab[10] – have also drawn attention to the important role that *fatāwā* issued by the muftī (i.e., the chief muftī or the officially appointed provincial one) played in the legal procedure. Most of these studies have identified the same pattern: in most cases in which the judge deemed the ruling relevant to the case under adjudication, the litigant who brought the *fatwā* to the court won the case.

To clarify this point further, the appearance of the officially appointed muftīs' rulings in the court record should be contrasted with the relative absence of rulings by those without a state appointment, with the exception of rulings by those jurisconsults who had been co-opted by the learned hierarchy and whose works had entered the imperial jurisprudential canon, as we have seen in the case of Khayr al-Dīn al-Ramlī (in Chapter 4). This is not to say, however, that the rulings of the nonappointed muftīs were not brought to court. But if they were, they were not recorded (or even mentioned) in the court record. Their absence from the record suggests that consulting these rulings was not considered part of the formal procedure in court. It is therefore difficult to assess the impact of the rulings issued by nonappointed jurists on the judge's resolution, but it is clear, as will be discussed, that the rulings of prominent nonappointed muftīs were influential, both in and outside the court.

[9] Sharaf al-Dīn Mūsā b. Yūsuf al-Anṣārī, *Nuzhat al-khāṭir wa-bahjat al-nāẓir* (Damascus: Manshūrat Wizārat al-Thaqāfa, 1991), 1:169–71. On Muḥammad b. Hilāl, see al-Muḥibbī, *Khulāṣat al-athar*, 3:227–28.

[10] Boğaç Ergene, *Local Court, Provincial Society and Justice in the Ottoman Empire: Legal Practice and Dispute Resolution in Cankiri and Kastamonu (1652–1744)* (Leiden: Brill, 2003), 139–40, 149–50; Haim Gerber, *State, Society, and Law in Islam: Ottoman Law in Comparative Perspective* (Albany: State University of New York Press, 1994), chap. 3; Hülya Canbakal, "Birkaç Fetva Bir Soru: Bir Hukuk Haritasına Doğru," in *Şinasi Tekin'in Anısına Uygurlardan Osmanlıya* (Istanbul: Simurg, 2005), 258–70; Ronald C. Jennings, "Kadi, Court, and Legal Procedure in 17th C. Ottoman Kayseri: The Kadi and the Legal System," *Studia Islamica* 48 (1978): 133–36; Ronald C. Jennings, "Limitations of the Judicial Powers of the Kadi in 17th C. Ottoman Kayseri," *Studia Islamica* 50 (1979), 156–59.

Moreover, in places where prominent muftīs who did not hold an official appointment operated and were influential enough, imperial subjects – Jewish subjects, in this case – made use of these muftīs to promote their legal interests. While the Jews of sixteenth-century Jerusalem knew the advantages of obtaining a ruling from the officially appointed provincial muftī for promoting their legal interests in court, some of their coreligionists addressed their questions to other muftīs who did not hold a state appointment whenever they thought the latter's ruling would promote their legal interests. Late in the sixteenth century, for example, two Jews from Alexandria, Samuel b. Shams b. Isḥāq and Salomon b. Mūsā b. Isḥāq, appeared before the Ḥanafī judge. The case was about certain commercial affairs and debts that should not concern us here. After the case was adjudicated in court, someone, possibly one of the litigants, brought a copy of the resolution (*ṣūra*) to the eminent sixteenth-century muftī Muḥammad b. ʿUmar Shams al-Dīn al-Ḥānūtī, who was not an officially appointed muftī.[11] The Jewish merchants' decision to approach al-Ḥānūtī demonstrates the weight his rulings carried in court, or, alternatively, points to the authoritativeness of his rulings among Muslims and non-Muslims alike.

The weight of the rulings of the officially appointed muftīs, and especially those of the chief imperial jurisconsults, is also reflected in the procedures for petitioning the Sublime Porte, as another example from sixteenth-century Jerusalem illustrates. In 1550 one of the officials in the district of Jerusalem petitioned the Porte, claiming that the Jews of the city had leased parts of the land he was given by the Ottoman state as salary (*tîmâr*) for their cemetery and that he had not been paid as had been agreed. Before petitioning the Porte, the *tîmâr* holder sought, and received, the opinion of the chief muftī at the time, Ebû's-Suʿûd Efendi. Based on the muftī's ruling and the petition, an imperial edict was issued and sent to Jerusalem. Upon the arrival of this edict, which also included the chief muftī's ruling, the judge of Jerusalem summoned the parties. After examining the documents presented by the litigants and the testimonies in support of their claims, the judge ruled in favor of the *tîmâr* holder. It is not fully clear why the *tîmâr* holder decided to submit his question to the chief muftī before petitioning the Porte.[12] The important point is that the

[11] Muḥammad b. ʿUmar b. Shams al-Dīn al-Ḥānūtī, *Fatāwā al-Ḥānūtī*, Bayezit Library MS Veliyüddin 1494, 428r–429v. On Muḥammad b. ʿUmar b. Shams al-Dīn al-Ḥānūtī, see al-Muḥibbī, *Khulāṣat al-athar*, 4:76–77.

[12] Cohen and Ben Shimon-Pikali, *Jews in the Moslem Religious Court*, 1:92.

latter assumed that the chief muftī's ruling would strengthen his stance, first in the Porte and later in court. Although it is practically impossible in most cases to reconstruct the entire story behind the *fatāwā* in the collections of the chief muftīs, it stands to reason that at least in some cases the solicitors intended to petition the Porte.[13]

It should be stressed that, as the above case illustrates, those who submitted their questions to the chief muftī were not always members of the imperial ruling elite. When the Ashkenazi Jews of Jerusalem wanted to renovate their synagogue in the city in the late seventeenth century, they addressed the chief muftī Feyżullah Efendi and obtained a *fatwā* approving the renovation.[14] Then they petitioned the Porte, and, as in the *tîmâr* holder's case, their petition resulted in an imperial edict sent to the court in Jerusalem.[15] Moreover, the content of many questions preserved in the collections of the chief imperial muftīs raise the possibility that the questions were posed by commoners, or were posed on their behalf. For instance, a question posed to Menteşîzâde Efendi (who served as chief muftī from 1715 to 1716) deals with a member of the ruling elite (*ahl al-ʿurf*) who "oppressively" seizes the money of a minor inheritor.[16]

The Jews of Jerusalem, like other solicitors who addressed the officially appointed jurisconsults, demonstrated remarkable familiarity with the legal procedures. Other cases indicate that solicitors were also familiar with specific legal arguments and tried to manipulate these arguments in their favor. Two *fatāwā*, one by Kemâlpaşazâde and the other by Ebû's-Suʿûd Efendi, concerning the permissibility of certain Sufi practices may

[13] On the practice of obtaining a ruling before petitioning the Porte, see Abdurrahman Atçil, "Procedures in the Ottoman Court and the Duties of the Kadis" (MA thesis, Bilkent University, Ankara, 2002), 21–22; Başak Tuğ, "Politics of Honor: The Institutional and Social Frontiers of 'Illicit' Sex in Mid-Eighteenth-Century Ottoman Anatolia" (PhD diss., New York University, 2009), 111–23.

[14] It is unclear, however, who submitted their question to the chief muftī. They may have sent an envoy or asked their coreligionists to solicit the chief muftī's opinion and to petition the Porte on their behalf. A scribal manual from seventeenth-century Jerusalem records epistles sent from the Jews of Jerusalem to the Jews in Istanbul. In these missives, the Jews of Jerusalem instruct their Istanbulian counterparts to obtain rulings from the muftī, that is, the *şeyḫülislâm*, for various purposes. Some of the epistles reflect the close contacts between certain unidentifiable members of the Istanbulian Jewish community and the chief muftī (and other senior jurists and officials). Minna Rozen, "Influential Jews in the Sultan's Court in Istanbul in Support of Jerusalem Jewry in the 17th Century" [in Hebrew], *Michael* 7 (1981): 394–430; Minna Rozen, *The Jewish Community of Jerusalem in the Seventeenth Century* [in Hebrew] (Tel Aviv: Tel Aviv University and the Ministry of Defense Publishing House, 1984), 419–21.

[15] Cohen and Ben Shimon-Pikali, *Jews in the Moslem Religious Court*, 1:87–89.

[16] Menteşîzâde, *Fetâvâ*, 521r.

illustrate this point.[17] Although Kemâlpaşazâde's *fatwā* is cited in Ebû's-Su'ûd's collection following the latter's answer, they should be treated as two separate *fatāwā* issued in two distinct moments. In Ebû's-Su'ûd's collection, his answer precedes that of his predecessor. Here I will reverse the order and read the *fatāwā* chronologically, but the connection made by Ebû's-Su'ûd is important and will be discussed as well.

Here, then, is Kemâlpaşazâde's *fatwā*:

Question: What is the opinion of jurists of the Prophetic religion and the sages of the jurisprudence of Muṣṭafā – may Allāh strengthen them with the grace He has bestowed upon them from the strong authority to render judgment and [may He] set them straight in what He imposed on them of correct decision[s] – about a group of Sufis [*ṭā'ifa mutaṣawwifa*] who are commemorating God and are sitting in circles in the manner they have always done, making utterance[s] [such as]: "There is no God" [but Allāh?], "He," or "Oh, Allāh." And they raise their voice at their preferred times. After the *dhikr* [commemoration of God] takes them over they utter and move, so sometimes they whirl with the *dhikr* right and left. [At] other [times] they fall with the *fikr* [thought of God] according to [the] manner in which Allāh treats them [*'āmalahum Allāh*] – may His glory and beauty be glorified – sometimes they are drawn by divine guidance and they

[17] Kemâlpaşazâde was one of the leading jurists in the central lands of the empire who in the early decades of the sixteenth century compiled treatises dealing with specific practices, such as the dance during *dhikr* sessions (Ibrāhīm al-Ḥalabī is another such jurist). Chronicles from the Arab lands also record *fatāwā* issued by leading, mostly non-Ḥanafī, jurists approving of certain debated Sufi practices, such as the use of drums and music in their *dhikr*. Although the jurists mentioned in the chronicles did not discuss the issue of dancing directly, as did those in the question, it appears that the question posed to Kemâlpaşazâde is part of this ongoing debate concerning the legality of a host of Sufi practices – a debate that, as we have just seen, cuts across legal schools and regions. See Aḥmad Shams al-Dīn Kemâlpaşazâde, *Risāla fī al-raqṣ*, Süleymaniye Library MS Denizli 114–1, 225r–228r; Ibrāhīm b. Muḥammad al-Ḥalabī, *Risāla fī al-raqṣ*, Süleymaniye Library MS Es'ad Efendi 1690, 214v–225r; Najm al-Dīn Muḥammad b. Muḥammad al-Ghazzī, *al-Kawākib al-sā'ira bi-a'yān al-mi'a al-'āshira* (Beirut: Jāmi'at Bayrūt al-Amīrikiyya, 1945–58), 3:16–20; al-Ghazzī, *Luṭf al-samar*, 2:595–600, 656–59. For Aleppo, see Muḥammad b. Ibrāhīm b. al-Ḥanbalī, *Durr al-ḥabab fī tārīkh a'yān Ḥalab* (Damascus: Wizārat al-Thaqāfa, 1972–74), 2 (part 1): 416. This debate continued until the eighteenth century (and perhaps even later). 'Abd al-Ghanī al-Nābulusī defended controversial Sufi practices. In his treatise on this issue, he also invokes Khayr al-Dīn al-Ramlī's approval of the loud dhikr. 'Abd al-Ghanī al-Nābulusī, *Jam' al-asrār fī radd al-ṭa'n 'an al-ṣūfiyya al-akhyār ahl al-tawājjud bi'l-adhkār* (Beirut: Dār al-Muḥabba, 2000). For al-Ramlī's response, see ibid., 68–72. See also Ahmet T. Karamustafa, *God's Unruly Friends: Dervish Groups in the Islamic Later Middle Period, 1200–1500* (Salt Lake City: University of Utah Press, 1995); Derin Terzioğlu, "Sufis in the Age of State Building and Confessionalization, 1300–1600," in *The Ottoman World*, ed. C. Woodhead (London: Routledge, 2011), 86–99; Zeynep Yürekli, *Architecture and Hagiography in the Ottoman Empire: The Politics of Bektashi Shrines in the Classical Age* (Farnham, Surrey, UK: Ashgate, 2012).

strike the ground with their feet, leaping [around], and the disapprover regarded all this and claimed that it amounted to the dance [*raqṣ*] that the entertainers perform blatantly. [In response the Sufis] say: "We do this [leaping] in ecstasy and involuntarily losing of ourselves in accordance with the correct Sunna and good intentions of our [?] *shaykhs*." [In a situation such that] the Sufis perform the *dhikr* in their presence and they do not prevent them [from doing so]; rather, they even find delight and comfort in watching and hearing them, and the observable way they are when [attending] their *samāʿ* [a Sufi session that includes music, dancing, and chanting as a means of reaching closer to God] testifies to this; and we have seen that some of the jurists [permitted?] the *dhikr* in their sessions, so in them they perform the *dhikr* according to the above-mentioned Sunna, and we have seen many of our masters the jurists, the most excellent of their time, issued *fatāwā* permitting [this practice]. We have found in several books compiled by the well-guided jurists [who follow the] the Ḥanafī and Shāfiʿī customs that they permitted this and showed how it [the *dhikr*] has great virtue and immense benefit. We have tested [?] this and witnessed numerous times what they have shown [?] and [witnessed] that the disapproved occurs only sporadically; so is [this] permissible for them or not?

Answer: There is nothing wrong in their ecstatic being if it is sincere and there is nothing [legally] problematic in their sway if they are sincere. You have undertaken to do foot-service [?], and it is legitimate for one asked by his master to do by way of permit, under the circumstances mentioned, at the *dhikr* and *samāʿ* what has been mentioned is permissible during the *dhikr* and the *samāʿ* for the knowledgeable/enlightened Sufis [*ʿārifīn*] who spent their time [doing] the most excellent acts of those who follow the path [*sālikīn*], and who possess [the ability] to hold themselves [while they face] ignobility [*qabā'iḥ al-aḥwāl*].... If they mention Him they lament [their distance from Him]; if they "witness" Him they find peace; if they graze in [?] the presence of His proximity they travel about [?] – when ecstasy overcomes them with His bouts of mastering [them], they drink from the sources of His will. Some of them receive the divine night-visits and fall to the ground and lose their poise; some are struck by lightning flashes of grace and move and are content; some are approached by love from the harbingers of [divine] intimacy and follow [that path] and lose themselves; and [verse]

He whose ecstasy is true ecstasy/does not need the word of the singer
[He finds in] himself eternal bliss /and ongoing drunkenness without a wine vat.

This is my answer and God knows best.[18]

The question sent to Kemâlpaşazâde, assuming that it was addressed to him personally, is intriguing. It deals with several Sufi practices whose permissibility stood at the center of a heated debate in the early sixteenth century.[19] What makes this question even more intriguing is that the Sufis

[18] Ebû's-Suʿûd Efendi, *Fetâvâ*, Süleymaniye Library MS Ismihan Sultan 226, 189r–189v.

[19] Aḥmad Shams al-Dīn Kemâlpaşazâde, *Risāla fī al-raqṣ*, Süleymaniye Library MS Denizli 114–1, 225r–228r; Ibrāhīm b. Muḥammad al-Ḥalabī, *Risāla fī al-raqṣ*, Süleymaniye Library MS Esʿad Efendi 1690, 214v–225r.

had reportedly asked other Ḥanafī and Shāfiʿī jurists for their opinion concerning these practices. It is also evident from the Sufis' report that these jurists had contended that the practices were licit and in congruence with the Prophetic tradition. The address to the imperial chief muftī, therefore, may be interpreted as an invitation to participate in an ongoing debate that troubled many sixteenth-century jurists and scholars, both Ḥanafī and non-Ḥanafī.

Against this backdrop, the questioner decided to address the jurists in Istanbul. Nothing is known about his (or their) identity. He may have been a local Arab subject who realized that he might find strong allies for his opinion in the imperial capital. Alternatively, he might have been an Ottoman official or judge who wanted to confirm what the opinion of the chief muftī was. By addressing the *şeyḫülislâm* and obtaining his opinion in Arabic, the solicitor perhaps thought he could counter the argument of jurists from the Arab lands who disapproved of such practices. It is likely, however, that the questioner considered the chief muftī to be the leading authority to resolve this dispute, even if the chief muftī's response did not necessarily convince the other jurists or the Sufis themselves.

Interestingly the question to Kemâlpaşazâde and his subsequent answer are included in the answer of his successor, Ebû's-Suʿûd Efendi, several decades later. After the address, the questioner inquires about

> a group [*qawm*] that recites "There is no God but Allāh," "He" [*Huwa*], and "Oh, Allāh," while chanting and uttering vociferously; at times they raise [their voices] and at times they lower [them] according to what suits these unlawful acts and the corrupt performance; they do not hope for God with respect, but they pursue illegal innovations [*bidaʿ*] as their banner. Issue your opinion, may [God] reward you and may God turn you into the most exalted in the protection of the master of the messengers [the Prophet].

Ebû's-Suʿûd Efendi gives the following answer:

> What is mentioned [in your question] is a despicable invention and a loathsome illicit invented deceit. They will fall into the abysses of distraction and downfall, [as] they took delight in those who corrupt the words and turn the recitation of the Qurʾān [*al-mathānī*] into [?] singing. Alas he who attributed [this act] to the evident Truth [God], when they [the Sufis who perform these illicit acts] do not cease their forbidden acts, and those who do not reintroduce the word [idea] of oneness to their rightly guided practice [*nahj*] shall suffer [lit. touched upon by] a severe punishment. [But] [you] who lament [?] this [act] and incite the believers against it, [there is nothing wrong in] beautifying the sounds of the beautiful Qurʾān without insertion or exchange. And God said: The Truth will lead the way

and "For me [Allāh] is sufficient and the best disposer of affairs" (Qur'ān 3:173). [Cites Kemâlpaşazâde's answer.][20]

There are interesting parallels between the question posed to Kemâlpaşazâde and that posed to Ebû's-Su'ûd Efendi, as well as significant differences. Taken together, the two *fatāwā* (that is, the questions and the answers) convey a sense of the dialogic nature of the process of the solicitation and dispensing of the muftī's opinion. As this case demonstrates, at times it was a dialogue that went on for decades. Furthermore, it seems that both the questioner and Ebû's-Su'ûd were aware that there was an ongoing exchange between solicitors from the Arab lands and chief imperial muftīs over this issue. From the solicitor's vantage point, the fact that the Sufis in his question say exactly the same phrases their counterparts are reported to have said in the question posed to Kemâlpaşazâde indicates that these phrases were employed with the intention of framing the debate. Nevertheless, unlike the earlier questioner, the latter adds adjectives that clearly point to his strong disapproval of the Sufi practices. It is possible that the questioner denounced certain Sufi practices as illegal innovations (*bid'a* pl. *bida'*), precisely because he was familiar with Kemâlpaşazâde's ruling, and attempted to lead Ebû's-Su'ûd to diverge from his predecessor's opinion. From the muftī's perspective, the citation of his predecessor's rulings points to his awareness of the history of the exchange and to its particular geographical setting, since both Ebû's-Su'ûd's and Kemâlpaşazâde's rulings were penned in Arabic. Moreover, Ebû's-Su'ûd's reference to the *fatwā* issued by Kemâlpaşazâde establishes the latter as precedent, although Ebû's-Su'ûd's ruling leaves room for speculation as to the degree of his agreement with his predecessor.[21]

Sometimes solicitors addressed officially appointed jurisconsults, usually provincial muftīs, in order to defend local practices within the imperial framework. Consider the following example: In his guide to ritual practices, *Hadiyyat Ibn al-'Imād li'l-'ubbād al-'ibād*, the officially appointed muftī of Damascus 'Abd al-Raḥmān b. Muḥammad al-'Imādī (d. 1641) reports an encounter he had with Es'ad Efendi (d. 1625), who passed through Damascus on his way to the holy cities.[22] Es'ad Efendi was not satisfied with the quality of the water in the Damascene cisterns

[20] Ebû's-Su'ûd Efendi, *Fetâvâ*, Süleymaniye Library MS Ismihan Sultan 226, 189r–189v.

[21] Similar dynamics may be discerned in two *fatāwā* from the second half of the seventeenth century. See Minḳarîzâde Yaḥyâ Efendi, *Fetâvâ*, Süleymaniye Library MS Hekimoğlu 421, 53r; Menteşîzâde, *Fetâvâ*, 77r.

[22] On Es'ad Efendi, see Abdülkadir Altunsu, *Osmanlı Şeyhülislamları* (Ankara: Ayyıldız Matbaası, 1972), 58–59.

for ablution. The quality of the water was so bad, in Es'ad Efendi's view, that he wanted to order the cisterns' renovation. The implication of Es'ad Efendi's view of the quality of the water was that the ablutions of the Damascenes were not valid. Al-'Imādī, as he recounts, defended the quality of the water, and thereby the validity of the Damascenes' ablutions, by citing an approving passage from one of Ibn Nujaym's works.[23] Several decades later, another officially appointed muftī, the Damascene 'Alā' al-Dīn al-Ḥaṣkafī, also pointed to differences in certain legal issues between Greater Syria and the core lands of the empire, and implicitly approved of the Damascene practice.[24] In other words, addressing local officially appointed muftīs was at times a good solution for securing the legality of local practices within the imperial context.

Prior to the Ottoman conquest in 1516–17, the overwhelming majority of the inhabitants of the Arab lands had very little, if any, contact with the evolving Ottoman learned hierarchy and legal system.[25] The Ottoman conquest led to the introduction of new legal institutions, such as the institution of the chief imperial muftī, into the Arab lands, and the imperial capital became an important political, scholarly, and legal center. The cases we have examined so far illustrate the increasing familiarity of a growing number of imperial subjects with the Ottoman learned hierarchy and the imperial legal institutions in general, and particularly with the

[23] See Ibn al-'Imād's opinion and 'Abd al-Ghanī al-Nābulusī's support of this ruling. 'Abd al-Ghanī al-Nābulusī, *Nihāyat al-murād fī sharḥ Hadiyyat Ibn al-'Imād* (Limassol, Cyprus: al-Jaffān wa'l-Jābī, 1995), 276–80.

[24] Muḥammad b. 'Alī b. Muḥammad al-Ḥiṣnī 'Alā' al-Ḥaṣkafī, *al-Durr al-muntaqā fī sharḥ al-Multaqā* (Beirut: Dār al-Kutub al-'Ilmiyya, 1998), 2:323.

[25] Some Mamluk subjects were familiar with at least some institutions of the burgeoning Ottoman legal system. Fifteenth-century and early sixteenth-century chronicles and biographical dictionaries include biographies of leading jurists who operated in the Ottoman realms and entered the Mamluk lands. At the same time, Mamluk subjects (such as merchants and scholars) traveled to Anatolia and to the Ottoman domains in the late fifteenth century. See, for instance, Ibn Ṭawq, *Yawmiyyāt Shihāb al-Dīn Aḥmad b. Ṭawq* (Damascus: Institut français de Damas, 2000–7), 2:947–48; Emire Cihan Muslu, "Ottoman-Mamluk Relations: Diplomacy and Perceptions" (PhD diss., Harvard University, 2007), 1–86. 'Alī b. Yūsuf al-Buṣrawī mentions in his chronicle an incident that sheds some light on the ongoing contacts between the jurists in the Ottoman realms and their colleagues in the Mamluk sultanate. In 1490, during the Ottoman-Mamluk war, the Ottoman chief muftī Mollâ 'Arab sent his own envoy to inform the Mamluk commanders that he and other jurists in the Ottoman lands were not pleased with Bâyezîd II's decision to attack the Mamluk sultanate. Mollâ 'Arab was, it should be mentioned, one of those jurists who traveled between the Mamluk and the Ottoman domains. 'Alī b. Yūsuf al-Buṣrawī, *Ta'rīkh al-Buṣrawī: ṣafaḥāt majhūla min Tārīkh Dimashq fī 'aṣr al-mamālīk, min sanat 871 H li-ghāyat 904 H* (Beirut: Dār al-Ma'mūn li'l-Tūrath, 1988), 140.

institution of the chief imperial muftī and his officially appointed provincial colleagues. To be sure, some of the solicitors, such as the *tîmâr* holder, were members of the imperial judicial or ruling elites who resided in the Arab lands. On the other hand, it is clear that commoners, such as the Jews of Jerusalem, knew enough to address the officially appointed muftī of the city. As has been argued earlier, the consistency with which certain authorities were addressed indicates that imperial subjects had access to "legal knowledge" that informed their consumption of justice.

This is not to suggest, however, that every subject (or even every member of the ruling or judicial elites) was equally familiar with the various authorities and the advantages their opinions might offer for his or her case. Some probably made use of the various muftīs more skillfully than others. It is also probable that at least some solicitors were loyal followers of specific muftīs, regardless of these muftīs' position in the new "legal landscape." Moreover, as Boğaç Ergene's study of the courts of Kastamonu and Çankırı has shown, there were some barriers that might have impeded easy access to the imperial legal system and its jurisconsults.[26] These included the geographical distance to the town where the officially appointed muftī operated, let alone the distance to the imperial capital; the costs of the procedure; and access to legal experts who could assist in formulating the question and provide legal guidance.[27]

Without underestimating the significance of these impediments, and without blurring the differences between imperial subjects in terms of their familiarity with and access to the legal procedure, one has to acknowledge that many subjects did have access to the legal system in general and to officially appointed muftīs in particular. Although unsuccessful attempts to obtain a muftī's ruling most likely remain underdocumented as do rulings that the solicitors considered unsatisfactory, other

[26] Ergene, *Local Court*.

[27] In the earlier stages of the institution of the *şeyḫülislâm*, it seems that the *fatāwā* were issued gratis. However, with the growing bureaucratization of the office, fees were imposed to finance the services of the scribes and secretaries. It is hard to assess to what degree these fees prevented people from obtaining a *fatwā*. But out of the forty-nine *fatāwā* in Arabic, a significant proportion deal with endowments or appointments to positions. Although it might be risky to deduce statistical data on the basis of this finding, it might suggest that, at far as the Arab subjects of the empire are concerned, propertied subjects tended to use the channel of the *şeyḫülislâm* more frequently. This, however, calls for further research. According to Hezârfen (writing around mid-seventeenth century), the fee for a *fatwā* was seven *akçe*. The fee was intended to cover the expenses of the scribes (*resm-i müsevvid, kâtiblerindir*). Uriel Heyd, "Some Aspects of the Ottoman Fetva," *Bulletin of the School of Oriental and African Studies* 32, no. 1 (1969): 52–53.

cases, such as the case of the sixteenth-century Jews of Jerusalem, suggest that commoners were familiar with the legal procedure or at least had access to judicial guidance. The subjects' decision to solicit the opinion of the chief muftī, given the alternatives they had at their disposal, may be interpreted as their recognition of the weight that the ruling of the officially appointed muftīs carried within the Ottoman legal system, and perhaps even as a sign of their own acceptance of these muftīs' authority. In other words, the process should be described both from the perspective of the imperial legal system that sought to gain recognition and from the vantage point of the system's "users." It is thus necessary to dwell on how imperial subjects, and especially those who were not members of the ruling or judicial elite, acquired knowledge about the legal procedure and learned when and how to address officially appointed muftīs.

Several channels whereby potential solicitors could have learned what muftī would better serve their interests emerge from the sources. (It is fairly safe to assume that there were also other venues in which legal knowledge was transmitted and disseminated.) The imperial legal court was one of the sites in which non-jurists were most frequently exposed to legal rulings. When *fatāwā* are mentioned in court records, the records describe this procedure in performative terms. In court records from the core lands of the empire, for example, litigants are reported to have presented the *fatwā* (the verb used is *ibrâz eylemek*).[28] Moreover, litigants are said to have declared in court they had obtained a ruling from a muftī (*fetvâm var diyü*).[29] After the presentation of the ruling, the court records often relate how the judge read the *fatwā* in court and deliberated its compatibility with the case under adjudication. In addition, the scribes at times included the *fatwā* in the record, copies of which were often given to the litigants. Litigants may have brought to court other rulings issued by nonappointed muftīs, in which case they had the opportunity to see which rulings carried greater weight in court. Moreover, as demonstrated by the edict issued following the petition of the *tîmâr* holder from

[28] Canbakal, "Birkaç Fetva Bir Soru"; Bilgin Aydın and Ekrem Tak, eds., *İstanbul Kadı Sicilleri Üsküdar Mahkemesi 1 Numaralı (H. 919–927/M. 1513–1521)* (Istanbul: İSAM Yayınalr, 2008), 349; Rıfat Günalan, Mehmet Âkif Aydın, and Coşkun Yılmaz, eds., *İstanbul Kadı Sicilleri Üsküdar Mahkemesi 2 Numaralı (H. 924–927/M. 1518–1521)* (Istanbul: İSAM Yayınalr, 2008), 149; Rıfat Günalan, Mehmet Akman, and Fikret Sarıcaoğlu., *İstanbul Kadı Sicilleri Üsküdar Mahkemesi 26 Numaralı (H. 970–971/M. 1562–1563)* (Istanbul: İSAM Yayınalr, 2008), 355, 412.

[29] Günalan et al., *İstanbul Kadı Sicilleri Üsküdar Mahkemesi 2 Numaralı*, 345; Günalan, *İstanbul Kadı Sicilleri Üsküdar Mahkemesi 26 Numaralı*, 303–4.

Jerusalem, rulings of the chief muftī were also cited in imperial edicts. The edicts were sent to provincial courts, where they were read publicly. In short, the imperial courts – and more broadly the imperial legal system – were instrumental in the consolidation and propagation of the authority of the rulings issued by the *şeyḫülislâm* and officially appointed provincial muftīs.

The growing familiarity of imperial subjects with the officially appointed muftī was facilitated by the growing bureaucracy that aided him, and by his secretaries. This bureaucracy played an instrumental role in the dissemination of legal knowledge. Important provincial centers, such as Damascus, had at least one muftī secretary (*amīn*). It is not fully clear when the first secretary was appointed, but it is clear that by the end of the sixteenth century a secretary operated in Damascus.[30] As we have seen, this secretary was in charge of communicating the muftī's rulings to the court, and most likely to other solicitors as well. It is likely that the secretary was also the one to articulate the solicitor's question and present it to the muftī. Thus the secretaries played a pivotal role in mediating between the solicitor and the jurisprudential discourse.[31]

The muftīs' secretaries were also important because they recorded and preserved the muftī's rulings. They were, in a sense, the archivists of the muftī. Therefore, they could have provided the solicitor with information about past rulings, which he or she could have used when articulating his question to the muftī. Furthermore, they may have kept other important rulings such as the rulings of the chief muftīs. It is also worth mentioning that the court records could have occasionally served the same end, since rulings dispensed by both the provincial and the chief muftīs were recorded there.

Finally, collections of rulings issued by certain muftīs played an important role in disseminating legal knowledge. Since these collections circulated across the empire, they served as "public archives," at least in learned circles. Jurists and scholars (and possibly others) could, and

[30] Another Damascene secretary was Ibrahim b. ʿAbd al-Raḥmān al-Dimashqī, also known as al-Su'ālātī (d. 1683). He was appointed to compile the questions for the Ḥanafī muftī of Damascus. Al-Muḥibbī, *Khulāṣat al-athar*, 1:41–42.

[31] This process is similar to the process described by Brinkley Messick in his *The Calligraphic State*. Brinkley Messick, *The Calligraphic State: Textual Domination and History in a Muslim Society* (Berkeley: University of California Press, 1992). Nevertheless, in some cases it is evident from the questions posed to the chief muftī about specific passages from jurisprudential texts that the questioner himself was a member of the learned circles. Ebû's-Suʿûd Efendi, *Fetâvâ*, 29r; Ṣunʿullah Efendi, *Fetâvâ*, Süleymaniye Library MS Reşid Efendi 269, 53v.

probably did, consult these collections when drafting their questions. In these collections, jurists could find how to address the chief muftī, the opinions of the current chief muftī's predecessors, and often the jurisprudential texts previous muftīs had consulted. In other words, the collections served as an important tool to cement the coherence of the institution of the officially appointed muftīship and its jurisprudential production.[32]

Writing Ottoman *Fatāwā* in Arabic

In addition to the considerable institutional efforts the imperial learned hierarchy made to cement the authority of its members, its particular branch within the Ḥanafī school, and its legal institutions, it also undertook to tap into the discourse of authority that prevailed throughout the empire's Arab provinces. In particular, it increasingly used certain discursive patterns in Arabic to address officially appointed jurisconsults across the Arab lands and the empire more generally. Consider, for example, the following *fatwā* issued by the sixteenth-century chief imperial muftī Çivizâde:

Question: What is the opinion of the *Shaykh al-Islām* and the magnificent master – may God glorify him in the world with the veneration of the most important master of masters – concerning an orchard whose revenues have been exploited for more than two centuries by the endower's [?] descendants and now a powerful man forcefully took over the [orchard] and uprooted its plants and destroyed its building. [Then] he planted [there] trees and built what he wanted without the permission of the guardian [*mutawallī*] [of the *waqf*]. Should the orchard be taken from him and left according to what it used to be in the past? And what is the verdict concerning the plants and the buildings? Issue your opinion [*aftūnā*], may you be rewarded [*ma'jūrīn*].

Answer: Yes, the orchard should be taken from him and should remain as it used to be in the past. Should another person who is entitled [to be a beneficiary] not appear, [the man] who took over [the orchard] should be accountable for what he uprooted and destroyed.[33]

[32] Writing in late eighteenth-century Istanbul, the dragoman of the Swedish embassy, Ignatius Mouradega d'Ohsson, states that in "every court throughout the empire" there are at least two or three *fatāwā* collections in addition to a copy of Ibrāhīm al-Ḥalabī's *Multaqā al-abḥur*. All the collections he lists are of rulings issued by seventeenth- and eighteenth-century chief jurisconsults. It is difficult to confirm this statement at this point. Still, it reflects the efforts made by the Ottoman dynasty and its learned hierarchy to promulgate the rulings of current and former chief muftīs. Ignatius Mouradega d'Ohsson, *Tableau general de l'Empire othman* (Paris: L'imprimerie de monsieur, 1788), 1:52–54.

[33] Muḥyîddîn Muḥammed b. İyâs el-Menteşevî Çivîzâde, *Fetâvâ*, Süleymaniye Library MS Kadizade Mehmed 251, 20r.

The stylistic conventions, beyond the language choice of Arabic, set this and similar *fatāwā* apart from the rulings issued in Ottoman Turkish *fatāwā* and, in fact, from those in many contemporary (or roughly contemporary) collections produced in the Arab lands. It should be stressed that despite the fact that Çivizâde's *fatāwā* are not among the earliest of those high-ranking members of the imperial learned hierarchy issued in Arabic, they differ stylistically from an earlier *fatwā* issued by Kemâlpaşazâde, which we have examined above; they also differ from another *fatwā* issued by Çivizâde himself, which was not included in the collection and has come down to us in the form of a document.[34] These differences are pertinent to the discussion here, for they illustrate the gradual development of the conventions that would characterize the Ottoman Arabic *fatāwā* across the next two centuries and perhaps even during the rest of Ottoman rule in the Arab lands.

We shall return to the earlier versions of the formula deployed to address the chief muftī, but first it would be useful to examine the conventions employed in the collections from Çivizâde's onward.[35] My inquiry into these conventions is inspired by Uriel Heyd's seminal study of the Ottoman *fatwā*. Heyd was the first, as far as I know, to have noticed the conventions that concern us here. However, he tended to interpret these conventions in terms of continuity and traced some of them to earlier periods.[36] The purpose of this examination is twofold: to expand on some issues that remained somewhat underdeveloped in Heyd's work concerning these conventions, and, second, and perhaps more importantly, to demonstrate how certain dynamics that accompanied the consolidation of the authority of the *şeyḫülislâm* and his subordinates in the Arab lands are reflected in the adoption of these conventions.

Let us start with the question (*istiftā'*). The question often opens with a formula addressing the head of the imperial learned hierarchy, the *şeyḫülislâm*: "what is the opinion of our lord [*mawlānā*] *Shaykh al-Islām*" (*mā qawl mawlānā shaykh al-Islām*). As Heyd has noted, this

[34] *İlmiye Salnamesi* (Istanbul: Maṭba'a-i 'Âmire, 1916), 363.

[35] There are some deviations from these conventions. Ebû's-Su'ûd's *fatwā* (*İlmiye Salnamesi*, 382) is one example. In the eighteenth-century collection *Behcetü'l-Fetâvâ* by Yenişerhirli, there are several *fatāwā* in Arabic that ask about the opinion of the Ḥanafī imāms (Abū Ḥanīfa and his companions, Abū Yūsuf and Muḥammad al-Shaybānī). See 'Abdullah Yenişehirli, *Behctetü'l-Fetâvâ Ma'an-Nüḳûl* (Istanbul: Matba'a-i Amire, 1872), 61, 62, 64. There are, however, other *fatāwā* in the collection that follow the general opening "what is the opinion of his honor *mawlānā* Shaykh al-Islām" (see ibid., 188).

[36] Heyd, "Fetva," 40–41.

formula appears in pre-Ottoman, and specifically Mamluk, *fatāwā*.[37] In his manual for the muftī and the questioner, the thirteenth-century jurist Abū Zakarīyā Yaḥyā b. Sharaf al-Nawawī (d. 1277) mentions this formula as the proper one to address a muftī.[38] This address is usually followed by praises and hyperbolic titles. In the other four Arabic *fatāwā* in Çivizâde's collection there are some variations: "what is the opinion of the knowledgeable [*ʿālim*], active [*ʿāmil*], and distinguished [*fāḍil*] *shaykh* – may God increase his glory in the two instances [*ānayn*] [i.e., this world and the hereafter] with the glory of the master of the two existences [*kawnayn*]";[39] "what is the opinion of the *shaykh*, the most erudite [*ʿallāma*], the sea of the two seas, the most perceptive [*fahhāma*], may God prolong his life until the Day of Judgement";[40] and "what is the opinion of the *Shaykh al-Islām* and the Muslims, the pillar of the verifiers [of truth], the best of the inquirers into the nuances [*zubdat al-mudaqqiqīn*] – may God let the people enjoy his presence until the Day of Judgment."[41] In later collections from the sixteenth and the seventeenth centuries, the formula "what is the opinion of the *Shaykh al-Islām*" is still occasionally followed by a long series of epithets: "what is the opinion of our lord, our master, and our exemplary model [*qidwa*], he who clarifies our problems, he who tears open the symbols of our complex issues [*fātiq rumūz mufaṣṣalātina*], the seal of the later [jurists] [*al-mutaʾakhkhirīn*]";[42] or "what is the opinion of the *Shaykh al-Islām* – may God let us enjoy his longevity until the Day of Resurrection."[43]

This convention for addressing officially appointed muftīs in the Ottoman era was not, however, frequently employed in the Mamluk period, nor was it very commonly used across the Arab provinces of the empire in later centuries. For example, during his journey to Istanbul while in the Syrian town of Ḥims, the Shāfiʿī Badr al-Dīn al-Ghazzī was asked for his legal opinion concerning a *waqf*-related issue. He recorded the question as it was submitted to him and his answer in his travelogue. For the purpose at hand, it is important to note that the *fatwā* opens

37 Ibid.
38 Abū Zakariyā Yaḥyā b. Sharaf al-Nawawī, *Adab al-fatwā wa'l-muftī wa'l-mustaftī* (Damascus: Dār al-Fikr, 1988), 83–84.
39 Çivizâde, *Fetâvâ*, 20r.
40 Ibid., 20v.
41 Ibid.
42 Ebû's-Suʿûd, *Fetâvâ*, 188r.
43 Menteşîzâde, *Fetâvâ*, 225r.

directly with the question without any address, attributes, or epithet.[44] Furthermore, the questions in the collections of provincial Greater Syrian officially appointed muftīs, such as the late seventeenth-century Ismāʿīl al-Ḥāʾik and ʿAbd al-Raḥīm b. Abī al-Luṭf, do not usually open with this formula.[45] It is precisely for this reason that the evolution of a standardized formula to address the chief muftī and his provincial subordinates merits attention.

After the address comes the question. The Ottoman *fatāwā*, as Heyd and others have pointed out, followed several conventions, which were meant to express the question in the most general terms.[46] When a question was asked concerning a specific scenario, the parties involved were represented by a set of fixed names (Zeyd, ʿAmr, Bekr, Beshîr, or Bishr for men and Hind and Zeyneb for women).[47] In the Arabic *fatāwā*, including in the *fatāwā* recorded in the collections of the *şeyḫülislâms*, names are rarely mentioned. Instead, the question is posed in general terms. During the sixteenth and the seventeenth centuries, however, the Zeyd/ʿAmr convention appears in several *fatāwā* in Arabic.[48] The question in Arabic is

[44] Badr al-Dīn Muḥammad al-Ghazzī, *al-Maṭāliʿ al-Badriyya fī al-manāzil al-Rūmiyya* (Beirut: al-Muʾassasa al-ʿArabiyya li'l-Dirāsāt wa'l-Nashr, 2004), 51. Ibn Ṭūlūn records another legal ruling issued by the Damascene Burhān al-Dīn al-Nājī in 1531. The question opens with a general address to the "lords, the jurists, the imāms of the religion [Islam]." Shams al-Dīn Muḥammad b. ʿAlī b. Ṭūlūn, *Ḥawādith Dimashq al-yawmiyya ghadāt al-ghazw al-ʿUthmānī li'l-Shām, 926–951H: Ṣafaḥāt mafqūda tunsharu li'l-Marra al-ūlā min Kitāb Mufākahat al-khillān fī ḥawādith al-zamān li-Ibn Ṭūlūn al-Ṣāliḥī* (Damascus: Dār al-Awāʾil, 2002), 223.

[45] Sharaf al-Dīn b. Ayyūb al-Anṣārī (d. 1590), who served as Shāfiʿī judge in Damascus, records several *fatāwā* that do not employ the address to the muftī in the questions. Sharaf al-Dīn b. Ayyūb al-Anṣārī, *Nuzhat al-khāṭir wa-bahjat al-nāẓir* (Damascus: Manshūrāt Wizārat al-Thaqāfa, 1991), 1:170–71. On the other hand, in a ruling issued by Khayr al-Dīn al-Ramlī preserved in a Jerusalem court record, the question opens with the official address. It is possible, however, that the scribe added this address when recording the ruling in the *sijill*. See Cohen and Ben Shimon-Pikali, *Jews in the Moslem Religious Court*, 1:453–54.

[46] Heyd, "Fetva," 39–41. It is worth mentioning Ebûʾs-Suʿûd Efendi's instructions as to how to draft a *fatwā* properly. Ebûʾs-Suʿûd Efendi, *Ebûʾs-Suʿûd Efendi Haẓretleri'nin Fetvâ Kâtiblerine Üslub Kitâbeti Taʿlîmdir*, Süleymaniye Library MS Esad Efendi 1017–1, 96r–99r.

[47] Heyd, "Fetva," 41. Heyd lists other names as well, but they are less common. For men: Khâlid, Velîd, Saʿîd, and Mubârak. For women: Ḥadîce, Ayşe, Umm Kulsum, Rabîʿe, Saʿîde, and Meryem.

[48] For example: Feyżullah b. Muḥammed Efendi, *Fetâvâ-i Feyżullah Efendi*, Süleymaniye Library MS Laleli 1267, 133v; Şunʿullah Efendi, *Fetâvâ*, 52r. It is worth noting that by the mid-seventeenth century this convention had gained some currency among muftīs from the Arab lands as well, as the collections of the *fatāwā* issued by the Palestinian muftīs Muḥammad al-Timurtāshī (d. 1595) and Khayr al-Dīn al-Ramlī (d. 1671) attest.

occasionally concluded with the phrase "issue your opinion [to us], may you be rewarded" (*aftūnā maʾjūrīn*),[49] or with the formula "may God the generous king reward you" (*athābakum Allāh al-malik al-wahhāb*),[50] rarely to be found in questions in Ottoman Turkish.

As is the case with other *fatāwā* in the Ottoman collections from the late fifteenth century onward, the question is usually articulated as a yes/no question. Accordingly, the answers tend to be brief. In the Arabic *fatāwā* the answer is usually brief, similar to the yes/no (*olur/olmaz*) answer in the Ottoman Turkish rulings. From time to time, however, the officially appointed muftī provides a somewhat longer answer, especially when he is asked for instructions on a particular matter or the case requires further clarification.[51] The important point is that the chief muftī penned his answer in Arabic, whenever the question was posed in Arabic. In other words, in such cases, the chief muftī assumed that the solicitor himself, or the ultimate audience, did not understand Ottoman Turkish.

These conventions also appear in questions posed to Greater Syrian officially appointed provincial muftīs and in their subsequent answers. A question in Arabic posed to Muʿîdzâde (d. 1575), the officially appointed Ḥanafī muftī of Damascus, opens with "what is the opinion of the *shaykh* of the *shaykh*s of Islam" and contains most of the features described above.[52] *Fatāwā* bearing similar conventions are also preserved in the court records of Jerusalem from the sixteenth and the seventeenth centuries. These *fatāwā*, it should be emphasized, were issued by the officially appointed muftī of Jerusalem. Since the *fatāwā* in the collections of the provincial muftīs – at least those from the seventeenth century – do not

Muḥammad b. ʿAbd Allāh al-Timurtāshī, *Fatāwā al-Timurtāshī*, Süleymaniye Library MS Esʿad Efendi 1114, 145v; al-Ramlī, *al-Fatāwā al-Khayriyya*, 1:33, 155; 2:11, 47, 63. It is worth mentioning that as early as the late fifteenth/early sixteenth century, the Zeyd/ʿAmr convention was employed, albeit very infrequently, across the Arab lands. For example, the Shāfiʿī Zakarīyā al-Anṣārī's (d. 1521) *fatāwā* collection uses this convention. Zakarīyāb. Muḥammad al-Anṣārī, *al-Iʿlām wa'l-ihtimām bi-jamʿ fatāwā Shaykh al-Islām* (Damascus: Dār al-Taqwā, 2007), 57–58.

49 For example: Çivizâde, *Fetâvâ*, 20r–20v; Ebû's-Suʿûd, *Fetâvâ*, 29r; Menteşîzâde, *Fetâvâ*, 77r, 83v.

50 For example: Feyżullah b. Muḥammed Efendi, *Fetâvâ-i Feyżullah Efendi*, Süleymaniye Library MS Laleli 1267, 65r.

51 Heyd, "Fetva," 41–42. For translated *fatāwā*, see Colin Imber, *Ebu's-Suʿud: The Islamic Legal Tradition* (Stanford, CA: Stanford University Press, 1997).

52 Meḥmed Muʿîdzâde, *Fetvâ*, Süleymaniye Library MS Fazil Ahmed Paşa 1581–1, 1v–7r. On Muʿîdzâde, see Muḥammad Khalīl b. ʿAlīb. Muḥammad b. Muḥammad al-Murādī, *ʿUrf al-bashām fī man waliya fatwā Dimashq al-Shām* (Damascus: Majmaʿ al-Lugha al-ʿArabiyya, 1979), 34–35.

usually open with these formulae, it appears that the scribe at the court added them when he recorded the *fatāwā*. One possible explanation for the use of this formula in the questions to the officially appointed muftīs (even when the solicitors themselves did not employ it) is that they were all members of the learned hierarchy, thus the provincial muftī represented the chief muftī.

The particular characteristics of the Arabic *fatwā* are significant precisely because they diverge from Ottoman Turkish conventions. One should bear in mind that the distinctive features of the Ottoman *fatwā* are the product of Ottoman muftīs' major efforts, beginning in the first half of the fifteenth century, to standardize the Ottoman *fatwā*. A *fatwā* issued by Şemsuddîn Fenârî (d. 1431), the first jurist to be appointed to the office of the chief muftī in the Ottoman realms, already displays most of the characteristics of the Ottoman *fatwā*.[53] Moreover, as I have already suggested, it is clear that the emergence of a distinctive, identifiable Ottoman *fatwā* marks a clear break from linguistic, scribal, and jurisprudential conventions that had prevailed across the Arab lands prior to the Ottoman conquest as well as after. In addition, the Ottoman *fatwā* differed from the *fatāwā* written in other parts of the Islamic world at the time, such as in North Africa.[54] Against this background, the fact that *fatāwā* in Arabic with their particular characteristics are preserved in Ottoman collections in their original language and with their particular stylistic patterns is telling.

The importance the chief muftīs and other members of the Ottoman imperial learned hierarchy attributed to the unique features of the Arabic *fatwā* is also evident from the fact that they were recorded in toto in the collections of the chief muftīs. Moreover, they were often recorded in their entirety in court records, as we shall see in the following discussion. It is worth dwelling on the decision to preserve the Arabic *fatāwā* with all their unique features. After all, even if the question and the answer were penned in Arabic, the scribes who included these *fatāwā* in the collection for their "legal content" could have translated the *fatwā* into Ottoman Turkish and removed the seemingly redundant formulae and phrases.

53 *İlmiye Salnamesi*, 323. On Fenâri, see Altunsu, *Osmanlı Şeyhülislamları*, 1–3; Richard C. Repp, *The Müfti of Istanbul: A Study in the Development of the Ottoman Learned Hierarchy* (London: Ithaca Press, 1986), 73–98.

54 On *fatāwā* in North Africa in the fifteenth century, see David S. Powers, *Law, Society, and Culture in the Maghrib, 1300–1500* (Cambridge: Cambridge University Press, 2002).

This is an appropriate point to return to Uriel Heyd's discussion of the Ottoman Arabic *fatāwā*. As I have already pointed out, in his study, Heyd noticed specific discursive patterns in those Ottoman *fatāwā* that were in Arabic, and he traced some of these patterns back to pre-Ottoman *fatāwā* collections, mostly from the Mamluk period. While Heyd does not explicitly describe these patterns in terms of persistence, endurance, or continuity, the fact that he does not explain the recurrence of pre-Ottoman patterns in the new Ottoman context suggests that he perceived their inclusion in the Ottoman collections in such terms. Understanding the reappearance of pre-Ottoman discursive patterns merely in terms of continuity, however, obscures the gradual process or dialogue through which these pre-Ottoman discursive patterns were standardized in the Ottoman context.

Questions sent to both Kemâlpaşazâde (d. 1533) and Çivizâde, for instance, reflect the dialogic evolution of specific patterns to address the chief and other officially appointed muftīs in Arabic. In the questions, the solicitors do not address the *şeyḫülislâm* but rather address a group of jurists, the "jurists of the Prophetic religion [*al-dīn al-Nabawī*] and the sages of the jurisprudence of Muṣṭafā [i.e., the Prophet, *ḥukamāʾ al-sharʿ al-Muṣṭafāwī*]," [55] or "the Ḥanafī lords, the jurists [*al-sādāt al-ʿulamāʾ al-Ḥanafiyya*]." [56] A reader of the collection could have known that Kemâlpaşazâde answered the question because he signed his name at the end of the answer. In Çivizâde's case, his signature appears after his answer at the bottom of the document. It is difficult, however, to determine whether the questioners had in mind a group of jurists to whom they addressed their question. What is clear, on the other hand, is that this formula soon disappeared and was replaced by a formula that would last for centuries. But since the address of the chief muftī evolved over the

[55] Ebû's-Suʿûd, *Fetâvâ*, 189r. The term "al-sharʿ al-Muṣṭafāwī" is fairly rare in the Arab context. The name Muṣṭafā was not in use in the Arab lands as the title of the Prophet. This seems like an Anatolian (perhaps Persianate) practice. Its use here might suggest that the Arab questioner employed this term for Ottoman ears. I am thankful to Everett Rowson for drawing my attention to this point.

[56] *İlmiye Salnamesi*, 363. Late fifteenth-century questions in Arabic addressed to the chief muftī Mollâ ʿArab also reflect the fluidity of the address. Mollâ ʿArab is addressed as the "master of the jurists" by one solicitor, whereas the other opens the question with "what is the opinion of the jurists of Islam and the virtuous [scholars] of the people ..." Mevlânâ Alâeddîn Alî al-ʿArabî al-Ḥalabî (Mollâ ʿArab), *Fetâvâ-i Mevlânâ ʿArab*, Süleymaniye Library MS Bağdatlı Vehbi 585, 14v, 51v. Furthermore, a question in Arabic recorded in the collection of Zenbilli ʿAlî Cemâlî, Mollâ ʿArab's successor, does not include any honorific title. Zenbilli ʿAlî Cemâlî, *Fetâvâ-i Zenbilli ʿAlî Cemâlî*, Süleymaniye Library MS Fatih 2388, 31r.

course of several decades, "continuity" fails to explain the conscious decision to follow specific patterns and dismiss others. Understanding this decision would help reveal some important dynamics that accompanied the consolidation of the authority of the *şeyhülislâm*, and, more broadly, the imperial learned hierarchy in the Arab lands during the first two centuries following the Ottoman conquest.

As has been described in the previous chapters, the Ottoman conquest created a new "legal landscape" across the Arab lands, which was partly an outcome of the introduction of a new understanding of the muftīship into the Arab provinces. On the other hand, in the "legal landscape" of the Arab lands in the sixteenth and even the seventeenth century, some prominent muftīs who did not hold a state appointment were not prevented from issuing their legal rulings, and so the chief muftī was one authority, albeit privileged in some circles, among many (Ḥanafī and non-Ḥanafī alike). It is in this context, I would argue, that the conventions of the Arabic *fatāwā* in the chief muftīs' *fatāwā* collections should be read and understood.

The address that opens many of the Arabic questions is of particular relevance to illustrate this point. As noted, this address already appears in treatises from the Mamluk period, such as al-Nawawī's. But in the Mamluk context, and in later centuries throughout the Ottoman Empire's Arab lands, the title *shaykh al-Islām*, which was occasionally attached to jurists, was one title in a fairly wide range of honorific titles that organized an informal scholarly hierarchy that was at least ideally based on the repute of the jurist and on his peers' appreciation of his scholarly excellence. Prominent jurists, such as the Egyptian Shāfiʿī jurist Zakarīyā b. Muḥammad al-Anṣārī (d. 1520), received the title *shaykh al-Islām*.[57] In the Ottoman context, on the other hand, by the sixteenth century the title "şeyhülislâm" designated the head of the imperial learned hierarchy.[58] By employing extant formulae that circulated throughout the Arab lands, the Ottoman learned hierarchy tapped into an existing discourse of authority and tamed it to its needs.

[57] Al-Ghazzī, *al-Kawākib al-sā'ira*, 1:196–207. For a more general survey of the history of the term "Shaykh al-Islām," see Richard W. Bulliet, "The Shaikh al-Islām and the Evolution of Islamic Society," *Studia Islamica* 35 (1972): 53–67.

[58] The title was already in use in the first half of the fifteenth century. See, for instance, Fenârî's endowment deed. Note that in the deed the title is only part of a long series of epithets and titles. Mustafa Bilge, *İlk Osmanlı Medreseleri* (Istanbul: İstanbul Üniversitesi Edebiyat Fakültesi Yayınları, 1984), 223.

Making use of various discourses prevalent across the Arab lands was not a unique practice of the imperial learned hierarchy. As Cihan Muslu's recent study of Ottoman-Mamluk diplomacy from the fourteenth century to the early sixteenth century has convincingly demonstrated, the Ottoman chancellery was aware of Mamluk honorific titles. The Ottoman diplomatic correspondence with the Mamluk sultans in the preconquest period clearly indicates that the Ottomans were familiar with these conventions and manipulated them skillfully.[59] It seems that a similar familiarity could be attributed to the Ottoman learned hierarchy.[60]

One may also situate the evolution of the Ottoman Arabic *fatwā* in another, though related, context. As we have seen in the previous chapters, from the mid-sixteenth century, scholars and jurists who were affiliated with the Ottoman learned hierarchy produced several important works, all written in Arabic, in response to the challenges posed by the incorporation of the Arab lands into the empire and the need to cement the authority of the chief muftī and, more generally, of the imperial learned hierarchy within the expanding imperial framework. Since many of the intended readers were Arab jurists (and more specifically Arab Ḥanafī jurists) who did not read Ottoman Turkish, the intellectual genealogies were compiled in Arabic.

In the same vein, the attempt to develop specific conventions for the Arabic *fatwā* may be read as part of a wider effort by the imperial learned hierarchy to facilitate access to the imperial legal system for the newly incorporated subjects who knew only Arabic. This effort is reflected in other legal venues as well. For example, the adjudication in the imperial courts across the Arab provinces was conducted in Arabic. The cases, moreover, were also recorded in Arabic in the court records (*sicill*). Even

[59] Muslu, *Ottoman-Mamluk*, 87–140.

[60] The Ottoman familiarity with the Mamluk "discourse of authority" in the first half of the fifteenth century is reflected in the question Murâd II sent to the Egyptian jurists concerning his attack on the Karamanid principality. The question opens with "what is the opinion of the lords the jurists ..." (*mā taqūlu al-sādāt al-ʿulamā'*). İsmail Hakki Uzunçarşılı, "Karamanoğulları Devri Vesikalarından İbrahim Bey'in Karaman İmareti Vakfiyesi," *Belleten* 1 (1937): 129–33. Interestingly enough, he asked jurists affiliated with the other Sunnī schools as well. On this correspondence, see Muslu, *Ottoman-Mamluk*, 15. On the emphasis many Ottoman sources place on titulature, including on that of the *şeyḫülislâm*, see İsmail Hakki Uzunçarşılı, *Osmanlı Devletinin İlmiye Teşkilatı* (Ankara: Türk Tarih Kurumu Basımevi, 1988), 204–5. In the introduction to his collection of letters, Ferîdûn Bey lists the honorifics and titulature one should employ when mentioning or addressing the chief muftī. Ferîdûn Bey, *Mecmûʿa-i Münşeât-i Selâtîn* (Istanbul: Dârüttibâʿattil'âmire, 1265–74 [1848–57]), 1:11. See also Akgündüz, *XIX. Asır Başlarına Kadar Osmanlı Devleti'nde Şeyhülislamlık*, 165–68.

in some places in the Turkish-speaking core lands of the empire, it seems, when one of the litigants spoke Arabic or at least requested the resolution to be written in Arabic, the case was recorded in Arabic in the *sicill*. In late sixteenth-century Ankara, for instance, cases were occasionally recorded in Arabic (among many other cases that were recorded in Ottoman Turkish).[61] Although this requires further research, it is possible to interpret the standardization of an imperial "legal vocabulary" in Arabic as part of a larger attempt to vernacularize law across the empire during the sixteenth and seventeenth century.[62] Moreover, despite the use of Arabic, the evolution of particular features advanced, to borrow Gülru Necipoğlu's term, a readable and reproducible "Ottomanness."[63]

To conclude, the particular features of the Ottoman Arabic *fatāwā* may be read as part of a concerted effort made by members of the imperial learned hierarchy to consolidate its authority in the context of an expanding imperial framework. Because of its explicit dialogic nature involving both the questioner and the muftī, the *fatwā*, unlike other genres, functioned as a kind of propaganda that required the active participation of its target (i.e., the questioner), for she had to deploy the aforementioned conventions in her question (or at least was presented in the court records and the *fatāwā* collections as if she did).

Viewed from this perspective, the *fatwā* was not merely a channel to transmit the opinion of the muftī to the inquirer but an instrument that served additional ends. These ends, however, should not be perceived as external to the "legal content." As we have seen in Chapter 1, the Ottoman view of the institution of the muftī differed substantially from the view prevalent across the Arab lands of the empire: from the Ottoman perspective, the chief muftī defined which opinion within the Ḥanafī school

[61] Halit Ongan, *Ankara'nın 1 Numaralı Şer'iye Sicili: 21 Rebiülahır 991–Evahir-i Muharrem 992 (14 Mayıs 1583–12 Şubat 1584)* (Ankara: Türk Tarih Kurumu Basımevi, 1958), 41, 45, 86, 102; Halit Ongan, *Ankara'nın İki Numaralı Şer'iye Sicili: 1 Muharrem 997–8 Ramazan 998 (20 Kasım 1588–11 Temmuz 1590)* (Ankara: Türk Tarih Kurumu Basımevi, 1974), 48, 65, 82, 105, 111, 114, 116, 123, 125.

[62] I thank James Baldwin for drawing my attention to this process. Also on the vernacularization of the court records (in this case, from Arabic to Ottoman Turkish) in the core lands of the empire in the fifteenth and the sixteenth centuries, see İklil Oya Selçuk's study of late fifteenth-century Bursa: İklil Oya Selçuk, "State and Society in the Marketplace: A Study of Late Fifteenth-Century Bursa" (PhD diss., Harvard University, 2009), 45–46, 93–96.

[63] I have borrowed the notion of readability from Gülru Necipoğlu, "A Kânûn for the State, a Canon for the Arts: Conceptualizing the Classical Synthesis of Ottoman Art and Architecture," in *Soliman le Magnifique et son temps*, ed. Gilles Veinstein (Paris: La documentation français, 1992), 195–213.

his subordinates should follow, while in the legal landscape of the Arab provinces from the sixteenth to the eighteenth century, there were multiple jurisprudential authorities. It was in this context that the chief muftī and the officially appointed muftīs had to establish their authority, and the discursive patterns that accompanied and supplemented the institutional development served this end.

Nonappointed Muftīs and the Imperial Jurisprudential Landscape

I wish to turn at this point to the jurists and religious scholars who did not hold an official state appointment and were not affiliated with the imperial learned hierarchy. To return to the case study of the Damascenes asking about the water allocation of a river, their decision to solicit the opinion of a nonappointed jurisconsult, the Palestinian muftī al-Ramlī (perhaps in addition to other jurists), was not unique or extraordinary. For a fuller appreciation of this incident and others like it, it is necessary to examine it in light of the complex relationship between the Ottoman learned hierarchy and its legal institutions on the one hand, and on the other, the prominent Greater Syrian muftīs who did not hold a state appointment. All these incidents indicate that pre-Ottoman jurisprudential and authoritative networks, on which the authority of these nonappointed jurists depended, had an audience and following well into the centuries of Ottoman rule.

What follows examines the activity of eminent muftīs – such as Muḥammad al-Timurtāshī (d. 1595), Khayr al-Dīn al-Ramlī (d. 1660), and the late seventeenth-century/early eighteenth-century ʿAbd al-Ghanī al-Nābulusī (d. 1731) – who were not appointed by the state, but were well respected both across Greater Syria and in other parts of the empire. It also is meant to cast light on the conditions that enabled their unmolested activity. Although these muftīs are better known and their activity is better documented, they seem to represent a larger group of Ḥanafī jurists who were not affiliated with or appointed by the Ottoman learned hierarchy, such as al-Timurtāshī's son Ṣāliḥ b. Muḥammad al-Timurtāshī[64] and grandson Muḥammad b. Ṣāliḥ al-Timurtāshī.[65] In addition, there

[64] On Ṣālih al-Timurtāshī, see *Tarjamat Ṣāliḥ al-Timurtāshī*, Süleymaniye Library MS Esʿad Efendi 2212–1, 5r–6v; al-Muḥibbī, *Khulāṣat al-athar*, 2:230–31.

[65] On Muḥammad b. Ṣāliḥ al-Timurtāshī, see al-Muḥibbī, *Khulāṣat al-athar*, 3:459–60. Another fascinating example is Ibrāhīm b. Muḥammad b. al-Ṭabbākh (d. 1597). A

were probably nonappointed muftīs who were not considered as authoritative as the three that concern us here. Future studies on less dominant muftīs may qualify some of my conclusions here and contribute to a more nuanced map of jurisprudential authority in the Ottoman lands.[66]

Establishing Authority

The jurisprudential authority of the muftīs who did not hold a state appointment rested on their affiliation with particular traditions or branches within the Ḥanafī school that were mostly rooted in the Arab lands of the empire and predated the Ottoman rule there. This affiliation was manifest through social interactions across time and space and especially in the connection between students and specific teachers. In this respect, the authority of these muftīs differed from that of members of the imperial learned hierarchy. As I have suggested in Chapter 2, however, over the course of the late fifteenth and the sixteenth centuries, the imperial learned hierarchy channeled the authority of a chain (or several chains) of transmission within the Ḥanafī school of law, and with the consolidation and rise of the hierarchy, the importance of the connection between a specific teacher and a student for the transmission of authority and knowledge declined. Instead, the learned hierarchy as a

protégé of Maʿlûlzâde Meḥmet Efendi (and serving him during his appointment as the chief judge in Damascus), Ibn al-Ṭabbākh returned to Damascus (his hometown) after a relatively short teaching career in the Ottoman madrasa system (his highest rank was a forty-*akçe* madrasa). In Damascus he worked in the service of the governor Sinân Paşa and was in charge of the distribution of salaries to the city's jurists (*ʿulūfat al-ʿulamāʾ bī-khazīnat al-Shām*) and was appointed to other teaching and preaching positions there. More significantly, his relations with many of the Damascene jurists, and possibly with other jurists as well, were tense (al-Muḥibbī, *Khulāṣat al-athar*, 1:46–47). In 1594, during his stay in Damascus, Ibn al-Ṭabbākh started issuing legal opinions that were subsequently collected under the title *ʿAyn al-muftī li-ghayn al-mustaftī*. In his rulings, he severely criticized the judges of his time, even stating that jurists should avoid serving as judges because of the incapability of judges to rule justly in his time (Ibrāhīm b. Muḥammad b. al-Ṭabbākh, *ʿAyn al-muftī li-ghayn al-mustaftī*, Süleymaniye Library MS Reşid Efendi 1115, 7v–8r). Because of these views, al-Muḥibbī describes Ibn al-Ṭabbākh as bigoted. Nevertheless, copies of his work circulated across the empire. One copy is located in Sarajevo (Hüsrev Bey Library MS 3069) and at least one more copy is now in Istanbul (Süleymaniye Library MS Reşid Efendi 1115). Moreover, the quality of the Istanbulian copy (a neat and decorated copy) suggests that at least in some circles Ibn al-Ṭabbākh's rulings were well received.

[66] Consider the "*fatwā* giver" (*fetvâcı*) in the mosque of Ayntab as an example of such a local authority. Leslie Peirce, *Morality Tales: Law and Gender in the Ottoman Court of Aintab* (Berkeley: University of California Press, 2003), 115.

whole became increasingly important as the channel of the authority of the school (or, to be precise, of the specific sub-school).[67]

In the case of the jurists who did not hold a state appointment, the immediate affiliation with specific traditions remained significant. It shaped both their lived experiences and the biographical texts that document and report about these experiences, as well as their textual production and rulings. These jurists' biographies and their jurisprudential production, in turn, circulated throughout the empire, and specifically throughout its Arab provinces, and served to constitute and propagate their affiliation with specific authoritative and jurisprudential traditions within the school. In this respect, the function of these legal documents resembled that of the rulings of the officially appointed jurisconsults.

To be sure, not all these texts were intended for the same audience. The circulation of the jurisprudential texts was perhaps limited to scholarly circles. The rulings, on the other hand, clearly reached a wider audience. The jurists' biographies, too, circulated in scholarly circles, but at least some contained almost hagiographic materials that might have reached a wider audience. Consider, for example, the dreams that both al-Timurtāshī and al-Ramlī are said to have dreamed. According to al-Timurtāshī's anonymous seventeenth-century biographer, in one of his dreams the Prophet appears in his residence in Gaza. During this encounter, al-Timurtāshī sucks the Prophet's tongue[68] – an allusion to other pious figures in Islamic history that are said to have performed the same act. The early eighteenth-century biographer and chronicler al-Muḥibbī mentions one of al-Ramlī's dreams in which the eponymous founder of the Shāfiʿī school, Muḥammad b. Idrīs al-Shāfiʿī (d. 820), releases al-Ramlī from his school and urges him to follow the Ḥanafī school.[69] The narration of the dream is intended to emphasize al-Ramlī's special status, as he is represented as a symbolic gift from the eponymous founder of the Shāfiʿī school to his Ḥanafī counterpart. Members of the imperial learned hierarchy, it is worth pointing out, also referred to dreams to establish their authority. In 1520, long before his appointment to the chief imperial muftiship, while holding the post of the military justice of Rumeli, Ebû's-Suʿûd Efendi had

[67] Interestingly enough, both al-Timurtāshī and al-Nābulusī studied with teachers who were members of the imperial learned hierarchy, although neither officially entered the hierarchy's training path. It is unclear at this point to what extent they could claim, on the basis of their studies with these teachers, affiliation to the sub-school endorsed by the imperial learned hierarchy.

[68] *Tarjmat Muḥammad al-Timurtāshī*, 2v–3r.

[69] Al-Muḥibbī, *Khulāṣat al-athar*, 2:134.

a dream. In the dream, which Snjezana Buzov has studied in detail, Ebû's-Su'ûd witnesses a session presided over by the Prophet, ten of his companions, and leading fifteenth- and sixteenth-century jurists and scholars, such as Molla Câmî and Kemâlpaşazâde, who served as *şeyḫülislâm* at the time. The Prophet points at Ebû's-Su'ûd and says that he will become the *şeyḫülislâm*.[70]

The importance of the affiliation with specific traditions within the school is reflected in the efforts invested by various jurists from the Arab lands, including al-Timurtāshī and al-Ramlī, to study with specific teachers. These efforts are also documented in detail in their textual biographies. The anonymous biographer and al-Muḥibbī both mention al-Timurtāshī's teachers in Egypt: "the muftī of Egypt" (*muftī al-diyār al-Miṣriyya*), al-Shaykh Amīn al-Dīn ʿAbd al-ʿĀl; the prominent Egyptian muftī Najm al-Dīn b. Nujaym; and the renowned member of the imperial learned hierarchy Kınalızâde.[71] The first two were eminent jurists in the Arab lands, while the third, at least potentially, linked al-Timurtāshī to the tradition of the imperial hierarchy. As in his biography of al-Timurtāshī, in his biographical entry of al-Ramlī, al-Muḥibbī lists his biographee's teachers, including renowned Ḥanafī jurists such as Muḥammad Sirāj al-Dīn al-Ḥanūtī (d. 1601)[72] and Aḥmad b. Muḥammad b. Amīn al-Dīn b. ʿAbd al-ʿĀl (d. ca. 1630).[73] Among the most important of al-Ramlī's teachers was ʿAbd Allāh b. Muḥammad al-Naḥrīrī (d. 1617), one of the most prominent Ḥanafīs who taught in al-Azhar,[74] and who, in addition to his public lectures in al-Azhar, taught al-Ramlī and his brother privately.[75]

Muftīs who did not hold a state appointment referred in their rulings to teachers with whom they had studied across the Arab lands. By invoking the opinion of a prominent authority, the jurist reasserted his affiliation to a specific authoritative network and, in turn, his support of specific opinions. In his *fatāwā*, al-Timurtāshī refers to several late fifteenth- and sixteenth-century Egyptian authorities, such as Burhān al-Dīn al-Karakī,[76]

70 Buzov, "The Lawgiver and His Lawmakers," 175–76, 246–47.

71 *Tarjmat Muḥammad al-Timurtāshī*; al-Muḥibbī, *Khulāṣat al-athar*, 4:19.

72 Al-Muḥibbī, *Khulāṣat al-athar*, 3:154.

73 Ibid., 1:518–21.

74 Ibid., 3:64.

75 Ibid., 2:134.

76 Al-Timūrtāshī, *Fatāwā*, 21r. On Burhān al-Dīn Ibrāhīm al-Karakī (d. 1516), see al-Ghazzī, *al-Kawākib al-sā'ira*, 1:112–13. al-Timurtāshī calls him "the shaykh of our shaykh."

Muḥammad al-Ḥānūtī,[77] Nūr al-Dīn al-Maqdisī,[78] and *Shaykh al-Islām* al-Aqṣarā'ī.[79] Al-Ramlī, too, as we have seen in Chapter 4, extensively cites Muḥammad al-Ḥānūtī as well as the Damascus-based al-Shihāb al-Ḥalabī.

Biographical entries portray the jurists not only as recipients but also as transmitters of specific traditions. Since the biographies were written posthumously, in addition to capturing the widely recognized excellence of these jurists and their importance as teachers during their lifetime, they also work to establish the authority of the students, with the biographers quite meticulously listing the students of each muftī. al-Timurtāshī's anonymous biographer provides a fairly long list of students. In addition to his son Ṣāliḥ, al-Timurtāshī's anonymous biographer provides a fairly long list of students from Gaza and Jerusalem; other sources indicate that Damascenes studied with al-Timurtāshī as well.[80] The list of al-Ramlī's students includes "*mawālī* [jurists who were affiliated with the Ottoman learned hierarchy], prominent *'ulamā'* [*al-'ulamā' al-kibār*], muftīs, teachers [*mudarrisūn*], and compilers of texts [*aṣḥāb al-ta'ālīf wa'l-mashāhīr*]."[81] Moreover, his students came from Jerusalem, Gaza, Damascus, Mecca, and Medina.[82] He also had some students from the central lands of the empire, such as Muṣṭafâ Paşa, the son of the grand vezir Meḥmet Köprülü, who asked al-Ramlī to grant him a permit to transmit religious knowledge (*ijāza*) for his brother, the grand vezir Aḥmed Köprülü (d. 1673).[83]

It is also worth paying attention to these muftīs' responses to other jurists' opinions and rulings. The response or opposition of a Greater Syrian muftī who did not hold an official appointment to, for example, the opinion of the Ottoman chief muftī or even to that of another officially appointed provincial muftī draws attention to the challenges the muftīs may have perceived to their own authority within a context of competition over a constituency of followers. This is not to suggest, however, a

[77] Al-Timurtāshī, *Fatāwā*, 108r. For more on Muḥammad al-Ḥanūtī, see al-Muḥibbī, *Khulāṣat al-athar*, 4:76–77.

[78] al-Timurtāshī, *Fatāwā*, 38r.

[79] Ibid., 170r.

[80] The officially appointed muftī of Damascus, Darwīsh al-Ṭālūwī, obtained an *ijāza* from al-Timurtāshī. See Darwīsh Muḥammad b. Aḥmad al-Ṭālūwī, *Sāniḥāt dumā al-qaṣr fī muṭāraḥāt banī al-'aṣr* (Beirut: 'Ālam al-Kutub, 1983), 2:118–19.

[81] Al-Muḥibbī, *Khulāṣat al-athar*, 2:135.

[82] Ibid., 2:135–36.

[83] Ibid., 2:136.

strict functionalist reading of the jurisprudential discourse. Muftīs might have genuinely believed that their opinions were sounder and preferable on the basis of their readings of the authoritative texts, without taking into consideration the support of their communities. References to their peers' rulings are significant, nonetheless, because they reveal which adversaries/peers certain muftīs deemed important enough to comment on in their rulings. al-Timurtāshī, for instance, responded to some of the rulings of the sixteenth-century chief jurisconsult Ebû's-Su'ûd Efendi,[84] and to the *fatāwā* issued by (presumably) the officially appointed muftī of Damascus.[85] Other instances of scholarly exchange between different jurisconsults include al-Ramlī's correspondence with the *şeyḫülislâm* at the time, Minḳârizâde, concerning an epistle the former wrote on questions of oath under the pain of being declared an infidel (*kāfir*).[86]

The spatial spread of the questioners who sent their questions to a particular muftī provides an interesting testimony to the eminence of a certain muftī in different localities and to the circulation of his rulings. For demarcating this area, I use the information about the places of origin as recorded in the *fatāwā* collections themselves. Granted, it is impossible to determine the provenance of every question. In fact, in most cases this piece of information remains obscure. But in many cases, the questions reveal important details about the questioner and his geographical location. The questions and the muftī's answers also occasionally provide clues about competing authorities that the questioners might have consulted or, at least, whose opinions they were familiar with.

al-Timurtāshī's *fatāwā* collection records questions sent from Gaza,[87] where al-Timurtāshī lived; Damascus;[88] and Jerusalem.[89] Al-Ramlī's *fatāwā* collection offers even richer information concerning the provenance of the questions. Al-Ramlī received questions from places as distant from one another as Medina[90] to Istanbul,[91] and Damascus[92] to Dumyat (Damietta).[93] Questions were also sent from the Palestinian cities of

[84] al-Timurtāshī, *Fatāwā*, 12r.
[85] Ibid., 73r.
[86] Al-Muḥibbī, *Khulāṣat al-athar*, 2:131–32. Moreover, Minḳârîzâde, in his *fatāwā* collection, cites al-Ramlī as an authoritative reference.
[87] al-Timurtāshī, *Fatāwā*, 163v.
[88] Ibid., 46r–47v.
[89] Ibid., 204v.
[90] Al-Ramlī, *al-Fatāwā al-Khayriyya*, 1:85.
[91] Ibid., 2:11.
[92] Ibid., 2:22.
[93] Ibid., 1:136–37.

Hebron,[94] Gaza, (including from al-Timurtāshī's son Ṣāliḥ),[95] Jerusalem,[96] Nablus,[97] and Safed.[98] As for al-Nābulusī, he received questions from the Hijaz,[99] Nablus,[100] Safed,[101] Jerusalem,[102] and most likely Damascus. These examples clearly indicate that questioners were willing to send their questions over long distances when they sought the opinion of a specific muftī, whose opinion carried, or at least was thought to carry, special weight. As al-Muḥibbī explains in his biography of al-Ramlī, "Rarely would any problem arise in Damascus or other main cities without him being consulted for an opinion about it, despite the availability of many other muftīs."[103] As we have seen in the previous sections, the questions sent to the *şeyḫülislâm* from the Arab lands demonstrate exactly this phenomenon.[104]

[94] Ibid., 2:19.

[95] Ibid., 1:100, 2:227.

[96] Ibid., 1:181; 2:170, 237, 239, 241.

[97] Ibid., 1:6; 2:38–39, 113.

[98] Ibid., 1:214.

[99] ʿAbd al-Ghanī al-Nābulusī, *al-Jawāb al-sharīf li-Ḥaḍrat al-Sharīf*, Süleymaniye Library MS Esʿad Efendi 1762, 252r–259v.

[100] ʿAbd al-Ghanī al-Nābulusī, *al-Ajwiba ʿalā 161 Suʾālan* (Damascus: Dār al-Fārābī al-ʿArīb, 2001).

[101] ʿAbd al-Ghanī al-Nābulusī, *al-Jawāb al-muʿtamad ʿan suʾālāt wārida min al-Ṣafad*, Süleymaniye Library MS Esʿad Efendi 3606, 239v–243r.

[102] ʿAbd al-Ghanī al-Nābulusī, *Jawāb suʾālayn waradat ʿalayhi min al-Quds al-Sharīf*, Süleymaniye Library MS Çelebi Abdullah Efendi 385, 67r–71v.

[103] Judith E. Tucker, "The Exemplary Life of Khayr al-Dīn al-Ramlī," in *Auto/Biography and the Construction of Identity and Community in the Middle East*, ed. Mary Ann Fay (New York: Palgrave, 2001), 16.

[104] It is worth comparing the "topography of authority" of the muftīs who did not hold a state appointment to that of their officially appointed colleagues in the provinces. As to cases with the officially appointed Damascene muftīs, it is difficult to determine the exact origin of the questions sent to them, for the questions rarely reveal this fact. Questions that provide some information about a concrete location, however, indicate that the questioners were from Damascus (al-Ḥāʾik, *al-Shifāʾ*, 57v–58r, 65r, 105v). Moreover, biographical dictionaries and other sources describe the officially appointed muftīs as the muftīs of a specific locality. (For example: al-Muḥibbī, *Khulāṣat al-athar*, 1:442–45, 552–55; 2:114–16. The son of the appointed Ḥanafī muftī of Jerusalem, ʿAbd al-Rahīm b. Abī Lutf al-Maqdisī, identifies his father as the muftī of Jerusalem. See ʿAbd al-Rahīm b. Abī Luṭf al-Maqdisī, *al-Fatāwā al-Raḥīmiyya fī wāqiʾāt al-sāda al-Ḥanafiyya*, Firestone Library [Princeton] MS Mach Yehuda 4154, 3v.) On the other hand, the officially appointed Ḥanafī muftī of Jerusalem ʿAbd al-Raḥīm b. Abī al-Luṭf received several questions from Damascus and even from Tripoli. For questions from Damascus, see ibid., 65r, 70r, 80r, 93r–94v, 97–98v; for the question from Tripoli, see ibid., 191r. It is interesting to note that all these *fatāwā* dealt with *waqf*-related issues.

The Nonappointed Muftīs' Rulings

There remain some crucial questions: What was the position of the muftīs who were not appointed by the Ottoman sultan (and dynasty) vis-à-vis other official judicial and administrative authorities, namely, judges and Ottoman officials? Did these officials respect their opinion? Why did questioners assume obtaining these muftīs' opinion would help promote their interests? And what was the relationship between the nonappointed muftīs?

To be sure, most of the muftīs who did not hold an official appointment were loyal subjects of the Ottoman Empire, despite occasional disputes and disagreements with members of the imperial learned hierarchy and other state authorities.[105] They all considered the Ottoman sultan the imām in all the cases in which Ḥanafī jurisprudence relegated the authority to the holder of this title, as in matters of appointments of judges. al-Timurtāshī even penned a short treatise on the virtues of the Ottoman dynasty, in which he praises the Ottomans for pacifying the newly conquered territories, undertaking charitable projects, and supporting scholars and jurists.[106] In 1694 al-Nābulusī, too, compiled a poem praising the Ottoman dynasty and the Ottoman sultan at the time, Aḥmet II (r. 1691–95).[107]

al-Timurtāshī's and al-Ramlī's *fatāwā* collections provide some answers to the aforementioned questions. Cases in which a judge addressed these muftīs directly are quite rare. Nevertheless, such a consultation was, it seems, a possibility that *qāḍīs* were aware of. The *qāḍī* of the Egyptian town of Dumyat, for instance, asked for al-Ramlī's opinion concerning a *waqf*-related issue that stood at the center of a controversy in Egypt. So did the *qāḍīs* of Gaza and Hebron.[108] It is difficult to identify the *qāḍīs* that solicited the muftī's opinion, but it is possible that they were local jurists who were appointed either by the provincial chief *qāḍī*, who was sent from Istanbul, or directly by the sultan. Although such cases are few, it is remarkable that an officially appointed *qāḍī* sought the opinion of a muftī who was not appointed by the sultan

[105] Barbara Rosenow von Schlegell, "Sufism in the Ottoman Arab World: Shaykh ʿAbd al-Ghanī al-Nābulusī (d. 1143/1731)" (PhD diss., University of California, Berkeley, 1997), 96–101.

[106] Muḥammad al-Timurtāshī, *Faḍāʾil Āl ʿUthmān*, Süleymaniye Library MS Esʿad Efendi 2337.

[107] See von Schlegell, "Sufism in the Ottoman Arab World," 96–101.

[108] Al-Ramlī, *al-Fatāwā al-Khayriyya*, 1:136–37, 100; 2:19.

in order to settle a jurisprudential dispute (although at least some of al-Ramlī's opinions were adopted by high ranking members of the imperial learned hierarchy).[109]

Much more common are cases in which the muftīs were asked about court resolutions.[110] It is important to keep in mind that some of the questions might have been hypothetical, and their main purpose might have been to help a solicitor assess his/her odds if she/he decided to petition against the judge or to ask for a *fatwā* from an officially appointed muftī. But it is also possible that the solicitors actually returned to the court, or went to another, with al-Timurtāshī's or al-Ramlī's opinion in hopes of changing the previous resolution. In some cases, these muftīs' rulings seem to have abrogated the court's resolution. Al-Ramlī's biography gives a glimpse of this practice: "If someone was ruled against in a non-sharīʿa fashion, the person could come with a copy of the *qāḍī*'s ruling and Khayr al-Dīn [al-Ramlī] could issue a *fatwā* that nullified that ruling, and it was his *fatwā* that would be implemented."[111] (Al-Muḥibbī's definition of "non-sharīʿa fashion" remains somewhat unclear.) It is also questionable whether judges always changed their rulings following a *fatwā* from al-Ramlī, but the impression that this was the case lasted for decades after al-Ramlī's death. On the other hand, as Judith Tucker has argued, legal rulings by these Greater Syrian muftīs were rarely brought to court, or at least rarely recorded in the court records.[112]

Others sought the nonappointed muftīs' opinions regarding state officials, ranging from provincial administrators to the sultan himself. These questions can be divided into two, often interrelated, categories – questions about appointments to positions and questions about the officials' comportment. The following question posed to al-Timurtāshī at some point between 1566 and 1599 serves as an example of the first type:

> [The muftī] was asked about a man who had been registered in the register of the sultan of Islam [*daftar sulṭān al-Islām*, i.e., the Ottoman sultan] as the sole preacher [*khaṭīb*]. This was recorded in the old imperial register [*al-daftar*

[109] It is possible that the practice of asking nonappointed muftīs was more common in Egypt. Ibn Ghānim al-Maqdisī was asked by the chief judge of Egypt, ʿAbd al-Ghanī, for his opinion. Al-Ḥānūtī, *Fatāwā al-Ḥānūtī*, 454r–456v.

[110] For example: al-Ramlī, *al-Fatāwā al-Khayriyya*, 1:131, 2:91.

[111] Tucker, "The Exemplary Life," 15–16.

[112] Judith E. Tucker, *In the House of the Law: Gender and Islamic Law in Ottoman Syria and Palestine* (Berkeley: University of California Press, 1998), 20–21.

al-khaqāni al-qadīm] [of the reign of] the deceased sultan Süleymân Khân. This manner [of having a single preacher per mosque] persisted until the time of our sultan now. Then a new preacher came [to serve as preacher] with the previous preacher [*al-khaṭīb al-sābiq*]. So [the position of the] preacher in this mosque was [manned] by two [preachers], one preaching in the [first] week and the other in the [second] week. The [position of the] other preacher and prayer leader [*al-khaṭīb wa'l-imām al-thānī*] had not been recorded in the old register. The sultan – may God grant him victory – introduced the new preacher and left the previous preacher in the former position. Is it permissible to introduce [changes] to the endowment? Will you permit both [appointment] edicts? Will the sultan or in turn whoever has the authority be rewarded [by God] [*yuthābu wa-yu'jaru*]? And if he [the sultan] issued a new appointment deed for the position of the preacher and the imām, should it be prevented and rejected? Issue your opinion for us.

[The muftī] answered: It is illicit to introduce [changes] in the endowment, as our deceased masters [*mashāyikhinā*] have declared. What is [written] in *al-Dhakhīra* and other [texts] supports that: "If a judge appointed a person as a servant to a mosque without the stipulation of the endower [while he is] aware of [this fact], the judge is not allowed to do so [to appoint] and the servant is not allowed to assume [the position]," despite the fact that the mosque needs the servant, for it is possible that a servant would be hired without an appointment by the judge. God knows best.[113]

al-Timurtāshī's answer clearly condemns the sultanic appointment. Since the positions were all recorded and allocated by the imperial bureaucracy, the case raises intriguing questions as to the intentions of the solicitor. It is possible that the solicitor wanted to know what the opinion of a respected jurisprudential figure was before he addressed an officially appointed provincial muftī or perhaps even the imperial chief muftī. The important point is that solicitors thought that obtaining al-Timurtāshī's opinion would serve their goals, even if the muftī's answer did not always fulfill their expectations.

Many solicitors resorted to these muftīs to express their anxiety about oppressive, or what they considered oppressive, officials. Al-Ramlī, for example, was asked about a *sipâhî* (a cavalryman who was allocated lands and villages as salary) who acted oppressively against the villagers and against endowed property.[114] But, as an interesting question preserved in al-Ramlī's collection suggests, at times the *sipâhî*s themselves, or someone on their behalf, addressed the Palestinian muftī:

[The muftī] was asked about a group of *sipâhîs* in the town of Nablus who were told, "You have been registered for the campaign." They then gave their

[113] al-Timurtāshī, *Fatāwā*, 48r–48v.
[114] Al-Ramlī, *al-Fatāwā al-Khayriyya*, 1:99. On oppressive *qāḍīs*, see ibid., 1:141, 2:148.

leaders who were going off on the campaign permission [to pay to get the *sipâhîs* exempted, saying] that if they [the leaders] met with ... the governor of Damascus ... and extracted from His Grace what is called a *buyuruldu* to the effect that they did not have to campaign in accordance with the imperial edict, [then] whatever exemption payment they [the leaders] made to the state, whether small or large, they [the *sipâhîs*] would pay it [as reimbursement] to them [the leaders] in any case. If it becomes clear that they are not registered, do they [still] have to pay [the leaders] or not, legally?

Answer: They do not have to do that (seeing as they made it dependent on their being registered for the campaign, but they were in fact not registered), since their giving [the leaders] permission to pay the exemption fee was conditional on that. "No condition, no conditioned" – clearly. But God knows best.[115]

Those solicitors clearly believed that al-Ramlī's opinion would outweigh those of other muftīs. Perhaps al-Ramlī's connections with higher officials, both at the local level, such as with the governor of Gaza,[116] and at the imperial level, such as his contacts with some members of the Köprülü family and with the *şeyḫülislâm*, might have led solicitors to assume that al-Ramlī could channel their complaints effectively.

Ultimately, questioners could have played the "local" muftīs against each other, although, it appears, these cases are quite rare. For the most part, later nonappointed jurists cited their predecessors approvingly.[117] A controversy concerning the inclusion of the descendants of an endower's daughters in his family endowment is an example of these fairly uncommon instances. This controversy stems from the existence of two contradictory sayings, both attributed to Abū Ḥanīfa, and thus ostensibly of equal weight. Writing in Egypt soon after the Ottoman conquest, Zayn al-Dīn b. Ibrāhīm b. Nujaym (d. 1563) was asked whether the daughters' descendants (*awlād al-banāt*) should benefit from the revenues of a *waqf*. The collector of Ibn Nujaym's *fatāwā* added an important comment following Ibn Nujaym's opinion, briefly describing the controversy:

If the endower stipulated: "I have endowed [this endowment] to my children and to the children of my children," the daughters' descendants [*awlād al-banāt*] are not included. On [the basis of this principle] the *fatwā* [should be issued]. Al-Ṭarsūsī[118] in his *Fawā'id*[119] chose this [opinion] from one of two transmitted

[115] Ibid., 2:38–39.
[116] Al-Muḥibbī, *Khulāṣat al-athar*, 2:135.
[117] Al-Ramlī, for instance, cites al-Timurtāshī's *Tanwīr al-abṣar* and *Minaḥ al-ghaffār*. See Chapter 4 of this volume.
[118] Ibrāhīm b. ʿImād al-Dīn al-Ṭarsūsī (d. 1356).
[119] *Al-Fawā'id al-fiqhiyya al-Badriyya*. See Carl Brockelmann, GAL, Suplementband II, 87.

sayings [*riwāyatayn*] from Abū Ḥanīfa. But *Shaykh al-Islām* ʿAbd al-Barr [Ibn al-Shiḥna][120] preferred in his commentary on the *Manẓūma* [*Sharḥ al-Manẓūma*][121] the inclusion [of the daughters' descendants].[122]

al-Timurtāshī, was asked about another case regarding a dispute between an endower's grandchildren:

[The muftī] was asked about an incident that took place in the well-protected [city of] Damascus. A man endowed [an endowment and stipulated it to] his children, to his grandchildren, and to his descendants. After them [if his lineage perishes] he [stipulated the revenues] to the poor. The judge approved the validity of this endowment. The [right to exploit the revenues of] the endowment devolved to the sons of the [endower's] male [descendants] and the sons of the [endower's] female [descendants]. Then there was a legal dispute between the sons of the male descendants [*awlād al-awlād*] and the sons of the female descendants [*awlād al-banāt*] [brought before] a Ḥanafī judge, who issued a sharʿī resolution to devolve the endowment to the descendants of the sons and to exclude the descendants of the daughters from the [beneficiaries] of the endowment. After a while, the sons of the [endower's] daughter had a dispute with the sons of the [endower's] sons and they brought the case before some judges, who ruled for the inclusion of the daughter's descendants [in the endowment] and abrogated the ruling of the first *qāḍī* not to include the daughter's descendants. Is it permissible [for the second judge] to do so or not? If the first ruling is based on what several jurists have approved [*ṣaḥḥaḥa*] and stated that [according to this opinion a muftī should] issue [his] *fatwā* [*ʿalayhi al-fatwā*], is it sound and reliable or not? [Is] the second [opinion] null [*wa-lā ʿibra biʾl-thānī*]? Issue your opinion.

[The muftī] answered: Know that if [in a certain] issue there are two sound opinions, it is permissible for the muftī and the *qāḍī* to issue *fatāwā* and rule according to one of these [opinions].... Our master *Shaykh al-Islām* [Ibn Nujaym] in his commentary on *al-Kanz* [*al-Baḥr al-rāʾiq*] in [the chapter on] endowments (*Kitāb al-Waqf*) [wrote]: "The son of the daughter should not be included in the endowment for the descendent[s] [neither] individually nor collectively, [according] to the prevailing view of the school (*ẓāhir al-riwāya*), which is the sound [opinion] for issuing *fatāwā*." The descendants of the daughters should not be included according to the prevailing view of the school, and according to this opinion the *fatwā* should be issued.... [discussion of the opinion of other Ḥanafī authorities] ... the first ruling by the Ḥanafī *qāḍī* against the inclusion of the daughters' descendent is sound and reliable and should be implemented. No judge is allowed to abrogate [*naqḍ*] this required [ruling] [*al-mūjab*].[123]

120 On ʿAbd al-Barr b. al-Shiḥna (d. 1515), see Ibn al-Ḥanbalī, *Durr*, 1 (part 2): 843–47.
121 Ibn al-Shiḥna wrote several commentaries on *manẓūmas*. See Carl Brockelman, GAL, Suplimentband II, 94.
122 Zayn al-Dīn b. Ibrāhīm b. Nujaym, *al-Fatāwā al-Zayniyya*, Süleymaniye Library MS Carullah 917, 31v.
123 al-Timurtāshī, *Fatāwā*, 46r–47r.

This intriguing question posed to the muftī discloses fascinating details about how both parties – the descendants of the endower's son and the descendants of his daughters – made use of the legal tools at their disposal.

The first *qāḍī*, who was Ḥanafī, ruled in favor of the descendants of the sons. Then their adversaries, the descendants of the daughters, identified another venue that would rule in *their* favor.[124] It is not clear, however, if the second *qāḍī* or *qāḍīs* were Ḥanafīs, although they might have been. Apparently, the second *qāḍī*'s ruling was in fact valid and was implemented. This led the descendant of the endower's son to seek support that would restore the ruling of the first *qāḍī*. To this end, they decided to address al-Timurtāshī.

In his detailed and lengthy reply, al-Timurtāshī surveys numerous opinions, including Ibn Nujaym's, on this issue. From the outset he argues that when there are two sound opinions it is permissible for the muftī and the *qāḍī* to choose either one. Against Ibn Nujaym's opinion he lists other authoritative texts, such as *Fatāwā Qaḍīkhān* and *al-Fatāwā al-Sirājiyya*, which support the inclusion of the daughters' progeny. Eventually, despite the debate between different Ḥanafī authorities, al-Timurtāshī favors the resolution of the first *qāḍī* to exclude the daughters' descendants. He reasons that the two opinions transmitted from Abū Ḥanīfa are not of equal jurisprudential weight, since "[according] to the transmitted opinion [*riwāya*] of al-Khaṣṣāf and Hilāl they [i.e., the daughters' descendants] should be included, whereas according to the prevailing view of the madhhab [*ẓāhir al-riwāya*] they should not, and upon this [opinion] the *fatwā* should be issued (*ʿalayhi al-fatwā*)."[125] Like Ibn Nujaym, al-Timurtāshī approves the first *qāḍī*'s resolution.

Although it is possible that the decision to address al-Timurtāshī was arbitrary, it is not unlikely that the solicitors knew what his opinion on this issue was. Another possibility is that al-Timurtāshī was chosen as an agreed-upon arbitrator. In that case, al-Timurtāshī, as well as other muftīs, should be perceived as an alternative legal site in which disputes were sometimes adjudicated. It is also plausible, though, that litigants thought that al-Timurtāshī's opinion would abrogate the *qāḍī*'s opinion in court, by challenging the latter's interpretation of the law.

[124] This practice was well documented by Boğaç Ergene for the seventeenth and eighteenth centuries. See Ergene, *Local Court*, 106–8.

[125] al-Timurtāshī, *Fatāwā*, 47r–47v.

Several decades later, Khayr al-Dīn al-Ramlī offered a different solution to a similar case in one of his rulings. Although he acknowledges, as al-Timurtāshī does, that the two opinions are not equally sound, he supports the somewhat weaker opinion, that of al-Khaṣṣāf and Hilāl, because "in these times [*hādhihi al-aʿṣār*] it is appropriate to prefer the opinion [*riwāya*] that asserts the inclusion because this is their [the Ottoman] custom [*ʿurfihim*] and they do not know any [other practice] but this one."[126] In other words, the difference between al-Timurtāshī's and al-Ramlī's answers registers a controversy that refused to die out. Both opinions were already fully developed and in circulation for centuries in the Arab lands. Each of these opinions had its own supporters among the muftīs, allowing solicitors to navigate their case between the different muftīs and multiple legal sites to promote their legal (and other) interests.

Al-Ramlī's answer may explain why the solicitors who approached al-Timurtāshī decided to do so. The Gaza-based muftī apparently defended a local practice. Occasionally, Greater Syrian muftīs defended legal arguments that contradicted or at least posed an alternative to the arguments advocated by the learned hierarchy and prevailing in the core lands of the empire.[127] al-Timurtāshī, for instance, clearly distinguishes between the customary practice in the Shām of taking oath on the pain of divorce and the customary practice in Anatolia as it appears in Ebû's-Suʿûd's *fatāwā*, speculating that the eminent *şeyḫülislâm* ruled the way he did because the oath (*ḥilf*) is not known in "their lands" (*fī diyārihim*), that is, in the central lands of the empire.[128] And as we have seen in the previous chapter, officially appointed muftīs in Damascus, and probably elsewhere, also defended local practices and at times even explained their legal rationale to members of the imperial learned hierarchy.

Concluding Remarks

Looking at the interactions between the jurists, their followers, and other authorities helps situate the scholarly debates between the followers of

[126] Al-Ramlī, *al-Fatāwā al-Khayriyya*, 1:150. To support his opinion, he cites a *fatwā* by Shihāb al-Dīn al-Ḥalabī, who in turn cites a *fatwā* by *qāḍī al-quḍāt* Nūr al-Dīn al-Ṭarabulusī.

[127] For a more general discussion of this issue in Ḥanafī jurisprudence, see Baber Johansen, "Coutumes locales et coutumes universelles," *Annales islamologiques* 27 (1993): 29–35.

[128] Muḥammad b. ʿAbd Allāh al-Timurtāshī, *Muʿīn al-muftī ʿalā jawāb al-mustafatī* (Beirut: Dār al-Bashā'ir al-Islāmiyya, 2009), 203–4.

the different branches within the Ḥanafī school of law in a broader context and points to the success of the nonappointed muftīs in preserving and negotiating their authority within the evolving imperial framework. The decision of different solicitors, including solicitors who were not members of scholarly circles, to approach these muftīs indicates the prestige and reputation these muftīs enjoyed not only among scholars and jurists but also among nonscholars. Such prestige is a particularly remarkable achievement, given the perceived benefits of consulting officially appointed muftīs.

The picture that emerges, then, is a dynamic one, in which official legal institutions are used to counter provincial jurists who did not hold an official appointment, and vice versa. In her study of seventeenth- and eighteenth-century muftīs, Judith Tucker contends that "there is little evidence to suggest that the muftī and qāḍī worked hand-in-glove." She explains, "Unlike their core-region counterparts, most Syrian and Palestinian muftīs served the court system only as a secondary endeavor; their primary mission was that of delivering legal advice to the local community of which they were a part."[129] This might have often been the case, especially as far as the nonappointed muftīs are concerned, although it is clear that the opinions of prominent nonappointed muftīs were also influential, including in certain courts across Greater Syria. Therefore, dividing the muftīs according to the core regions/province dichotomy seems to miss the complexity of the Greater Syrian legal landscape in particular and of the empire in general. As Mundy and Smith compellingly show, to a large extent it is affiliation with the Ottoman dynasty that marks the difference between the muftīs in Greater Syria and across the Ottoman lands.[130]

As we have seen in Chapter 1, the officially appointed muftīs monopolized the institutional authority to issue enforceable legal opinions within the imperial legal system. For this reason, the Ottoman state did not prevent prominent Greater Syrian jurists and muftīs who did not hold an official appointment from issuing their own legal opinions. This fact is even more striking given the opposition some of these nonappointed jurists and muftīs voiced in their opinions on certain legal rulings by chief

[129] Tucker, *In the House of the Law*, 21.

[130] Martha Mundy and Richard Saumarez-Smith have noticed this treatise; see Martha Mundy and Richard Saumarez-Smith, *Governing Property, Making the Modern State: Law, Administration, and Production in Ottoman Syria* (London: I. B. Tauris, 2007), 11–39.

muftīs and judges. Nevertheless, it appears that for the most part the Ottoman authorities were not troubled by the activity of eminent muftīs who did not hold a state appointment, and even at times adopted their rulings and writings. Possibly, the nonappointed jurists' activity continued unmolested because they were not members of the imperial learned hierarchy and thus their opinions were not institutionally enforceable. On the other hand, it may be interpreted in other, not necessarily mutually exclusive ways, such as the Ottoman ruling elite's inability to eliminate every alternative legal venue or the learned hierarchy's self-confidence as a dominant actor in the imperial legal landscape.

In terms of the solicitors, it is noteworthy that they sought to obtain for various reasons the opinion of the hierarchy's chief jurisprudential authority (and his representative in the province). By doing so, they invited the imperial learned hierarchy to intervene in their or their community's affairs. Concurrently, it is likely that in certain circumstances the same question was addressed to both imperial and locally acclaimed authorities. Although it is difficult to assess the degree to which every solicitor considered all the available muftīs, it seems that some were aware of and used multiple officially appointed and not officially appointed muftīs.

The reconstruction of the "topography of jurisprudential authority" of the Ottoman Bilād al-Shām could serve as a fruitful direction for examining the boundaries of the Ottoman learned hierarchy within the Ottoman domains. Moreover, it could enable a mapping out of a concrete spatial spread of specific perceptions of the school of law and Ḥanafī legal doctrines within the Ottoman imperial framework, while drawing attention to the overlapping geographies of different arguments within a single province.

Conclusion

The Second Formation of Islamic Law

The previous chapters have tried to reconstruct several interrelated debates between various Ḥanafī jurists who adhered to different understanding of the school of law and of the relations between the Ottoman dynasty and the jurists. These debates, which occurred in multiple sites and temporalities, assumed different forms. In some cases, they were amicable exchanges, in others, fierce disputes. Taken together, these disagreements reveal some hitherto understudied doctrinal and institutional aspects of the Ottoman adoption of a particular branch of the Ḥanafī legal school and of the notion of an official madhhab.

The Ottoman adoption of this particular branch within the madhhab was not merely an act of state patronage. It was an active intervention by the Ottoman dynasty in the structure of the school of law and its doctrines. In this sense, the Ottoman adoption of the school was very different from the support that earlier Muslim sovereigns and dynasts extended to jurists and religious scholars. As we have seen in this study, the Ottoman adoption-development of an official madhhab was accompanied by the evolution of several institutional and administrative practices, such as the appointment of muftīs and the development of an imperial learned hierarchy. These new practices and institutions, in turn, were a product of and legitimized through Ottoman dynastic law (*ḳânûn*). In other words, the emergence of the Ottoman official madhhab depended to a considerable extent on the existence of the notion of dynastic law.

As opposed to several studies that have tended to perceive Islamic and Ottoman dynastic laws as two independent legal-political discourses that had to be reconciled, this book argues that the emergence of the official madhhab calls for a more nuanced historicization of the relationship between the Ottoman notion of dynastic law and the pre-Ottoman (or, as I will suggest in the following discussion, pre-Mongol) notion of Islamic law. My intention here is not to suggest that the emergence of the official school of law was instrumental. Nor am I implying that the jurists who were affiliated with the Ottoman dynasty participated in a cynical collaboration. After all, the Ottoman dynasty invested enormous efforts in developing its learned hierarchy and engaged intensely in several Islamic discourses. At the same time, it seems to me necessary to account for the Ottoman commitment, at least to some degree, to their dynastic law.

It is precisely for this reason that the Ottoman case may assist us in further exploring some of the dynamics of what John Woods aptly describes as the era of "great experimentation and innovation in political thought, a time in which standard Sunni theories were subjected to the Turko-Mongol influences."[1] In the following pages, I attempt to situate the debates examined throughout this study within the context of the eastern Islamic lands in the post-Mongol period. This attempt is in many ways tentative and provisional, as the study of Islamic law in other parts of the eastern lands in that period is still in its embryonic stage. But there are several similarities between the imperial legal systems that merit attention and justify this exercise, and I hope that this comparison will encourage others to work with the framework I am proposing in this conclusion. Be the case as it may, I am encouraged to pursue this line of inquiry by the fact that the study of the eastern Islamic lands in the post-Mongol period as a somewhat coherent unit has proven to be illuminating in numerous other issues and disciplines, such as political thought, mysticism, and art and architecture.[2]

Looking East: The Ottoman Case in a Comparative Perspective

Among the legal systems of the early modern Muslim world, the Ottoman system is the best studied. This may explain the central place it occupies in many accounts of Islamic legal history. In what follows, I aim to expand the scope of inquiry and suggest that the history of the Ottoman

[1] John E. Woods, *The Aqquyunlu: Clan, Confederation, Empire: A Study in 15th/9th Century Turko-Iranian Politics* (Minneapolis, MN: Bibliotheca Islamica, 1976), 5.

[2] For example: Nicola Di Cosmo, Allen J. Frank, and Peter B. Golden, eds., *The Cambridge History of Inner Asia: The Chinggisid Age* (Cambridge: Cambridge University Press, 2009).

legal system and learned hierarchy should be situated in the broader context of the eastern Islamic lands of that period. To this end, I would like to point to some key issues that figure in the modern scholarship on other roughly contemporary polities (and, to a lesser extent, in primary sources produced throughout the eastern Islamic lands) and that bear significant similarities to the Ottoman case and its historiography.

My intention is not to obscure substantial differences between the polities. Among these differences one can list the size of the polities; their political organization; and the social, ethnic, and denominational composition of their populations. Nor is my intention to produce a comprehensive comparative account of the differences and similarities. This clearly would be too ambitious. Furthermore, I am not implying that the notions of law (and sovereignty) that concern us here were the only source of political inspiration that Muslim dynasts and emperors across the eastern Islamic lands could and did draw on. Nor am I suggesting that the discourse and ideas I am tracing here were always the most dominant throughout the region during this time period. In most polities throughout the eastern Islamic lands in the centuries following the Mongol invasions, one can find multiple, at times contradictory, discourses and ideals of sovereignty, kingship, and law. In the fifteenth and sixteenth centuries, Ottoman sultans, for example, participated in other discourses – Byzantine, Mamluk, and Mediterranean – of sovereignty and kingship,[3] while the Mughal dynasty adopted many practices and discourses of kingship that prevailed across the subcontinent and beyond.[4]

My objective is to draw attention to the circulation across the post-Mongol eastern Islamic lands of specific discourses and views concerning the relationship between dynastic and Islamic (Sunnī) law. The particular structure and discourse of authority, the Sunnī school of law (and, more specifically, the Ḥanafī school of law), led me to focus on the Sunnī dynasties. Much of what will be said in the following pages, however, may also be applied to Safavid Iran, the major Shi'ī counterpart of the Ottomans.[5]

[3] Emire Cihan Muslu, "Ottoman-Mamluk Relations: Diplomacy and Perceptions" (PhD diss., Harvard University, 2007); Gülru Necipoğlu, "Süleyman the Magnificent and the Representation of Power in the Context of Ottoman-Hapsburg-Papal Rivalry," *Art Bulletin* 71, no. 3 (1989): 401–27.

[4] Lisa Balabanlilar, *Imperial Identity in the Mughal Empire: Memory and Dynastic Politics in Early Modern South and Central Asia* (London: I. B. Tauris, 2012); A. Azfar Moin, *The Millennial Sovereign: Sacred Kingship and Sainthood in Islam* (New York: Columbia University Press, 2012).

[5] See Rula Jurdi Abisaab, *Converting Persia: Religion and Power in the Safavid Empire* (London: I. B. Tauris, 2004); Devin J. Stewart, "The First *Shaykh al-Islām* of the Safavid

Methodologically, the comparison of the Sunnī polities has to overcome several challenges. First, there are gaps in the modern historiography of these polities. Second, there is considerable variation in the amount and nature of the primary sources from different parts of the eastern Islamic lands; for example, within the Ḥanafī school of law from the Ottoman lands, there is a sizable corpus of biographical dictionaries that are dedicated to senior members of the imperial learned hierarchy as well as several works that document the intellectual genealogies of the hierarchy, whereas, to the best of my knowledge, other scholarly circles across the eastern Islamic lands did not produce such works. These gaps raise two fundamental questions: How should one treat the missing parts of the puzzle? And, second, what is the relationship between the missing and existing parts?

While not downplaying the challenges these gaps pose, a comparative approach may also offer ways to bridge them, as the existing parts of the puzzle are indicative of important similarities and shared patterns. These similarities, I believe, may also permit extrapolating, albeit cautiously and tentatively, about the missing parts. In other words, the historiographical move I am suggesting is bidirectional: on the one hand, I would like to suggest that the Ottoman adoption of a particular branch within the Ḥanafī school be studied as part of a legal culture shared by other polities and dynasties throughout the continent, their particularities notwithstanding; on the other hand, I use the Ottoman case to contextualize and explain similar administrative and legal practices in other polities across central and south Asia. To be more concrete, I would like to examine two practices that recur in different contexts across the eastern Islamic lands throughout the post-Mongol period (as well as in the modern historiography) and are central to my understanding of the Ottoman adoption and development of an official school of law: the appointment of muftīs by the ruling dynasty and the imperial canonization of jurisprudential texts. Furthermore, I am interested in investigating these developments as the outcome of the rise of dynastic law in the post-Mongol eastern Islamic lands.[6]

The most striking pattern is the rise of the officially appointed muftīship throughout the region. As early as the first decades of the fifteenth century,

Capital of Qazvin," *Journal of the American Oriental Society* 116, no. 3 (1996): 387–405; Maryam Moazzen, "Shi'ite Higher Learning and the Role of the Madrasa-yi Sultani in Late Safavid Iran" (Ph.D. diss, University of Toronto, 2011).

6 Very little is known about educational institutions and the career tracks of jurists in central Asia and the Mughal Empire in that period.

the Timurid ruler Shāhrukh (d. 1447) appointed a *shaykh al-Islām* for his domains. This office, which was held by the members of two families, the descendants of Burhān al-Dīn al-Marghīnānī and Saʿd al-Dīn al-Taftāzānī, was intended to oversee all the juridical activity throughout the Timurid lands.[7] Interestingly enough, the appointment of the first Timurid *shaykh al-Islām* parallels similar developments in the Ottoman lands. Roughly around this time, the Ottoman sultan Murâd II appointed Mollâ Şemseddîn Fenârî (d. 1431) to the newly created office of the chief muftī of the Ottoman lands, the *şeyḫülislâm*.[8]

A century later, around 1514, the itinerant jurist and chronicler Fażl Allāh b. Rūzbahān (d. 1519) wrote a treatise in which he advised the new Özbek khān on how to conduct the affairs of his state. In the chapter on the administration of the religious and judicial offices, the jurist advises the khān to appoint a chief jurisprudential authority, a *shaykh al-Islām*:

> When the sultan [*pādīshāh*] charges the *shaykh al-Islām* with the task of preserving the religious sciences, and grants him the letter of authority, then he [the *shaykh al-Islām*] should investigate the affairs of the jurists [*ʿulamāʾ*] of the [his] dominion. He must keep [the sultan] informed of their level of knowledge and intelligence, their way of teaching, their power of independent reasoning [*ijtihād*], the ability to issue legal opinions and teach [*quvvet-e iftāʾ ve-tedrīs-e īshān*].[9]

The *shaykh al-Islām*, in other words, was to preside over what Ibn Rūzbahān envisioned as the khān's learned hierarchy and to operate on his behalf to guarantee that the hierarchy functions properly. In this capacity, Ibn Rūzbahān maintains, the khān and the *shaykh al-Islām* have authority to inspect and examine the competence and knowledge of their appointed jurists. Furthermore, Ibn Rūzbahān envisioned a mosaic of officially appointed muftīships, each covering a well-defined territory:

> Whenever a muftī is appointed, he is allowed to receive a salary from the treasury [*bayt al-māl*]. If he is appointed [to this office], he must not charge any fee [for his services].... If within the distance of a qaṣr [roughly 48 miles] a post of a learned muftī is vacant, it is an obligation [of the sultan] to appoint a muftī in a town, for otherwise all inhabitants of that place will be sinful.[10]

[7] Beatrice Forbes Manz, *Power, Politics and Religion in Timurid Iran* (Cambridge: Cambridge University Press, 2007), 213; Shiro Ando, "The *Shaykh al-Islām* as a Timurid Office: A Preliminary Study," *Islamic Studies* 33, nos. 2–3 (1994): 253–55.

[8] Richard C. Repp, *The Müfti of Istanbul: A Study in the Development of the Ottoman Learned Hierarchy* (London: Ithaca Press, 1986), 73–124.

[9] Fażl Allāh b. Rūzbahān, *Sulūk al-Mulūk* (Tehran: Intishārāt-i Khvārazmī, 1984), 96.

[10] Ibid., 114–15.

The administrative practice prescribed by Ibn Rūzbahān was apparently implemented, perhaps even before his compilation of this work. By the mid-sixteenth century, there was a dynasty-appointed muftī in Bukhara and probably in other major urban centers across the khanate.[11] The Özbek appointment of muftīs was quite similar – although, it seems, not identical – to that in the Mughal realms. There, too, the officially appointed muftīs, though apparently there was no chief imperial muftī.[12]

Related to the rise of the officially appointed muftī is, of course, the growing importance of his legal opinions (*fatāwā*). As we have seen in the discussion of the Ottoman case, the rulings of the officially appointed muftī were instrumental in regulating which opinions and doctrines within the Ḥanafī school of law members of the Ottoman learned hierarchy were to apply. This seems to be the reason for the appointment of muftīs in other parts of the eastern Islamic lands as well. Some of these rulings were collected and circulated throughout the different polities, and in some cases, as with the Mughal seventeenth-century collection *al-Fatāwā al-ʿĀlamgīriyya*, well beyond their boundaries.

Let me dwell on the example of *al-Fatāwā al-ʿĀlamgīriyya*, the collection of rulings that was compiled in Mughal India during the reign of Aurangzeb (r. 1658–1707, also known as ʿĀlamgīr) and named after him. The collection still awaits thorough study, but it seems that the notion behind this project was to determine what legal opinions the jurists affiliated with the Mughal dynasty were to follow. As we have seen in Chapter 1, this was also the idea behind the appointment of muftīs in the Ottoman Empire and the collecting of their rulings. If *al-Fatāwā al-ʿĀlamgirīyya* is the Mughal equivalent of the collections of the Ottoman chief imperial muftīs, then the dynastic sponsorship – which is clearly reflected in the title of the collection – possibly made this collection enforceable throughout the empire's legal system.[13]

[11] One of these muftīs was Muḥammad b. Ḥusām al-Dīn al-Quhistānī (d. 1554), the author of *Jāmiʿ al-Rumūz*. Muḥammad b. ʿAbd al-Rahmān al-Ghazzī, *Dīwān al-Islām* (Beirut: Dār al-Kutub al-ʿIlmiyya, 1990), 4:35–36; ʿAbd al-Ḥayy b. Aḥmad b. al-ʿImād, *Shadharāt al-Dhahab fi Akhbār Man Dhahab* (Beirut: Dār al-Kutub al-ʿIlmiyya, 1980), 8:300.

[12] Rafat M. Bilgrami, *Religious and Quasi-Religious Departments of the Mughal Period (1556–1707)* (New Delhi: Munshiram Manoharlal Publishers, 1984); M. L. Bhatia, *Administrative History of Medieval India: A Study of Muslim Jurisprudence under Aurangzeb* (New Delhi: Radha Publications, 1992).

[13] Alan N. Guenther, "Ḥanafī Fiqh in Mughal India: The *Fatāwá-i ʿAlāmgīrī*," in *India's Islamic Traditions, 711–1750*, ed. Richard M. Eaton (Oxford: Oxford University Press, 2003), 209–30. As Joseph Schacht has pointed out, the title also alludes to similar earlier projects, such as the fourteenth-century *al-Fatāwá al-Tatārkhāniyya* and others. Joseph

Aurangzeb requested that the jurists he summoned consult the jurisprudential texts he held in his imperial library. Although very little is known about the circulation of jurisprudential and other texts throughout the eastern Islamic lands, it is worth dwelling on this request. In the Ottoman Empire, the sultan, and later the chief imperial muftī, specified what texts constituted the imperial jurisprudential canon. It is quite possible that Aurangzeb's request was intended to specify the texts comprising the distinctive Mughal imperial canon. To be sure, the different imperial canons shared many texts, but an interesting comment from the mid-nineteenth century suggests that there were also substantial differences: in his account of the administration of law in colonial India, William H. Morley related that "many works according to the doctrines of Abu Hanifa have been written, and are received as authorities in the Turkish [Ottoman] empire. These I apprehend would be admissible if quoted in our Courts in India where the parties to a suit are of the Hanafi persuasion."[14] In other words, although jurisprudential texts circulated throughout the eastern Islamic lands (and beyond), it appears that the different dynasties succeeded in creating identifiable imperial textual geographies within the Ḥanafī school of law across the region.

The appointment of muftīs by the state/dynasty, the rise in the importance of these muftīs' rulings, and the different textual geographies within the Ḥanafī school across the eastern Islamic lands suggest that the Ottoman adoption and development of a specific branch within the Ḥanafī school was not a unique case. If my interpretation of these examples is correct, it appears that in the post-Mongol period, rulers and dynasties across the eastern Islamic lands sought to regulate in an unprecedented manner the structure of the school of law and the doctrines that the school's affiliated jurists were expected to follow. From the perspective of Islamic legal history, it appears, the post-Mongol period was the era of the state madhhab.

Schacht, "On the Title of the *Fatāwā al-ʿĀlamgīriyya*," in *Iran and Islam: In Memory of the Late Vladimir Minorsky*, ed. C. E. Bosworth (Edinburgh: Edinburgh University Press, 1971), 475–78. Despite the Mughal sponsorship, *al-Fatāwá al-ʿĀlamgirīyya* was widely consulted in other parts of the Ḥanafī world, especially in the Ottoman Empire (ibid., 475).

14 Willian H. Morley, *The Administration of Justice in British India, Its Past History and Present State: Comprising an Account of the Laws Peculiar to India* (London: William & Norgate, Stevens & Norton, Lepage & Co., 1858), 294.

The Chinggisid Heritage

So far I have used the term "post-Mongol" quite freely to denote the chronological framework of my inquiry. The Mongol invasions of the thirteenth century, which culminated in the conquest of Baghdad in 1258 and the execution of the ʿAbbasid caliph al-Mustaʿṣim, introduced new notions of sovereignty and law to the eastern Islamic lands. Of particular relevance is the image of Chinggis Khān as a world conqueror that enjoyed a divine mandate to rule and legislate. In this sense, the term "post-Mongol" is intended to draw attention to the ongoing dialogues – despite their different manifestations over time and space – that sultans, emperors, and dynasties held with their real and imagined Mongol past and Chinggisid heritage. More specifically, I am interested both in the ways different sovereigns throughout this period envisioned and interpreted Chinggis Khān's political-legal legacy and in the relationship between this legacy and the pre-Mongol Islamic notions of law. I propose that the adoption and development of an official madhhab is one of the results of the dialogues the different dynasties held with their Chingissid heritage and particularly with the post-Mongol notion of dynastic law.

The fact that many of these dynasties perceived Chinggis Khān and the law that was associated with him as a historical and legal point of reference, even when they tried to shift the focus to other dynastic ancestors (as was the case with the Timurids, the Ottomans, and the Mughals),[15] suggests that we are not dealing with merely parallels and similarities, but rather with, to paraphrase Sanjay Subrahmanyam's words, a "connected legal history."[16] In what follows, I seek to reconstruct in fairly broad strokes some of the historical and discursive connections and dialogues that spanned the different polities of the eastern Islamic lands of the period.

[15] Despite the importance of Timur in their worldview, the Timurids and the Mughals emphasized Timur's and, by extension, their link to Chinggis Khān and his lineage. On the significance of Timur in Mughal India and central Asia, see Stephen F. Dale, *The Garden of the Eight Paradises: Bābur and the Culture of Empire in Central Asia, Afghanistan and India (1483–1530)* (Leiden: Brill, 2004); Balabanlilar, *Imperial Identity*; Moin, *Millennial Sovereign*, 23–55; Ron Sela, *The Legendary Biographies of Tamerlane: Islam and Heroic Apocrypha in Central Asia* (Cambridge: Cambridge University Press, 2011).On the importance of Chinggis Khān in central Asia, see Robert D. McChesney, *Central Asia: Foundations of Change* (Princeton, NJ: Darwin Press, 1996), 117–48.

[16] Sanjay Subrahmanyam, "Connected Histories: Notes toward a Reconfiguration of Early Modern Eurasia," *Modern Asian Studies* 31 (1997): 735–62.

The Chinggisid universalist notion of sovereignty rested on the view that the divine dispensation to rule the world was given to Chinggis Khān and his descendants. Fittingly, Chinggis Khān was perceived as divine legislator. Two concepts capture this notion of sovereignty: Chinggisid *yasa* and the Turkic *töre* (or *törä*). The definition of these concepts and the nature of the Mongol *yasa* have attracted a great deal of scholarly attention over the years and are beyond the scope of this study.[17] Suffice it to say that the Chinggisid *yasa* was not, apparently, a fixed written legal code, but rather "an evolving body of individual decrees, regulations, and practices that had been instituted or sanctioned by Chinggis Khān … a kind of unwritten 'constitution.'"[18]

These notions did not lose their appeal in the centuries following the demise of the Mongol empire, even though all the successor dynasties in the eastern Islamic lands considered themselves Islamic. This self-perception is reflected in different attempts to draw on pre-Mongol Islamic ideals of sovereignty and kingship in combination with Chinggisid political ideals. Yet despite – or, perhaps, because of – the tensions, the rulers of the successor states upheld key Mongol-Chinggisid ideals of law and sovereignty.

It is also worth pointing out that the rulers of the successor states, especially when they were not descendants of Chinggis Khān, modified these ideals to varying degrees. For example, members of the ruling and scholarly elites in the Ottoman and the Timurid lands, two of the better-studied polities among those that emerged in the centuries following the demise of the Mongol empire in the fourteenth century, were concerned with articulating their respective claims of sovereignty. Although the dynasts of both polities were not descendants of Chinggis Khān, scholars and rulers in these lands maintained an ongoing dialogue with Chinggisid ideals of sovereignty and law. Writing in the early fifteenth century in the

[17] David Ayalon, "The Great Yasa of Chingiz Khān. A Reexamination (Part A–D)," *Studia Islamica* 33 (1971): 97–140; 34 (1971): 151–80; 36 (1972): 113–58; 38 (1973): 107–56; David Morgan, "The 'Great "Yasa" of Chingiz Khān' and Mongol Law in the Ilkhānate," *Bulletin of the School of Oriental and African Studies* 49, no. 1 (1986): 163–76; David Morgan, "The 'Great Yasa of Chinggis Khān' Revisited," in *Mongols, Turks and Others*, ed. R. Amitai and M. Biran (Leiden: Brill, 2005), 291–308; Caroline Humphrey and A. Hürelbaatar, "The Term *Törü* in Mongolian History," in *Imperial Statecraft: Political Forms and Techniques of Governance in Inner Asia, Sixth-Twentieth Centuries*, ed. David Sneath (Bellingham: Center for East Asian Studies, Western Washington University, 2006), 265–93.

[18] Maria E. Subtelny, *Timurids in Transition: Turko-Persian Politics and Acculturation in Medieval Iran* (Leiden: Brill, 2007), 16–17.

Ottoman lands, Tâcü'ddîn İbrâhîm b. Ḫıżır Aḥmedî (d. 1413)[19] dedicates several couplets to the Mongol legal heritage:

> Concerning the justice (ʿ*adl*) of the Mongol Sultans:
> Hear now the explanation of what it was.
> They did not mention the fact that
> Chinggis Khān clearly oppressed the people.
> They [the Mongol rulers] oppressed them with the law [*ḳânûnıla*],
> But they did not paint their hands with blood.
> Lawful oppression and confiscation
> Are amenable to the people as a form of justice.[20]

Aḥmedî's couplets may be read as an attempt to appropriate a Mongol discourse of sovereignty (law and justice) in order to praise the Ottoman sultans, "those of just nature ... [who] were both Muslims and dispensers of justice." The term Aḥmedî uses for "law," "ḳânûn," was at times employed by Ottoman authors to refer to the Mongol *yasa*.[21] However, in Aḥmedî's eyes, it is the just Ottoman ḳânûn that distinguished the Ottoman dynasts from its Mongol counterparts. In other contemporary sources, the promulgation of laws (*yasa* or ḳânûn) is perceived as a sign of the sultan's sovereignty. In a work commissioned by the Ottoman sultan Meḥmet I's vezir and presented to the sultan in 1414, the author, ʿAbdülvâsiʿ Çelebi, recounts the succession struggles, before Meḥmet assumed power, between the future sultan and his brother Mûsâ. In his description of Meḥmet's campaign in Thrace, ʿAbdülvâsiʿ Çelebi states that "everywhere he [Meḥmet] went, he made laws [*yasağ*] for justice."[22] The important point is that even though Aḥmedî and ʿAbdülvâsiʿ Çelebi do not explicitly refer to a distinctive Ottoman *yasa*, they are employing the Mongol-Chinggisid discourse of sovereignty to assert Ottoman sovereignty.

The notion of dynastic law (framed in terms of *yasa* or *töre*) indeed was already circulating at that time across the eastern Islamic lands. To the east, in the Timurid domains, the descendants of Timur referred to the

[19] On Aḥmedî, see Kemal Silay, introduction to *History of the Kings of the Ottoman Lineage and Their Holy Raids against the Infidels*, by Tâcü'ddîn İbrâhîm b. Ḫıżır Aḥmedî (Cambridge, MA: Department of Near Eastern Languages and Literatures, 2004), xiii–xiv.

[20] Aḥmedî, *History of the Kings*, 1. For the Turkish, see ibid., 25.

[21] Cornell H. Fleischer, *Bureaucrat and Intellectual in the Ottoman Empire: The Historian Mustafa Âli (1541–1600)* (Princeton, NJ: Princeton University Press, 1986), 284.

[22] Dimitris J. Kastritsis, *The Sons of Beyazid: Empire Building and Representation in the Ottoman Civil War of 1402–1413* (Leiden: Brill, 2007), 224. On ʿAbdülvâsiʿ Çelebi and his work, see ibid., 217–20.

"*törä* [or *töre*] of the Lord of the auspicious conjunction" (*törä-i ṣāḥib-qirānī*) and to "the triumphant *törä*." As Maria Subtelny has explained, "[the *törä*] appears to have overlapped and complemented the Chinggisid *yasa*, as the formula 'in accordance with the *yasa* of Chinggis Khān and the törä of His Excellency, Lord of the auspicious conjunction,' which was frequently cited by Timurid chroniclers, indicates." Nevertheless, it appears that in some instances the Timurid *töre* differed from the Mongol *yasa* and referred to specific Timurid customs. But much like the Mongol *yasa*, the Timurid *töre* was an evolving corpus of regulations, customs, and practices that were introduced by Timur and observed by his descendants and followers.[23]

Similarly, by the fifteenth and sixteenth centuries, members of the Ottoman dynasty explicitly referred to their own *törä*. In a correspondence between Meḥmet I and Timur's son Shāhrukh concerning Ottoman succession practices, which is preserved in Ferîdûn Bey's (d. 1583) *Münşeâtü'l-Selâṭîn*, the issue of the Ottoman *töre* is raised:

> [Shāhrukh to Meḥmet I:] "As required by the Ottoman law [*töre*], you have removed from contention all of your brothers. This type of activity between blood brothers is not in accordance with the Mongol [Ilkhānī] traditions [*töre*]."
>
> [Meḥmet I to Shāhrukh:] "Your advice with regard to brothers is well taken. However, from the very beginnings of the Ottoman state, our forefathers have used the hand of experience to solve their problems."[24]

Although the authenticity of some of the documents in the collection has been questioned over the centuries, it clearly reflects the way in which some members of the scholarly elite in the sixteenth century, and probably even earlier, perceived the rise of the Ottoman dynastic law and the relationship between the Mongol *yasa/töre* and the *töre* of various local dynasties. Shāhrukh presents himself as the defender of Chinggisid (Ilkhānī) traditions, while emphasizing the contradiction between these traditions and the Ottoman töre, thus implying a hierarchy between the Mongol *yasa/töre* and the Ottoman *töre* (and others). Meḥmet I's reply, on the other hand, suggests that by the fifteenth century, local dynastic traditions had gained currency at the expense of the more universalist

[23] Subtelny, *Timurids in Transition*, 16–17.

[24] Ferîdûn Bey, *Münşeâtü'l-Selâṭîn* ([Istanbul?], 1858), 1:143–44. The translation appears in Halil Inalcık, *The Middle East and the Balkans under the Ottoman Empire: Essays on Economy and Society* (Bloomington, IN: Indiana University Turkish Studies and Turkish Ministry of Culture Joint Series, 1993), 57. On Ferîdûn Bey, see J. H. Mordtmann and V. L. Menage, "Ferîdûn Bey," *Encyclopedia of Islam*, 2nd ed.

Chinggisid approach. But regardless of the different approaches toward the Chinggisid tradition, the correspondence indicates that the latter still served as a point of reference in claims of legitimacy. Last, the exchange between the two post-Mongol rulers shows that dynasties not only articulated their notions of sovereignty in relation to their (real or imagined) Mongol past, they also negotiated and debated these ideals with their contemporaries, thus partaking in a shared discourse concerning sovereignty and law.[25]

In the sixteenth century, which witnessed the emergence of four major polities – the Ottomans, the Safavids, the Özbeks, and the Mughals – dynastic laws became the predominant norm. Thus each of the dynasties followed political, legal, and administrative norms they could trace to a real or imagined ancestral origin (whether the early Ottoman sultans, Chinggis Khān, or Timur). These legal principles became the cornerstone in each dynasty's perception of itself vis-à-vis other dynasties. Furthermore, in the multiethnic and diverse landscapes of these empires, these political-legal traditions enabled the dynasts to instill a sense of imperial coherence and order.[26]

From the perspective of Islamic legal history, the rise of distinctive dynastic legal traditions provoked debates between members of the ruling elites and judicial circles across the eastern Islamic lands concerning the relationship between these dynastic traditions and Islamic law. Fifteenth- and sixteenth-century chronicles, legal treatises, and other sources attest to the tensions and difficulties the amalgamation of various legal, political, and religious traditions entailed, or at least, was perceived to entail. As the authors of these chronicles and treatises observed, there were serious contradictions and tensions between the political-legal heritage of Chinggis Khān and certain pre-Mongol perceptions of Islamic law.

The perceived tensions between these discourses also necessitated the delineation of the boundaries of each of the legal corpuses. Since the Mongol invasions, different jurists would condemn the new rulers for not following the sharīʿa. For example, the late fourteenth-century/early fifteenth-century jurist Aḥmad b. Muḥammad b. ʿArabshāh (d. 1450), one of the most adamant critics of Timur, accused the latter of trying

[25] The famous fifteenth-century Aqquynulu ruler Uzun Ḥasan also issued his own *yasaknāmes* and *ḳânûnnāmes* in his territories. See Stephen F. Dale, *The Muslim Empires of the Ottomans, Safavids, and Mughals* (Cambridge: Cambridge University Press, 2010), 82–83.

[26] Fleischer, *Bureaucrat and Intellectual*, 290.

to "extinguish the Light of God and the Pure Faith [of Islam] with the law of Chinggis Khān." According to Ibn ʿArabshāh, Timur's adherence to the *yasa* led Syrian jurists to consider him an infidel.[27] On the other hand, Timur's son Shāhrukh, who is said to have been a devout Muslim, declared the abrogation of the Mongol *yasa* in 1441 and "reinstated the sharīʿa, and had wine from the taverns publicly poured onto the ground."[28] Some of Timur and Shāhrukh's descendants in Mughal India also emphasized their commitment to the sharīʿa. In a quite well-known passage in his memoir, the founder of the Mughal dynasty in India, Bābur (d. 1530), explains:

> Previously our ancestors had shown unusual respect for the Chinggisid code (*torah*). They did not violate this code sitting and rising at councils and courts, at feasts and dinners. [However] Chinggis Khān's code is not a *naṣṣ qāṭiʿ* (categorical text) that a person must follow. Whenever one leaves a good custom, it should be followed. If ancestors leave a bad custom, however, it is necessary to substitute a good one.[29]

Bābur, then, acknowledges his ancestors' adherence to the Chinggisid heritage, but at the same time he downplays its importance, for it is not, in his mind, a divinely ordained law, as opposed to Islamic law, which he held to be divinely revealed. Moreover, the last sentence may be read as an expression of Bābur's urge to correct his ancestors' misconduct.

To the north, in the Özbek domains, contemporary chronicles record similar tensions between the Chinggisid yasa and the sharīʿa. The early sixteenth-century jurist and chronicler Ibn Rūzbahān, whom we have already met, mentions participating in a debate in Samarqand concerning inheritance practices. Against the opinions of several leading jurists, the Özbek dynast Shaybānī (or Shībānī) Khān ruled for a solution that, in Ibn Rūzbahān's and possibly other jurists' eyes, was "incompatible with the sharīʿa," for it originated from the Chinggisid *yasa*.[30] Likewise, sources from the Ottoman lands preserve this distinction between ḳânûn and *sharīʿa*: in the early sixteenth century, the chief imperial muftī had to insist on the implementation of both dynastic law (*ḳânûn*) and *sharīʿa*.[31]

27 Subtelny, *Timurids in Transition*, 18.

28 Manz, *Power, Politics and Religion*, 28. On the conversion of the Ilkhāns to Islam and its ideological implications, see Anne F. Broadbridge, *Kingship and Ideology in the Islamic and Mongol Worlds* (Cambridge: Cambridge University Press, 2008), chap. 3.

29 Dale, *Garden of the Eight Paradises*, 171.

30 Ken'ichi Isogai, "Yasa and Sharīʿah in Early 16th Century Central Asia," *L'heritage timourdie Iran-Asia central – Inde XVe-XVIIIe siècles* 3–4 (1997): 91–103.

31 Zenbilli ʿAlî Cemâlî, *Fetâvâ*, Süleymaniye Library MS Fatih 2390, 75r.

Furthermore, in the decades after the Ottoman conquest of the Arab lands in 1516–17, jurists from the empire's Arab provinces accused their colleagues from the core lands of the empire of following the *yasa* (i.e., ḳânûn), implying that it was not compatible with the *sharīʿa*.[32]

Most studies of these debates have focused on the tensions between the dynastic and Islamic law as two independent discourses. This study, on the other hand, suggests that the tensions between dynastic law and the pre-Mongol ideal of Islamic law (as jurists' law) – and the debates these tensions produced – offer important clues to the circumstances in which the notion of the official state madhhab emerged. The official/dynastic school of law (or branch within the school) was the response that dynasts and state-affiliated jurists developed to cope with the challenges that the encounter between the Chinggisid and pre-Mongol Islamic (Sunnī) notions of law posed.

Situating the Post-Mongol Period in the Grand Narratives of Islamic Legal History

Despite its importance, the rise of the official madhhab across the eastern Islamic lands in the post-Mongol period has not received sufficient attention in the grand narratives of Islamic legal history. In part, this relative disregard may be attributed to the emphasis most grand narratives of Islamic legal history tend to place on the so-called formative period of Islamic law and on the legal reforms of the nineteenth century. According to this accepted view, nineteenth-century states increasingly codified Islamic law as part of a wider set of modernizing reforms. As a result, these grand narratives argue, the fluidity and diversity that characterized

[32] Michael Winter, "Ottoman Qadis in Damascus in the 16th–18th Centuries," in *Law, Custom, and Statute in the Muslim World: Studies in Honor of Aharon Layish*, ed. Ron Shaham (Leiden: Brill, 2007), 89–90; Reem Meshal, "Antagonistic Sharīʿas and the Construction of Orthodoxy in Sixteenth-Century Ottoman Cairo," *Journal of Islamic Studies* 21, no. 2 (2010): 182–212. On the other hand, it appears that dynasts attempted to tap into the Islamic Sunnī discourse of legal authority. In his report of the debate between the Özbek khān and the jurists, Ibn Rūzbahān accuses the former of exerting his own discretion (performing *ijtihād*), although he was not entitled to do so (Isogai, "Yasa and *Sharīʿah*"). This is an interesting comment, for it suggests that some jurists used the legal discourse of authority that was central to the organization and regulation of the school of law (namely, independent discretion to interpret revelation, *ijtihād*, and following/imitation of more knowledgeable authorities, *taqlīd*) to limit the authority of the khān to derive new laws. Interestingly enough, several decades later, in Mughal India, the emperor Akbar also employed Islamic authoritative discourse and claimed the right to derive new laws on the basis of *ijtihād* (Moin, *Millennial Sovereign*, 139–40).

the premodern *sharīʿa* from its earliest centuries diminished. In addition to the codification of law, the state's appointment of jurists and especially of muftīs is perceived as part of this modernization of Islamic law by the state, which modeled its legal ideals and institutions after "Western" notions of law. In the colonial context, namely, that of the Indian subcontinent, it is the colonial administrators who are considered the main contributors to the decline in the fluidity and diversity of the "pre-modern *sharīʿa*."[33] In short, these narrative take the intervention of the state in regulating the content of the law as one of their most important organizing principles.

I fully agree that the intervention of the state is critical for the periodization of Islamic legal history. Nevertheless, as I have tried to show in this book, the developments of the post-Mongol period raise questions about some central elements of the aforementioned narratives. As I have suggested, the rise of the official madhhab, along with the development of legal hierarchies and the different dynastic states' appointment of muftīs, reflects a growing interest on the part of the post-Mongol dynasties to intervene in regulating the structure of the school (or, more precisely, the branch within the school) they adopted and developed. Moreover, it appears that in some cases, as in the Ottoman Empire, sultans and dynasties were quite successful in obtaining this goal.

This is not to say that there were no major developments in the nineteenth century that justify treating it as a separate period in Islamic legal history. But one has to acknowledge that the intensive intervention of the state in regulating the school of law and, by extension, Islamic law antedates the nineteenth century. As far as the nature of the school of law and the right sovereigns assumed to regulate it are concerned, the narrative I am offering is one of much greater continuity between (1) the pre- and the post-nineteenth-century periods and (2) Islamic and non-Islamic governmental practices. To illustrate this continuity, suffice it to consider the following decree, which was issued in Egypt in 1865:

It has been brought to our attention that some John Does issues fatwas related to sharīʿa cases dealt with in the shariʿa courts, in the awqaf ministry and particularly in the Supreme Council of Adjudication. It also transpires that the parties

[33] For example: Muhammad Qasim Zaman, *The Ulama in Contemporary Islam: Custodian of Change* (Princeton, NJ: Princeton University Press, 2002), chap. 1; Wael B. Hallaq, *Sharīʿah: Theory, Practice, Transformations* (Cambridge: Cambridge University Press, 2009); Chibli Mallat, *Introduction to Middle Eastern Law* (Oxford: Oxford University Press, 2009).

who obtain such fatwas believe them to be valid and see them as an authoritative source that would enable them to achieve their goal – ignorant and unaware of the fact that these fatwas have neither value nor significance whatsoever.... This phenomenon causes grave problems and great dispute between the parties, and these John Does assume the honorable position of muftis for their own personal profit.[34]

Rudolph Peters and, more recently, Liat Kozma have offered different interpretations of this decree.[35] While the former has interpreted the decree as the state's attempt to ban those jurists whose knowledge of *sharīʿa* was deficient, the latter has read it as the (modernizing) Egyptian state's attempt to "monopolize and systemize." Moreover, according to Kozma, "it was the notion of regularization itself with which the central authorities were concerned."[36] The importance both accounts place on regulation is correct. I find, however, Kozma's "regulation for the sake of regulation" argument somewhat lacking. If my interpretation of the post-Mongol legal reality in the eastern Islamic lands (of which Egypt was part, following its incorporation into the Ottoman Empire in the sixteenth century) is correct, it seems that much like their Istanbul-based contemporary and earlier colleagues, the jurists (as well as other actors) who were affiliated with the Egyptian state wanted to regulate the content of a particular *sharīʿa*, or, more accurately, of a particular school of law, which was to be applied within the confines of the state's official legal system. Put differently, the "modernizing" Egyptian state was employing administrative logic and practices that had been in place by that time for centuries.

Similar continuities are discernable in the colonial context of the Indian subcontinent in the late eighteenth and early nineteenth century. This is not to downplay the significance of the changes and innovations the British colonial authorities did introduce to the administration of law in the subcontinent. It is to suggest, however, that the British colonial authorities tapped into and made use of Mughal notions of sovereignty and law. The Mughal state regulated the doctrines of the Ḥanafī school and specified (in fact, codified) which were to be followed. This continuity is reflected, for example, in the emphasis the British administrators

[34] Cited in Liat Kozma, *Policing Egyptian Women: Sex, Law, and Medicine in Khedival Egypt* (Syracuse, NY: Syracuse University Press, 2011), 12.

[35] Rudolph Peters, "Muḥammad al-ʿAbbāsī al-Mahdī (d. 1897), Grand Mufti of Egypt, and His al-Fatāwá al-Mahdīyya," *Islamic Law and Society* 1 (1994): 66–82; Kozma, *Policing Egyptian Women*, 11–12.

[36] Kozma, *Policing Egyptian Women*, 12.

in early colonial India placed on specific jurisprudential texts that were considered particularly authoritative under the Mughals.[37]

To conclude, the dominant grand narratives of the history of Islamic law in the eastern Islamic lands and their periodization seem to overlook some of the developments I have discussed here. My intention has been to offer a different analytical framework that would call into question a set of dichotomies that serve to organize many of these grand narratives of Islamic legal history: state or dynastic law/jurist law, modern/premodern, and Western/non-Western. Moreover, the account offered here of the emergence of the concept of the state madhhab in the post-Mongol period may modify our understanding of the legal reforms of the nineteenth century. This is not to say that post-Mongol legal notions and practices were not invested with new meanings, further developed, or contextualized in new genealogies (such as the West or modernity). In fact, the suggested framework, and particularly its emphasis on continuity, offers an opportunity to examine how different categories and genealogies – Western and non-Western, modern and premodern – intersect and overlap in the same administrative or legal practice.

[37] Robert Travers, *Ideology and Empire in Eighteenth-Century India: The British Bengal* (Cambridge: Cambridge University Press, 2007), 124–25.

Appendix A

The Classification of the Authorities of the Ḥanafī School

In addition to reconstructing the genealogy of the imperial learned hierarchy, the *ṭabaqāt* works compiled by members of the imperial learned hierarchy classified the authorities of the Ḥanafī school. The classification of the authorities of the different Sunnī jurisprudential schools has a long history that predates the Ottoman period, but it appears that in the Ottoman context Kemâlpaşazâde's treatise on the authorities of the school played a particularly prominent role, as many later authors responded to this treatise by offering their own taxonomies.[1]

It is not fully clear why, when, and in what capacity Kemâlpaşazâde compiled his treatise on the hierarchy of the authorities of the school. Nevertheless, his appointment as the chief imperial jurisconsult and the fact that during his lifetime he was considered a prominent jurist contributed to its immense popularity, which is reflected in the numerous copies of the treatise located in many libraries and in the attention it attracted from Kemâlpaşazâde's contemporaries and successors – as well as modern scholars. Although in many ways the authors who responded to Kemâlpaşazâde's treatise with their own versions follow

[1] In addition to his *ṭabaqāt* work, Kınalızâde wrote two treatises that deal with the hierarchy of the authorities of the Ḥanafī school. Although they diverge in certain points from Kemâlpaşazâde's treatise, they bear clear similarities to it. Kınalızâde ʿAlî Çelebi, *Risāla fī masāʾil ṭabaqāt al-Ḥanafiyya*, Süleymaniye Library MS Reisülküttab 1221, 52v–54r; H. Yunus Apaydın, "Kınalı-zade'nin, Hanefi Mezhebini Oluşturan Görüşlerin Toplandığı Ederlerin Gruplandırılmasına Dair bir Risalesi," in *Kınalı-zade Ali Efendi (1510–1572)*, ed. Ahmed Hulusi Köker (Kayseri: Erciyes Üniversitesi Matbbası, 1999), 96–100; Menderes Gürkan, "Müctehidlerin Tasnifinde Kemalpaşazade ile Kınalızade arasında bir Mukayese," in ibid., 83–95.

Kemâlpaşazâde's classification, they occasionally diverge from it. What follows is an attempt to summarize the major similarities and differences between the taxonomies.

Kemâlpaşazâde's classification of the authorities of the school consists of seven ranks, with the jurists' authority to exercise independent reasoning (*ijtihād*) decreasing as their rank decreases. In this sense, the general narrative is one of decline or, alternatively, of the consolidation of the school's authority. The first rank, the rank of those allowed to employ the utmost degree of independent reasoning in order to reach a ruling (*mujtahidīn fī al-sharʿ*), includes the eponymous founders of the Sunnī legal schools (including the schools that did not survive). The jurists of this rank established the fundamental principles (*uṣūl*) and derived legal rulings (*furūʿ*) on the basis of the Qurʾān, the Sunna, consensus, and analogy (*qiyās*).

The members of the second rank, such as Abū Yūsuf and Muḥammad al-Shaybānī, are already members of a school, the Ḥanafī school in this case. These jurists are considered mujtahids, but they have to follow the principles set by Abū Ḥanīfa, despite their numerous disagreements with him. The jurists of the third rank, who lived from the ninth century to the twelfth, are also considered mujtahids, but they practice *ijtihād* only in particular cases that were not addressed by Abū Ḥanīfa. Like their predecessors in the second rank, they are committed to the principles set by the eponymous founder of the school.

From the fourth *ṭabaqa* onward, the jurists are no longer considered mujtahids. Because of their mastery of the principles defined by Abū Ḥanīfa and their understanding of how rules were derived by members of earlier *ṭabaqāt*, the jurists of the fourth rank are allowed to practice *takhrīj*, an activity that entails a limited form of *ijtihād* whereby the jurist confronts the established opinions of the founder of the school and those of his companions to resolve juridical ambiguities and point out which opinion is preferable.

The last three *ṭabaqāt* are those of the followers (*muqallids*) of the eponym. The *muqallids* of the fifth rank, who lived in the eleventh and twelfth centuries, are known as the people of *tarjīḥ* (*aṣḥāb al-tarjīḥ*), which means that they are allowed to choose a preferable solution among the several solutions offered by their predecessors. Members of the sixth rank, who lived in the thirteenth and fourteenth centuries, are able to classify the extant opinions according to their soundness and authoritativeness. More importantly, since many of them compiled authoritative legal manuals (*al-mutūn al-muʿtabara min al-mutaʾakhkhirīn*), they weeded out less authoritative and weaker opinions. The last *ṭabaqa*, the seventh, includes the lowliest followers, including poorly trained jurists, who are incapable of "differentiating right from left." Although not stated explicitly, it seems that Kemâlpâşâzâde assumes that he and his peers are members of the seventh *ṭabaqa*.[2]

As mentioned, Kemâlpaşazâde's successors wrote their own versions of the classification of the authorities of the school, which were based explicitly or implicitly on the former's treatise. In the introduction to his genealogy of the Ḥanafī school, Kınalızâde explains that he includes a classification of the school's authorities to assist the muftī in his rulings, for the latter should follow the rulings of the school according to Kemâlpaşazâde's hierarchy of authorities.[3] His treatise, Kınalızâde argues, can assist the perplexed muftī in applying the soundest opinion among the opinions at his disposal.[4] Nevertheless, despite clear similarities, Kınalızâde diverges from Kemâlpaşazâde's treatise in some points. For instance, he lists only six ranks of jurists instead of Kemâlpaşazâde's seven-rank typology.

Several decades later, in his introduction to his genealogy of the Ḥanafī school, Kefevî also provides his reader with his own classification of the authorities of the school. As in Kemâlpaşazâde's taxonomy, Abū Ḥanīfa is not included in the taxonomy of the Ḥanafī jurists and is in the same *ṭabaqa* with the eponymous founders of the other Sunnī legal schools. The justification for this decision is that the eponyms do not follow the principles of other jurists, as the jurists who are affiliated with a school are required to do. The major difference between Kefevî's taxonomy and that of his predecessors is that he divides the Ḥanafī jurists into five ranks, as opposed to the seven and six ranks that Kemâlpaşazâde and Kınalızâde offered, respectively. The first rank, according to Kefevî, includes the jurists who were the direct disciples of Abū Ḥanīfa, such as Abū Yūsuf, Muḥammad al-Shaybānī, Zufar, and others. They form the

[2] Ibn Kamāl Pāshā (Kemâlpaşazâde), *Risālat ṭabaqāt al-mujtahidīn*, New York Public Library MS M&A 51891A, 195v–196v. Hallaq, *Authority*, 14–17. Hallaq also compares Kemâlpâşâzâde's classification to classifications in the other Sunnī legal schools (ibid., 1–23). Zouhair Ghazzal, *The Grammar of Adjudication: The Economics of Judicial Decision Making in Fin-de-Siècle Ottoman Beirut and Damascus* (Beirut: Institut français du Proche-Orient, 2007), 48–49.

[3] Edirneli Meḥmet Kâmî cites this classification almost verbatim. Edirneli Meḥmet Kâmî, *Mahāmm al-fuqahāʾ fī ṭabaqāt al-Ḥanafiyya*, Süleymaniye Library MS Aşir Efendi 422, 41v–43r.

[4] Kınalızâde ʿAlāʾ al-Dīn ʿAlī Çelebī Amr Allāh b. ʿAbd al-Qādir al-Ḥumaydī al-Rūmī al-Ḥanafī, *Ṭabaqāt al-Ḥanafiyya* (Amman: Dār Ibn al-Jawzī, 2003–4), 93–98.

first *ṭabaqa* because of their competence to derive rulings on the basis of the principles set by Abū Ḥanīfa. In addition, the jurists of this rank further elaborated the principles jurists should follow in their rulings. The second *ṭabaqa* consists of leading jurists of later centuries such as al-Khaṣṣāf, al-Taḥāwī, al-Karkhī, al-Ḥilwānī, al-Sarakhsī, and Qāḍīkhān. These jurists may employ their jurisprudential capacities, but only in cases where there is no explicit ruling by Abū Ḥanīfa. In the third rank are jurists, such as Muḥammad b. Abī Bakr al-Razī, who are allowed to employ *takhrīj*; that is, they were allowed, based on juristic competence, to explicate unclear issues, though they must follow the principles set by Abū Ḥanīfa. In the fourth rank are Ḥanafī jurists who may determine, whenever there is a disagreement between Abū Ḥanīfa and his disciples, which opinion is preferable. The last rank includes jurists who are familiar with the various categories concerning the soundness of an opinion within the Ḥanafī school.[5] Although not stated explicitly, it seems that Kefevî considers himself and his contemporaries to be part of the fifth rank of jurists.

[5] Maḥmûd b. Süleymân Kefevî, *Katāʾib aʿlām al-akhyār min fuqahāʾ madhhab al-Nuʿmān al-mukhtār*, Süleymaniye Library MS Esʿad Efendi 548, 2r–2v.

Appendix B

Kefevî's Chains of Transmission*

1. Kefevî > al-Sayyid Muḥammad b. ʿAbd al-Qādir> Nūr al-Dīn al-Qarāṣūʾī > Sinān Pāşā Yūsuf b. Khuḍur Bey > Khuḍur Bey b. Jalāl al-Dīn >Muḥammad b. Armağān (Molla Yegân) > Shams al-Dīn Muḥammad b. Ḥamza al-Fenārī > Muḥammad b. Muḥammad b. Maḥmūd al-Bābartī > Qiwām al-Dīn Muḥammad al-Kālī > al-Ḥusayn b. ʿAlī al-Saghnāqī > Ḥāfiẓ al-Dīn Muḥammad b. Naṣr al-Bukhārī > Muḥammad b. ʿAbd al-Sattār al-Kardarī > ʿAlī b. Abī Bakr al-Marghīnānī > Ḥusām al-Dīn ʿUmar b. ʿAbd al-ʿAzīz b. ʿUmar b. Māza > ʿAbd al-ʿAzīz b. ʿUmar > Abū Bakr Muḥammad b. Aḥmad b. Abī Sahl al-Sarakhsī > ʿAbd al-ʿAzīz b. Aḥmad al-Ḥilwānī > al-Ḥusayn b. ʿAlī al-Nasafī > Muḥammad b. al-Faḍl al-Bukhārī > ʿAbd Allāh b. Muḥammad al-Subadhmūnī > Abū Ḥafṣ al-Ṣaghīr Abū ʿAbd Allāh > Abū Ḥafṣ al-Kabīr al-Bukhārī > Muḥammad [al-Shaybānī] > Abū Ḥanīfa.
2. Kefevî > Muḥammad b. ʿAbd al-Wahhāb > Aḥmad b. Sulaymān b. Kamāl Pāşā > Muṣliḥ al-Dīn al-Qasṭalānī > Khuḍur Bey b. Jalāl al-Dīn> Muḥammad b. Armağān (Molla Yegân) > Shams al-Dīn Muḥammad b. Ḥamza al-Fenārī > Muḥammad b. Muḥammad b. Maḥmūd al-Bābartī > Qiwām al-Dīn Muḥammad al-Kālī (?) > al-Husayn b. ʿAlī al-Saghnāqī > Ḥāfiẓ al-Dīn Muḥammad b. Naṣr al-Bukhārī > Muḥammad b. ʿAbd al-Sattār al-Kardarī > ʿAlī b. Abī Bakr al-Marghīnānī > Husām al-Dīn ʿUmar b. ʿAbd al-ʿAzīz b.

* Maḥmûd b. Süleymân Kefevî, *Katāʾib aʿlām al-akhyār min fuqahāʾ madhhab al-Nuʿmān al-mukhtār*, Süleymaniye Library MS Esad Efendi 548, 41v.

'Umar b. Māza > 'Abd al-'Azīz b. 'Umar > Abū Bakr Muḥammad b. Aḥmad b. Abī Sahl al-Sarakhsī > 'Abd al-'Azīz b. Aḥmad al-Ḥilwānī > al-Ḥusayn b. 'Alī al-Nasafī > Muḥammad b. al-Faḍl al-Bukhārī > 'Abd Allāh b. Muḥammad al-Subadhmūnī > Abū Ḥafṣ al-Ṣaghīr Abū 'Abd Allāh > Abū Ḥafṣ al-Kabīr al-Bukhārī > Muḥammad [al-Shaybānī] > Abū Ḥanīfa.

3. Kefevî > 'Abd al-Raḥmān > Sa'd Allāh b. 'Īsā b. Amīr Khān > Muḥammad b. Ḥasan al-Samsūnī > Ḥasan b. 'Abd al-Ṣamad al-Samsūnī > Ilyās b. Yaḥyā b. Ḥamza al-Rūmī > Muḥammad b. Muḥammad b. Maḥmūd al-Ḥāfiẓī al-Bukhārī Khāwāja Muḥammad Pārsā > Ḥāfiẓ al-Ḥaqq wa-l-Dīn Abū Ṭāhir Muḥammad b. Muḥammad b. al-Ḥasan al-Ṭāhirī > Ṣadr al-Sharī'a 'Ubayd Allāh b. Mas'ūd b. Tāj al-Sharī'a Maḥmūd b. Aḥmad > Tāj al-Sharī'a Maḥmud b. Aḥmad b. 'Ubayd Allāh > Shams al-Dīn Aḥmad b. Jamāl al-Dīn 'Ubayd Allāh b. Ibrāhīm al-Maḥbūbī > 'Ubayd Allāh b. Ibrāhīm b. 'Abd al-Malik Jamāl al-Dīn al-Mahbuni (also known as Abū Ḥanīfa) > 'Imād al-Dīn 'Umar b. Bakr b. Muḥammad al-Zaranjarī > Bakr b. Muḥammad al-Zaranjarī > 'Abd al-'Azīz b. Aḥmad al-Ḥilwānī > Abū 'Alī al-Nasafī > Muḥammad b. al-Faḍl > Abū al-Ḥarth 'Abd Allāh al-Subadhmūnī > Abū Ḥafṣ al-Ṣaghīr > Abū Ḥafṣ al-Kabīr > Muḥammad [al-Shaybānī] > Abū Ḥanīfa.

Appendix C

Minkârîzâde's and al-Ramlī's Bibliographies

General Comments

The bibliographies are organized in alphabetical order. I have not been able to identify all the works that appear in the muftīs' bibliographies. At times, there are several works with the same titles. The bibliographies are based on Minkârîzâde's fatāwā collection (MS Hekimoğlu 421) and on al-Ramlī's published collection. Some of the identifications are based on the electronic catalogue of the Süleymaniye Library. In addition, when possible, I have included reference to one (or more) of the following works:

- GAL – Carl Brockelmann, *Geschichte der Arabischen Litteratur*. Leiden: Brill, 1937–42.
- IQ – Ibn Quṭlūbughā, Qāsim, *Tāj al-tarājim fī man ṣannafa min al-Ḥanafiyya*. Damascus: Dār al-Ma'mūn lil-Turāth, 1992.
- KZ – Kâtip Çelebi, *Kashf al-ẓunūn ʿan asāmī al-kutub wa-al-funūn*. Istanbul: Milli Eğitim Basımevi, 1971.
- Mahāmm – Edirneli Muḥammed Kâmî, *Mahāmm al-fuqahāʾ fī ṭabaqāt al-Ḥanafiyya*. Süleymaniye Library MS Aşir Efendi 422.
- Qurashī – ʿAbd al-Qādir b. Muḥammad al-Qurashī, *al-Jawāhir al-muḍiyya fī ṭabaqāt al-Ḥanafiyya*, 2 vols. Cairo: Dār Iḥyāʾ al-Kutub al-ʿArabiyyah, 1978.
- Muḥibbī – Muḥammad Amīn ibn Faḍl Allāh al-Muḥibbī, *Khulāṣat al-athar fī aʿyān al-qarn al-ḥādī ʿashar*, 4 vols. Beirut: Dār al-Kutub al-ʿIlmiyyah, 2006.
- Ghazzī – Najm al-Dīn Muḥammad b. Muḥammad al-Ghazzī, *al-Kawākib sāʾira bi-aʿyān al-miʾa al ʿāshira*, 3 vols. Beirut: Jāmiʿat Bayrūt al-Amīrikiyya, 1945–58.

Minkârîzâde's Bibliography

1. *Adab al-awṣiyā ʾ fī furūʿ* by ʿAlî b. Muḥammad al-Jamālī (d. 1524). [KZ, 1: 45]. There is another work with the same title by Ghiyāth al-Dīn Abū Muḥammad Ghānim b. Muḥammad al-Baghdādī (d. 1620) [GAL S. II: 502].
2. *Adab al-qāḍī* by Aḥmad b. ʿUmar al-Khaṣṣāf (d. 874–875).
3. *Aḥkām al-awqāf wa-l-ṣadaqāt* by Aḥmad b. ʿUmar al-Khaṣṣāf (d. 874–875).
4. *Aḥkām al-ṣighār* by Majd al-Dīn Abī al-Fatḥ Muḥammad b. Maḥmūd al-Asrūshnī (d. ca. 1232) [KZ, 1: 19].
5. *Aḥkām fī al-fiqh al-Ḥanafī* by Aḥmad b. Muḥammad b. ʿUmar al-Nāṭifī al-Ḥanafī (d. 1054) [KZ, 1: 22].
6. *Al-Shifāʾ*(?).
7. ʿAlī al-Maqdisī (Ibn Ghānim) (d. 1596) – unknown work.
8. *Anfaʿ al-wasāʾil ilā taḥrīr al-masāʾil* by Najm al-Dīn Ibrāhīm b. ʿAlī b. Aḥmad al-Ḥanafī al-Ṭarsūsī (d. 1357) [KZ, 1: 183].
9. *Al-Ashbāh wa'l-naẓāʾir* by Zayn al-Dīn Ibrāhīm Ibn Nujaym (d. 1563) [KZ, 1: 98–99].
10. *Badāʾiʿ al-ṣanāʾiʿ fī tartīb al-sharāʾiʿ* by ʿAlāʾ al-Dīn Abī Bakr b. Masʿūd al-Kāsānī (d. 1191).
11. *Al-Baḥr al-rāʾiq* by Zayn al-Dīn Ibrāhīm Ibn Nujaym (d. 1563). A commentary on *Kanz al-daqā ʾiq*. [KZ, 2: 1515].
12. *Al-Bidāya (Bidāyat al-mubtadā fī al-furūʿ)* by ʿAlī b. Abī Bakr al-Marghīnānī (d. 1196 or 7) An abridged summary (*mukhtaṣar*) of *Mukhtaṣar al-Qudūrī* and *al-Jāmiʿ al-ṣaghīr* [IQ, 148; KZ, 1: 227–28].
13. *Al-Ḍamānāt al-Fuḍayliyya* by Fuḍayl Çelebi b. ʿAlī b. Aḥmad al-Jamālī Zenbillīzāde (Fużayl Çelebi b. ʿAlî b. Aḥmed el-Cemâlî Zenbillîzâde) (d. 1583) [KZ, 2: 1087].
14. *Ḍamānāt Ghānim* (al-Baghdādī) (*Majmaʿ Ḍamānāt*) by Abū Muḥammad b. Ghānim Baghdādī (d. 1620).
15. Ebû's-Suʿûd Efendi – most likely one the *fatāwā* collection of Ebû's-Suʿûd Efendi (d. 1574) [KZ, 2: 1220].
16. Fakhr al-Dīn al-Rāzī (d. 1210) – unspecified work.
17. *Fatāwā Abī al-Layth al-Samarqandī* by Naṣr b. Muḥammad al-Ḥanafī Abū al-Layth al-Samarqandī (d. 985) [KZ, 2: 1220].
18. *Al-Fatāwā al-ʿAttabiyya* by Zayn al-Dīn Aḥmad b. Muḥammad b. ʿUmar al-ʿAttābī al-Bukhārī (Abū Naṣr) (d. 1190) [GAL S. I: 643; KZ, 2: 1226].

19. *Al-Fatāwā al-Bazzāziyya* by Ḥāfiz al-Dīn Muḥammad b. Muḥammad al-Kardarī (d. 1433) [KZ, 1: 242].
20. *Fatāwā al-Burhānī* (*Dhakhīrat al-Fatāwā/al-Dhakhīra al-Burhāniyya*) by Burhān al-Dīn Maḥmūd b. Aḥmad b. ʿUmar b. ʿAbd al-ʿAzīz b. ʿUmar b. Māza al-Bukhārī (d. 1219). This is an abridged version of his al-Muḥīṭ al-Burhānī. [KZ, 1: 823].
21. *Al-Fatāwā al-Qāʿidiyya* by Muḥammad b. ʿAlī b. Abī al-Qāsim al-Khujandī (d.?) [KZ, 2: 1228].
22. *Al-Fatāwā al-Ṣayrafiyya* by Majd al-Dīn Esʿad b. Yūsuf al-Ṣayrafī (d.?) [KZ, 2: 1225–26].
23. *Al-Fatāwā al-Sirājiyya* by Sirāj al-Dīn ʿUmar b. Isḥāq al-Hindī al-Ghaznawī (d. 1372) [KZ, 2: 1224].
24. *Al-Fatāwā al-ṣughrā* by Ḥusām al-Dīn ʿUmar b. ʿAbd al-ʿAzīz al-Bukhārī al-Ṣadr al-Shahīd (d. 1141) [KZ, 2: 1224–25].
25. *Al-Fatāwā al-Tātārkhāniyya* by ʿĀlim b. ʿAlāʾ al-Dihlawī al-Ḥanafī (d. 1384 or 1385) [KZ, 1: 268].
26. *Al-Fatāwā al-Walwālijiyya* by ʿAbd al-Rashīd b. Abī Ḥanīfa al-Walwālijī (d. ca. 1145) [KZ, 2: 1230–31].
27. *Al-Fatāwā al-Ẓahīriyya ʿalā madhhab al-sādat al-Ḥanafiyya* by Muḥammad b. Aḥmad b. ʿUmar al-Ḥanafī Ẓahīr al-Dīn al-Bukhārī (d. 1222) [KZ, 2: 1226].
28. *Fatāwā Ibn Nujaym* by Zayn al-Dīn Ibrāhīm Ibn Nujaym (d. 1563) [KZ, 2: 1223].
29. *Fatāwā Khayr al-Dīn al-Ghazzī* (al-Ramlī) [probably not the extant collection] (d. 1671).
30. *Fatāwā Qāḍīkhān* by Fakhr al-Dīn Ḥasan b. Manṣūr b. Maḥmūd al-Ūzjandī (d. 1195) [KZ, 2: 1227–28].
31. *Fatāwā Qārī al-Hidāya* by Sirāj al-Dīn ʿUmar b. ʿAlī al-Kinānī Qārī al-Hidāya (d. 1422) [KZ, 2: 1227].
32. *Fatḥ al-qadīr* by Muḥammad b. ʿAbd al-Wāḥid b. al-Humām. A commentary on the *Hidāya* (d. 1459 or 1460).
33. *Fayḍ al-Karakī* by Ibrāhīm b. ʿAbd al-Raḥmān b. Muḥammad b. Ismāʿīl b. al-Karakī (d. 1516) [KZ, 2: 1304–5].
34. *Fetâvâ-i Çivizâde* by Muḥyiddîn Muḥammed b. Ilyâs el-Menteşevî Çivizâde (d. 1547).
35. *Al-Fuṣūl al-ʿImādiyya* (*Fuṣūl al-iḥkām li-uṣūl al-aḥkām*) by Jamāl al-Dīn ʿAbd al-Raḥīm b. ʿImād al-Dīn b. ʿAlī al-Marghīnānī (d. 1253) [KZ, 2: 1270–71].
36. *Fuṣūl fī al-Muʿādalāt* by Muḥammad b. Maḥmūd b. al-Ḥusayn al-Ustrūshanī (d. 1234) [KZ, 2: 1266].

37. *Ghāyat al-bayān wa nādirat al-aqrān* by Qiwām al-Dīn Amīr Kātib b. Amīr 'Umar al-Itqānī (d. 1356). This work is a commentary on al-Marghīnānī's *Hidāya.*
38. *Ghurar al-aḥkām* and *Durar al-ḥukkām fī Sharḥ Ghurar al-aḥkām*, both by Muḥammad b. Feramerz b. ʿAlī Molla Hüsrev (d. 1480) [KZ, 2: 1199–1200].
39. *Ḥāshiya Saʿdiyya* [possibly Saʿdî Çelebi's gloss on the tafsīr of al-Bayḍāwī].
40. *Ḥāshiyat al-Qudūrī* (?).
41. *Ḥāwī* by al-Tarahidī (?).
42. *Ḥāwī al-munya* by al- Najm al-Dīn Mukhtār b. Maḥmūd al-Ghazmīnī al-Zāhidī al-Ḥanafī (d. 1259).
43. *Al-Ḥāwī al-Qudsī by* Jamāl al-Dīn Aḥmad b. Muḥammad b. Saʿīd al-Ḥanafī al-Ghaznawī (d. 1196) [KZ, 1: 627].
44. *Al-Ḥāwī fī al-fatāwā* by Muḥammad b. Ibrāhīm al-Ḥanafī (d. 1106).
45. *Al-Hidāya* by ʿAlī b. Abī Bakr al-Marghīnānī (d. 1196 or 1197) [KZ, 2: 2031–40].
46. *Al-Ikhtiyār* by Abū al-Faḍl Majd al-Dīn ʿAbd Allāh b. Maḥmūd (b. Mawdūd) al-Mawṣilī (d. 1284). A commentary on *al-Mukhtār fī furūʿ al-Ḥanafiyya* [KZ, 2: 1622].
47. *Al-ʿInāya fī sharḥ al-Hidāya* by Akmal al-Dīn Muḥammad b. Maḥmūd al-Bābartī (d. 1384). A commentary on al-Marghīnānī's *Hidāya.*
48. *Al-Isʿāf* [*Al-Isʿāf fī aḥkām al-awqāf*] by Burhān al-Dīn Ibrāhīm b. Mūsā b. ʿAbd Allāh al-Ṭarablusī (d. 1516). [KZ, 1: 85].
49. *Al-Jāmiʿ* by Aḥmad b. 'Ubayd Allāh b. Ibrāhīm al-Maḥbūbī Ṣadr al-Sharīʿa (d. 1232) [KZ, 1: 563–64].
50. *Al-Jāmiʿ al-fatāwā* by Kırk Emre al-Ḥamīdī (d. 1475) [KZ, 1: 565–66].
51. *Jāmiʿ al-fuṣulayn* by Badr al-Dīn Maḥmūd b. Qāḍī Simāwna (d. 1416?) [KZ, 1: 566–67].
52. *Jāmiʿ al-rumūz* by Shams al-Dīn Muḥammad b. Ḥusām al-Dīn al-Quhistānī (d. 1554). A commentary on *al-Nuqāya.*
53. *Al-Jāmiʿ al-ṣaghīr* by Muḥammad b. Ḥasan b. Farkad al-Ḥanafī al-Shaybānī (d. 804) [KZ, 1: 561–62].
54. *Jawāhir al-fatāwā* by Rukn al-Dīn Muḥammad b. ʿAbd al-Rashīd al-Kirmānī (d. 1169) [KZ, 1: 615].
55. *Al-Jawhara al-nāʾira* (or *al-munīra*) *fī Sharḥ Mukhtaṣar al-Qudūrī* by Abū Bakr b. ʿAlī al-Ḥaddādī (d. 1397). This is an abridged version of his *al-Sirāj wa'l-wahhāj.* [KZ, 2: 1631].

56. *Al-Kāfī fī furū' al-Ḥanafiyya* by al-Ḥākim al-Shahīd Muḥammad b. Muḥammad al-Ḥanafī (d. 945) [KZ, 2: 1387].
57. *Kanz al-daqā'iq* by 'Abd Allāh b. Aḥmad al-Nasafī (d. 1310) [KZ, 2: 1515–17].
58. *Kashf al-asrār* by Abū al-Ḥusayn 'Alī b. Muḥammad al-Pazdawī (d. 1089) [GAL S. I: 637; KZ, 1: 112].
59. *Khizānat al-akmal fī al-furū'* by Abū Ya'qūb Yūsuf b. 'Alī b. Muḥammad al-Jurjānī al-Ḥanafī. The author started working on this text in 1128. [KZ, 1: 702].
60. *Khizānat al-fatāwā* by Ṭāhir b. Aḥmad al-Bukhārī al-Sarakhsī (d. 1147). There is another work with the same title by 'Alī b. Muḥammad b. Abī Bakr al-Ḥanafī (d. 1128). [KZ, 1: 702–3].
61. *Khizānat al-fiqh* by Abū al-Layth al-Samarqandī (d. 983) [KZ, 1: 703].
62. *Khizānat al-muftīyīn fī al-furū'* by al-Ḥusayn b. Muḥammad al-Samīqānī al-Ḥanafī (d. 1339) GAL S. II: 204; KZ, 1: 703].
63. *Khizānat al-riwāyāt* – might be the work by Jakan al-Ḥanafī of Gujarat (d.?) [KZ, 1: 702].
64. *Khulāṣat al-Fatāwā* by Iftikhār Ṭāhir b. Aḥmad b. 'Abd al-Rashīd Ṭāhir al-Bukhārī (d. 1147) [KZ, 1: 718].
65. Al-Kirmānī, possibly Qiwām al-Dīn Abū Mas'ūd b. Ibrāhīm al-Kirmānī (d. 1348), the author of a commentary on *Kanz al-daqā'iq*. [KZ, 2: 1516].
66. *Kitāb al-Mabsūṭ* by Muḥammad b. Aḥmad al-Sarakhsī (d. 1090) [KZ, 2: 1580].
67. *Kitāb al-Mabsūṭ* by Muḥammad b. Ḥusayn b. Muḥammad b. al-Ḥasan al-Bukhārī, also known as Bakr Khohar Zāde (d. 1090) [IQ, 213; KZ, 2: 1580].
68. *Kitāb al-Wāqi'āt min al-fatāwā* by Ḥusām al-Dīn 'Umar b. 'Abd al-'Azīz al-Bukhārī al-Ṣadr al-Shahīd (d. 1141) [KZ, 2: 1998].
69. *Lawāzim al-quḍāt* by Dakhī Efendi (*Lawāzim al-quḍāt wa'l-ḥukkām fī iṣlāḥ umūr al-anām*) by Muṣṭafā b. Muḥammad b. Yardim b. Saruhan al-Sirūzī al-Dīkhī (Muṣṭafā b. Muḥammed b. Yardim b. Saruhan es-Sirozî ed-Dikhî) (d. 1679).
70. *Al-Maḥallī* – possibly Jalāl al-Dīn Muḥammad b. Aḥmad al-Maḥallī's (d. 1459) commentary on *Jam' al-jawami' fī uṣūl al-fiqh* by Tāj al-Dīn 'Abd al-Wahhāb b. 'Alī b. al-Subkī (d. 1369). Al-Subkī's work is a mukhtaṣar on uṣūl. Although both the author and the commentator were Shāfi'ī, it seems their works were popular among Ḥanafīs. [KZ, 1: 595].

71. *Majma' al-baḥrayn wa-multaqā al-nahrayn* by Muẓaffar al-Dīn Aḥmad b. 'Alī al-Baghdādī Ibn al-Sā'ātī (d. 1293) [KZ, 2: 1599–1601].
72. *Majma' al-fatāwā* by Aḥmad b. Muḥammad b. Abī Bakr al-Ḥanafī (d.?). A collection of *fatāwā* issued by various jurists, from al-Ṣadr al-Shahīd to 'Alī al-Jamālī. [KZ, 2: 1603].
73. *Majma' al-nawāzil* (?).
74. *Mi'rāj al-dirāya fī Sharḥ al-Hidāya* by Muḥammad b. Muḥammad Kākī (d. 1348 or 9). [KZ, 2: 2035].
75. *Minaḥ al-ghaffār* by Shams al-Dīn Muḥammad al-Timurtāshī (d. 1595) [KZ, 1: 501].
76. *Al-Muḥīṭ (al-Burhānī)* by Burhān al-Dīn Maḥmūd b. 'Alī b. al-Ṣadr al-Shahīd (d. 1174). [KZ, 2: 1619–20].
77. *Al-Muḥīṭ al-Raḍawī fī fiqh al-Ḥanafī* by Raḍī al-Dīn Muḥammad b. Muḥammad al-Sarakhsī (d. 1149) [KZ, 2: 1620].
78. *Al-Muḥīṭ* by al-Sarakhsī by Shmas al-A'imma Muḥammad b. Aḥmad b. Abī Sahl al-Sarakhsī (d. 1046) [KZ, 2: 1620].
79. *Mukhtaṣar al-Qudūrī* by Abū al-Ḥusayn Aḥmad b. Muḥammad al-Qudūrī al-Baghdādī (d. 1037).
80. *Mukhtaṣar al-Ṭaḥāwī* by Abū Ja'far Aḥmad b. Muḥammad b. Salāma al-Ḥajrī al-Ṭaḥāwī (d. 933) [GAL S. I: 293; KZ, 2: 1627–28].
81. *Al-Muntaqā* by Ibrāhīm b. 'Alī b. Aḥmad b. Yūsuf b. Ibrāhīm Abū Isḥāq, also known as Ibn 'Abd al-Ḥaqq al-Wāsiṭī (d. 1343) [IQ, 11–12]. There is another work entitled *al-Muntaqā fī furū' al-Ḥanafiyya* by al-Ḥākim al-Shahīd (d. 945). [KZ, 2: 1851–52].
82. *Munyat al-muftī* by Yūsuf b. Abī Sa'īd Aḥmad al-Sijistānī (d. 1240) [GAL S. I, 653; KZ, 2: 1887].
83. *Munyat al-muṣalli wa-ghunyat al-mubtadī* by Sadīd al-Dīn al-Kāshgharī (d. 1305) [KZ, 2: 1886–87].
84. *Nāfi'* [*al-Fiqh al-nāfi'*] by Naṣr al-Dīn Muḥammad b. Yūsuf Abū al-Qāsim (d. 1258) [IQ, 175–76; KZ, 2: 1921–22].
85. *Naqd al-fatāwā* by Muḥammad b. Ḥamza al-'Alā'ī (d.?) [Mahāmm, 143r].
86. *Naqd al-masā'il fī jawāb al-sā'il* by Istanbullu 'Alī b. Muḥammad Riḍā'ī (Rižâî) (d. 1629) [KZ, 2: 1974].
87. *Nawāzil fī furū' al-Ḥanafiyya* by Naṣr b. Muḥammad al-Ḥanafī Abu al-Layth al-Samarqandī (d. 985) [KZ, 2: 1981].

88. *Al-Nihāya fī furū' al-fiqh al-Ḥanafī* by Ḥusām al-Dīn Ḥusayn b. 'Alī al-Ṣighnāqī (d. 1311). A commentary on al-Marghīnānī's Hidāya.
89. *Qunyat al-munya li-tatmīm al-Ghunya* by Najm al-Dīn Mukhtār b. Maḥmūd al-Ghazmīnī al-Zāhidī al-Ḥanafī (d. 1259) [KZ, 2: 1357].
90. Shams al-Dīn al-Wafā'ī(?).
91. *Sharḥ al-Jāmi' al-Ṣaghīr* by al-Timurtāshī(?).
92. *Sharḥ al-Mabsūṭ*(?).
93. *Sharḥ al-Majma'* by 'Abd al-Laṭīf b. 'Abd al-'Azīz Ibn Malak (Firişteoğlu) (d. 1395). A commentary on *Majma' al-baḥrayn*. [KZ, 2: 1601; GAL, S. II: 315].
94. *Sharḥ al-Muḥkī* (?).
95. *Sharḥ al-Sirājiyya* by Aḥmad b. Yaḥyā b. Muḥammad b. Sa'd al-Dīn al-Taftāzānī (d. 1510) [GAL, S. II: 309].
96. *Sharḥ al-Ziyādāt* by Fakhr al-Dīn Ḥasan b. Manṣūr b. Maḥmūd al-Ūzjandī (d. 1195) [GAL S. I: 645].
97. *Sharḥ Mukhtaṣar al-Qudūrī* by Najm al-Dīn Mukhtār b. Maḥmūd al-Zāhidī (d. 1259) [KZ, 2: 1631].
98. *Sharḥ Mukhtaṣar al-Ṭāḥāwī* by 'Alā' al-Dīn b. Muḥammad b. Ismā'īl al-Ḥanafī al-Isbijābī (d. 1140) [KZ, 2: 1627–28].
99. Shaykh al-Islām al-Arzsadī (?).
100. *Tabyīn al-ḥaqā'iq fī Sharḥ Kanz al-daqā'iq* by Fakhr al-Dīn 'Uthmān b. 'Alī al-Zayla'ī (d. 1342 or 1343). A commentary on *Kanz al-daqā'iq* [KZ, 2: 1515].
101. *Tafsīr al-Qur'ān* by Muḥammad ibn Abī Bakr al-Rāzī (d. 1261).
102. *Al-Tajrīd fī al-khilāfiyyāt* by Aḥmad b. Muḥammad b. Aḥmad al-Baghdādī al-Qudūrī (d. 1036) [KZ, 1: 346].
103. *Al-Tajziya* (?).
104. *Tarjīḥ al-bayānāt* by Ibn al-Ghānim al-Baghdādī (d. 1620). There is another work with the same title by Muḥammad b. Muṣṭafā al-Vānī (d. 1591). [KZ, 1: 398].
105. *Taṣḥīḥ al-Qudūrī* by Qāsim Ibn Quṭlūbughā (d. 1474).
106. *Tatamat al-fatāwā* by Burhān al-Dīn Maḥmūd b. Aḥmad b. 'Abd al-'Aziz al-Ḥanafī (d. 1219).
107. *Yatimat al-dahr fī fatāwā al-'aṣr* by 'Alā' al-Dīn Muḥammad al-Ḥanafī (d. 1247).
108. Zekarîyâ Efendi – unspecified work by Ankarali Zekeriyâ Efendi.

Al-Ramlī's Bibliography

1. 'Abd al-'Azīz b. Aḥmad b. Ṣāliḥ al-Ḥilwānī (d. 1057) – unspecified work. [al-Qurashī, 2: 429–30].
2. Abū al-Faḍl al-Kirmānī (d. 1148) – the author of *al-Jāmi' al-kabīr* and *al-Tajrīd*. [al-Qurashī, 2: 388–390; IQ, 122].
3. Abū al-Layth al-Samarqandī (d. 985) – unspecified work.
4. Abū Bakr Muḥammad b. al-Faḍl [Qurashī, 1, 102].
5. Abū Ḥamīd (?).
6. Abū Ḥasan al-Karkhī (d. 950) (mentioned in al-Qurashī, 2, 493–94) – unspecified work.
7. Abū Ja'far [Aḥmad b. Muḥammad b. Salāma al-Ḥajrī al-Ṭaḥāwī (d. 933)] – unspecified work.
8. Abū Qāsim [possibly: *Nāfi'* [*al-Fiqh al-nāfi'*] by Naṣr al-Dīn Muḥammad b. Yūsuf Abū al-Qāsim (d. 1258)].
9. *Adab al-qāḍī* by Aḥmad b. 'Umar al-Khaṣṣāf (d. 874–75).
10. Aḥmad ibn Muḥammad Ibn Ḥajar al-Haytamī (d. 1566) (Shāfi'ī).
11. 'Alī al-Maqdisī (Ibn Ghānim) (d. 1596) – unspecified work.
12. 'Alī al-Sughdī (d. 1068), possibly *Nutaf fī al-fatāwā* [KZ, 2: 1925].
13. *Anfa' al-wasā'il ilā taḥrīr al-masā'il* by Najm al-Dīn Ibrāhīm b. 'Alī b. Aḥmad al-Ḥanafī al-Ṭarsūsī (d. 1357) [KZ, 1: 183].
14. *Al-Ashbāh wa'l-naẓā'ir* by Zayn al-Dīn Ibrāhīm Ibn Nujaym (d. 1563).
15. *Al-Asrār* by Najm al-Dīn (?).
16. *Badā'i' al-ṣanā'i' fī tartīb al-sharā'i'* by 'Alā' al-Dīn Abī Bakr b. Mas'ūd al-Kāsānī (d. 1191).
17. *Al-Baḥr al-rā'iq* by Zayn al-Dīn Ibrāhīm Ibn Nujaym (d. 1563). A commentary on *Kanz al-daqā'iq*. [KZ, 2: 1515].
18. *Ḍaw' al-sirāj*, *Sharḥ al-farā'iḍ* – unknown author [Mahāmm, 106v].
19. *Al-Ḍiyā' al-ma'nāwiyya 'alā al-Muqaddima al-Ghaznawiyya* by Abū al-Baqā' Muḥammad b. Aḥmad b. al-Ḍiyā' al-Qurashī (d. 1450). A commentary on *al-Muqaddima* by Aḥmad b. Muḥammad al-Ghaznawī. [KZ, 2: 1802].
20. Ebū's-Su'ūd Efendî [probably his *Fetâvâ*] (d. 1574).
21. *Al-Fatāwā al-'Attābiyya* by Zayn al-Dīn Aḥmad b. Muḥammad b. 'Umar al-'Attābī al-Bukhārī (Abū Naṣr) (d. 1190) [GAL S. I: 643].

22. *Al-Fatāwā al-Bazzāziyya* by Ḥāfiz al-Dīn Muḥammad b. Muḥammad al-Kardarī (d. 1433) [KZ, 1: 242].
23. *Fatāwā al-Burhānī* (*Dhakhīrat al-Fatāwā/al-Dhakhīra al-Burhāniyya*) by Burhān al-Dīn Maḥmūd b. Aḥmad b. ʿUmar b. ʿAbd al-ʿAzīz b. ʿUmar b. Māza al-Bukhārī (d. 1219). This is an abridged version of his al-Muḥīṭ al-Burhānī. [KZ, 1: 823].
24. *Fatāwā al-Ḥijja al-kāfira*? [KZ, 2: 1222].
25. *Al-Fatāwā al-kubrā* by Ḥusām al-Dīn ʿUmar b. ʿAbd al-ʿAzīz al-Bukhārī al-Ṣadr al-Shahīd (d. 1141) [KZ, 2: 1228–29].
26. *Fatāwā al-Nasafī* by Najm al-Dīn b. ʿUmar b. Muḥammad al-Nasafī [KZ, 2: 1230].
27. *Fatāwā al-Nawawī* by Muḥammad Ra'fat ʿUthmān Nawawī (Shāfiʿī) [KZ, 2: 1230].
28. *Fatāwā al-Shurunbulālī* by Ḥasan al-Shurunbulālī (d. 1659) [Muḥibbī, 2:38–39].
29. *Al-Fatāwā al-Sirājiyya* by Sirāj al-Dīn ʿUmar b. Isḥāq al-Hindī al-Ghaznawī (d. 1372) [KZ, 2: 1224].
30. *Al-Fatāwā al-ṣughrā* by Ḥusām al-Dīn ʿUmar b. ʿAbd al-ʿAzīz al-Bukhārī al-Ṣadr al-Shahīd (d. 1141) [KZ, 2: 1224–25].
31. *Al-Fatāwā al-Tātārkhāniyya* by ʿĀlim b. ʿAlā' al-Dihlawī al-Ḥanafī (d. 1384 or 1385) [KZ, 1: 268].
32. *Al-Fatāwā al-Walwālijiyya* by ʿAbd al-Rashīd b. Abī Ḥanīfa al-Walwālijī (d. ca. 1145) [KZ, 2: 1230–31].
33. *Al-Fatāwā al-Ẓahīriyya ʿalā madhhab al-sādat al-Ḥanafiyya* by Muḥammad b. Aḥmad b. ʿUmar al-Ḥanafī Ẓahīr al-Dīn al-Bukhārī (d. 1222) [KZ, 2: 1226].
34. *Fatāwā Amīn al-Dīn ʿAbd al-Āl* (d. 1563) (also known as *al-Fatāwā al-Amīniyya*).
35. *Fatāwā Ibn Nujaym* (d. 1563) [KZ, 2: 1223].
36. *Fatāwā Ibn Quṭlūbughā* (d. 1480).
37. *Fatāwā Muḥammad al-Timurtāshī* (d.1595).
38. *Fatāwā Qāḍīkhān* by Fakhr al-Dīn Ḥasan b. Manṣūr b. Maḥmūd al-Ūzjandī (d. 1195) [KZ, 2: 1227–28].
39. *Fatāwā Rashīd al-Dīn* by Rashīd al-Dīn al-Wattār (d. 1201) [KZ, 2: 1223].
40. *Fatāwā Zakariyā al-Anṣārī* (d. 1520) (Shāfiʿī).
41. *Al-Fawā'id al-Zayniyya* by Ibn Nujaym (d. 1563) [KZ, 2: 1296].
42. *Al-Fawākih al-Badriyya fī al-aqḍiyya al-ḥukmiyya* by Ibn al-Ghars Muḥammad al-Ḥanafī (d. 1525) [KZ, 2: 1293].

43. *Fayḍ al-Karakī* by Ibrāhīm b. ʿAbd al-Raḥman b. Muḥammad b. Ismāʿīl b. al-Karakī (d. 1516) [KZ, 2: 1304–5].
44. *Al-Fuṣūl al-ʿImādiyya* (*Fuṣūl al-iḥkām li-uṣūl al-aḥkām*) by Jamāl al-Dīn ʿAbd al-Raḥīm b. ʿImād al-Dīn b. ʿAlī al-Marghīnānī (d. 1253) [KZ, 2: 1270–71].
45. *Al-Ghāya* by Aḥmad b. Ibrāhīm al-Sarūjī (d. 1310) [GAL, S. I: 646/35].
46. *Ghurar al-aḥkām* and *Durar al-ḥukkām fī sharḥ Ghurar al-aḥkām*, both by Muḥammad b. Feramerz b. ʿAlī al-Ḥanafī Molla Hüsrev (d. 1480) [KZ, 2: 1199–1200].
47. *Ḥāshiyat al-Pazdawī* (?).
48. *Ḥāshiyat Ibn Qāsim* (?).
49. *Ḥashiyat Sharḥ al-Wiqāya* by Yaʿqūb Paşa (d. 1486) [KZ, 2: 2022].
50. *Ḥawāshī al-Majmaʿ* by Ibn Quṭlūbughā (d. 1474).
51. *Ḥāwī al-munya* by al- Najm al-Dīn Mukhtār b. Maḥmūd al-Ghazmīnī al-Zāhidī al-Ḥanafī (d. 1259).
52. *Al-Ḥāwī al-Qudsī* by Jamāl al-Dīn Aḥmad b. Muḥammad b. Saʿīd al-Ḥanafī al-Ghaznawī (d. 1196) [KZ, 1: 627].
53. *Hidāya* by ʿAlī b. Abī Bakr al-Marghīnānī (d. 1196 or 1197) [KZ, 2: 2031–40].
54. Ibn al-Ghars – possibly *al-Fawākih al-Badriyya fī al-ʿaqḍiyya al-ḥukmiyya* by Ibn al-Ghars Muḥammad al-Ḥanafī (d. 1525) [KZ, 2: 1293].
55. *Al-Īḍāḥ* by al-Jurjānī – possibly ʿAbd al-Qāhir al-Jurjānī's (d. 1078) Kitāb al-Muqtaṣid fī Sharḥ al-Īḍāḥ (?).
56. *Al-Ikhtiyār* by Abū al-Faḍl Majd al-Dīn ʿAbd Allāh b. Maḥmūd (b. Mawdūd) al-Mawṣilī (d. 1284). A commentary on *al-Mukhtār fī furūʿ al-Ḥanafiyya*. [KZ, 2: 1622].
57. *Al-ʿInāya fī Sharḥ al-Hidāya* by Akmal al-Dīn Muḥammad b. Maḥmūd al-Bābartī (d. 1384). A commentary on al-Marghīnānī's Hidāya.
58. *Al-Isʿāf fī aḥkām al-awqāf* by Burhān al-Dīn Ibrāhīm b. Mūsā b. ʿAbd Allāh al-Ṭarablusī (d. 1516). [KZ, 1: 85].
59. *Iṣlāḥ al-īḍāḥ* by Shams al-Dīn Aḥmad Kemâlpâşâzâde (d. 1533) [KZ, 1: 109].
60. ʿIzz al-Dīn ʿAbd al-Salām (?).
61. Jalāl al-Dīn al-Suyūṭī (d. 1505) – unspecified work.
62. *Al-Jāmiʿ al-aṣghar* by Muḥammad b. Walīd al-Samarqandī (d.?) [KZ, 1: 535].

63. *Jāmiʿ al-fatāwā* by Abū al-Layth al-Samarqandī (d. 985) [Mahāmm, 74v].
64. *Jāmiʿ al-Fuṣulayn* by Badr al-Dīn Maḥmūd b. Qāḍī Simāwna (d. 1416?) [KZ, 1: 566–67].
65. *Al-Jāmiʿ al-kabīr* by Muḥammad al-Shaybānī (d. 804) [KZ, 1: 567–70].
66. *Jawāhir al-fatāwā* by Rukn al-Dīn Muḥammad b. ʿAbd al-Rashīd al-Kirmānī (d. 1169) [KZ, 1: 615].
67. *Al-Jawhara al-nāʾira* (or *al-Munīra) fī Sharḥ Mukhtaṣar al-Qudūrī* by Abū Bakr b. ʿAlī al-Ḥaddādī (d. 1397). This is an abridged version of his *al-Sirāj wa'l-wahhāj*. [KZ, 2: 1631].
68. *Al-Kāfī fī furūʿ al-Ḥanafiyya* by al-Ḥākim al-Shahīd Muḥammad b. Muḥammad al-Ḥanafī (d. 945) [KZ, 2: 1387].
69. *Kanz al-daqāʾiq* by ʿAbd Allāh b. Aḥmad al-Nasafī (d. 1310) [KZ, 2: 1515–17].
70. *Khizānat al-akmal fī al-furūʿ* by Abū Yaʿqūb Yūsuf b. ʿAlī b. Muḥammad al-Jurjānī al-Ḥanafī. The author started working on this text in 1128. [KZ, 1: 702].
71. *Khizānāt al-fatāwā* by ʿAlī b. Muḥammad b. Abī Bakr al-Ḥanafī (d. 1128).
72. *Khizānat al-fatāwā* by Ṭāhir b. Aḥmad al-Bukhārī al-Sarakhsī (d. 1147). There is another work with the same title by ʿAlī b. Muḥammad b. Abī Bakr al-Ḥanafī (d. 1128). [KZ, 1: 702–3].
73. *Khizānat al-fiqh* by Abū al-Layth al-Samarqandī (d. 985) [KZ, 1: 703].
74. *Khulāṣat al-fatāwā* by Iftikhār Ṭāhir b. Aḥmad b. ʿAbd al-Rashīd Ṭāhir al-Bukhārī (d. 1147) [KZ, 1: 718].
75. [*Khulāṣat*] *al-Nawādir al-fiqhiyya* by Abū al-Layth al-Samarqandī (d. 985) [Mahāmm, 85r].
76. *Al-Kināyāt* by Fakhr al-Dīn ʿUthmān b. ʿAlī al-Zaylaʿī (d. 1342 or 3) (?).
77. *Kitāb al-Wāqiʿāt min al-fatāwā* by Ḥusām al-Dīn ʿUmar b. ʿAbd al-ʿAzīz al-Bukhārī al-Ṣadr al-Shahīd (d. 1141) [KZ, 2: 1998].
78. *Lisān al-ḥukkām fī maʿrifat al-aḥkām* by Abū Walīd Ibrāhīm b. Muḥammad Ibn al-Shiḥna al-Ḥalabī (d. 1477) [KZ, 2: 1549].
79. *Al-Mabsūṭ* (*al-Mabsūṭ fī al-furūʿ*) by Shams al-A'imma b. Bakr Muḥammad b. Abī Sahl Aḥmad al-Sarakhsī (d.1056) [KZ, 2: 1580].

80. *Majmaʿ al-baḥrayn wa-multaqā al-nahrayn* by Muẓaffar al-Dīn Aḥmad b. ʿAlī al-Baghdādī Ibn al-Sāʿātī (d. 1293) [KZ, 2: 1599–1601].
81. *Majmaʿ al-fatāwā* by Aḥmad b. Muḥammad b. Abī Bakr al-Ḥanafī (d.?). A collection of *fatāwā* issued by various jurists, from al-Ṣadr al-Shahīd to ʿAlī al-Jamālī. [KZ, 2: 1603].
82. *Majmūʿat Muʾayyadzade* (al-Amāsī) [Mahāmm, 137r].
83. *Minaḥ al-Ghaffār* by al-Timurtāshī (d. 1595) [KZ, 1: 501].
84. *Minhāj al-Ḥanafiyya* by ʿUmar b. Muḥammad b. ʿUmar b. Muḥammad b. Aḥmad al-ʿUqaylī (d. 1180) [IQ, 169].
85. *Muʿīn al-ḥukkām* by ʿAlāʾ al-Dīn Abī Ḥasan ʿAlī b. Khalīl al-Ṭarabulusī (d. 1440) [KZ, 2: 1745].
86. *Muʿīn al-ḥukkām* by Ibn Aflatūn (possibly Derviş Muḥammed Eflatûnzâde) (d. 1530) [Mahāmm, 103r].
87. *al-Mudāmarāt* (*Sharḥ al-Qudūrī*) by Yūsuf b. ʿUmar b. Yūsuf al-Ṣufī al-Kamaruzī (?) (d. 1428) [Mahāmm, 134v].
88. Muḥammad b. Aḥmad, Abū Jaʿfar al-Nasafī (?) [IQ, 305].
89. Muḥammad b. ʿAbd Allāh Abū Jaʿfar al-Hindūwānī (d. 972) – unspecified work.
90. Muḥammad b. ʿAbd al-Raḥmān b. Abī Layla (d. 768) [Mahāmm, 43v].
91. Muḥammad b. ʿUmar Shams al-Dīn b. Sirāj al-Dīn al-Ḥānūtī (d. 1601) – possibly his *fatāwā* collection. [Muḥibbī, 4: 76–77].
92. Muḥammad b. Aḥmad al-Ramlī (d. 1596) – probably *Fatāwā al-Ramlī* (Shāfiʿī).
93. *Al-Muḥīṭ* (*al-Burhānī*) by Burhān al-Dīn Maḥmūd b. ʿAlī b. al-Ṣadr al-Shahīd (d. 570/1174).
94. *Al-Mujtabā fī uṣūl al-fiqh* by al-Zāhidī (d. 1259). A commentary on al-Qudūrī. [KZ, 2: 1592].
95. *Mukhtaṣar al-Qudūrī* by Abū al-Ḥusayn Aḥmad b. Muḥammad al-Qudūrī al-Baghdādī (d. 1037) [KZ, 2: 1631–34].
96. *Mukhtaṣar fī furūʿ al-Ḥanafiyya* by Abū Bakr Muḥammad b. ʿAbd Allāh ibn al-Ḥusayn al-Nāsiḥī (d. 1091) [Mahāmm, 137v].
97. *Multaqā al-abḥur* by Ibrāhīm al-Ḥalabī (d. 1549) [KZ, 2: 1814–16].
98. *Al-Multaqaṭ* by Ṣadr al-Islām (Khoharzade) (d. late eleventh century) (?).
99. *Al-Muntaqā* by Ibrāhīm b. ʿAlī b. Aḥmad b. Yūsuf b. Ibrāhīm Abū Isḥāq, also known as Ibn ʿAbd al-Ḥaqq al-Wāsiṭī (d. 1343) [IQ, 11–12].

100. *Mushtamil al-aḥkām fī al-fatāwā al-Ḥanafiyya* by Fakhr al-Dīn al-Rūmī Yaḥyā b.... al-Ḥanafī (d. 1459) [KZ, 2: 1692].
101. *Al-Nahr al-fā'iq* (*Sharḥ Kanz al-daqā'iq*) by 'Umar b. Ibrāhīm Ibn Nujaym (d. 1596 or 1597). A commentary on *Kanz al-daqā'iq*.
102. *Nawāzil fī furū' al-Ḥanafīyya* by Naṣr b. Muḥammad al-Ḥanafī Abu al-Layth al-Samarqandī (d. 985) [Mahāmm, 142v–143r].
103. *Al-Nihāya fī furū' al-fiqh al-Ḥanafī* by Ḥusām al-Dīn Ḥusayn b. 'Alī al-Ṣighnāqī (d. 1311). A commentary on al-Marghīnānī's *Hidāya*.
104. Pazdawī (d. 1089) – possibly Kashf al-asrār by Abū al-Ḥusayn 'Alī b. Muḥammad al-Pazdawī (d. 1089) [GAL S. I: 637].
105. *Qunyat al-munya li-tatmīm al-ghunya* by Najm al-Dīn Mukhtār b. Maḥmūd al-Ghazmīnī al-Zāhidī al-Ḥanafī (d. 1259) [KZ, 2: 1357].
106. *Rasā'il Ibn Nujaym* (d. 1563).
107. Al-Sa'd al-Dayrī (d. 1462) – unspecified work.
108. Shams al-Dīn Muḥammad al-Shirbinī (d. 1569) (Shāfi'ī) [Ghazzī, 3: 79–80].
109. *Sharḥ al-Durar* by Ibn Quṭlūbughā (d. 1474). A commentary on Molla Hüsrev's Durar al-aḥkām.
110. *Sharḥ al-Kanz* by 'Alī b. Ghānim al-Maqdisī (d. 1574). A commentary on *Kanz al-daqā'iq*. [KZ, 2: 1516].
111. *Sharḥ al-Majma'* by 'Abd al-Laṭīf b. 'Abd al-'Azīz Ibn Malak (Firişteoğlu) (d. 1395). A commentary on *Majma' al-baḥrayn*. [KZ, 2: 1601; GAL, S. II: 315].
112. *Sharḥ al-Rawḍ* by Shaykh al-Islām Zakarīyā al-Anṣārī (d. 1520). A commentary on al-Nawawī's *al-Rawḍ* (Shāfi'ī).
113. *Sharḥ Manẓūmat Ibn Wahbān* by 'Abd al-Barr Ibn al-Shiḥna (d. 1512) [KZ, 2: 1865–66].
114. *Sharḥ Mukhtaṣar al-Ṭāḥāwī* by 'Alā' al-Dīn b. Muḥammad b. Ismā'īl al-Ḥanafī al-Isbijābī (d. 1140) [KZ, 2: 1627–28].
115. Shihāb al-Dīn Aḥmad b. Muḥammad b. Aḥmad b. Idrīs al-Ḥalabī (d. 1627) [Muḥibbī, 1: 337] – unspecified work.
116. *Al-Sirāj al-wahhāj* by Abū Bakr b. 'Alī b. Muḥammad al-Zabīdī al-Ḥanafī al-Ḥaddād (d. 1397). A commentary on *Mukhtaṣar al-Qudūrī*. [Mahāmm, 99v].
117. *Tabyīn al-ḥaqā'iq fī Sharḥ Kanz al-daqā'iq* by Fakhr al-Dīn 'Uthmān b. 'Alī al-Zayla'ī (d. 1342 or 1343).

118. *Tahdhīb al-wāqiʿāt* by Jamāl al-Dīn Aḥmad b. ʿAlī al-Qalānisī (d. 1304) [KZ, 1: 517].
119. *Al-Tajrīd al-Burhānī fī furūʿ al-Ḥanafiyya* – unknown author [Mahāmm, 68v].
120. *Tanwīr al-abṣār wa-jāmiʿ al-biḥār* by al-Timurtāshī (d. 1595) [KZ, 1: 501].
121. Taqiyy al-Dīn ʿAlī b. ʿAbd al-Kāfī al-Subkī – unspecified work.
122. *Taṣḥīḥ al-Qudūrī* by Qāsim Ibn Quṭlūbughā (d. 1474).
123. *Tuḥfat al-mulūk fī al-furūʿ* by Zayn al-Dīn Muḥammad b. Abī Bakr Ḥasan al-Rāzī (d. 1261) [KZ, 1: 374–75].
124. *ʿUyūn al-masāʾil* by Abū al-Layth al-Samarqandī (d. 985) [KZ, 2: 1187].
125. Walī al-Dīn al-ʿIrāqī (?).

Selected Bibliography

Primary Sources

Fatawa Collections

ʿAbdullah Yenişehirli. *Behcetü'l-Fetâvâ maʿan-nüḳûl.* Istanbul: Maṭbaʿa-i ʿÂmire, 1872.

Al-Anṣārī, Zakariyā b. Muḥammad. *Al-Iʿlām wa-l-ihtimām bi-jamʿ fatāwā Shaykh al-Islām.* Damascus: Dār al-Taqwā, 2007.

Çatalcalı ʿAlî Efendi. *Fetâvâ-ı Çatalcalı.* Süleymaniye Library MS Aya Sofya 1572.

Ebû's-Suʿûd Efendi. *Fetâvâ.* Süleymaniye Library MS Ismihan Sultan 226.

Esʿad Efendi. *Fetâvâ-i Esʿad Efendi.* Süleymaniye Library MS Kasidecizade 277.

Feyżullah b. Muḥammed Efendi. *Fetâvâ-i Feyżiyye maʿan-Nuḳûl.* Istanbul: Dâr ü't-Ṭibaʿâti'l-ʿÂmîre, 1266 [1850].

Fetâvâ-i Feyżullah Efendi. Süleymaniye Library MS Laleli 1267.

Al-Ḥā'ik, Ismāʿīl b. ʿAlī b. Rajab b. Ibrāhīm. *Al-Shifā' al-ʿalīl bi-fatāwā al-marḥūm al-Shaykh Ismāʿīl.* Dār Isʿāf al-Nashashibī (Jerusalem) MS 9mim-53dal.

al-Ḥānūtī, Muḥammad b. ʿUmar b. Shams al-Dīn. *Fatāwā al-Ḥānūtī.* Beyazit Library MS Veliyüddin 1494.

Ibn Abī Luṭf al-Maqdisī, ʿAbd al-Raḥīm. *Al-Fatāwā al-Raḥīmiyya fi waqiʿāt al-sadā al-Ḥanafiyya.* Firestone Library (Princeton) MS Mach Yehuda 4154.

Ibn al-Bazzāz, Muḥammad b. Muḥammad al-Kardarī. *al-Fatāwā al-Bazzāziyya*, 6. vols. Pishavar: Nurani Kutubkhanah, 1970[?].

Ibn al-Ṭabbākh, Ibrāhīm b. Muḥammad al-Dimashqī al-Hanafī. *ʿAyn al-muftī li-ghayn al-mustaftī.* Hüsrev Bey Library (Sarajevo) MS 3069.

ʿAyn al-muftī li-ghayn al-mustafī. Süleymaniye Library MS Reşid Efendi 1115.

Ibn Nujaym, Zayn al-Dīn ibn Ibrāhīm. *Al-Fatāwā al-Zayniyya.* Süleymaniye Library MS Carullah 917.

Kemâlpâşâzâde. *Fetâvâ.* Süleymaniye Library MS Darulmesnevi 118.

Meḥmet ʿAtaullah Efendi. *Fetâvâ-ı ʿAtâiyye.* Süleymaniye Library MS H. Hüsnü Paşa 427.

Meteşîzâde ʿAbdurraḥim Efendi. *Fetâvâ*. Süleymaniye Library MS Haci Selim Aga 440.
Minkarîzâde Yaḥyâ Efendi. *Fetâvâ*. Harvard Law School Library MS 1402.
Fetâvâ. Süleymaniye Library MS Aşir Efendi 137.
Fetâvâ. Süleymaniye Library MS Haci Selim Ağa 449.
Fetâvâ. Süleymaniye Library MS Hekimoğlu 421.
Mollâ ʿArab, Mevlânâ ʿAlâeddîn ʿAlî al-ʿArabî al-Ḥalabî. *Fetâvâ-i Mevlânâ ʿArab*. Süleymaniye Library MS Bağdatlı Vehbi 585.
Muḥyîddîn Muḥammed b. İyâs el-Menteşevî Çivîzâde. *Fetâvâ*. Süleymaniye Library MS Kadizade Mehmed 251.
Al-Ramlī, Khayr al-Dīn. *Al-Fatāwā al-Khayriyya li-nafʿ al-bariyya ʿalā madhhab al-Imām al-Aʿẓam Abī Ḥanīfa al-Nuʿmān*. 2 vols. Cairo: al-Maṭbaʿah al-Kubrā al-Miṣriyya bi-Bulāq, 1882.
Saʿdî Efendi. *Fetâvâ-ı* Saʿdî. Amasya Beyazit Kütüphanesi MS 439.
Ṣunʿullah Efendi. *Fetâvâ*. Süleymaniye Library MS Reşid Efendi 269.
Al-Timurtāshī, Muḥammad ibn ʿAbd Allāh. *Fatāwā* al-Timurtāshī. Süleymaniye Library MS Esʿad Efendi 1114.
Yaḥyâ Efendi. *Fetâvâ*. Süleymaniye Library MS Ayasofya 1569.
Zenbilli, ʿAlî Cemâlî. *Fetâvâ*. Süleymaniye Library MS Fatih 2390.
Fetâvâ-i Zenbilli ʿAlî Cemâlî. Süleymaniye Library MS Fatih 2388.

Ṭabaqāt

Al-Ḥalabī, Ibrāhīm b. Muḥammad b. Ibrāhīm. *Mukhtaṣar al-jawāhir al-muḍiyya fī ṭabaqāt al-Ḥanafiyya*. Süleymaniye Library MS Esad Efendi 605–001.
Ibn Quṭlūbughā, Qāsim. *Tāj al-tarājim fī man ṣannafa min al-Ḥanafiyya*. Damascus: Dār al-Maʾmūn li'l-Turāth, 1992.
Ibn Ṭūlūn, Shams al-Dīn Muḥammad. *Al-Ghuraf al-ʿāliyya fī akhkhirī al-Ḥanafiyya*. Süleymaniye Library MS Şehid Ali Paşa 1924.
Kâmî, Edirneli Meḥmet. *Mahāmm al-fuqahāʾ fī ṭabaqāt al-Ḥanafiyya*. Süleymaniye Library MS Aşir Efendi 422.
Mahāmm al-fuqahāʾ fī ṭabaqāt al-Ḥanafiyya. Süleymaniye Library MS Pertev Paşa 495.
Mahāmm al-fuqahāʾ fī ṭabaqāt al-Ḥanafiyya. Süleymaniye Library MS Carullah 896.
Kefevî, Maḥmûd b. Süleymân. *Katāʾib aʿlām al-akhyār min fuqahāʾ madhhab al-Nuʿmān al-Mukhtār*. Süleymaniye Library MS Esad Efendi 548.
Kemâlpaşazâde. *Risālat ṭabaqāt al-mujtahidīn*. New York Public Library MS M&A 51891A, 195v–196v.
Kınalızâde ʿAlāʾ al-Dīn ʿAlī Çelebī Amr Allāh b. ʿAbd al-Qādir al-Ḥumaydī al-Rūmī al-Ḥanafī. *Ṭabaqāt al-Ḥanafiyya*. Amman: Dār Ibn al-Jawzī, 2003–2004. Also published as Taşköprüzâde, Aḥmad b. Muṣṭafā. *Ṭabaqāt al-fuqahāʾ*, 2nd ed. Mosul: Maṭbaʿat al-Zahrāʾ al-Ḥadīthah, 1961.
Al-Qārī al-Harawī, ʿAlī b. Sulṭān. *Al-Athmār al-janniyya fī asmāʾ al-Ḥanafiyya*. 2 vols. Baghdad: Jumhūrīyat al-ʿIrāq, Diwān al-Waqf al-Sunnī, Markaz al-Buḥūth wa'l-Dirāsāt al-Islāmiyya, 2009.

Al-Qurashī, ʿAbd al-Qādir b. Muḥammad. *Al-Jawāhir al-muḍiyya fī ṭabaqāt al-Ḥanafiyya*. 2 vols. Cairo: Dār Iḥyāʾ al-Kutub al-ʿArabiyya, 1978.
Ṣolâk-zâde, Khalīl al-Rūmī. *Tuḥfat al-tarājim*. Beyazit Library MS Velyüddin 1606.
Al-Tamīmī, Taqī al-Dīn b. ʿAbd al-Qādir. *Al-Ṭabaqāt al-saniyya fī tarājim al-Ḥanafiyya*. Süleymaniye Library MS Aya Sofya 3295.
Al-Ṭabaqāt al-saniyya fī tarājim al-Ḥanafiyya. 4 vols. Riyad: Dār al-Rifāʿī, 1983.

Other Primary Sources

Anonymous. *Asmāʾ al-kutub al-khizāna al-ʿāmira*. Magyar Tudományos Akadémia, Könyvtár (Hungary), MS Török F 59.
Ḥırzu'l-Mülûk. In *Osmanlı Devlet Teşkilâtına dair Kaynaklar*, ed. Yaşar Yücel. Ankara: Türk Tarih Kurumu, 1988.
İlmiye Salnamesi. Istanbul: Maṭbaʿa-i ʿÂmire, 1916.
Mecmuʿa. Süleymaniye Library MS Fazil Ahmed Paşa 1581–1.
Tarjmat Muḥammad al-Tīmurtāshī. Süleymaniye Library MS Esad Efendi 2212–1.
Waqfiyyat Khāṣakī Khūram (Ḫürem) Sulṭān ʿalā al-Ḥaramayn al-Sharīfayn Makka al-Mukarrama wa'l-Madīna al-Munawwara. Karak: Mu'assasat Rām lil-Tiknūlūjiyā wa'l-Kumbiyūtar, 2007.
Abudrrahman Abdi Paşa. *Abdurrahman Abdi Paşa Vekâyiʿ-nâmesi*. Istanbul: Çamlıca, 2008.
Aḥmedî, Tâcü'ddîn İbrâhîm b. Ḫıżır. *History of the Kings of the Ottoman Lineage and Their Holy Raids against the Infidels*. Cambridge, MA: Department of Near Eastern Languages and Literatures, 2004.
Akgündüz Ahmed, ed. *Osmanlı Kanunnâmeleri ve Hukukî Tahlilleri*. 9 vols. Istanbul: Fey Vakfı, 1990.
Al-Anṣārī, Sharaf al-Dīn Ibn Ayyūb. *Nuzhat al-khāṭir wa-bahjat al-nāẓir*. 2 vols. Damascus: Manshūrāt Wizārat al-Thaqāfah, 1991.
Âşıḳ Çelebi, Muḥammad b. ʿAlī Zayn al-ʿĀbidīn b. Muḥammad b. Jalāl al-Dīn b. Ḥusayn b. Ḥasan b. ʿAlī b. Muḥammad al-Raḍawī. *Dhayl al-Shaqāʾiq al-nuʿmāniyya*. Cairo: Dār al-Hidāya, 2007.
Meşâʿirü'ş-Şuʿarâ. Istanbul: İstanbul Araştırmaları Enstitüsü, 2010.
Aydın, Bilgin, and Ekrem Tak, eds. *İstanbul Kadı Sicilleri Üsküdar Mahkemesi 1 Numaralı (H. 919–927/M. 1513–1521)*. Istanbul: İSAM Yayınları, 2008.
Al-Bābānī, Ismāʿīl Bāshā. *Īḍāḥ al-maknūn fī al-dhayli ʿalā Kashf al-ẓunūn ʿan asāmī al-kutub wa'l-funūn*. 2 vols. Istanbul: Milli Eğitim Basımevi, 1945–47.
Al-Baghdādī, Abū Muḥammad b. Ghānim b. Muḥammad. *Majmaʿ al-Ḍamānāt fī madhhab al-Imām al-Aʿẓam Abī Ḥanīfa al-Nuʿmān*. Cairo: Dār al-Salām li'l-Ṭibāʿah wa'l-Nashr wa-Tawzīʿ, 1999.
Al-Bahnasī, Najm al-Dīn Muḥammad b. Muḥammad. *Sharḥ Multaqā al-abḥur*. New York Public Library MS M&A 51893A.
Al-Bāqānī, Maḥmūd b. Barakāt. *Majrā al-anhur ʿalā Multaqā al-abḥur*. Süleymaniye Library MS Pertev Paşa 196.

Al-Biqāʿī, Ibrāhīm b. Ḥasan. *ʿInwān al-zamān bi-tarājim al-shuyūkh wa-l-aqrān*. 5 vols. Cairo: Maṭbaʿat Dār al-Kutub wa'l-Wathā'iq al-Qawmiyya, 2006.

ʿUnwān al-ʿunwān bi-tajrīd asmā' al-shuyūkh wa-baʿḍ al-talāmidhah wa-l-Aqrān. Beirut: Dār al-Kitāb al-ʿArabī, 2002.

Al-Būrīnī, al-Ḥasan b. Muḥammad. *Tarājim al-aʿyān min abnā' al-zamān*. Staatsbibliothek zu Berlin MS Weetzstein II 29.

Tarājim al-aʿyān min abnā' al-zamān. 2 vols. Damascus: al-Majmaʿ al-ʿIlmī al-ʿArabī bi-Dimashq, 1959–63.

Al-Buṣrawī, ʿAlī b. Yūsuf. *Tārīkh al-Buṣrawī: ṣafaḥāt majhūlah min tārīkh Dimashq fī ʿaṣr al-Mamālīk, min sanat 871 H li-ghāyat 904 H*. Damascus: Dār al-Ma'mūn lil-Turāth, 1988.

Celālzāde, Muṣṭafā (Ḳoca Nişāncı). *Ṭabaḳāt ül-Memalīk ve Deracāt ül-Mesālik*. Wiesbaden: Franz Steiner Verlag GMBH, 1981.

Cohen, Amnon, and Elisheva Ben Shim'on-Pikali. *Jews in the Moslem Religious Court: Society. Economy and Communal Organization in the XVIIth Century*. 2 vols. Jerusalem: Yad Izhak Ben-Zvi, 2010 [in Hebrew].

Defterdâr Sarı Mehmed Paşa. *Zübde-i Vekiʿât (1066–1116)*. Ankara: Türk Tarih Kurumu Basımevi, 1995.

Ebû's-Suʿûd Efendi. *Ebû's-Suʿûd Efendi Haẓretleri'nin Fetvâ Kâtiblerine Üslub Kitâbeti Taʿlîmdir*. Süleymaniye Library MS Esad Efendi 1017–1, 96r–99r.

Evliya Çelebi. *Evliya Çelebi Seyahatnâmesi: Topkapı Sarayı Bağdat 304 Yazmasının transkripsiyonu, dizini*. 10 vols. Istanbul: Yapı Kredi Yayınları, 1996–2007.

Eyyûbî. *Menâḳib-i Sulṭan Süleyman (Risâle-i Pâdişâh-nâme)*. Ankara: Kültür Bakanlığı, 1991.

Ferîdûn Bey. *Mecmûʿa-i Münşeât-i Selâtîn*. 2 vols. Istanbul: Dârü't-Ṭibaʿâti'l-ʿÂmire, 1265–74 [1848–57].

Gelibolulu Muṣṭfâ ʿÂlî. *Künh ül-Ahbâr*. 5 vols. Istanbul: Dârü't-Ṭibaʿâti'l-ʿÂmîre, 1860–61.

Künhü'l-Ahbâr, c. II: Fatih Sultan Mehmed Devri 1451–1481. Ankara: Türk Tarih Kurumu, 2003.

Al-Ghazzī, Badr al-Dīn Muḥammad. *Al-Maṭāliʿ al-Badriyya fī al-manāzil al-Rūmiyya*. Beirut: al-Mu'assasa al-ʿArabiyya li'l-Dirāsāt wa'l-Nashr, 2004.

Al-Ghazzī, Muḥammad b. ʿAbd al-Raḥmān. *Dīwān al-Islām*. 4 vols. Beirut: Dār al-Kutub al-ʿIlmiyya, 1990.

Al-Ghazzī, Najm al-Dīn Muḥammad b. Muḥammad. *Al-Kawākib al-sā'ira bi-aʿyān al-mi'a al-ʿāshira*. 3 vols. Beirut: Jāmiʿat Bayrūt al-Amīrikiyya, 1945–58.

Luṭf al-samar wa-qaṭf al-thamar: min tarājim aʿyān al-ṭabaqa al-ūlā min al-qarn al-ḥādī ʿashar. 2 vols. Damascus: Wizārat al-Thaqāfah wa-al-Irshād al-Qawmī, 1981–82.

Al-Ghazzī, Raḍī al-Dīn Muḥammad b. Aḥmad. *Kitāb bahjat al-nāẓirīn ilā tarājim al-muta'akhkhirīn min al-Shāfiʿiyya al-bāriʿīn*. Beirut: Dār Ibn Ḥazm, 2000.

Günalan, Rıfat, Mehmet Akman and Fikret Sarıcaoğlu, *İstanbul Kadı Sicilleri Üsküdar Mahkemesi 26 Numaralı (H. 970–971/M. 1562–1563)*. Istanbul: İSAM Yayınları, 2008.

Günalan, Rıfat, Mehmet Âkif Aydın and Coşkun Yılmaz, eds. *İstanbul Kadı Sicilleri Üsküdar Mahkemesi 2 Numaralı (H. 924–927/M. 1518–1521)*. Istanbul: İSAM Yayınları, 2008.

Al-Ḥalabī, Ibrāhīm ibn Muḥammad. *Risāla fī al-raqṣ*. Süleymaniye Library MS Es'ad Efendi 1690, 214v–225r.

Al-Ḥamawī, Muṣṭafā ibn Fatḥ Allāh. *Fawā'id al-irtiḥāl wa-natā'ij al-safar fi akhbār al-qarn al- ḥādī 'ashar*. 6 vols. Beirut: Dār al-Nawādir, 2011.

Hasan Beyzade, Ahmet. *Hasan Bey-zâde târîhi*. 3 vols. Ankara: Türk Tarih Kurumu Basımevi, 2004.

Al-Ḥaṣkafī, Aḥmad ibn Muḥammad Ibn al-Mullā. *Mut'at al-adhhān min al-tamattu' bi-l-iqrān bayna tarājim al-shuyūkh wa'l-aqrān*. 2 vols. Beirut: Dār Ṣādir, 1999.

Al-Ḥaṣkafī, Muḥammad ibn 'Alī ibn Muḥammad al-Ḥiṣnī al-ma'rūf bi'l-'Alā'. *Al-Durr al-muntaqā fī sharḥ al-Multaqā*. 4 vols. Beirut: Dār al-Kutub al-'Ilmiyya, 1998.

Hezârfen Hüseyin Efendi. *Telhîsü'l-Beyân fî Ḳavânîn-i Âl-i Osmân*. Ankara: Türk Tarih Kurumu Basımevi, 1998.

Ibn al-'Ābidīn, Muḥammad Amīn b. 'Umar. *Majma' rasā'il al-imām Ibn 'Ābidīn al-Ḥanafī*. 2 vols. Cairo: al-Maktaba al-Azhariyya li'l-turāth, 2012.

Thabat Ibn al-'Ābidīn al-musammā 'Uqūd al-lālī fī asānīd al-'awālī (takhrīj li-asānīd shaykhihi Muḥammad Shākir al-'Aqqād). Beirut: Dār al-Bashā'ir al-Islāmiyya, 2010.

Ibn al-Ḥanbalī, Muḥammad ibn Ibrāhīm. *Durr al-ḥabab fī tārīkh a'yān Ḥalab*. 2 vols. Damascus: Wizārat al-Thaqāfa, 1972–74.

Ibn al-Ḥimṣī, Shihāb al-Dīn Aḥmad ibn Muḥammad ibn 'Umar. *Ḥawādith al-zamān wa-wafāyāt al-shuyūkh wa'l-aqrān*. 3 vols. Beirut: al-Maktaba al-'Aṣriyya, 1999.

Ibn al-'Imād, 'Abd al-Ḥayy b. Aḥmad. *Shadharāt al-dhahab fi akhbār man dhahab*. 4 vols. Beirut: Dār al-Kutub al-'Ilmiyya, 1980.

Ibn al-Mibrad, Yūsuf b. Ḥasan. *Al-Jawhar al-munaḍḍad fi ṭabaqāt muta'akhkhirī aṣḥāb Aḥmad*. Cairo: Maktabat al-Kanjī, 1987.

Ibn al-Shiḥna, Ibrāhīm b. Abī al-Yamn Muḥammad b. Abī al-Faḍl. *Lisān al-ḥukkām fi ma'rifat al-aḥkām*. Cairo: Muṣṭafā al-Bābī al-Ḥalabī, 1973.

Ibn Bālī Manq, 'Alī. *Al-'Iqd al-manẓūm fī dhikr afāḍil al-Rūm*. Beirut: Dār al-Kitāb al-'Arabī, 1975.

Ibn Ḥajar al-'Asqalānī, Aḥmad b. 'Alī. *Inbā' al-ghumr fi anbā' al-'umr*. 3 vols. Cairo: al-Majlis al-A'lāli'l-Shu'ūn al-Islāmiyya, 1972.

Ibn Ḥijjah al-Ḥamawī al-Azrārī, Taqiyy al-Dīn Abī Bakr b. 'Alī. *Kitāb qahwat al-inshā'*. Beirut: Klaus Schwarz Verlag, 2005.

Ibn Nujaym, Zayn al-Dīn b. Ibrāhīm. *Al-Ashbāh wa'l-naẓā'ir 'alā madhhab Abī Ḥanīfa al-Nu'mān*. Beirut: Dār al-Fikr al-Mu'āṣir, 1999.

Al-Baḥr al-rā'iq sharḥ Kanz al-daqā'iq. 9 vols. Beirut: *Dār al-Kutub al-'Ilmiyya*, 1997.

Ibn Rūzbahān, Fażl Allāh. *Sulūk al-mulūk*. Tehran: Khvārazmī, 1984.

Ibn Taghrībirdī, Abū al-Maḥāsin Yūsuf. *Al-Manhal al-ṣāfī wa-l-mustawfā ba'da al-wāfī*. 12 vols. Cairo: Maṭba'at Dār al-Kutub al-Miṣriyya, 1956.

Ibn Ṭawq, Shihāb al-Dīn Aḥmad. *Yawmiyāt Shihāb al-Dīn Aḥmad ibn Ṭawq*. 4 vols. Damascus: Institut Français du Damas, 2000–7.
Ibn Ṭūlūn al-Ṣāliḥī, Shams al-Dīn Muḥammad b. ʿAlī. *Al-Fulk al-mashḥūn fī aḥwāl Muḥammad b. Ṭūlūn*. Beirut: Dār Ibn Ḥazm, 1996.
Ḥawādith Dimashq al-yawmiyya ghadāt al-ghazw al-ʿUthmānī lil-Shām, 926–951H: ṣafaḥāt mafqūda tunsharu lil-marra al-ūlā min Kitāb Mufākahat al-khillān fī ḥawādith al-zamān li-Ibn Ṭūlūn al-Ṣāliḥī. Damascus: Dār al-Awāʾil, 2002.
Mufākahat al-khillān fī ḥawādith al-zamān: tārīkh Miṣr wa'l-Shām. 2 vols. Cairo: al-Muʾassasa al-Miṣriyya al-ʿĀmma li'l-Taʾlīf wa'l-Tarjama wa'l-Ṭibāʿa wa'l-Nashr, 1962–64.
Al-Qalāʾid al-jawhariyya fī tārīkh al-Ṣāliḥiyya. 2 vols. Damascus: Majmaʿ al-Lugha al-ʿArabiyya, 1949–56.
Al-ʿImādī. ʿAbd al-Raḥmān b. Muḥammad al-Dimashqī. *Hadiyyat Ibn al-ʿImād li-ʿubbād al-ʿibād*. Süleymaniye Library MS Laleli 1185.
Al-ʿImādī. Hāmid b. ʿAlī. *Ṣalāḥ al-ʿālam bi-iftāʾ al-ʿālim* (Amman: Dār ʿAmmār, 1988).
ʿÎsâ-zâde. *ʿÎsâ-zâde Târîhi: Metin ve Tahlîl*. Istanbul: İstanbul Fetih Cemiyeti, 1996.
Al-Jīnīnī, Ṣāliḥ. *Thabat Ṣāliḥ al-Jīnīnī*. Staatsbibliothek zu Berlin MS Weetzstein II 413, 77r–86r.
Kâtip Çelebi. *Fezleke-i Tarîh*. 2 vols. Istanbul: Cerîde-i Ḥavâdiṡ Maṭbaʿası, 1870–871.
Kashf al-ẓunūn ʿan asāmī al-kutub wa-l-funūn. 2 vols. Istanbul: Milli Eğitim Basımevi, 1972.
Kemâlpaşazâde. *Al-Iḍāḥ fī sharḥ al-Islāḥ fī al-fiqh al-Ḥanafī*. Beirut: Dār al-Kutub al-ʿIlmiyya, 2007.
Risāla fī al-raqṣ. Süleymaniye Library MS Denizli 114–1, 225r–228r.
Kınalızâde ʿAlî Çelebi. *Risāla fī masāʾil ṭabaqāt al-Ḥanafiyya*. Süleymaniye Library MS Reisülküttab 1221, 52v–54r.
Koçi Bey. *Risale-i Koçi Bey*. Istanbul: Ahmet Vefik Paşa, 1863.
Al-Maḥāsinī, Ismāʿīl. (Anonymous Chronicle). Edited under the title "Ṣafaḥāt fī tārīkh Dimashq fī al-qarn al-ḥādī ʿashar al-hijrī." *Revue de l'Institut des manuscits Arabes* 6 (May–November 1960): 80–160.
Al-Maḥbūbī, ʿUbayd Allāh b. Masʿūd (Ṣadr al-Sharīʿa). *Mukhtaṣar al-Wiqāya*. 2 vols. Beirut: Dār al-Kutub al-ʿIlmiyya, 2005.
Mecdî Meḥmet Edendî. *Hadâiku'ṣ-Ṣakâik*. In *Ṣakâik-iNuʿmâniye ve Zeyilleri*, ed. Abdülkadir Özcan. Istanbul: Çağrı Yayınları, 1985.
Mekkî Efendi, and Ahmed Neylî Efendi. *Yavuz Sultan Selim'in Emriyle Hazırlanan İbn Arabi Müdafaası*. Istanbul: Gelenek, 2004.
Morley, Willian H. *The Administration of Justice in British India, Its Past History and Present State: Comprising an Account of the Laws Peculiar to India*. London: William & Norgate, Stevens & Norton, Lepage & Co., 1858.
Müeyyedzâde ʿAbd al-Raḥmān al-Amāsī. *Majmūʿat al-masāʾil*, Süleymaniye Library MS Nafiz Paşa 16.
Al-Muḥibbī, Muḥammad Amīn ibn Faḍl Allāh ibn Muḥibb al-Dīn. *Dhayl Nafḥat al-rayḥāna wa-rashḥat ṭilāʾ al-ḥāna*. Cairo: ʿĪsā al-Bābī al-Ḥalabī, 1971.

Khulāṣat al-athar fī a'yān al-qarn al-ḥādī 'ashar. 4 vols. Beirut: Dār al-Kutub al-'Ilmiyya, 2006.
Mu'îdzâde, Meḥmed. *Fetvâ*. Süleymaniye Library MS Fazil Ahmed Paşa 1581–1.
Munajjim Bāshī, Aḥmad ibn Luṭf Allāh. *Kitāb jāmi' al-duwal: Qism salāṭīn Āl 'Uthmān ilā sanat 1083 H.* 3 vols. Mecca: s.n., 2009.
Al-Murādī, Muḥammad Khalīl ibn 'Alī ibn Muḥammad ibn Muḥammad. *'Arf al-bashām fī-man waliya fatwā Dimashq al-Shām*. Damascus: Majma' al-Lugha al-'Arabiyya, 1979.
Kitāb Silk al-durar fī a'yān al-qarn al-thānī 'ashar. 4 vols. Beirut: Dār al-Bashā'ir al-Islāmiyya, 1988.
Müstakîmzâde Süleymân Sa'deddin. *Devḥatü-l-Meşâyih: Einleitung und Edition*. 2 vols. Stuttgart: Steiner Verlag, 2005.
Al-Nābulusī, 'Abd al-Ghanī b. Ismā'īl. *Al-Ajwiba 'alā 161 su'ālan*. Damascus: Dār al-Fārābī al-'Arīb, 2001.
Jam' al-asrār fī radd al-ṭa'n 'an al-ṣūfiyya al-akhyār ahl al-tawājjud bi'l-adhkār. Beirut: Dār al-Muḥabba, 2000.
Al-Jawāb al-mu'tamad 'an su'ālāt wārida min al-Ṣafad. Süleymaniye Library MS Es'ad Efendi 3606, 239v–243r.
Jawāb su'ālayn Warada 'alayhi min al-Quds al-Sharīf. Süleymaniye Library MS Çelebi Abdullah Efendi 385, 67r–71v.
Al-Jawāb al-sharīf li'l-Ḥaḍrat al-Sharīf fī anna madhhab Abī Yūsuf wa-Muḥammad huwa Madhhab Abī Ḥanīfa. Süleymaniye Library MS Esad Efendi 1762–1.
Nihāyat al-murād fī sharḥ Hadiyyat Ibn al-'Imād. Limassol, Cyprus: al-Jaffān wa'l-Jābī, 1995.
Al-Radd al-wafī 'alā jawāb al-Ḥaṣkafī 'alā mas'alat al-khiff al-Ḥanafī. Süleymaniye Library MS Esad Efendi 1762.
Sharḥ al-Ashbāh wa'l-naẓā'ir. Süleymaniye Library MS Hamidiye 502.
Na'îmâ, Mustafa. *Târih-i Na'îmâ: Ravzatü'l-Hüseyin fî Hulâsati Ahbâri'l-Hâfikayn*. 4 vols. Ankara: Türk Tarih Kurumu, 2007.
Naṣūḥü's-Silāḥī (Maṭrākçī). *Beyān-ı Menāzil-i Sefer-i 'Irāḳeyn-i Sulṭān Süleymān Ḫān*. Ankara: Türk Tarih Kurumu, 1976.
Al-Nawawī, Abū Zakariyā Yaḥyā b. Sharaf. *Adab al-fatwā wa-l-muftī wa-l-mustaftī*. Damascus: Dār al-Fikr, 1988.
Nev'îzâde 'Atâî. *Hadâiku'l-Hakâik fî Tekmileti'ş*, in *Şakaik-i Nu'maniye ve zeyilleri*, ed. Abdülkadir Özcan. Istanbul: Çağri Yayınları, 1989.
Ongan, Halit. *Ankara'nın 1 Numaralı Şer'iye Sicili: 21 Rebiülahır 991-Evahir-i Muharrem 992 14 Mayıs 1583–12 Şubat 1584)*. Ankara: Türk Tarih Kurumu Basımevi, 1958.
Ankara'nın İki Numaralı Şer'iye Sicili: 1 Muharrem 997–8 Ramazan 998 (20 Kasım 1588–11 Temmuz 1590). Ankara: Türk Tarih Kurumu Basımevi, 1974.
Orhonlu, Cengiz. *Osmanlı Tarihine Âid Belgeler*. Istanbul: Edebiyat Fakültesi Basımevi, 1970.
Peçevî, İbrâhîm. *Târîḫ-i Peçevî*. 2 vols. Istanbul: Maṭba'a-i 'Âmire, 1283 [1866].
Qalqashandī, Aḥmad b. 'Alī. *Ṣubḥ al-a'shā fī ṣinā'at al-inshā'*. 14 vols. Cairo: al-Mu'assasa al-Misriyya al-'Āmma lil-Ta'līf wa'l-Tarjama wa'l-Ṭibā'a wa'l-Nashr, 1964.

Al-Qaramānī, Aḥmad Çelebi b. Sinān. *Tārīkh salāṭīn Āl 'Uthmān*. Damascus: Dār al-Naṣā'ir, 1985.

Al-Ramlī, Khayr al-Dīn (collected by Najm al-Dīn al-Ramlī). *Kitāb al-Lā'lī al-duriyya fī al-fawā'id al-Khayriyya 'alā Jāmi' al-fuṣūlayn, ta'līf Mawlānā Shaykh al-Islām al-wālid Khayr al-Dīn*. Khalediyya Library (Jerusalem) MS 523/fiqh/450.

Al-Sakhāwī, Muḥammad b. 'Abd al-Raḥmān. *Al-Ḍaw' al-lāmi' li-ahl al-qarn al-tāsi'*. 12 vols. Beirut: Dār Maktaba al-Ḥayāt, 1966.

Al-Ṣayrafī, 'Alī b. Dāwūd al-Jawharī. *Inbā' al-haṣr bi-abnā' al-'aṣr*. Cairo: Dār al-Fikr al-'Arabī, 1970.

Selânikî, Muṣṭafâ. *Târîh-i Selânikî*. 2 vols. Istanbul: İstanbul Üniversitesi Edebiyat Fakültesi, 1989.

Şeyḫî Meḥmed Efendi. *Vekâyi'ü'l-Fudalâ*, in *Şakaik-i Nu'maniye ve zeyilleri*, ed. Abdülkadir Özcan. Istanbul: Çağri Yayınları, 1989.

Shaykhīzāde (Şeyḫîzâde), 'Abd al-Raḥmān b. Muḥammad b. Sulīmān. *Majma' al-anhur fī sharḥ Multaqā al-abḥur*. 4 vols. Beirut: Dār al-Kutub al-'Ilmiyya, 1998.

Silâḥdâr Fındıklılı Meḥmet Ağa. *Silâḥdâr Târîḫi*. 2 vols. Istanbul: Devlet Maṭba'ası, 1928.

Al-Suyūṭī, Jalāl al-Dīn 'Abd al-Raḥmān b. Abī Bakr. *Al-Munjam fi al-mu'jam*. Beirut: Dār Ibn Hazm, 1995.

Al-Ṭalūwī, Darwīsh Muḥammad b. Aḥmad. *Sāniḥāt dumā al-qaṣr fī muṭāraḥāt banī al-'aṣr*. 2 vols. Beirut: 'Ālam al-Kutub, 1983.

Al-Ṭarābulusī, Dīn Abī al-Ḥasan 'Alī ibn Khalīl. *Mu'īn al-ḥukkām fīmā yataraddadu bayna al-khaṣmayn min al-aḥkām*. Cairo: Muṣṭafā al-Bābī al-Ḥalabī, 1973.

Ṭaşköprüzâde, Aḥmad b. Muṣṭafá. *Al-Shaqā'iq al-nu'māniyya fī 'ulamā' al-dawla al-'Uthmāniyya*. Beirut: Dār al-Kitāb al-'Arabī, 1975.

Miftāḥ al-sa'āda wa-miṣbāḥ al-siyāda fi mawḍū'āt al-'ulūm. 2 vols. Cairo: Dār al-Kutub al-Ḥadītha, 1968.

al-Timurtāshī, Muḥammad b. 'Abd Allāh. *Faḍā'il Āl 'Uthmān*. Süleymaniye Library MS Es'ad Efendi 2337.

Mu'īn al-muftī 'alā jawāb al-mustafatī. Beirut: Dār al-Basha'ir al-Islāmiyya, 2009.

Mus'ifat al-ḥukkām 'alā al-aḥkām. Amman: Dār al-Fatḥ li'l-Dirāsāt wa'l-Nashr, 2007.

Al-'Ulaymī, 'Abd al-Raḥmān b. Muḥammad. *Al-Uns al-jalīl bi-tārīkh al-Quds wa-l-Khalīl*. 2 vols. Najaf: al-Maṭba'a al-Ḥaydariyya, 1968.

Uşşâkîzâde es-Seyyid İbrâhîm Hasîb Efendi. *Uşşâkîzâde Tarihi*. 2 vols. Istanbul: Çamlıca, 2005.

Secondary Literature

Abisaab, Rula. *Converting Persia: Religion and Power in the Safavid Empire*. London: I. B. Tauris, 2004.

Abou el-Haj, Rifa'at A. "Aspects of the Legitimation of Ottoman Rule as Reflected in Preambles of Two Early *Liva Kanunnameler*." *Turcica* 21–23 (1991): 372–83.

Abou el-Haj, Rifa'at A.. *The 1703 Rebellion and the Structure of Ottoman Politics*. Istanbul: Nederlands Historisch-Archaeologisch Isntitut te Istanbul, 1984.

Ahmed, Shahab. "Mapping the World of a Scholar in Sixth/Twelfth Century Bukhāra: Regional Tradition in Medieval Islamic Scholarship as Reflected in a Bibliography." *Journal of the American Oriental Society* 120, no. 1 (2000): 24–43.

Ahmed, Shahab, and Nenad Filipovic. "The Sultan's Syllabus: A Curriculum for the Ottoman Imperial Medreses Prescribed in a Fermān of Qānūnī Süleymān, Dated 973 (1565)." *Studia Islamica* 98–99 (2004): 183–218.

Akgündüz, Murat. XIX. Asır Başlarına Kadar Osmanlı Devleti'nde Şeyhulislâmlık. Istanbul: Beyan Yayınları, 2002.

Aksoy, Hasan. "Kınalızâde Ali Efendi," *TDVIA*.

Alam, Muzaffar. *The Language of Political Islam in India: c. 1200–1800*. Chicago: University of Chicago Press, 2004.

Altunsu, Abdülkadir. *Osmanlı Şeyhülislamları*. Ankara: Ayyıldız Matbaası, 1972.

Ando, Shiro. "The Shaykh al-Islām as a Timurid Office: A Preliminary Study." *Islamic Studies* 22, nos. 2–3 (1994): 253–80.

Anooshahr, Ali. "Writing, Speech, and History for an Ottoman Biographer." *Journal of Near Eastern History* 69, no. 1 (2010): 43–62.

Apaydın, H. Yunus. "Kınalı-zade'nin, Hanefi Mezhebini Oluşturan Görüşlerin Toplandığı Ederlerin Gruplandırılmasına Dair bir Risalesi." In *Kınalı-zade Ali Efendi (1510–1572)*, ed. Ahmed Hulusi Köker, 96–100. Kayseri: Erciyes Üniversitesi Matbbası, 1999.

Ârif Bey. "Devlet-i Osmaniyye'nin Teessüs ve Takarrürü Devrinde İlim ve Ulema." *Darülfünün Edebiyat Fakültesi Mecmuası* 2 (1916): 137–44.

Atcil, Abdurrahman. "The Formation of the Ottoman Learned Class and Legal Scholarship (1300–1600)." PhD diss., University of Chicago, 2010.

"Procedures in the Ottoman Court and the Duties of the Kadis." MA thesis, Bilkent University, Ankara, 2002.

"The Route to the Top in the Ottoman *Ilmiye Hierarchy of the Sixteenth Century*." *Bulletin of SOAS* 72, no. 3 (2009): 489–512.

Ayalon, David. "The Great Yasa of Chingiz Khān. A Reexamination (Part A–D)." *Studia Islamica* 33 (1971): 97–140; 34 (1971): 151–80; 36 (1972): 113–58; 38 (1973): 107–56.

Ayalon, Yaron. "Plagues, Famines, Earthquakes: The Jews of Ottoman Syria and Natural Disasters." PhD diss., Princeton University, 2009.

Babinger, F. s.v. "Nishandji." *EI²*.

Bakhit, Muhammad 'Adnan. *The Province of Damascus in the Sixteenth Century*. Beirut: Librarie du Liban, 1982.

Balabanlilar, Lisa. *Imperial Identity in the Mughal Empire: Memory and Dynastic Politics in Early Modern South and Central Asia*. London: I. B. Tauris, 2012.

Baldwin, James E. "Islamic Law in an Ottoman Context: Resolving Disputes in Late 17th/early 18th- century Cairo." PhD diss., New York University, 2010.

Baltacı, Cahid. *XV–XVI. Yüzyıllarda Osmanlı Medreseleri*. 2 vols. Istanbul: Marmara Üniversitesi İlahiyat Fakültesi Vakfı, 2005.
Barbir, Karl K. "All in the Family: The Muradis of Damascus." In *Proceedings of the IIIrd Congress on the Social and Economic History of Turkey*, ed. Heath W. Lowry and Ralph S. Hattox, 327–53. Istanbul: ISIS Press, 1990.
Behrens-Abouseif, Doris. *Egypt's Adjustment to Ottoman Rule: Institutions, Waqf, and Architecture in Cairo, 16th and 17th Centuries*. Leiden: Brill, 1994.
Benton, Lauren. *Law and Colonial Cultures: Legal Regimes in World History 1400–1900*. Cambridge: Cambridge University Press, 2002.
A Search for Sovereignty: Law and Geography in European Empire, 1400–1900. Cambridge: Cambridge University Press, 2010.
Berkey, Jonathan. *The Transmission of Knowledge in Medieval Cairo: A Social History of Islamic Education*. Princeton, NJ: Princeton University Press, 1992.
Berlekamp, Persis. *Wonder, Image, and Cosmos in Medieval Islam*. New Haven, CT: Yale University Press, 2011.
Bhatia, M. L. *Administrative History of Medieval India: A Study of Muslim Jurisprudence under Aurgangzeb*. New Delhi: Radha Publications, 1992.
Bilge, Mustafa. *İlk Osmanlı Medreseleri*. Istanbul: İstanbul Üniversitesi Edebiyat Fakültesi Yayınları, 1984.
Bilgrami, Rafat M. *Religious and Quasi-Religious Departments of the Mughal Period (1556–1707)*. New Delhi: Munshiram Manoharlal Publishers, 1984.
Bosworth, C. E. "Rum." *EI*².
Broadbridge, Anne F. *Kingship and Ideology in the Islamic and Mongol Worlds*. Cambridge: Cambridge University Press, 2008.
Brockelmann, Carl. *Geschichte der Arabischen Litteratur*. Leiden: Brill, 1937–42.
Brockopp, Jonathan E. *Early Maliki Law: Ibn ʿAbd al-Hakam and His Major Compendium of Jurisprudence*. Leiden: Brill, 2000.
Brown, Jonathan. *The Canonization of al-Bukhārī and Muslim*. Leiden: Brill, 2007.
Bulliet, Richard W. "The Shaikh al-Islām and the Evolution of Islamic Society." *Studia Islamica* 35 (1972): 53–67.
Burak, Guy. "The Abū Ḥanīfah of His Time: Islamic Law, Jurisprudential Authority and Empire in the Ottoman Domains (16th–17th Centuries)." PhD diss., New York University, 2012.
"Dynasty, Law and the Imperial Provincial Madrasa: The Case of *al-Madrasa al-ʿUthmāniyya* in Ottoman Jerusalem." *International Journal of Middle East Studies* 45, no. 1 (2013).
"Faith, Law and Empire in the Ottoman 'Age of Confessionalization' (15th–17th Centuries): The Case of 'Renewal of Faith.'" *Mediterranean Historical Review* 28, no. 1 (2013): 1–23.
"Reflections on Censorship, Canonization and the Ottoman Practices of *Takriz* and *Imza*" (forthcoming).
Buzov, Snjezana. "The Lawgiver and His Lawmakers: The Role of Legal Discourse in the Change of Ottoman Imperial Culture." PhD diss., University of Chicago, 2005.

Calder, Norman. "al-Nawawi's Typology of Muftis and Its Significance for a General Theory of Islamic Law." *Islamic Law and Society* 3, no. 2 (1996): 137–64.

Studies in Early Muslim Jurisprudence. Oxford: Clarendon Press, 1993.

Canbakal, Hülya. "Birkaç Fetva Bir Soru: Bir Hukuk Haritasına Doğru." In *Şinasi Tekin'in Anısına Uygurlardan Osmanlıya*, 258–70. Istanbul: Simurg, 2005.

Chamberlain, Michael. *Knowledge and Social Practice in Medieval Damascus, 1190–1350*. Cambridge: Cambridge University Press, 1994.

Cici, Recep. "Osmanlı Klasik Dönemi Fıkıh Kitapları." *Türkiye Araştırmaları Literatür Dergisi* 3, no. 5 (2005): 215–48.

Cohen, Amnon, and Elisheva Ben-Shimon-Pikali. *Jews in the Moslem Religious Court: Society, Economy and Communalx Organization in the XVIth Century (Documents from Ottoman Jerusalem)*. Jerusalem: Yad Izhak Ben-Zvi, 1993.

Conermann, Stephan. "Ibn Ṭūlūn (d. 955/1548): Life and Works." *Mamluk Studies Review* 8, no. 1 (2004): 115–40.

Cooperson, Michael. *Classical Arabic Biography: The Heirs of the Prohpets in the Age of al-Ma'mun*. Cambridge: Cambridge University Press, 2000.

Crecelius, Daniel. "The Waqf of Muhammad Bey Abu al-Dhahab in Historical Perspective." *International Journal of Middle East Studies* 23, no. 1 (1991): 57–81.

Cuno, Kenneth M. "Was the Land of Ottoman Syria Miri or Milk? An Examination of Juridical Differences within the Ḥanafī School." *Studia Islamica* 81 (1995): 121–52.

Dale, Stephen F. *The Garden of the Eight Paradises: Bābur and the Culture of Empire in Central Asia, Afghanistan and India (1483–1530)*. Leiden: Brill, 2004.

Dale, Stephen F. *The Muslim Empires of the Ottomans, Safavids, and Mughals*. Cambridge: Cambridge University Press, 2010.

Dalkıran, Sayın. *Ibn-i Kemâl ve Düşünce Tarihimiz*. Istanbul: Osmanlı Araştrıma Vakfı (OSAV), 1997.

Di Cosmo, Nicola, Allen J. Frank, and Peter B. Golden, eds. *The Cambridge History of Inner Asia: The Chinggisid Age*. Cambridge: Cambridge University Press, 2009.

el-Rouayeb, Khaled. "The Myth of the Triumph of Fanaticism in the Seventeenth-Century Ottoman Empire." *Die Welt des Islams* 48 (2008): 196–221.

"Opening the Gate of Verification: The Forgotten Arab-Islamic Florescence of the Seventeenth Century." *International Journal of Middle East Studies* 38, no. 2 (2006): 263–81.

El Shamsy, Ahmed. *The Canonization of Islamic Law: A Social and Intellectual History*. Cambridge: Cambridge University Press, 2013.

"The *Ḥāshiya* in Islamic Law: A Sketch of the Shāfi'ī Literature," *Oriens* 41 (2013): 289–315.

Ephrat, Daphna. *A Learned Society in a Period of Transition: The Sunni 'Ulama' in Eleventh-Century Baghdad*. Albany: State University of New York Press, 2000.

Ergene, Boğaç. *Local Court, Provincial Society, and Justice in the Ottoman Empire: Legal Practice and Dispute Resolution in Çankırı and Kastamonu (1652–1744)*. Leiden: Brill, 2003.

Erünsal, İsmail E. *Ottoman Libraries: A Survey of the History, Development and Organization of Ottoman Foundation Libraries*. Cambridge, MA: Department of Near Eastern Languages and Literatures, Harvard University, 2008.

Erünsal, İsmail E.. "909 (1503) Tarihli Defter-i Kütüb." In *The Archival Sources of Turkish Literary History*, ed. Cemal Kafadar and Gönül Alpay Tekin, 251–70. Cambridge, MA: Department of Near Eastern Languages and Literatures, Harvard University, 2008.

Fadel, Muhammad. "The Social Logic of *Taqlīd* and the Rise of the *Mukhtaṣar*." *Islamic Law and Society* 3, no. 2 (1996): 193–233.

Fernandes, Leonor. "Between Qadis and Muftis: To Whom Does the Mamluk Sultan Listen?" *Mamluk Studies Review* 6 (2002): 95–108.

Fitzgerald, Timothy J. "Ottoman Methods of Conquest: Legal Imperialism and the City of Aleppo, 1480–1570)." PhD diss., Harvard University, 2009.

Fleischer, Cornell H. *Bureaucrat and Intellectual in the Ottoman Empire: The Historian Mustafa Âli (1541–1600)*. Princeton, NJ: Princeton University Press, 1986.

Gencer, Yasemin. "İbrahim Müteferrika and the Age of the Printed Manuscript." In *The Islamic Manuscript Tradition: Ten Centuries of Book Arts in Indiana University Collections*, ed. Christiane Gruber, 154–93. Bloomington: Indiana University Press, 2010.

Gerber, Haim. *Islamic Law and Culture 1600–1840*. Leiden: Brill, 1999.

State, Society, and Law in Islam: Ottoman Law in Comparative Perspective. Albany: State University of New York Press, 1994.

Ghazzal, Zouhair. *The Grammar of Adjudication: The Economics of Judicial Decision Making in Fin-de-Siècle Ottoman Beirut and Damascus*. Beirut: IFPO, Institut Francais du Proche-Orient, 2007.

Gilliot, Cl. "Ṭabaḳāt." *EI²*.

Gomez-Rivas, Camilio. "The Fatwās of Ibn Rushd al-Jadd to the Far Maghrib: Urban Transformation and the Development of Islamic Legal Institutions Under the Almoravids." PhD diss., Yale University, 2009.

Greene, Molly. *A Shared World: Christians and Muslims in the Early Modern Mediterranean*. Princeton, NJ: Princeton University Press, 2000.

Guenther, Alan N. "Ḥanafī Fiqh in Mughal India: The *Fatāwá-i ʿĀlāmgīrī*." In *India's Islamic Traditions, 711–1750*, ed. Richard M. Eaton 209–230. New Delhi: Oxford University Press, 2003.

Gürkan, Menderes. "Müctehidlerin Tasnifinde Kemalpaşazade ile Kınalızade arasında bir Mukayese." In *Kınalı-zade Ali Efendi (1510–1572)*, ed. Ahmed Hulusi Köker, 83–95. Kayseri: Erciyes Üniversitesi Matbbası, 1999.

Haarman, Ulrich. "The Library of a Fourteenth Century Jerusalem Scholar." *Der Islam: Zeitschrift für Geschichte und Kultur des islamischen Orients* 61 (1984): 327–33.

Hafsi, Ibrahim. "Recherches sur le genre *Ṭabaqāt* dans la litterature Arabe." *Studia Arabica* 23 (1976): 227–65.

"Recherches sur le genre *Ṭabaqāt* dans la litterature Arabe." *Studia Arabica* 24 (February 1977): 1–41.

"Recherches sur le genre *Ṭabaqāt* dans la litterature Arabe." *Studia Arabica* 24 (June 1977): 150–86.

Hagen, Gottfried. "Translation and Translators in a Multilingual Society: A Case Study of Persian-Ottoman Translations, Late 15th to Early 17th Century." *Eurasian Studies II/1* (2003): 95–134.

Halbertal, Moshe. *People of the Book: Canon, Meaning, and Authority*. Cambridge, MA: Harvard University Press, 1997.

Hallaq, Wael B. *Authority, Continuity, and Change in Islamic Law*. Cambridge: Cambridge University Press, 2004.

Hallaq, Wael B. "From Fatāwā to Furū': Growth and Change in Islamic Substantive Law." *Islamic Law and Society* 1, no. 1 (1994): 29–65.

The Origin and Evolution of Islamic Law. Cambridge: Cambridge University Press, 2005.

Sharī'ah: Theory, Practice, Transformations. Cambridge: Cambridge University Press, 2009.

Al-Ḥanafī, Lu'ayy ibn 'Abd al-Raūf al-Khalīlī. *La'ālī' al-mahār fī takhrīj maṣādir Ibn 'Ābidīn fī ḥāshīyatihi Radd al-muḥtār, dhikr li-mā fī al-Ḥāshīya min muṣannafāt wa-rasā'il makhṭūṭah aw maṭbū'ah ma'a al-ta'rīf bi-hā wa-biaṣḥābihā*. 2 vols. Amman: Dār al-Fatḥ li'l-Dirāsāt wa'l-Nashr, 2010.

Has, Şükrü Selim. "A Study of Ibrahim al-Halebi with Special Reference to the Multaqa." PhD diss., University of Edinburgh, 1981.

"The Use of Multaqa'l-Abḥur in the Ottoman Madrasas and in Legal Scholarship." *Osmanlı Araştırmaları* 7–8 (1988): 393–418.

Hathaway, Jane. *The Politics of Household in Ottoman Egypt: The Rise of the Qazdağlıs*. Cambridge: Cambridge University Press, 1997.

Heinrichs, Wolfhart P. "'Abd al-Raḥmān al-'Abbāsī (al-Sayyid 'Abd al- Raḥīm) (12 June 1463–1555 or 1556)." In *Essays in Arabic Literary Biography 1350–1850*, ed. Joseph E. Lowry and Devin J. Stewart, 12–20. Wiesbaden: Harrassowitz Verlag, 2009.

Heyd, Uriel. *Ottoman Documents on Palestine 1552–1615*. Oxford: Clarendon Press, 1960.

"Some Aspects of the Ottoman Fetvâ." *Bulletin of the School of Oriental and African Studies* 32 (1969): 35–56.

Studies in Old Ottoman Criminal Law. Oxford: Clarendon Press, 1973.

Hirschler, Konrad. *The Written Word in the Medieval Arabic Lands: A Social and Cultural History of Reading Practices*. Edinburgh: Edinburgh University Press, 2012.

Humphrey, Caroline, and A. Hürelbaatar. "The Term Törü in Mongolian History." In *Imperial Statecraft: Political Forms and Techniques of Governance in Inner Asia, Sixth-Twentieth Centuries*, ed. David Sneath, 265–93. Bellingham: Center for East Asian Studies, Western Washington University, 2006.

Hurvitz, Nimrod. *The Formation of Hanbalism: Piety into Power*. London: RouteledgeCurzon, 2002.

İhsanoğlu, Ekmeleddin. "The Initial Stage of the Historiography of Ottoman Medreses (1916–1965): The Era of Discovery and Construction." In *Science,*

Thechnology and Learning in the Ottoman Empire: Western Influence, Local Institutions, and the Transfer of Knowledge, ed. Ekmeleddin İhsanoğlu, 41–85. Burlington, VT: Ashgate/Variorum, 2004.

Imber, Colin. *Ebu's-Su'ud: The Islamic Legal Tradition*. Stanford, CA: Stanford University Press, 1997.

Inaclik, Halil. "Rumi." *EI*².

"Kanun." *EI*².

Isogai, Ken'ichi. "Yasa and Shari'a in Early 16th Century Central Asia." In *L'Heritage timouride: Iran-Asie Centrale-Inde XVe-XVIIIe siècles* ¾, ed. Maria Szuppe, 91–103. Tashkent: IFÉAC; Aix-en-Provence: Édisud 1997.

Isutsu, Toshihiko. *The Concept of Belief in Islamic Theology*. Yokohama: Yurindo Publishing, 1965.

İzgi, Cevat. *Osmanlı Medreselerinde İlim*. 2 vols. Istanbul: İz Yayıncılık, 1997.

Jackson, Sherman A. *Islamic Law and the State: The Constitutional Jurisprudence of Shihāb al-Dīn al-Qarāfī*. Leiden: Brill, 1996.

Jaques, R. Kevin. *Authority, Conflict, and the Transmission of Diversity in Medieval Islamic Law*. Leiden: Brill, 2006.

Jennings, R. C. "Kadi, Court, and Legal Procedure in 17th c. Ottoman Kayseri." *Studia Islamica* 48 (1978): 133–72.

"Limitations of the Judicial Powers of the Kadi in 17th C. Ottoman Kayseri." *Studia Islamica* 50 (1979): 151–84.

Johansen, Baber. "Coutumes Locales et Coutumes Universelles aux Sources des Règles Juridiques en Droit Musulman Hanéfite." *Annales Islamologiques* 27 (1993): 29–35.

"Formes de langage et fonctions publiques: stéréopypes, témoins et offices dans la preuve par l'écrit en droit musulman." *Arabica* 44, no. 3 (1997): 333–76.

The Islamic Law on Land Tax and Rent: The Peasants' Loss of Property Rights as Interpreted in the Ḥanafite Legal Literature of the Mamluk and Ottoman Periods. London: Croom Helm, 1988.

"Legal Literature and the Problem of Change: The Case of the Land Rent." In *Islam and Public Law*, ed. Chibli Mallat, 29–47. London: Graham & Trotman, 1993.

"Secular and Religious Elements in Hanafite Law. Function and Limits of the Absolute Character of Government Authority." In *Islam et politique au Maghreb*, ed. E. Gellner and J. C. Vatin, 281–303. Paris: Editions du CNRS, 1981.

Joseph, Sabrina. *Islamic Law on Peasant Usufruct in Ottoman Syria: 17th to Early 19th Century*. Leiden: Brill, 2012.

Judd, Steven C. "Al-Awzāʿī and Sufyān al-Thawrī: The Umayyad Madhhab?" In *The Islamic School of Law: Evolution, Devolution, and Progress*, ed. Peri Bearman, Rudolph Peters, and Frank E. Vogel, 10–25. Cambridge, MA: Harvard University Press, 2005.

Kafadar, Cemal. "A Rome of One's Own: Reflections on Cultural Geography and Identity in the Lands of Rum." *Muqarnas* 24 (2007): 7–25.

Kafescioğlu, Çiğdem. *Constatntinopolis/Istanbul: Cultural Encounter, Imperial Vision, and the Construction of the Ottoman Capital*. University Park: Pennsylvania State University Press, 2009.

"'In the Image of Rūm': Ottoman Architectural Patronage in Sixteenth-Century Aleppo and Damascus." *Muqarnas* 16 (1999): 70–96.

Karamustafa, Ahmet T. *God's Unruly Friends: Dervish Groups in the Islamic Later Middle Period, 1200–1500*. Salt Lake City: University of Utah Press, 1995.

Kastritsis, Dimitris J. *The Sons of Beyazid: Empire Building and Representation in the Ottoman Civil War of 1402–1413*. Leiden: Brill, 2007.

Kaya, Eyyup Said. "Continuity and Change in Islamic Law: The Concept of Madhhab and the Dimensions of Legal Disagreement in Hanafi Scholarship of the Tenth Century." In *The Islamic School of Law: Evolution, Devolution, and Progress*, ed. Peri Bearman, Rudolph Peters, and Frank E. Vogel, 26–40. Cambridge, MA: Harvard University Press 2005.

Khoury, Dina Rizk. *State and Provincial Society in the Ottoman Empire: Mosul, 1540–1834*. Cambridge: Cambridge University Press, 1997.

Koç, Yunus. "Early Ottoman Customary Law: The Genesis and Development of Ottoman Codification." In *Shattering Tradition: Custom, Law and the Individual in the Muslim Mediterranean*, eds. Walter Dostal and Wolfgang Kraus., 75–121. London: I.B. Tauris, 2005.

Kohlberg, Etan. *A Medieval Muslim Scholar at Work: Ibn Ṭāwūs and His Library*. Leiden: Brill, 1992.

Kosei, Morimoto. "What Ibn Khaldūn Saw: The Judiciary of Mamluk Egypt." *Mamluk Studies Review* 6 (2002): 109–35.

Kozma, Liat. *Policing Egyptian Women: Sex, Law, and Medicine in Khedival Egypt*. Syracuse, NY: Syracuse University Press, 2011.

Krstić, Tijana. *Contested Conversion to Islam: Narratives of Religious Change in the Early Modern Ottoman Empire*. Stanford, CA: Stanford University Press, 2011.

Lane, Andrew. "'Abd al-Ghanī al-Nābulusī (1641–1731): Experience of a Sufi Shaykh on the Margins of Society." In *Marginal Voices in Literature and Society: Individual and Society in the Mediterranean Muslim World*, ed. Robin Ostle, 89–116. Strasbourg: European Science Foundation in collaboration with Maison mediterraneenne des sciences de l'homme d'Aix-en-Provence, 2000.

Lellouch, Benjamin. *Les Ottomans en Égypte: Historiens et Conquerants au XVIe siècle*. Louvain: Paris, 2006.

Levanoni, Amalia. "A Supplementary Source for the Study of Mamluk Social History: The *Taqārīẓ*." *Arabica* 60, nos. 1–2 (2013): 146–77.

Liechti, Stacy. "Books, Book Endowments, and Communities of Knowledge in the Bukharan Khanate." PhD diss., New York University, 2008.

Makdisi, George. *The Rise of Colleges: Institutions of Learning in Islam and the West*. Edinburgh: Edinburgh University Press, 1981.

"*Ṭabaqāt*-Biography: Law and Orthodoxy in Classical Islam." *Islamic Studies* 32, no. 4 (1993): 371–96.

Mallat, Chibli. *Introduction to Middle Eastern Law*. Oxford: Oxford University Press, 2009.

Mandaville, Jon E. "The Muslim Judiciary of Damascus in the late Mamluk Period." PhD diss., Princeton University, 1969.

"Usurious Piety: The Cash Waqf Controversy in the Ottoman Empire." *International Journal of Middle East Studies* 10, no. 3 (1979): 289–308.

Manz, Beatrice Forbes. *Powers, Politics, and Religion in Timurid Iran*. Cambridge: Cambridge University Press, 2007.

Miklós Maróth. "The Library of Sultan Bayazit II." In *Irano-Turkic Cultural Contacts in the 11th–17th Centuries*, ed. Éva M. Jeremiás, 111–32. Piliscsaba, Hungary: Avicenna Institute of Middle Eastern Studies, 2003.

Masud, Muhammad Khalid. "The Significance of Istifta' in the Fatwa Discourse." *Islamic Studies* 48, no. 3 (2009): 341–66.

Masud, Muhammad Khalid, Brinkley Messick, and David S. Powers, eds. *Islamic Legal Interpretation: Muftīs and Their Fatwás*. Cambridge, MA: Harvard University Press, 1996.

"Muftīs, Fatwás, and Islamic Legal Interpretation." In *Islamic Legal Interpretation: Muftīs and Their Fatwás*, ed. Muhammad Khalid Masud, Brinkley Messick, and David S. Powers, 3–32. Cambridge, MA: Harvard University Press, 1996.

McChesney, R. D. *Central Asia: Foundations of Change*. Princeton, NJ: Darwin Press, 1996.

"A Note on the Life and Works of Ibn 'Arabshāh." In *History and Historiography of Post-Mongol Central Asia and the Middle East: Studies in Honor of John E. Woods*, ed. Judith Pfeiffer and Sholeh A. Quinn, 205–49. Wiesbaden: Harrassowitz Verlag, 2006.

Meier, Astrid. "Perceptions of a New Era? Historical Writing in Early Ottoman Damascus." *Arabica* 51, no. 4 (2004): 419–34.

Melchert, Christopher. *The Formation of the Sunni Schools of Law, 9th–10th Centuries CE*. Leiden: Brill, 1997.

Melis, Nicola. "A Seventeenth-Century Ḥanafī Treatise on Rebellion and *Jihād* in the Ottoman Age." *Eurasian Studies* 11, no. 2 (2003): 215–26.

Meservey, Sabra F. "Feyżullah Efendi: An Ottoman Şeyhülislam." PhD diss., Princeton University, 1965.

Meshal, Reem. "Antagonistic Sharī'as and the Construction of Orthodoxy in Sixteenth-Century Ottoman Cairo." *Journal of Islamic Studies* 21, no. 2 (2010): 183–212.

Messick, Brinkley. *The Calligraphic State: Textual Domination and History in a Muslim Society*. Berkeley: University of California Press, 1993.

"The Muftī, the Text and the World: Legal Interpretation in Yemen." *Man* 12, no. 1 (1986): 102–19.

Mikhail, Alan. "An Irrigated Empire: The View from Ottoman Fayyum." *International Journal of Middle Eastern Studies* 42, no. 4 (2010): 569–90.

Minkov, Anton. *Conversion to Islam in the Balkans: Kisve Bahasi Petitions and Ottoman Social Life, 1670–1730*. Leiden: Brill, 2004.

Moazzen, Maryam. "Shi'ite Higher Learning and the Role of the Madrasa-yi Sultani in Late Safavid Iran." PhD diss., University of Toronto, 2011.

Moin, A. Azfar. *The Millennial Sovereign: Sacred Kingship and Sainthood in Islam*. New York: Columbia University Press, 2012.

Mordtmann, J. H., and V. L. Menage. "Ferîdûn Bey." *EI*[2].

Morgan, David. "The 'Great "Yasa" of Chingiz Khān' and Mongol Law in the Ilkhānate." *Bulletin of the School of Oriental and African Studies* 49, no. 1 (1986): 163–76.
"The 'Great Yasa of Chinggis Khān' Revisited." In *Mongols, Turks and Others*, ed. R. Amitai and M. Biran, 291–308. Leiden: Brill, 2005.
Mundy, Martha, and Richard Saumarez-Smith. *Governing Property, Making The Modern State Law, Administration and Production in Ottoman Syria*. London: I. B. Tauris, 2007.
Muslu, Emire Cihan. "Ottoman-Mamluk Relations: Diplomacy and Perceptions." PhD diss., Harvard University, 2007.
Necipoğlu, Gülru. *The Age of Sinan: Architectural Culture in the Ottoman Empire*. Princeton, NJ: Princeton University Press, 2005.
"A Kânûn for the State, a Canon for the Arts: Conceptualizing the Classical Synthesis of Ottoman Art and Architecture." In *Soliman le Magnifique et son temps*, ed. Gilles Veinstein, 195–213. Paris: La Documentation Français, 1992.
"Süleyman the Magnificent and the Representation of Power in the Context of Ottoman-Hapsburg-Papal Rivalry." *Art Bulletin* 71, no. 3 (1989): 401–27.
Nielsen, Jørgen S. *Secular Justice in an Islamic State: Maẓālim under the Baḥri Mamlūks 662/1264–789/1387*. Leiden: Nederlands Historisch-Archaeologisch Instituut te Istanbul, 1985.
Niyazioğlu, Aslı. "Ottoman Sufi Sheikhs Between this World and the Hereafter: A Study of Nev'īzāde 'Atā'ī's (1583–1635) Biographical Dictionary." PhD diss., Harvard University, 2003.
Nizri, Michael. *Ottoman High Politics and the Ulema Household*. New York: Palgrave Macmillan, 2014.
Opwis, Felicitas. "The Role of the Biographer in Constructing Identity and School: al-'Abbādi and his *Kitāb Ṭabaqāt al-Fuqahā' al-Shāfi'īyya*." *Journal of Arabic and Islamic Studies* 11, no. 1 (2011): 1–35.
Özbaran, Salih. *Bir Osmanlı Kimliği: 14.-17. Yüzyıllarda Rûm/Rûmi Aidiyet ve Imgeleri*. Istanbul: Kitab, 2004.
Özcan, Abdülkadir. "Idrîs-i Bitlisî." *TDVIA*.
Özel, Ahmet. "Kefevî, Mahmûd b. Süleyman." *TDVIA*.
Özen, Şükrü. "Osmanlı Döneminde Fetva Literatürü." *Türkiye Araştırmaları Literatür Dergisi* 3, no. 5 (2005): 249–378.
Özyılmaz, Ömer. *Osmanlı Medreselerinin Eğitim Programları*. Ankara: Kültür Bakanlığı, 2002.
Pakalın, Mehmet Zeki. *Osmanlı Tarih Deyimleri ve Terimleri Sözlüğü*. 3 vols. Istanbul: Milli Eğitim Basımevi, 1993.
Peirce, Leslie. "'The Law Shall Not Languish': Social Class and Public Conduct in Sixteenth-Century Ottoman Legal Discourse." In *Hermeneutics and Honor: Negotiating Female "Public" Space in Islamic/ate Societies*, ed. Asma Afasruddin, 140–58. Cambridge, MA: Harvard University Press, 1999.
Morality Tales: Law and Gender in the Ottoman Court of Aintab. Berkeley: University of California Press, 2003.

Peters, Rudolph. "Muḥammad al-'Abbāsī al-Mahdī (d. 1897), Grand Mufti of Egypt, and his *al-Fatāwá al-Mahdīyya*." *Islamic Law and Society* 1 (1994): 66–82.

"'What Does It Mean to Be an Official Madhhab?' Ḥanafīsm and the Ottoman Empire." In *The Islamic School of Law: Evolution, Devolution, and Progress*, ed. Peri Bearman, Rudolph Peters, and Frank E. Vogel, 147–58. Cambridge, MA: Harvard University Press, 2005.

Powers, David S. *Law, Society, and Culture in the Maghrib, 1300–1500*. Cambridge: Cambridge University Press, 2002.

Rabbat, Nasser O. "The Ideological Significance of the Dar al-'Adl in the Medieval Islamic Orient." *International Journal of Middle East Studies* 27, no. 1 (1995): 3–28.

Rafeq, Abdul Karim. "The Opposition of the Azhar 'Ulamā' to Ottoman Laws and its Significance in the History of Ottoman Egypt." In *Études sur les Villes du Proche-Orient XVIe–XIXe Siècle: Homage à André Raymond*, 43–54. Damascus: Institut français d'études arabes de Damas, 2001.

The Province of Damasucs, 1723–1783. Beirut: Khayats, 1966.

"The Syrian 'Ulamā', Ottoman Law, and Islamic Shari'a." *Turcica* 26 (1994): 9–32.

Rapoport, Yossef. "Legal Diversity in the Age of Taqlīd: The Four Chief Qāḍīs under the Mamluks." *Islamic Law and Society* 10, no. 2 (2003): 210–28.

"Royal Justice and Religious Law: Siyāsah and Shari'ah under the Mamluks." *Mamluk Studies Review* 16 (2012): 71–102.

Reinhart, A. Kevin. "Transcendence and Social Practice: Muftīs and Qāḍīs as Religious Interpreters." *Annales Islamologiques* 27 (1993): 5–25.

Repp, Richard C. *The Müfti of Istanbul: A Study in the Development of the Ottoman Learned Hierarchy*. London: Ithaca Press, 1986.

Richardson, Brian. *Manuscript Culture in Renaissance Italy*. Cambridge: Cambridge University Press, 2009.

Rosenthal, Franz. "'Blurbs' (taqrīẓ) from Fourteenth-Century Egypt." *Oriens* 27–28 (1981): 177–96.

A History of Muslim Historiography. Leiden: Brill, 1968.

Rozen, Minna. "Influential Jews in the Sultan's Court in Istanbul in Support of Jerusalem Jewry in the 17th Century." *Michael* 7 (1981): 394–430.

The Jewish Community of Jerusalem in the Seventeenth Century. Tel Aviv: Tel Aviv University and the Ministry of Defense Publishing House, 1984.

Sabev, Orlin (Orhan Salih). "Private Book Collections in Ottoman Sofia, 1671–1833." *Etudes Balkaniques* 1 (2003): 34–82.

Schacht, Joseph. "On the Title of the *Fatāwā al-'Ālamgīriyya*." In *Iran and Islam: In Memory of the Late Vladimir Minorsky*, ed. C. E. Bosworth 475–478. Edinburgh: Edinburgh University Press, 1971.

Sela, Ron. *The Legendary Biographies of Tamerlane: Islam and Heroic Apocrypha in Central Asia*. Cambridge: Cambridge University Press, 2011.

Selçuk, İklil Oya. "State and Society in the Marketplace: A Study of Late Fifteenth-Century Bursa." PhD diss., Harvard University, 2009.

Severcan, Şefaattın. "Kınalı-zade 'Ali Efendi." In *Kinali-Zade Ali Efendi (1510–1572)*, ed. Ahmet Hulusi Koker, 1–11. Kayseri: Erciyes Üniversitesi Matbaası, 1999.

Shefer-Mossensohn, Miri. *Ottoman Medicine: Healing and Medical Institutions, 1500–1700*. Albany: State University of New York Press, 2009.

Shoshan, Boaz. "Jerusalem Scholars ('Ulamā') and Their Activities in the Mamluk Empire." In *Palestine in the Mamluk Period*, ed. Joseph Drory, 86–97. Jerusalem: Yad Izhak Ben-Zvi, 1992.

Stewart, Devin. "The Doctorate of Islamic Law in Mamluk Egypt and Syria." In *Law and Education in Medieval Islam: Studies in Memory of Professor George Makdisi*, Joseph E. Lowry, Devin J. Stewart, and Shawkat M. Toorawa, 45–90. Cambridge: E.J.W. Gibb Memorial Trust, 2004.

"The First Shaykh al-Islām of the Safavid Capital of Qazvin." *Journal of the American Oriental Society* 116, no. 3 (1996): 387–405.

"The Structure of the *Fihrist*: Ibn al-Nadim as Historian of Islamic Legal and Theological Schools." *International Journal of Middle East Studies* 39, no. 3 (2007): 369–87.

Stilt, Kristen. *Islamic Law in Action: Authority, Discretion, and Everyday Experiences in Mamluk Egypt*. Oxford: Oxford University Press, 2012.

Stock, Brian. *The Implications of Literacy: Written Language and Models of Interpretation in the Eleventh and Twelfth Centuries*. Princeton, NJ: Princeton University Press, 1987.

Subrahmanyam, Sanjay. "Connected Histories: Notes toward a Reconfiguration of Early Modern Eurasia." *Modern Asian Studies* 31 (1997): 735–62.

Subtelny, Maria E. *Timurid in Transition: Turko-Persian Politics and Acculturation in Medieval Iran*. Leiden: Brill, 2007.

Subtelny, Maria Eva, and Anas B. Khalidov. "The Curriculum of Islamic Higher Learning in Timurid Iran in the Light of the Sunni Revival under Shah-Rukh." *Journal of the American Oriental Society* 115, no. 2 (1995): 210–36.

Tamari, Stephen E. "Teaching and Learning in 18th-Century Damascus: Localism and Ottomanism in an Early Modern Arab Society." PhD diss., Georgetown University, 1998.

Terem, Etty. "The New Mi'yar of al-Mahdi al-Wazzani: Local Interpretation of Family Life in Late Nineteenth-Century Fez." PhD diss., Harvard University, 2007.

Terzioğlu, Derin. "Sufi and Dissident in the Ottoman Empire: Miyāzī-i Miṣrī." PhD diss., Harvard University, 1999.

"Sufis in the Age of State Building and Confessionalization, 1300–1600." In *The Ottoman World*, ed. Christine Woodhead, 86–99. London: Routledge, 2011.

Tezcan, Baki. "The Definition of Sultanic Legitimacy in the Sixteenth Century Ottoman Empire: The Ahlak-i Ala'i of Kınalızâde Ali Çelebi (1510–1572)." MA diss., Princeton University, 1996.

"Dispelling the Darkness: The Politics of 'Race' in the Early Seventeenth-Century Ottoman Empire in the Light of the Life and Work of Mullah Ali." In *Identity and Identity Formation in the Ottoman World: A Volume of Essays in Honor of Norman Itzkowitz*, ed. Baki Tezcan and Karl Barbir, 73–95. Madison: University of Wisconsin Press, 2007.

"The Ottoman Mevali as 'Lords of the Law.'" *Journal of Islamic Studies* 20, no. 3 (2009): 383–407.

"The Ottoman Monetary Crisis of 1585 Revisited." *Journal of the Economic and Social History of the Orient* 52 (2009): 460–504.

The Second Ottoman Empire: Political and Social Transformation in the Early Modern World. Cambridge: Cambridge University Press, 2010.

"Some Thoughts on the Politics of Early Modern Ottoman Science." In *Beyond Dominant Paradigms in Ottoman and Middle Eastern/North African Studies*, ed. Donald Quataert and Baki Tezcan, 135–56. Istanbul: Center for Islamic Studies (İSAM), 2010.

Toledano, Ehud R. "The Emergence of Ottoman-Local Elites (1700–1900): A Framework of Research." In *Middle Eastern Politics and Ideas: A History from Within*, Ilan Pappé and Moshe Ma'oz, 145–62. London: Tauris Academic Studies, 1997.

Travers, Robert. *Ideology and Empire in Eighteenth-Century India: The British Bengal*. Cambridge: Cambridge University Press, 2007.

Tsafrir, Nurit. *The History of an Islamic School of Law: The Early Spread of Ḥanafīsm*. Cambridge, MA: Harvard University Press, 2004.

Tucker, Judith E. "The Exemplary Life of Khayr al-Dīn al-Ramlī." In *Auto/Biography and the Construction of Identity and Community in the Middle East*, ed. Mary Ann Fay, 9–17. New York: Palgrave, 2001.

Tucker, Judith E.. *In the House of the Law: Gender and Islamic Law in Ottoman Syria and Palestine*. Berkeley: University of California Press, 1998.

Tuğ, Başak. "Politics of Honor: The Institutional and Social Frontiers of "Illicit" Sex in Mid-Eighteenth-Century Ottoman Anatolia." PhD diss., New York University, 2009.

Tyan, Emile. *Histoire de L'organisation Judiciaire en Pays D'Islam*. Leiden: Brill, 1960.

Uğur, Ali. *The Ottoman 'Ulema in the mid-17th Century: An Analysis of the Vaḳā'i'ü'l-fużalā of Meḥmed Şeyhī Efendi*. Berlin: K. Schwarz, 1986.

Uzunçarşılı, İsmail Hakki. "Karamanoğulları Devri Vesikalarından İbrahim Bey'in Karaman İmareti Vakfiyesi." *Belleten* 1 (1937): 56–146.

Osmanlı Devletinin İlmiye Teşkilâtı. Ankara: Türk Tarih Kurumu Basımevi, 1988.

Van Leeuwen, Richard. *Waqfs and Urban Structures: The Case of Ottoman Damascus*. Leiden: Brill, 1999.

Varlık, Nükhet. "Disease and Empire: A History of Plague Epidemics in the Early Modern Ottoman Empire (1453–1600)." PhD diss., University of Chicago, 2008.

Voll, John. "Old 'Ulama Families and Ottoman Influence in Eighteenth Century Damascus." *American Journal of Arabic Studies* 3 (1975): 48–59.

von Schlegell, Barbara Rosenow. "Sufism in the Ottoman Arab World: Shaykh 'Abd al-Ghanī al-Nābulusī (d. 1143/1731)." PhD diss., University of California, Berkeley, 1997.

Vryonis, Speros. *The Decline of Medieval Hellenism in Asia Minor and the Process of Islamization from the Eleventh through the Fifteenth Century*. Berkeley: University of California Press, 1971.

Watenpaugh, Haghnar Zeitlian. *The Image of an Ottoman City: Imperial Architecture and Urban Experience in the 16th and 17th Centuries*. Leiden: Brill, 2004.

Wheeler, Brannon M. *Applying the Canon in Islam: The Authorization and Maintenance of Interpretive Reasoning in Ḥanafī Scholarship*. Albany: State University of New York Press, 1996.

Wiederhold, Lutz. "Blasphemy against the Prophet (*Sabb al-Rasul, Sabb al-Sahabah*): The Introduction of the Topic into Shāfiʿī Legal Literature and its Relevance for Legal Practice under Mamluk Rule." *Journal of Semitic Studies* 42, no. 1 (1997): 39–70.

"Legal-Religious Elite, Temporal Authority, and the Caliphate in Mamluk Society: Conclusions Drawn from the Examination of a 'Zahiri Revolt' In Damascus in 1386." *International Journal of Middle East Studies* 31, no. 2 (1999): 203–35.

Wilkins, Charles L. *Forging Urban Solidarities: Ottoman Aleppo 1640–1700*. Leiden: Brill, 2010.

Winter, Michael. "Ottoman Qāḍīs in Damascus in 16th-18th Centuries." In *Law, Custom, and Statute in the Muslim World: Studies in Honor of Aharon Layish*, ed. Ron Shaham, 87–109. Leiden: Brill, 2007.

Wittmann, Richard. "Before Qadi and Grand Vizier: Intra-Communal Dispute Resolution and Legal Transactions among Christians and Jews in the Plural Society of Seventeenth Century Istanbul." PhD diss., Harvard University, 2008.

Woodhead, Christine. "Puff and Patronage: Ottoman *Takriz*-Writing and Literacy Recommendation in the 17th Century." In *The Balance of Truth: Essays in Honour of Professor Geoffrey Lewis*, ed. Ciğdem Baalim-Harding and Colin Imber. Istanbul: Isis Press, 2000.

Woods, John E. *The Aqquyunlu: Clan, Confederation, Empire: A Study in 15th/9th Century Turko-Iranian Politics*. Minneapolis, MN: Bibliotheca Islamica, 1976.

Yazıcı, Gülgün. "Kâmî." *TDVIA*.

Yılmaz, Hüsyein. The Sultan and the Sultanate: Envisioning Rulership in Age of Süleymân the Lawgiver (1520–1566)." PhD diss., Harvard University, 2004.

Yürekli, Zeynep. *Architecture and Hagiography in the Ottoman Empire: The Politics of Bektashi Shrines in the Classical Age*. Farnham, Surrey, UK: Ashgate, 2012.

Zaman, Muhammad Qasim. "The Caliphs, the 'Ulamā' and the Law: Defining the Role and Function of the Caliph in the Early 'Abbāsid Period." *Islamic Law and Society* 4, no. 1 (1997): 1–36.

The Ulama in Contemporary Islam: Custodian of Change. Princeton, NJ: Princeton University Press, 2002.

Zecevic, Selma. "On the Margin of Text, On the Margin of Empire: Geography, Identity, and Fatwá-Text in Ottoman Bosnia." PhD diss., Columbia University, 2007.

Ze'evi, Dror. *An Ottoman Century: The District of Jerusalem in the 1600s*. Albany: State University of New York Press, 1996.

Producing Desire: Changing Sexual Discourse in the Ottoman Middle East, 1500–1900. Berkeley: University of California Press, 2006.

Zilfi, Madeline C. "Elite Circulation in the Ottoman Empire: Great Mollas of the Eighteenth Century." *Journal of the Economic and Social History of the Orient* 26, no. 3 (1983): 353–54.

Zilfi, Madeline C. "The Kadizadelis: Discordant Revivalism in Seventeenth-Century Istanbul." *Journal of Near Eastern Studies* 45, no. 4 (1986): 251–69.

"The Ottoman Ulema." In *Cambridge History of Turkey III: The Later Ottoman Empire, 1603–1839*, ed. Suraiya N. Faroqhi, 209–25. Cambridge: Cambridge University Press, 2006.

Politics of Piety: the Ottoman ulamā in the Postclassical Age (1600–1800). Minneapolis: Bibliotheca Islamica, 1988.

Index

Other Titles in the Series

Popular Culture in Medieval Cairo, Boaz Shoshan
Early Philosophical Shiism: The Ismaili Neoplatonism of Abū Ya'qūb Al-Sijistānī, Paul E. Walker
Indian Merchants and Eurasian Trade, 1600–1750, Stephen Frederic Dale
Palestinian Peasants and Ottoman Officials: Rural Administration Around Sixteenth-Century Jerusalem, Amy Singer
Arabic Historical Thought in the Classical Period, Tarif Khalidi
Mongols and Mamluks: The Mamluk–Īlkhānid War, 1260–1281, Reuven Amitai-Preiss
Hierarchy and Egalitarianism in Islamic Thought, Louise Marlow
The Politics of Households in Ottoman Egypt: The Rise of the Qazdağlis, Jane Hathaway
Commodity and Exchange in the Mongol Empire: A Cultural History of Islamic Textiles, Thomas T. Allsen
State and Provincial Society in the Ottoman Empire: Mosul, 1540–1834, Dina Rizk Khoury
The Mamluks in Egyptian Politics and Society, Thomas Philipp and Ulrich Haarmann (Eds.)
The Delhi Sultanate: A Political and Military History, Peter Jackson
European and Islamic Trade in the Early Ottoman State: The Merchants of Genoa and Turkey, Kate Fleet
Reinterpreting Islamic Historiography: Hārūn Al-Rashīd and the Narrative of the 'Abbāsid Caliphate, Tayeb El-Hibri
The Ottoman City Between East and West: Aleppo, Izmir, and Istanbul, Edhem Eldem, Daniel Goffman, and Bruce Masters
A Monetary History of the Ottoman Empire, Şevket Pamuk
The Politics of Trade in Safavid Iran: Silk for Silver, 1600–1730, Rudolph P. Matthee
The Idea of Idolatry and the Emergence of Islam: From Polemic to History, G. R. Hawting
Classical Arabic Biography: The Heirs of the Prophets in the Age of Al-Ma'mūn, Michael Cooperson
Empire and Elites after the Muslim Conquest: The Transformation of Northern Mesopotamia, Chase F. Robinson
Poverty and Charity in Medieval Islam: Mamluk Egypt, 1250–1517, Adam Sabra
Christians and Jews in the Ottoman Arab World: The Roots of Sectarianism, Bruce Masters
Culture and Conquest in Mongol Eurasia, Thomas T. Allsen
Revival and Reform in Islam: The Legacy of Muhammad Al-Shawkani, Bernard Haykel
Tolerance and Coercion in Islam: Interfaith Relations in the Muslim Tradition, Yohanan Friedmann
Guns for the Sultan: Military Power and the Weapons Industry in the Ottoman Empire, Gábor Ágoston
Marriage, Money and Divorce in Medieval Islamic Society, Yossef Rapoport
The Empire of the Qara Khitai in Eurasian History: Between China and the Islamic World, Michal Biran
Domesticity and Power in the Early Mughal World, Ruby Lal
Power, Politics and Religion in Timurid Iran, Beatrice Forbes Manz

Postal Systems in the Pre-Modern Islamic World, Adam J. Silverstein
Kingship and Ideology in the Islamic and Mongol Worlds, Anne F. Broadbridge
Justice, Punishment and the Medieval Muslim Imagination, Christian Lange
The Shiites of Lebanon Under Ottoman Rule, 1516–1788, Stefan Winter
Women and Slavery in the Late Ottoman Empire, Madeline Zilfi
The Second Ottoman Empire: Political and Social Transformation in the Early Modern World, Baki Tezcan
Non-Muslims in the Early Islamic Empire: From Surrender to Coexistence, Milka Levy-Rubin
The Legendary Biographies of Tamerlane: Islam and Heroic Apocrypha in Central Asia, Ron Sela
Law and Piety in Medieval Islam, Megan Reid
The Origins of the Shi'a: Identity, Ritual, and Sacred Space in Eighth-Century Kufa, Najam Haider
Politics, Law, and Community in Islamic Thought: The Taymiyyan Moment, Ovamir Anjum
The Power of Oratory in the Medieval Muslim World, Linda G. Jones
Animals in the Qur'an, Sarra Tlili
The Logic of Law Making in Islam: Women and Prayer in the Legal Tradition, Behnam Sadeghi
Empire and Power in the Reign of Süleyman: Narrating the Sixteenth-Century Ottoman World, Kaya Şahin
Women and the Transmission of Religious Knowledge in Islam, Asma Sayeed
The New Muslims of Post-Conquest Iran, Sarah Bowen Savant
The Mamluk City in the Middle East, Nimrod Luz
Disability in the Arab Ottoman World, 1500–1800, Sara Scalenghe
The Holy City of Medina: Sacred Space in Early Islamic Arabia, Harry Munt
Muslim Midwives: The Craft of Birthing in the Premodern Middle East, Avner Giladi
Doubt in Islamic Law: a History of Legal Maxims, Interpretation, and Islamic Criminal Law, Intisar A. Rabb